In the HIMALAYAS

In the HIMALAYAS

Journeys through Nepal, Tibet, and Bhutan

Fully revised and updated

Jeremy Bernstein

LYONS & BURFORD, PUBLISHERS

Library of Congress Cataloging-in-Publication Data
Bernstein, Jeremy, 1929-
In the Himalayas : journeys through Nepal, Tibet, and Bhutan / Jeremy Bernstein. —Fully rev. and updated.
p. cm.
Includes bibliographical references and index.
ISBN 1-55821-443-7
1. Himalaya Mountains Region—Description and travel. 2. Hiking-Himalaya Mountains Region. I. Title.
DS485.H6B44 1996
915.49604—dc20   96-2466
                                                                    CIP

Printed in the United States of America
10 9 8 7 6 5 4 3 2 1

Contents

Preface
to the 1996 Edition

This book, as its readers will discover, has a good deal to do with Buddhism—at least of the sort that is practiced in Nepal, Bhutan, and Tibet—the latter in the face of terrible obstacles. Therefore it may be appropriate to speak of its various incarnations and reincarnations—especially since I have never really recounted in print how it all came about in the first place. It all began with *The New Yorker* magazine—the old *New Yorker*—the real *New Yorker*. Soon after I joined its staff, in the very early 1960s, I got the idea of writing a sort of profile of the mountain guides of the Chamonix Valley in France. I had just published a long profile of the electronic computer, "The Analytical Engine," and its success—it won several prizes—emboldened me to ask William Shawn, the magazine's legendary editor, if he had any interest in a piece of writing on mountain climbing. It was quite clear—politeness aside—that on first hearing, mountain climbing was of even less interest to him than professional football—which, I believe, was never written about in the magazine. However, I was quite prepared in advance for this reaction and had given some thought as to what to do when, predictably, it occurred. By this time, although I was still in my middle thirties, I had been reading literature about the mountains for some twenty-five years. I knew a lot about the subject, especially about its history. So I asked Mr. Shawn if he had realized that, at least in the West, the mountain aesthetic was a rather recent invention. *This* caught his attention. When something caught Mr. Shawn's attention, he had a way of looking at you as if you had just announced the invention of fire.

Seizing the moment, I explained to him that the activity of mountain climbing, in the sense that we understand it, had been invented in the Chamonix Valley at the end of the eighteenth century with the attempts to climb Mont Blanc, the highest mountain in western Europe. Until that time, mountains were considered obstacles to travel and commerce, and their inhabitants almost subhuman. But it was in the nineteenth century, through the efforts of people like the British painter and art critic John Ruskin, that the mountain aesthetic was really articulated and mountains—especially snow-covered mountains—became "beautiful." Soon after, again through the activities largely of the British and their local alpine guides, they became "playgrounds." I was also able to assure Mr. Shawn that I was one of the most maladept mountain climbers known to man, so there was little chance of any piece of writing of mine on the subject turning into a vulgar account of the "rattling of the hardware"; it would be more like the rattling of my teeth. He then said that it appeared that such a project had real possibilities, so I set to work.

This coincided with the time when I was spending summers on a regular basis at the gigantic elementary particle physics laboratory—CERN—just outside of Geneva, my profession being that of physicist. During the week, I did my calculations in the Theory Division at CERN, but every weekend I went to Chamonix to climb and poke around. On one of these visits, I had a chance encounter with a Chamonix guide named Claude Jaccoux. This was, as it turned out, a case of "chance," in Pasteur's phrase, favoring the "prepared mind." Jaccoux is a few years younger than I am. Like me, he began his professional life as an academic—a teacher of French literature in the lycées of the Haute-Savoie, where he was born. Unlike me, he is a brilliantly gifted athlete, and when I first met him he had already achieved the reputation of being one of the most formidable mountain climbers and guides in Europe. We hit it off at once, and I spent much of that summer under Jaccoux's expert tutelage learning to do technical climbing and also about the guides and their history. Jaccoux introduced me to some of the great guides of the previous generation, such as, Armand Charlet, and the great guides of his generation, such as Gaston Rebuffat and Lionel Terray. I also met, and became very fond of, Jaccoux's then-wife, Michele, who, under her maiden name, Stamos, had been a member of the French national ski team. By the time the summer was over, I had gathered enough material for a small book—and indeed it became one, under the title *Ascent*.

This brings me to a few years later—the spring of 1967. By this time my three articles on Chamonix—*Ascent*—had been published in *The New Yorker*. I still treasure a note from Mr. Shawn telling me how much he had liked them. It was such a rich subject that it had almost written itself. During the interval between my writing of these articles and the spring of 1967, a plan began hatching in my head. Why not move our whole modus operandi to the Himalayas? Why didn't the three of us, Jaccoux, Michele, and I, go out to Nepal and do for that country and Himalayan climbing what I had done for the Chamonix Valley and its climbers? There were, however, three obstacles: time, money, and logistics.

I was, in the spring of 1967, an associate professor of physics at New York University. I was teaching full-time (two courses), doing re-search (I had two thesis students), and also writing extensively for *The New Yorker*. But I did not have tenure. As I was going about my various activities and professions, I was naively unaware of the fact that my dual career—physics and writing—was not only not consid-ered to be a virtue, but had generated a great deal of animosity among several important members of the physics department faculty, who seemed to regard this sort of thing as frivolous. The result was a soul-destroying departmental fight over my tenure which, after nearly two years, I had lost that spring. I did have another job lined up, at the Stevens Institute of Technology in New Jersey. However, I was in no mood to begin it. To paraphrase Voltaire, at that moment I would have enjoyed the spectacle of the last dean being strangled in the entrails of the last department chairman. Clearly, I needed to get away—as far away as possible. What better place than Nepal! The timing was, in short, perfect. That left the matters of money and logistics—which were, of course, intertwined.

At this point, I was very fortunate to be able to call upon the advice of my old graduate school roommate and close friend, John Franklin Noxon III. John, who died tragically a few years ago, was not only a great scholar of mountaineering literature but, as a first-rate climber, had also been selected for expeditions to Canada, Alaska, South America, and, most importantly, Nepal. He had, incidentally, appeared anonymously in my *New Yorker* articles. A week before we were awarded our Ph.D.'s in physics, John had led me on a nocturnal climb up the side of Memorial Hall at Harvard. I had described this, leaving John's name out, in the magazine as part of the great tradition of university-building ascents immortalized in that classic of mountaineering literature, *The Night Climbers of Cambridge* [England], written under the pseudonym of "Whippersnaith." What I did not reveal—there were still inhibitions at *The New Yorker*—was that, having arrived as close to the top of the roof as we deemed safe, John then micturated in the general direction of the Jefferson Physics Laboratory, a liberating gesture. In any event, John had in 1967 recently returned from Nepal and was a marvelous source of relevant information.

The most important thing that John told me was that a small group like ours—three, in fact—could now realize a trekking expedition to the base of Mount Everest. This had to do with a recent series of events in Nepal. A few climbers had decided that they were above the law and had mounted illegal expeditions from Nepal into Tibet. They probably regarded this as a jolly prank to be played on the guileless Nepalese, but it turned into a disaster. The Nepalese have always found themselves caught in the middle between China and India. The Chinese had occupied Tibet on Nepal's northern border and the fact that climbers—especially Americans—were sneaking into Tibet from Nepal was not something they took lightly. Indeed, they put so much pressure on the Nepalese that the government had banned mountain climbing in the country entirely. So, while people such as Woodrow Wilson Sayre—whose book *Four Against Everest* recounted one of these border-crossing japes—had a good laugh, the people of the high Himalayas—the Sherpas and the like—were reduced to near destitution by the loss of income from climbing expeditions.

Into this void there had stepped one James Owen Merion Roberts, then recently of the Second King Edward VII's Own Gurkha Rifles. I will have more to say about "Jimmy"—as he is known in Nepal—in the text, but let me here recount what he did. Roberts had a vision: There must be hardy, but inexperienced, people out there somewhere who, if given the proper arrangements, could, and would, walk to places like the base of Mount Everest under the guidance of Sherpas and with the logistical support of local porters. In short, Jimmy invented the activity of Nepalese trekking. To this end, he created a company called Mountain Travel, which hired the Sherpas and arranged trekking trips. Noxon had run into Jimmy in Nepal, where he had organized the logistics of an expedition in which Noxon had participated before the climbing ban had come into effect. He gave me Jimmy's address in Kathmandu, and early that spring I wrote to him to see what might be arranged for the following fall.

This, in theory, took care of the logistics, leaving only the matter of money. Noxon had given me some idea of the cost of such a trekking expedition—about ten dollars a day per person. He also told me that there were, at the time, two trekking routes that were open. One was the trek to the Everest base camp from Kathmandu—an operation that would take about five weeks, coming and going. Then there was a two-week trek open in western Nepal near Annapurna. Hence, we were looking at about fifty days of trekking—a cost for the three of us of about fifteen hundred dollars. There were also, of course, the airfares—about a thousand dollars each from Geneva, where I would be spending the summer. The rest of the time we would be living in hotels—substantially more expensive than being in the field. I, at least, was planning to spend the entire fall and early winter in Nepal, having informed my new employers that the press of business would keep me from beginning my service at Stevens before the spring semester. The money was beginning to mount up in a serious way. I figured that ten thousand dollars would about cover it—a very large amount, at least for me, in 1967. My annual academic salary was then about fifteen thousand. I didn't have ten thousand dollars. My only hope was *The New Yorker* and Mr. Shawn.

Here, once again, I was fortunate in my timing. It turned out that one, or more, of Mr. Shawn's sons had just been in Nepal. He, or they, had found the country fascinating but gotten sick and had to leave. Perhaps it was Wallace Shawn, who, in his film *My Dinner with Andre,* had some acerbic things to say about westerners going to Nepal to rearrange their spiritual furniture. In any event, Nepal had become one of the innumerable items on Mr. Shawn's inexhaustible list of interests. And here I was with a concrete proposal to visit and write about the place. He was very enthusiastic and asked me how much money it would take to mount our expedition. With some trepidation, I mentioned the figure of ten thousand dollars. Not batting an eyelash, Mr. Shawn said that a check for same would be forthcoming immediately. However, he was worried about our health and safety. Mr. Shawn was always worrying about the health and safety of his writers and artists. I assured him that we would eat only fruit that we had peeled ourselves and that we would carefully boil the water. Moreover, I told him, Jaccoux—as part of his guide's training—had had several courses in first aid, and we would take a medical kit with us sufficient to every contingency, short of brain surgery. With this, he appeared to be satisfied. This is how my first trip to Nepal, in 1967, came about.

There are a few experiences in life whose realization vastly surpasses one's expectations. Our 1967 trip to Nepal was one. None of us had ever been to the Orient. Everything was new—an adventure. I will never forget our first view of the Himalayan chain. After an interminable flight from Europe to New Delhi, which terminated by one of the plane's engines ingesting a large bird as we landed—as I got off it was being extracted, still smoking, from the turbine—we spent a night sleeping, or not sleeping, on benches in the Delhi airport. That was a calvary that all airborne incoming passengers to Nepal then suffered; the few who entered the country from India by road were even worse for the wear. (Now there are direct flights from Europe to Kathmandu.) The next morning we boarded an elderly, but serviceable, turboprop belonging to the Royal Nepal Air Lines for the two-hour flight north to Kathmandu.

Although it was September, there were still traces of the monsoon. The air in Delhi was as steamy as a sauna and large lakes of water covered the fields. There were not many passengers on the plane. Indeed, at one point we filled out landing cards, on which we had to state our purpose for coming to the country. The three of us checked "trekking." Some years later I obtained the government statistics on the number of official trekkers—people who had checked "trekking" on their entry forms—by year. For the year 1967 there were three— three!—official trekkers. They must have been us. The plane initially flew over flat, emerald, water-laden fields for about an hour. Then there appeared on the horizon what I, at first, took to be clouds. They were at an altitude substantially higher than the plane's. But they did not move. They floated, still as castles, in the sky. It finally dawned on me that these were mountains. I had never seen mountains like this. Despite years and years of reading about the Himalayas, I had had no idea that this was what they really looked like—giant, serrated castles of snow and rock soaring into the sky. To this day, I get goose bumps thinking about that first view. It is a feeling that comes back every time—now many—I first see these mountains again.

Kathmandu was also like nothing any of us had ever seen. It was a kind of mad mixture of the ancient and the modern. Each street was a discovery—a sort of living art museum. The sky above the city was a crystalline blue and the people seemed extraordinarily kind and attractive. It took a while to see that underneath all of this were layers of grinding poverty and neglect. The fact that the life span of the Nepalese was then less than forty years told all. But there were hopeful signs. In 1967, the Nepalese had known seventeen years of release from the oppression of a century-old autocratic regime whose concern had been only the feathering of its own nest. It is true that the country was not a democracy in the sense that we understand it, but the actual form of government seemed less important than the government's actions to try to improve the standard of living of the people. At the time, Nepal was, if anything, an underpopulated country with a food surplus. It was one of the few countries in Asia that was actually exporting food! There were, if one chose to pay attention to them, some ominous signs for the future—the population, for example, was growing much too rapidly—but in 1967 the future seemed very far away.

It was in this state of semi-euphoria that I wrote my *New Yorker* articles. They constituted the first modern attempt—at least in English—to give a three-dimensional portrait of this remarkable country. Before 1950, all such attempts had been heavily controlled by the regime, which did not allow foreign travelers to move freely about the country. One of the editors at the publishing firm of Simon and Schuster became interested in the *New Yorker* articles as the basis for a book. He, and I, had somewhat grandiose ideas about how such a book should be presented. This was reflected in its poetic title, *The Wildest Dreams of Kew*—taken from Rudyard Kipling's poem "In the Neolithic Age"—"And the wildest dreams of Kew / Are the facts of Kathmandu. . . ." To add to the obscurity of the title, we chose a very fey design for the cover, created by a then-celebrated design studio. It was quite unclear to anyone who glanced casually at the cover of the book what it was about.

As if this were not bad enough, my editor left Simon and Schuster before the book was actually published in 1970. I was assigned to a new editor, who upon meeting me told me that I was among his favorite writers, but he could never get my name straight. The net result was that the book was basically dumped by the company. For a while, I found it in bookstores—often in the garden section—and then it disappeared. Nonetheless, it had a small cult following. People began traveling to Nepal and doing the kinds of treks we had done. My book, *faute de mieux,* became a sort of guide. I would receive photographs from these trekkers of scenes that I had described in the book. Now, the book is a sort of minor-league collector's item, with a catalog price very much larger than its original price. This was the first incarnation.

The second incarnation occurred in the late 1980s. By this time, trekking in Nepal had become a big business. There were over a hundred agencies in Kathmandu and some twenty thousand— twenty thousand!—trekkers and climbers were annually visiting the Everest region alone. All of this had totally transformed the lives of the indigenous people. The effect that it had on the rest of the country and, above all, on the Kathmandu valley is indescribable. To give one example: As far as I could tell, in 1967 the number of automobiles in private hands in the Kathmandu valley could be counted on the fingers of two hands. One such vehicle was a red Sunbeam Alpine that was owned by Barbara Adams, a remarkable American expatriate who still lives in Kathmandu and with whom I have remained friends since 1967. She still has the car. But, in 1967, she more or less had the impossibly narrow roads of the city to herself.

I thought of this on my last visit to Kathmandu in the fall of 1994. On more than one occasion, indeed on almost all occasions, I found it next to impossible to cross the street—any street. There is now a cloacal flow of unregulated traffic. Cars, motorbikes, trucks, and bicycles compete for space that used to accommodate rickshaws. Their fumes have manufactured a deadly pall that hangs over the valley. The din, the near and actual collisions, the incessant circulation, are beginning to drive the city dwellers somewhat crazy. If someone had told me in 1967 that in less than thirty years, in the words of a journalist I know in Kathmandu, the "Kathmandu valley [would] become a kind of death trap of economic overaffluence, bad air quality, and all the ills that one associates with third-world megacities, albeit on a smaller scale," I would have said that *he* was crazy. It is true that I was able to communicate from Colorado with this journalist by electronic mail—e-mail to Kathmandu!—and that the life expectancy there has been raised to the middle fifties. But at what cost?

This was beginning to be evident in the mid-1980s, when I was again approached by Simon and Schuster about the prospect of bringing out a new edition of my old book—the first reincarnation. By this time, not only had Nepal changed drastically, but I had also made extended visits to Bhutan, Pakistan, and Tibet. It was clear to me that, while the history of Nepal had not changed, much else of what I had written in the late 1960s was way out of date. Therefore, what I did for the first reincarnation—which we called *In the Himalayas,* a much more sensible title—was to bring up to date, as best I could, the material on Nepal and to add to it new sections on Bhutan and Tibet. This book was published in 1989 and remarkably, essentially every last copy was sold.

I hasten to add that not that many copies were printed; they were, however, all scooped up. I had not been paying much attention to this until about a year ago, when I noticed that my own stock had dwindled down to a couple of copies. I had given a lot of the others away as presents. I decided to get a few more. I soon discovered that, not only was the book out of print, but even the publisher could not locate any copies. No one had any copies—at least not in this country. It might come as a surprise to people who have never visited Kathmandu to learn that it has a few of the finest bookstores I have ever seen—especially when comes to regional literature of all kinds. I doubt that there is a better selection of Himalayan literature anywhere than one can find, for example, in the Pilgrim Bookstore in Kathmandu. In the fall of 1994, I visited it, and some of the others, in search of my book. In the end, about a half-dozen copies were unearthed. I bought them all. They represent the extinction of a species.

This brings us to the spring of 1995. In March, I received, from out of the blue, a letter from Peter Burford—the publisher of this, the third incarnation—stating that he had come across the book and would like to consider bringing it back into print. I liked the idea very much. However, I did not think that simply reprinting the existing text would be satisfactory. Let me take one, of many, examples to explain why.

In the fall of 1988 I visited Bhutan. I was as euphoric about this tiny Himalayan kingdom as I had been about Nepal in 1967—and nearly as naive. In leaving the country, we had taken a horrific seven-hour, one-hundred-and-fifty-mile drive from its capital, Thimphu, to the Indian border town of Phuntsholing. It was made horrific by the topography. The Indian subcontinent, on its northward drift, collided with the Asian, and this collision produced the Himalayas. In Nepal, the Himalayan wall is prefigured from the south by a gradually rising, undulating series of relatively low altitude hills and mountains. They are not really a major impediment to north-south travel. One consequence is that the Nepalese population is a kind of racial continuum, ranging from Hindus in the south, who merge into the population of northern India, to Sherpas in north, who merge into the Tibetan population. Since the racial diversity is so enormous, and since it proceeds in such small steps, it has been, at least as I see it, paradoxically simpler to unify the country than it would have been if, say, the population had been manifestly biracial.

But in Bhutan, the topography is totally different. As viewed from an airplane, the country looks as if one had emptied an ocean, leaving the sea bottom exposed—this is the southern part of Bhutan—and then the sea bottom had been separated from the shore above by a series of giant cliffs. This is, in fact, what happened, and the cliffs are some seven thousand feet high. Because the terrain on this "shoreline" is so inhospitable, north-south travel is very difficult. That is why our drive was "horrific." That is also why the population of the country is essentially biracial. The northern part of Bhutan—the part to which most visitors go—is thinly populated and Buddhist. The southern part, on the other hand, is densely populated and Hindu. In fact, much of this Hindu population is of Nepalese origin.

The country, which is ruled from Thimphu in the north, is a Buddhist theocracy. Sometime in the late 1980s it must have occurred to the king and his advisers that much of the country's population—the southern portion—had entirely different traditions and did not even speak as the language of choice Dzongkha—a Tibetan dialect. While population statistics are very difficult to come by in this part of the world, it may even be that this group—Hindus of Nepalese origin—constitute the majority of the Bhutanese population. Confronted by this realization, the rulers experienced the sort of predictable xenophobic reaction that has occurred in many countries whose traditional populations have come to feel that their traditions, and even their languages, are being threatened by "foreigners." There is a good deal of disagreement as to what happened next. But it appears that many of these southern Bhutanese ended up in internment camps. I was aware of none of this in 1988 when I wrote my chapter on Bhutan, since it was just unfolding. I will describe what I know about it in a postscript to my Bhutanese chapter. But this is only one example.

Therefore, it did not seem appropriate simply to reprint *In the Himalayas* with some additions. What I decided to do was to go over the whole book from beginning to end, keeping what still seemed valid and interesting to me from its two previous incarnations, and changing whatever seemed out of date or uninteresting. That is what this third incarnation is.

Finally, I would like to acknowledge with gratitude some of the people who have helped me along the way. To explain in detail what they did would require another book. But let me thank Elizabeth Hawley, Barbara Adams, Lisa Choegyal, John and Diana McKinnon, Carol Laise, Ray Fort, Gene Borster, Robert Rieffel, "Jimmy" Roberts, Sonam Gyalpo, Garry Daintry, Jim Edwards, Leon Weil, Rishikesh Shah, and Kanak Mani Dixit. I would also like to acknowledge the interest and encouragement of Peter Burford, my publisher, and, above all, Claude Jaccoux, who has remained my mentor in all things alpine for more than thirty years, and my indulgent friend for all that time.

Jeremy Bernstein
April, 1996

Part One
NEPAL

1

The Jewel in the Lotus

Once upon a time there was a lake called the Serpent's Lake, for Karkotak, the king of the serpents, dwelt in it. It was a big, beautiful lake surrounded by lofty mountains. All the water plants except the lotus grew in it, and one day the Vipaswi Buddha came and threw a root of the lotus into the water.

"When this root shall produce a flower," declared the Buddha, "then Shoyambhu, the Self-Existent One, shall be revealed here in the form of a flame. Then the water in this lake shall go and there shall be a valley wherein shall flourish many towns and villages."

Years passed.

Lotus leaves were seen floating upon the water. And then the predicted flower bloomed in all its heavenly beauty, with a flame of five colors playing upon it.

Knowing that the Self-Existent One had been revealed in the lake, another Buddha, the Sikhi, made a pilgrimage to it with a large number of his followers. He went around the Serpent's Lake thrice and sat down to meditate at the top of a mountain; then he called together his disciples and told them of the future of the holy lake. He also informed them that it was time for him to leave the world, and amid the lamentations of the men the Sikhi Buddha plunged into the lake and was absorbed into the spirit of the Self-Existent One.

Another long period elapsed, and the Visambhu Buddha arrived at the lake. Like his predecessors, he was accompanied by numerous followers to the Self-Existent One, and then he declared to his retinue, "The bodhisattva shall duly arrive here and let the water out of the lake." With that, the Buddha departed.

About this time, in northern China, the Bodhisattva Manjusri was meditating upon world events. When he knew that the Self-Existent One had been revealed in the Serpent's Lake, he called his followers, among whom was a person of high rank named Dharmakar, and set out, accompanied by them, for the holy lake.

Arriving at the lake, Manjusri went around until he came to a low hill in the south. Then he drew his scimitar and cut a passage through the hill, and the water gushed out. The bodhisattva told his followers to settle down in the newly formed valley, and he departed, leaving Dharmakar to become Nepal's first ruler.

This is the legend of the origin of the Kathmandu valley. Like many Nepalese legends, there is a good deal about it that is true. Until about seven million years ago, according to the geologists, the Indian and Asiatic continents were separated by a sea, the Himalayan Sea, located about where the Himalayan chain is now. The Indian subcontinent drifted north, and when it collided with Asia, the soft alluvial sea bottom was squeezed up. Gradually, the Himalayan Sea was divided by the rising mountains into what are known as the Tibetan Sea, now a high desertic plain north of the mountains, and the Gangeatic Sea, now the flat plain of northern India, to the south. In the middle was left a fantastic land of high mountains, deep gorges, and magnificent rivers and lakes. The Kathmandu valley, which lies slightly to the east of the middle of modern Nepal, was—as is shown by fossils, as well as by the alluvial character of the rich soil in the valley—such a lake. (Most of the sizable lakes now left in Nepal are in the western part of the country.) The place near Kathmandu where Manjusri cut the mountains with his scimitar to liberate the waters is well known to every Nepali. It is the Chobar Gorge, three miles south of the city of Kathmandu. It is a remarkably sharp gorge, through which the sacred Bagmati River flows southward into the Ganges. The gorge is spanned by a steel suspension bridge with a wooden plank flooring; and, despite the fact that it is the oldest steel bridge in the country, dating back nearly a century, and that it sways and creaks when one walks over it, it is still one of the better footbridges in Nepal.

The Kathmandu valley floor ranges in altitude from four thousand to five thousand feet. The country as a whole exhibits the widest altitude variation of any country on earth—from 150 feet above sea level in the south near India to 29,028 feet, the currently measured altitude of the summit of Mount Everest, which lies on the border between Tibet and Nepal to the north. Since Nepal is about at the latitude of Florida, the country is tropical wherever the altitude is low. In a general sort of way, the average altitude increases as one goes from the south to the Himalayas on the northern frontier. The width of Nepal varies from 90 to 150 miles; it is, as a whole, a rectangularly shaped country, bounded by India on the west and Sikkim on the east, with the long side of the rectangle stretching about five hundred miles.

The south of Nepal is a flat region—an extension of the Gangeatic plain—known as the Terai. It varies from five to fifty-five miles in width and consists of rice paddies, forests, and jungles. (The Terai jungle used to be one of the most famous big-game hunting grounds in the world and still contains its share of tigers, cobras and pythons, crocodiles, and the one-horned Asian rhinoceros. Although now illegal, the killing of these animals continues; they are killed for their horns, which, when ground up, produce a powder that is sold abroad as an aphrodisiac.) After the lower forests, the Himalayan foothills, which rise ten thousand feet or more, begin, and extend up to the main Himalayan chain in the north. This part of the country is ribbed by gigantic gorges that were created by the rivers running southward from the Himalayas. The geological forces that produced the mountains twisted the rivers and the gorges and left an occasional large valley—a former lake. The Kathmandu valley, which has a population of about eight hundred thousand people, is the largest valley. (The total population of Nepal, which is estimated to be growing, on average, at about 2.6 percent a year—and nearly 6 percent in the south—is now close to twenty million. If this continues unchecked, the population will double every thirty years.) It is circular in shape and has an area of 218 square miles. Since the valley is neither very high nor very low, it has rather temperate weather, with temperatures that rarely exceed 90 degrees F in the hot months of May and June, and never get much below 36 degrees in the coldest month, January. Even in the winter months, the sun warms the air during the day, it almost never snows, and it is rarely necessary to put on a sweater before evening.

Throughout the history of the country, the Kathmandu valley has been the cultural and political locus of Nepal. In fact, until the last forty years, internal communication was so bad among the different communities in Nepal that a large fraction of the population was hardly aware that it belonged to any sort of nation at all. For most people in the hills or the Terai, Nepal meant the Kathmandu valley, and in 1958 King Mahendra Bir Bikram Shah Deva, then ruler of Nepal, in an attempt to stimulate a national awareness, issued a decree asking the population to refrain from using *Nepal* in reference to the valley alone.

It is simply not known who the original settlers of the valley were. It is believed that the aboriginal population was overrun and absorbed during a series of migrations into the valley, ending in the seventh century B.C. by an Indo-Mongoloid race known as the Kirantis, from whom the present occupants of the valley evolved. In B.C. 536, the Gautama Buddha was born in the village of Lumbini in what is now the southern part of Nepal—the Terai. Legend has it that the Buddha visited the Kathmandu valley. According to one account, he and his party were warned before leaving, "In Nepal the ground is nothing but rocks, and it is as humpy as the back of a camel. Surely you are not going to enjoy your journey." Whether because of the Buddha's visit or otherwise, the Kirantis became Buddhists, and by the third century B.C. some of the most famous Buddhist shrines in the valley— the stupas at Swayambhunath, a hill near Kathmandu where the first lotus took root and flowered, and at Bodnath, a small town a few miles northeast of Kathmandu—had been built. A *stupa* is a representation of the contemplating Buddha. In form it has a hemispherical bottom, the *garb,* representing Buddha's body. At the top of the hemisphere is a cube—Buddha's face. All the faces of the cube are painted to show the Buddha's eyes. His nose is often represented by a curious figure like a question mark that is usually interpreted as the Sanskrit symbol for "one"—as in the "oneness" or "uniqueness" of Buddha. In the middle of each of the four foreheads there is a third eye. In Bodnath, the four middle eyes have been fitted with electric light bulbs, which give the stupa an uncanny appearance when viewed at night. During the day, the outstanding feature of the stupas is the eyes, which, as one writer has remarked, have "a fascinating aspect of mingled meditation and detached watchfulness." They seem to follow you as you go around the base. Above the face is a series of coils, sometimes in metal and sometimes in stone, that represent Buddha's hair. The legend has it that the Buddha was meditating one day when it occurred to him that he was losing a certain amount of time from his contemplation by the necessity of getting periodic haircuts. At once, the story says, his hair became tightly coiled and turned blue and no further haircuts were required. In the countryside, especially in the north near Tibet, the landscape is dotted with stupas, many of which have, through age and neglect, lost their eyes, but still retain a haunting suggestion of the original face.

The community of Bodnath is built in a circle surrounding the central stupa. It has long been a place of pilgrimage for Buddhists, especially from Tibet. Since the Chinese takeover of Tibet in the 1950s, a certain number of Tibetan refugees have settled in Bodnath—there are about eight thousand Tibetan refugees left in Nepal out of the original group of fifteen thousand or so, the rest having remigrated to India, to join the Dalai Lama in Dharamsala, or to the West. The Tibetans in Nepal ply many of their traditional trades, such as farming and rug weaving. They are also extraordinarily persuasive salespeople, and any visitor to Nepal comes away with Tibetan statuary and *thangkas,* religious wall scrolls, which, he is often assured, were brought down from the *gompas*—monasteries—in Tibet. There is a thriving industry in the valley engaged in manufacturing imitation Tibetan monastery art, and it may be just as well for the visitor that it is now all but impossible to find the real thing, since it is against the law in Nepal to export anything that is more than a hundred years old.

The main Buddhist sanctuary in the valley is Swayambhunath, situated on the top of a wooded hill just west of Kathmandu. It is best approached by climbing the 300 steps that lead, rather steeply, to the summit. One first encounters a row of three very large, striking, and rather cruel looking Buddhas that have been painted in bright colors. Everywhere one looks, there are small, brown, and very aggressive monkeys. The monkey, like the cow, is a sacred, protected animal in Nepal, but one can sympathize with the children who play near Swayambhunath when they take occasional shots at them with small slingshots. On the top of the hill, there is a large cleared plateau, every square foot of which contains religious monuments. There is a huge stupa and dozens of small stupas; there is a large metal *dorje* (a symbolic lightning bolt); there are rows of prayer wheels that have *Om mani padme hum*—a sacred mantra often translated as "Hail to the jewel in the lotus"—engraved on the sides. The wheel, the wheel of life, represents for Buddhists the endless cycle of birth and rebirth. To turn a prayer wheel adds to one's *sonam*—a measure of the credit that a Buddhist hopes to accumulate in this present life in order to escape the pain of rebirth. In the mountainous countryside of Nepal, where the wheel as a mode of transportation is all but unknown, the only wheels one sees are waterwheels for grinding corn or millet, prayer wheels, and potters' wheels. In the high-mountain country near Tibet, one encounters prayer wheels that are turned by water in a stream; a bell rings each time a cycle is completed, and with the rushing stream it makes a lovely sound.

At the top of the hill at Swayambhunath one encounters a cross section of all the races in Nepal: Sherpas and Tibetans from the north; Newars, the racial group that succeeded the Kirantis, in the valley; Gurungs, Magars, Sunwars, Rais, and Limbus—the hill peoples from whom the Gurkha soldiers were traditionally recruited; and a few Tharus, who have come north from the Terai to visit Kathmandu. (There are at least thirty separate local languages in Nepal, and at least that many tribal groups. The official language of the country is Nepali, an Indo-Aryan language derived from Sanskrit, which most of the population can now speak or understand. Most of the population, however, is unable to read or write any language, and a number of local languages, such as Sherpa, a dialect of Tibetan, have no written counterparts.) Something like 90 percent of Nepalis are now Hindu or at least practice a religion that is a mixture of Buddhism, animism, and Hinduism—a mixture that is nearly pure Hinduism in the south, where there is also a tiny Muslim enclave, and becomes nearly pure Buddhism in the north near Tibet. However, almost all of the great religious shrines in the Kathmandu valley—there are more than twenty-seven hundred temples there—contain icons that belong to both major faiths. At Swayambhunath, for example, which is nominally a Buddhist shrine and indeed has an important monastery, also located at the top of the hill, there is a shrine dedicated to Sitala, the Hindu goddess of smallpox, at which both Hindus and Buddhists used to pray for protection (smallpox was eradicated from Nepal in 1975 after a very successful vaccination program). In all the complex and often bloody history of Nepal, there has never been a war fought along religious lines, and religious tolerance is both the law of the land and the practice of its people.

Buddhism was the religion of Nepal until about the fourth century A.D., when the valley fell under the influence of the Gupta kings of India, who were Hindus, and since that time the kings of Nepal have all been Hindu. Buddhism migrated northward, through Nepal into Tibet and China as increasing contacts developed among these countries in the seventh century. The first Chinese mission visited the Kathmandu valley in A.D. 643. The leader of the second Chinese mission, in 647, Wang Huen Tse, recorded his mixed feelings about "Ni-Po-Lo"—Nepal—and its inhabitants:

The kingdom of "Ni-Po-lo" is about four thousand Li in circumference [a "li" is about a third of a mile] and the capital about twenty. It is situated in the middle of snowy mountains and, indeed, presents an uninterrupted series of hills and valleys. Its soil is suited to the cultivation of grain and abounds in flowers and fruits. One finds there red copper, yaks and birds of the name ming ming. [Real yaks are never found below about thirteen thousand feet, so Wang Huen Tse was speaking either of yaks that he met while crossing the high passes leading from Tibet to Nepal, or of one of the crossbreeds between yaks and buffalo—such as the zopkio and zhum, the male and female offspring of such a union—which to the casual observer

look like yaks, but which can and do live at lower altitudes.]
Coins of red copper are used for exchange. The climate is very
cold. The national character is stamped with falseness and per-
fidy, the inhabitants are all of hard and savage nature: to them
neither good faith nor justice nor literature appeal, but they are
gifted with considerable skill in the arts. Their bodies are ugly
and their faces are mean. Among them are true believers [i.e.,
Buddhists] and heretics [i.e., Hindus]. Buddhist convents and the
temples of the Hindu gods touch each other. It is reckoned that
there are about two thousand religious who study both the
Greater and the Lesser Vehicle. The number of Brahmans and of
the nonconformists has never been ascertained exactly.

Curiously, Buddhism was, at the time of Wang Huen Tse's visit to
Ni-Po-Lo, a relatively new export from Nepal to Tibet and China.
Indeed, the ruler of Nepal, Amshuvarma, had only recently given his
daughter Bhirkuti in marriage to the Tibetan king, Songsten Gampo.
The king also took a Chinese princess in marriage. (The two brides
have become canonized in the Buddhist tradition and are now wor-
shiped in Nepal and Tibet as the Green and White Taras (Sanskrit)
or Drölma (Tibetan)—the goddesses of compassion. In both countries one sees beautiful statues of the Tara with her hand held out in
a gesture of offering.) Bhirkuti transmitted the Buddhist tradition to
Tibet and hence to China. In addition, at this time the greatest architectural innovation that has ever been produced by the Nepalese, the pagoda
temple, also moved north. According to Nepalese scholars, the pagoda
temple can be traced back four thousand years in Nepal. It is said to have
its origins in the practice of animal sacrifice.

There is still a great deal of ritual animal sacrifice in Nepal. On
Saturdays one can drive past the Chobar Gorge to Dashinkali, a
temple dedicated to Kali, the Hindu goddess of destruction, located
about ten miles south of the city. Here hundreds of Nepalese Hindus
come on foot and by truck, with ducks, chickens, and goats that are to
be sacrificed on the altar of Kali. The animals, which are led to the
altar in a strangely silent procession, are killed with a single stroke of
a *kukri,* the traditional Nepalese scimitar. (Almost every Nepalese boy

acquires a kukri as a sign of his manhood. The knives, kept razor sharp, are worn in the belt and are used for everything from felling small trees to killing buffalo. The Gurkha soldiers often use kukris in hand-to-hand combat with devastating effect.) After an animal sacrifice, the blood of the animal is used as a religious ornament and the animal is eaten. (Once, in the hills, I came across a small village, all of whose inhabitants were gathered around a buffalo that had been hit in the neck with an ax, another weapon of sacrifice, and was slowly dying while the fresh blood was being collected in a copper vessel.) In these ancient rites, the animals are often burned after being killed. It was necessary to design an altar that was sheltered, to keep the rain from extinguishing the fire. It was also necessary, however, to cut a hole in the roof, in order to let out the smoke. Hence, to keep the rain from entering the hole, a second roof was put on top of the first—thus, the pagoda. The Kathmandu valley is dotted with pagoda temples, often with three or four gilded roofs. At sunrise and sunset they glitter like jewels.

The city of Kathmandu is thought to have been founded in the eighth century. Its name, until the beginning of the sixteenth century, was Kantipur. At that time, according to legend, a sacred tree of Paradise took on human form during a religious procession and wandered among the spectators. The tree was recognized and held prisoner until it promised to give itself up, and to allow its wood to be used in the construction of a single pagoda temple. Thus, in the center of the town there is a pagoda temple that is said to have been built from the wood of the sacred tree. In Nepali *kath* means "wood" and *mandu* means "house."

The real history of modern Nepal begins in the thirteenth century, with the advent of the Malla kings. The Mallas, assumed to be of Indian origin, acquired control over a part of what is now western Nepal and over numerous feudal principalities in the Kathmandu valley. (In addition to Kathmandu itself, and the small Tibetan community of Bodnath, there are two other major communities in the valley: Patan, which has structures that date back to at least the third century B.C.; it is about three miles southeast of Kathmandu and the oldest city in the valley, with a population of about eighty thousand;

and Bhadgaon, which is about eight miles east of Kathmandu and has a population of about fifty thousand.) At one point, before the advent of the Mallas, each ward of Patan had its own king, while twelve kings ruled over Kathmandu and Bhadgaon. It appears that the Mallas were of Buddhist origin but adopted the Hinduism of the Newars, the race that succeeded the Kirantis in the valley. Now there are both Buddhist and Hindu Newars. What their origin is and when they came to the valley are not well established. Many of them have Mongolian features, indicating that they may have come down from the north. Both Buddhist and Hindu Newars have a caste system similar to but somewhat less rigid than the Indian system. *Nava* means "valley" in Newari, and it is sometimes thought that *Nepal* is derived from that word. The Newars have some especially interesting matrimonial customs. Sometime between the ages of seven and nine a Newar girl is symbolically married to a tree, so that, in the event she is later divorced or widowed, she retains her status as a married woman. At the time of her marriage, her husband presents her a gift of areca nuts, and if she later decides to divorce him, she merely has to leave an areca nut on his bed and the marriage is terminated.

The Malla kings were great patrons of the arts, and under their reign most of the pagoda temples and gilded statues that are now the glory of the valley were constructed by Newar craftsmen. The Newars excelled in both metal- and woodwork. A typical Newar house—and many that are now occupied in the valley date back to the time of the Mallas—is made of red brick, but the windows and roofs are decorated with marvelously intricate wood carvings. It is one of the sadder aspects of modern Nepal that the Newar arts are disappearing. The brassworkers have become plumbers, the woodworkers carpenters, and the wonderful old brick Newar houses are being plastered over with cement whenever their occupants can afford it.

The Malla dynasty reached its political apex under the rule of Yaksha Malla, which began in 1417 and lasted for forty-two years. He extended his domain into the west of Nepal and into present-day Tibet. At Yaksha Malla's death, his kingdom broke up again into lesser principalities, and it was not until the eighteenth century that Nepal was reunited. The three sons of Yaksha Malla each ruled over a part of his empire, with a resultant chaos of internecine warfare among their descendants that lasted three centuries. The greatest achievements of this period were in the proliferation of Newar masterpieces, as each Malla king vied with the others in the building of palaces and pagoda temples. In the beginning of the eighteenth century, Bhupatindra Malla had built in Bhadgaon the Nyatpola, a giant wooden pagoda temple with five roofs, which, despite the earthquakes that strike Nepal about once every thirty-five years—the last severe earthquake in Kathmandu was in 1934, and it caused the destruction of entire nearby villages as well as a great many buildings in the city itself—remains intact as one of the architectural marvels of the country. The entrance is guarded by a pair of legendary heroes ten times as strong as an ordinary man. Above them is a pair of elephants ten times stronger than they, and above the elephants are two lions ten times stronger than the elephants and above the lions are two dragons ten times stronger than the lions. (The fact that lions figure in both Nepalese and Tibetan iconography of this period presumably means that there were then lions in this part of Asia.) Finally, above the lions are two goddesses said to be ten times more powerful than the lions, and so one hundred thousand times more powerful than an ordinary man.

While the Mallas were fighting among each other and building statues of elephants and lions, another family dynasty was building its power in western Nepal. This was the Shah family, whose dynastic capital was Gorkha, now a fairly modest town some forty miles west of Kathmandu. The hill tribes who became the subjects of the Shah kings of Gorkha were, and are, superb fighters, and it is from among them that the so-called Gurkha soldiers are recruited. It was not until the middle of the nineteenth century that the British army in India began employing the Gurkhas as military mercenaries. (There are presently five Gurkha battalions—some eight thousand soldiers—in the British army. They are stationed in places such as Hong Kong, Great Britain, and Brunei. The government of Brunei has them on a "lease" arrangement from the British. The number is expected to be reduced to some twenty-five hundred in the next few years, and they may eventually be eliminated altogether. The Indians, on the other hand, have an estimated one hundred thousand mercenary Gurkhas in their army.) Until that time, they formed the army of the kings of Gorkha and were used by them in the conquest of the Mallas. In 1736, the ninth king of the house of Gorkha, Marbhupal Shah, made the first invasion of the Kathmandu valley. He was badly beaten by the Malla king and died in 1742. But his son Prithwi Narayan Shah, who became king at the age of twelve, took up where his father had failed, and by the time of his death, in 1775, he had succeeded in subjugating all of Nepal and establishing its borders pretty much as they are today.

Prithwi Narayan was a ruthless soldier. He began his conquest of the valley by laying siege, three times, to the town of Kirtipur, a small medieval village on top of a hill a few miles south of Kathmandu. Its inhabitants were firmly entrenched in their fortifications, but Prithwi Narayan offered a general amnesty if they surrendered. They did, and he promptly gave orders that the lips and noses of all males twelve and over be cut off, and that the name of the town be changed to Naskatipur—the "City of Cut Noses." Only the players of wind instruments were spared mutilation. The rest of the towns surrendered to the Gurkhas one after the other, and by 1768, Prithwi Narayan had conquered the entire valley and established the national capital of Nepal at Kathmandu. The present king, Birendra Bir Bikram Shah Dev, is the tenth Shah king to rule Nepal.

It was with Prithwi Narayan that the systematic exclusion of Europeans from Nepal began, a policy that was followed, with rare exceptions, until 1950. Before the rise of the Shahs, Nepal had been visited, more or less freely, by Europeans and especially by Christian missionaries. In 1661, a German Jesuit, Father Greuber, made a celebrated exodus from Beijing, from which he had been expelled, south through Tibet and into Nepal. His journal is a fascinating record of how the country appeared in the midseventeenth century. Like all travelers from Nepal to Tibet, he had to cross the high-mountain passes that traverse the Himalayan range, which forms the boundary between the two countries. Some of these passes are more than nineteen thousand feet in elevation, and the unacclimated traveler experiences serious problems from the lack of oxygen. As Father

Greuber wrote upon crossing such a pass, "This hill is of unsurpassed altitude, so high that travelers can scarcely breathe when they reach the top, so attenuated is the air. In summer no one can cross it without gravely risking his life because of the poisonous exhalations of certain herbs." One wonders what herbs Father Greuber had in mind. In any case, after a month's journey he reached the Nepalese town of Nesti, where he found that the inhabitants "live in the darkness of idolatry. There was no sign of the Christian faith. However, all things which are necessary for human life were abundant and one could there, as a matter of course, buy thirty or forty chickens for a crown." Six days later Father Greuber reached "Cadmendu," whose inhabitants offended his sensibilities even more than the residents of Nesti. "The women of this country are so ugly," he wrote, "that they resemble rather devils than human beings. It is actually true that from a religious scruple they never wash themselves with water but with an oil of a very unpleasant smell. Let us add that they themselves are no pleasanter and with the addition of this oil one would not say that they were human beings but ghouls." Prithwi Narayan summarized his own attitude toward missionaries in the formula: "First the Bible; then the trading stations; then the cannon." Even now, all religious missionary activity is forbidden by law in Nepal, although some missionary hospitals and schools are allowed to function so long as they do not make any attempt at conversion.

After the death of Prithwi Narayan, Nepal entered a period of internal political disorder and external expansion. The sons of Prithwi Narayan plotted against each other until finally, in 1786, Bahadur Shah, the youngest son, removed the legitimate heir and became the de facto ruler until 1795. It was under Bahadur Shah that Nepal had its first confrontation with Chinese power. In 1788 and 1791, Nepal invaded Tibet, at that time a domain of the Manchu emperors of China. In 1791, a Chinese army of seventy thousand expelled the Nepalese from Tibet and marched over the high Himalayan passes to within a short distance of Kathmandu. Undoubtedly, the Chinese then, and the British in the next century, could have annexed Nepal. But for one reason or another, perhaps the stubborn fighting qualities of the inhabitants, both powers chose to administer military lessons and then withdraw. In this case, in 1792, the Nepalese agreed to leave Tibet and to send a tribute mission to Beijing every five years, a practice that continued until 1908.

Bahadur Shah was the first *mukhtiyar,* "prime minister," to assume executive powers in the name of the king. From his reign, and indeed until that of the present king—who in 1990, after a brief revolution, gave up many of his traditional powers—the prime minister became, in Nepalese politics, an important and often dominant figure. Such were the rivalries between the king and his executive officer that none of the *mukhtiyars,* from Bahadur Shah who began his office in 1769, until the rise of the Ranas, the family that ruled Nepal with an iron hand as *hereditary* prime ministers from 1846 until 1951, died a natural death. All were assassinated or committed suicide. A British commentator, Laurence Oliphant, who made a rare visit to Nepal in the 1850s, observed that "the power of the prime minister is absolute until he is shot, when it becomes unnecessary to question the expediency of his measures"; he added that a man's chance of filling the office did not depend on his ability to form a ministry "so much as upon his accuracy in taking aim and his skill in seizing any opportunity offered by his rival of showing his dexterity in a manner more personal than pleasant."

The Shah kings adopted the practice, maintained up to the present king's grandfather, of marrying two queens at once. This introduced another source of confusion and intrigue into the government: The queens and their assorted offspring vying for political power. In their fascinating book *Democratic Innovations in Nepal,* Leo Rose and Bhuwan Joshi describe the court scene as it was in the early 1840s, when the power struggle produced a state of almost total chaos: "The royal household was at this time badly split between the King, the Junior Queen, and the Crown Prince. The King was anxious to fix the succession on the Crown Prince, but without his own abdication; the Junior Queen was conspiring to put her son on the throne in place of the son of the late Senior Queen; the Crown Prince was conspiring against both his father and his stepmother in his eagerness to be seated on the throne at the earliest opportunity." To make matters worse, during this period the Nepalese attempted to penetrate south into India, an effort that led to an inevitable confrontation with the British.

The first British entry into Nepal had come at the time of Prithwi Narayan. In 1767, the Malla king of Patan asked the British East India Company to send troops to help lift the siege that Prithwi Narayan had laid upon the city. A force under the command of one Captain Kinloch was sent north. Before they even made contact with the Gurkhas, however, they were stopped in the Terai by an impassable natural barrier that the jungle and swamp country interposed—malaria. In Captain Kinloch's day, the malaria-carrying mosquito was more than a match for any European army. As a British historian of Nepal put it, "Throughout the hours of daylight the Terai is safe enough. It is the evening that man may not spend in his most beautiful park. Sundown in the Terai has brought to an end more attempted raids into Nepal and has buried more political hopes than will ever be known."

In 1800, the Shah king, Girvana Jadha Bikram Shah, was deposed by his prime minister and fled to British India to organize, with the aid of the British, an attempt to regain the throne. But the new government, in order to avoid a direct confrontation with the British, signed a treaty in 1801 with the East India Company that gave the company special trading rights and, most significantly, permitted the British to establish a residency in Kathmandu. This residency, which in 1947 became the British embassy, has functioned, with a few interruptions, since 1801. It was the only real contact that the Nepalese government had with Europe or the West until 1951. The first Resident, however, lasted only a year—the Nepalese government made it impossible for him to function—and shortly after he was withdrawn, the Nepalese began raiding northern India from the Terai. The border situation deteriorated to such an extent that in November of 1814, Great Britain declared war on Nepal. After several setbacks, a British army under General Ochterlony defeated the Gurkhas in 1815 in the Garhwal hills. The Nepalese delayed in ratifying the treaty of armistice, and in 1816, General Ochterlony was ordered to take the capital, Kathmandu. There is little doubt that he could have done so, but in March of 1916 the Nepalese signed the Treaty of Segauli, which conceded portions of the Terai to the East India Company and established the British Resident in Kathmandu once and for all. One of the most extraordinary provisions of the treaty, Article 7, gave the British a veto right over any future employment of westerners in Nepal: "The Rajah of Nepal hereby engages never to take or retain in his service any British subject, nor the subject of any European or American State, without the consent of the British Government."

General Ochterlony, through his bitter struggles with the Gurkhas, had come to appreciate their exceptional qualities as soldiers, and he conceived the idea of recruiting them into the British army—if for no other reason than to keep them from making trouble in India. This was not done at once, on the grounds that the Gurkhas might have divided loyalties. (This concern surfaced again in 1989, when the Nepalese purchased military supplies from China. The Indians responded by closing several entry points into Nepal and restricting that country's importation of petroleum.) But in 1832, Sir Brian Hodgson, the second British Resident, again urged their recruitment, and in a communication to his government he wrote:

> *These Highland soldiers, who dispatch their meal in half an hour, and satisfy the ceremonial law by merely washing their hands and face and taking off their turbans before cooking, laugh at the pharisaical rigour of our sepoys, who must bathe from head to foot and make puja ere they begin to address their dinner, must eat nearly naked in the coldest weather, and cannot be marching trim again in less than three hours—the best part of the day. In war, the former carry several days' provisions on their backs, the latter would deem such an act intolerably degrading. The former see foreign service nothing but the prospect of gain and glory, the latter can discover in it nothing but pollution and peril from unclean men and terrible wizards and goblins and evil spirits. . . .*
>
> *I calculate that there are at this time in Nepal no less than 30,000 dhakeries, or soldiers off the roll by rotation, belonging to the Khas, Muggars and Gurung tribes. I am not sure that there exists any insuperable obstacle to our obtaining, in one form or another, the services of a large body of these men, and such are their energy of character, love of enterprise, and freedom from the shackles of cast, that I am well assured their services, if obtained, would soon come to be most highly prized.*

In 1857, when the Sepoy Mutiny broke out in India, the Nepalese offered to send Gurkha troops to the aid of the British. From that time on, the recruitment of Gurkha soldiers, which the British had been practicing clandestinely in Nepal for some time, became officially accepted by both governments. In 1908, the first Gurkha brigade in the British army was formed. It numbered about twelve thousand men, organized into ten regiments. In the First World War, the Nepalese government placed the whole of its military resources at the service of the British, and more than two hundred thousand Gurkhas fought in the war and suffered twenty thousand casualties. (Just before the war, the Nepalese prime minister complained to the British Resident, "We have forty thousand soldiers ready in Nepal and there is nothing to fight.") After the war, Colonel Kennion, the British Resident, made a speech of appreciation to the prime minister in which he said, "I cannot attempt to enumerate all that His Highness did during the four years of war and after. Let it suffice to say that in this great war, Nepal pulled her weight, and more than pulled her weight." The British historian and journalist Percival Landon, in his book *Nepal,* written in 1928, commented in a footnote to Colonel Kennion's speech, "It would be interesting to know what meaning the expression, so full of significance to any Englishman, actually conveyed to the minds of the Resident's hearers; for there is scarcely a country in the world in which there are so few pieces of water and boat racing is entirely unknown." (This comment may well have reflected the fact that Landon was not allowed to visit most of the country. Rafting the Nepalese rivers is now a common tourist activity.) In the Second World War, the Gurkhas served with the British on every front, and after the war, they were used to fight Communist guerrillas in places like Malaysia. Until 1977, the Indian government was said to have paid the Nepalese government some two million rupees a year (a Nepalese rupee is worth roughly two American cents) for the right to recruit Gurkha soldiers; it paid the British government a comparable amount. It used to be the case that the pensions and salaries paid to Gurkhas were a leading source of foreign exchange. But both tourism and the export of Tibetan rugs have now vastly surpassed the Gurkhas as a source of income from abroad.

By 1843, the political situation in Nepal had decayed into a state of nearly total chaos. There were three principal contending centers of power. There was the king, Rajendra Bir Bikram Shah, who has been described at best as weak and vacillating. There was the crown prince, Surendra Bikram Shah, the late senior queen's son, who was anxious to replace his father on the throne as soon as possible. And there was the junior queen, Lakshimi Devi, who, in a secret collaboration with General Mahatabar Singh Tapa, commander-in-chief of the army and prime minister, was attempting to put *her* son on the throne. The king sided alternately with the junior queen and the crown prince. In 1843, he made a formal declaration investing the junior queen with what amounted to the power to govern the country, and in December of 1844, the crown prince left Kathmandu for the Terai, vowing not to return until his father had turned over the throne to him. The king followed his son to the Terai and persuaded him to come back to Kathmandu by transferring some of his royal prerogatives to the crown prince. In addition, but still in the background, there was a young army officer, Jang Bahadur Kunwar, who later added the title *Rana* to his name, claiming descent from the Rajput Ranas of Rajasthan, in India, a famous Indian royal house. During the next three years, Jang Bahadur unleashed or profited from a series of events that catapulted him into absolute power in Nepal and have shaped the destiny of the country to the present day.

The first act of the drama occurred in May of 1845. Both the king and the junior queen had become apprehensive about the growing power of the prime minister, Mahatabar Singh, and in a rare collaborative effort they decided that he should be done away with. For this purpose they selected as executioner Jang Bahadur, who was Mahatabar Singh's nephew. It is not entirely clear whether—as Jang later claimed—he was ordered to shoot his uncle or be shot himself, or whether he realized that shooting his uncle would give him a new status with the royal family and so he accepted the job willingly. In any event, one night in May, Mahatabar was summoned to the palace on the pretext that the queen was ill, and when he arrived in her room he was shot dead by his nephew. For this act Jang was given command of a quarter of the Nepalese army. This was only the beginning. The queen had a lover in court, one Gagan Singh, who, through his liaison with her, had become the commander of seven Nepalese regiments and been put in charge of supervising all of the arsenals and magazines in the country. The queen's love affair became known to the king, who decided that Gagan Singh was to be assassinated. At 10 P.M. on the fourteenth of September, 1846, Gagan Singh was shot while kneeling in his room in prayer. It is not clear what role, if any, Jang Bahadur had in this assassination, but he took full advantage of it to precipitate the next act. The queen, upon hearing of the murder, was beside herself with rage and, on Jang's advice, summoned all of the civil and military officials in the capital to the Kot, or courtyard, of the Royal Palace. She proceeded to the Kot herself, armed with a sword, which she intended to use or have used to behead her lover's murderer. As the courtiers assembled, unarmed and unsuspecting, Jang Bahadur surrounded the Kot with his own troops. By 1 A.M., the Kot was full. What happened next is the subject of a great deal of controversy among historians of Nepal, and the various accounts tend to be flavored by a given historian's feelings toward the Ranas in general. In sifting through the different versions, one gets the impression that the queen, for reasons of her own, had fixed the guilt upon a government minister, one of those assembled in the Kot, named Birkishore Pande, who at once proclaimed his innocence. The queen nevertheless demanded that he be beheaded immediately and without trial. General Abhiman Singh, whom the queen commanded to carry out the execution, refused, and Jang Bahadur, taking advantage of the overall confusion, advised the queen to arrest General Singh, telling her, probably falsely, that Singh's troops were even then moving in on the palace and that there was no time to lose. Singh resisted arrest and was stabbed to death by one of Jang's soldiers. (One account says that he was cut in two by a single stroke of a sword at the hand of one of Jang's brothers.) At this juncture, the situation got out of control, and over the next few hours Jang's soldiers slaughtered most of the nobility in Nepal. This event, known as the Kot Massacre, eliminated in one swoop most of Jang's rivals for power. The king himself sought refuge in the British Residency, and the next day the queen conferred the title of prime minister on Jang Bahadur. Most of those government officials not already under Jang's control fled the country. Jang had seven brothers, and within a few days they held essentially all of the important government posts in Nepal. Indeed, for the next century Jang Bahadur and his descendants, the Ranas, controlled *everything* in Nepal as a sort of private preserve.

Jang Bahadur became, in the thirty years that he ruled Nepal, that country's first really international political figure. The Rana regimes—the "Ranacracy," as it is usually referred to now in Nepal— left so many scars and bitter memories that even today, although nearly half a century has passed since the Ranas were overthrown and the monarchy restored, historians of Nepal find it all but impossible to give an objective account of Jang Bahadur's life and career. There is no question, though, that he was a man of extraordinary physical courage and—while illiterate and uneducated—immense native intelligence, political shrewdness, and wit. Very soon after he seized power, the British realized that Jang was potentially an invaluable ally who, if cultivated, could guarantee stability on India's northern frontier. Thus, in 1850, Jang was invited to make a state visit to Great Britain to meet Queen Victoria. It is quite likely that Jang's party, which included four cooks and twenty-two domestic servants and which arrived in Britain in May of 1850, was the first group of Nepalis to cross the ocean and visit the West. The visit included a tour of the arsenals and munitions factories in Britain and a review of the troops—both of which were intended to, and did, convince Jang that it was hopeless to fight the British—as well as a night at the opera. The last, according to Percival Landon, produced an exchange with Queen Victoria that became the talk of London. As Landon tells it, "A distinguished prima donna had just given an exhibition of her powers and Jang Bahadur had applauded. The Queen, turning to him, said, 'But you have not understood what she was singing.' Jang Bahadur at once replied, 'No, Madam, nor do I understand what the Nightingales are saying.'"

After returning home—through France, where he demanded a review of a hundred thousand French troops, and through India, where he visited a number of Hindu shrines in order to obtain ritual purification for having crossed the waters to the lands of the infidel—

Jang, inspired by the example of Britain, made at least some attempt to reform the legal code of Nepal. Nepalese law had evolved from Hindu religious practices and local tribal customs. Mutilation was a common punishment for thievery—the thief was given his choice of having what was left of his arm bound or of bleeding to death—and executions were often carried out on the spot by the prosecutor. (Brahmans were, under all circumstances, exempt from capital punishment.) Slavery was legal, and in order to pay a debt, an individual could sell either himself or some member of his family into slavery. Civil disputes were frequently settled by a remarkable procedure involving a "water test" that took place in the Rani Pokhari, the "Queen's Tank," in Kathmandu. If the disputants were unable to otherwise settle their quarrel, the name of each was inscribed on a piece of paper, which was rolled into a ball. Each ball, with the name hidden, was then attached to a reed, which was immersed in the deep end of the pool. Two members of the *chamkhalak* caste (the leather-workers) were selected, one for each party in the dispute. They entered the tank, were assigned a reed, and, at a signal, immersed themselves simultaneously, head down, in the water. The first man to rise was declared the loser, and the paper ball attached to his reed was opened to see who had lost the case. Adultery was punishable by the summary execution of the male adulterer at the hand of the offended husband; *sati,* the practice among Hindu widows of offering themselves for burning on their husbands' funeral pyres, was common. Jang abolished the mutilation penalty and the water test; he made it illegal for a man to sell himself or his children into slavery, although it was not until 1924 that slavery as an institution was abolished in Nepal, and he discouraged the practice of sati. (Nevertheless, when he died in 1877, his three senior wives committed themselves to the pyre.) The method of punishing an adulterer was subtly modified—the adulterer was allowed a moment's head start to flee for his life, an advantage that was, in general, of small value, since friends of the husband were allowed to trip the adulterer as he tried to get away. A system of lower and higher courts was instituted, with Jang assigned ultimate judicial power, an intriguing feature of which was that a lower-court magistrate whose ruling was overturned was liable to fine, corporal punishment, and even decapitation.

On his return trip from England to Nepal, Jang encountered in Ceylon the English hunter and sportsman Laurence Oliphant, whose observations on the vulnerability of the prime ministers to gunshot were cited earlier. Oliphant was invited to accompany Jang on a hunting trip to the Terai and, ultimately, to Kathmandu; his account of the voyage, *A Journey to Kathmandu,* published in 1852[1], is one of the delights of Himalayan literature. Oliphant and his host did some fine tiger hunting in the Terai. The method then used to hunt tiger and other big game there does not appear to the casual observer to have given the beasts much of a chance. For weeks in advance of the shoot the animals were "beaten"—essentially, herded—by a ring of native "beaters" into a small area in the jungle, which was surrounded by men and tame elephants in order to keep the game inside. The

1. The book is long out of print, but in 1967 I had the good fortune to find it and several other out-of-print classics on Nepal in what was then a remarkable private library in Kathmandu belonging to one of Jang's descendants, Field Marshal Kaiser Shamsher Rana. (*Keshar* is a fairly common Nepalese first name, but the field marshal, who was the commander-in-chief of the Nepalese army and an admirer of Kaiser Wilhelm, preferred the western spelling.) The library, reputed to have been the largest private library in Asia, was housed in several rooms in the field marshal's mansion. People who knew him told me that the old gentleman—he died in 1964 at the age of seventy-two—delighted in working a conversation around to the point where he could say, "On page thus-and-so of the first volume of thus-and-so the author says. . . ," and quoting verbatim from one of his books, which he would then produce from the depths of his library to clinch the point. In addition to being a book collector, the field marshal was an avid hunter, and a visitor to the largest of the rooms in which the books are housed, on the first floor of the mansion, is stunned by the sight of an extremely lifelike stuffed tiger evidently ready to pounce. On one of my early visits, arranged by writing a note of request to the field marshal's widow, who then lived in the house, I came upon a live spotted deer in the library chewing on the fur of the tiger. The book collection is incredibly eclectic, ranging from *The Wizard of Oz* to an entire cabinet devoted to sex. In addition to an enormous ensemble of rare Tibetan manuscripts, the field marshal managed to collect probably every book on Nepal and Tibet ever written in any language. There were at that time not so many. The library has now been turned over to the Nepalese government by his widow. On my recent visits it had been cataloged, and the other visitors—some of whom seemed to be students—were making use of the books that are now available to the general community.

animals were then allowed a few weeks before the shoot to calm down and become accustomed to their new home. At the time of the shoot, bait, which for a tiger was a live buffalo, was staked out; the buffalo was literally staked to a post or a tree. When the tiger came to kill and eat the buffalo, the stake was surrounded by a ring of trained elephants, which kept the tiger trapped until the hunter, on the back of one of the elephants, could shoot it. About the only chance the tiger had was to panic and stampede an elephant. This was not too common, since a tiger is no match for an elephant—which, when attacked, simply lifts the tiger with its trunk and pounds it several times on the ground until it is dead. (On one of my visits to the Terai I had occasion to take an elephant ride in the jungle. At one point, the beast suddenly knelt on its forefeet as if in prayer. Later, when I asked why, I was told that this was the elephant's defensive fighting position and that it had probably scented a tiger, which, happily, had been scared off by the noise of our party.)

After the hunt, Oliphant and his host started the long trek over the mountains to Kathmandu. Oliphant described the trek in terms that will strike a chord of sympathy in anyone who has traveled in the Himalayas of Nepal on foot: "It was with no little regret then," he wrote, "that we made the almost interminable descent, apparently for the mere purpose of starting fair from the bottom of the valley, before we commenced the arduous climb in store for us over a range still higher than the one we had just traversed." Finally they came upon the Kathmandu valley. He was overwhelmed by its sheer beauty and wrote:

A tradition is current in Nepaul [Oliphant's spelling] *that the valley of Kathmandu was at some former period a lake, and it's difficult to say in which character it would have appeared the most beautiful. The knolls, wooded or terraced, with romantic old Newar towns crowning their summits—the five rivers of the valley winding amongst verdant meadows—the banks here and there precipitous where the soft clayey soil had yielded to the action of the torrent in the rains—the glittering city itself—the narrow paved ways leading between high hedges of prickly pear—the pagodas and temples studded in all directions, presented a scene as picturesque and perhaps more interesting than would have been afforded by the still lake embedded in wild mountains and frowned upon by snow-capped peaks.*

When I first came across this quotation in 1967, it seemed to me to apply to the Kathmandu I had just encountered. Now Oliphant's "narrow paved ways" are choked with motor vehicles spewing emissions that make Kathmandu a polluted inferno—a tragedy.

To return to the history. As Jang's guest in Kathmandu, Oliphant developed a thoroughgoing admiration for the foresight of his host when it came to dealing with potential conspiracies against his life. In particular, he wrote, "It is by no means an uncommon mode of execution in Nepaul to throw the unfortunate victim down a well: Jang had often thought that it was entirely the fault of the aforesaid victim if he did not come up again alive and unhurt. In order to prove the matter satisfactorily, and also to be prepared for any case of future emergency, he practiced the art of jumping down wells and finally perfected himself therein." Indeed, Jang claimed to have been thrown down a well at one point in his career before becoming prime minister, in an attempted assassination organized by the crown prince. By a prearranged plan he clung to the side until midnight, when he was rescued by some friends. (In Field Marshal Kaiser Shamsher Rana's copy of Oliphant, the word *dexterously,* used to describe Jang's acrobatics in the well, is printed upside down and backward, in a careful script, with red ink. The field marshal, who evidently thought well of his ancestor's feat, had crossed out the offending misprint and rewritten it.) On a tour of Jang's residence, Oliphant happened upon a portrait of Queen Victoria and also one of a gentleman with "keen eyes and high forehead" whom he did not recognize. Jang was helpful. "See," said Jang enthusiastically, "here is the Queen of England and she has not got a more loyal subject than I am." Then, turning to the picture of the man with the keen eyes and high forehead, he remarked, "That is my poor uncle Mahatabar Singh, whom I shot; it is very like him."

Jang Bahadur regarded the law of succession of the prime ministry, as established by the Sanad [decree] of 1856—which King Surendra, the former crown prince, signed, and which reduced the royal family to political impotence—as the masterstroke of his political career. In order to understand the circumstances under which the king issued a decree eliminating himself and his family, in perpetuity, from playing any sort of active role in the government of his country, one must understand a bit of what happened to the junior queen, to King Rajendra, and to Crown Prince Surendra after the Kot Massacre. No sooner had the queen proclaimed Jang Bahadur prime minister than she entered into a conspiracy with one of the few remaining noble families not decimated in the massacre—a conspiracy in which she intended to murder Jang, the king, *and* the crown prince. But one of the plotters gave away the show, and Jang had thirteen members of the family killed on the night of October 31, less than a month after the affair at the Kot. The queen was banished to Benares, and King Rajendra, apparently reasoning that, despite everything, he was safer with the queen than with Jang, went with her. He there organized a naive and futile attempt to regain his throne, and in May of 1847, Jang deposed him and elevated the crown prince to the throne, an arrangement that was endorsed by the British, giving it international status. Shortly thereafter the old king was arrested and brought back to Kathmandu, where he lived out the remainder of his life as a prisoner. The queen died in exile, and Jang maintained the new king, Surendra, as a puppet. During this period, a member of the staff of the British Residency wrote that "one may live for years in Nepal, without either seeing or hearing of the King." One may, indeed, wonder why Jang did not simply eliminate the monarchy once and for all rather than preserve at least its symbolic status. The answer is that in Nepal, the monarch was regarded as a direct descendant of the god Vishnu, so to have done away with kingship altogether would have aroused considerable hostility and perhaps open rebellion among the populace. So Jang was content to keep the king out of sight, but alive, in Kathmandu.

The law of succession introduced by Jang passed the office of prime minister not from father to son—as was the case with the royal house—but from brother to brother. The first to succeed was, therefore, the oldest surviving brother of the prime minister; then came the next oldest, and so on. When these had been exhausted, the job was to pass to the sons of Jang, then the sons of the oldest brother, and so on. The system was designed to ensure that Nepal would have a mature ruler at all times. Indeed, one of the problems that had plagued the Shah dynasty was that since many of the kings died young, their offspring were often infants when they inherited the crown, which meant that the country was ruled by the prime minister or the queen or one of the brothers of the king—whoever succeeded in eliminating the others, usually by assassination, from the race for power. As far as it went, Jang's scheme did at least ensure that there were no infant prime ministers. But Jang failed to anticipate the problems that arose from the fact that all of the Ranas had enormous numbers of children, legitimate and illegitimate. According to Dr. Daniel Wright, who was the surgeon attached to the British Residency during Jang's lifetime, Jang fathered at least a hundred children, including ten legitimate sons, while his youngest brother, Dhir Shamsher, had seventeen legitimate sons. A later-day British commentator who was shown a picture of a typical Rana general and his family remarked, "He is surrounded by so many children that the picture looks more like a photograph of a school than a family group." The situation reached such proportions that Chandra Shamsher Rana, who ruled as prime minister from 1901 to 1929, made a formal division of Rana offspring into three classes. The "A" class Ranas were children of Ranas and wives of equally high caste families. These families were allowed by the caste system to dine with the Ranas, and male "A" Ranas automatically became major generals at the age of twenty-one and could advance—at least in principle to commander-in-chief. The "B" class Ranas were born of mothers who were also legitimate wives but whose families were of lower, though good, caste. These families were allowed to take part in Rana social occasions but were not allowed to eat boiled rice with Ranas of higher caste. The "B" male offspring became, at the age of twenty-one, lieutenant colonels, but could never rise above the rank of full colonel. Finally, there were the "C" class Ranas, born of mistresses whose families, being of lower caste, were not allowed to eat with the Ranas at all. Various influential Ranas after Chandra Shamsher, however, made special exemptions for certain of their offspring of whom they were especially fond. Until the end of the Second World War, the Rana regime was so powerful that there was very little, and certainly no successful, resistance to it; such resistance as there was came, in most cases, however, from lower-class Ranas who felt frustrated by their inability to rise within the succession and hence made attempts to overthrow the system.

Jang was immensely pleased with the Sanad, which enunciated the law of succession, and he commented to his sons and brothers, "I have established a constitution unknown in the annals of gods or emperors by setting up a covenant, and you should not think of acting in contravention of the order of succession. Even if your superior and master takes to tying up goats to elephants' posts or vice versa or to paying no heed to merit, do not oppose him, but rather forsake the country and retire to a sacred place." Needless to say, no sooner had Jang died than his ten sons and the seventeen sons of Dhir Shamsher, along with various surviving members of Jang's family, began conspiring against each other for power. In 1885, Bir Shamsher, the oldest son of Dhir Shamsher, who had in the meanwhile died, organized a coup in which Jang's oldest and only surviving brother, the prime minister at the time, was shot, along with Jang's sons and their families. Bir Shamsher elevated himself to the prime ministry in a ceremony that was presided over by the then-king, Prithwi Vir Bikram Shah, who was five years old. From that time until the overthrow of the Ranas in 1951, all of the prime ministers came from the Shamsher branch of the family. (In Urdu, *sham* means "equal" and *sher* means "lion"—again the symbolism of the long-extinct Nepalese and Tibetan lion.) Jang was concerned not only about arranging the succession, but also about interlocking his family with the royal house through marriage. Indeed, three of his daughters were married to the king's oldest son, and *his* oldest son married the king's daughter. It became the practice of the Ranas to arrange marriages for the young kings as early as possible, and very often with Rana girls. Thus, for example, the present king's grandfather, King Tribhuvan, was married to two young girls when he was thirteen, and his father, Mahendra, was only fourteen years younger than his own late father. (Tribhuvan had fathered three sons by the time he reached sixteen.) King Mahendra, defying tradition, married only one wife, in 1940; when she died, he married her sister. They were Rana noblewomen. The present queen, Aishwarya Rajya Laxmi Davi Shah, is the oldest daughter of the late Lieutenant General Tandra Shumshare J. B. Rana. She married King Birendra, who was born in 1945, in 1970.

In 1854, the Nepalese, under Jang, invaded Tibet, and after a certain number of indecisive battles, the Chinese mediated an armistice, the Treaty of Thapathali, in which both governments pledged "respect" for the emperor of China. The treaty went on to say, "Tibet being merely a country of Monasteries of Lamas and a place for recitation of prayers and practice of religious austerities, should any foreign country invade Tibet in the future, Gorkha [i.e., Nepal] will afford such assistance and protection as it can." Be that as it may, when, in 1903, the British invaded Tibet, the Nepalese supplied them with yaks and porters, treaty or no treaty. One of Jang's more ingenious maneuvers in the war of 1854 was to obtain a declaration from the *rajguru,* the highest Hindu religious authority then in Nepal, that yaks were a species of deer, so that Gurkha soldiers could eat them without breaking the Hindu law against consuming beef. It was Jang who, in 1857, sent the Gurkhas to India to help suppress the mutiny; in recognition of this he was decorated by the British and, more important, Nepal received back the portions of the Terai that had been given to the British in 1816. Since it is agricultural produce from the Terai that feeds much of the country, it is quite possible that the return of these territories was the most significant act of foreign policy during the century of Rana rule.

In 1901, Bir Shamsher, the prime minister who had come into power after the assassination of Jang's older brother, died and was succeeded by Deva Shamsher. If Deva had been allowed to rule, the subsequent history of Nepal might well have been entirely different and the country could have been a half-century farther along in its development than it is today. Deva Shamsher was a progressive. He opened a network of primary schools in the Kathmandu valley, favored judicial reforms, and even hinted at the beginnings of some sort of popular democracy. He lasted four months in office and then, because of his ideas, was deposed by his younger half-brother at gunpoint and sent into exile. The only tangible result of Deva's ministry that has endured is the custom, initiated by him, of having cannons fired in Kathmandu to indicate high noon.

Chandra Shamsher was the first Rana prime minister to have a formal education. He studied at Calcutta University, where he learned English. (According to a contemporary account, Jang had made a few attempts to learn English during his lifetime and had a fondness throughout his life for having the English and Indian newspapers read and explained to him. There were no newspapers in Nepal.) Perhaps because he had been educated himself, Chandra Shamsher understood the dangers that an educated population would pose to an authoritarian government, and one of his first acts as prime minister was to close his brother's primary schools. Chandra also maintained the Rana tradition of excluding nearly all foreigners from Nepal. The rare exceptions were either guests of the British Resident or journalists and scholars such as Percival Landon and the great French orientalist Sylvain Levi, who wrote favorably about the regime. In his book *Nepal,* Percival Landon gives a list of all the Europeans who visited Nepal officially from 1881 to 1923; there were exactly 153. Even these visitors were not allowed to leave the Kathmandu valley, except for hunting in the Terai. Indeed, the second volume of Landon's monumental work begins with a sort of illustrated tour of the countryside, complete with photographs, which he received from the government, along with a text written in travelog style that he appears to have invented partly from his imagination and partly from what he was told to write. At one point, he asked Chandra why none of the English visitors to Nepal, including the Resident, were allowed to leave the valley, and why so few Englishmen were allowed to come to Nepal at all. He was told, "My friend, the English have at times difficulty in the government of India. These difficulties arise in no small measure from the fact that in these days of easy travel all English sahibs are not sahibs. Now, I am convinced that the prosperity of Nepal is bound up with the maintenance of British predominance in India, and I am determined that the sahib who is no sahib shall never enter Nepal and weaken my people's belief that every Englishman is a gentleman." As late as 1960, after a decade of intense effort by the post-Rana governments to improve the conditions in the villages in the countryside of

Nepal (following a century of total neglect under the Ranas), the life expectancy of a rural Nepali was twenty-six years, and two out of three children failed to survive infancy. It is small wonder that Chandra was not inclined to allow European journalists to learn firsthand about the lives of the Nepalese people.

Despite everything, it must be said that Chandra Shamsher brought the beginnings of western technology to Nepal, or, at least, to the Kathmandu valley. In 1904, Kathmandu was electrified, and in 1906, Lord Kitchener, the commander-in-chief of the British forces in India, who visited the valley, could write, "There I found marble palaces lighted by electricity and full of Nepalese officers who are . . . always in uniform like a continental nation." During Chandra's regime, the Ranas began construction of fantastic mansions modeled after French châteaux. Fixtures like the crystal clock, chandeliers, and illuminated fountain that decorated Chandra's own dining room, which is now used for state dinners, were carried across the mountains from India on the backs of coolies. Chandra's palace, the Singha Durbar, constructed in 1905 and modeled after the Palace of Versailles, contains more than fourteen hundred rooms. It now houses the offices of nearly the entire Nepalese government.[2]

The ruling elite were vaccinated against smallpox—which raged in epidemic proportions in the countryside. The disfigurement resulting from smallpox was a common sight when I first visited the country in 1967. A narrow-gauge railroad was constructed through part of the Terai, and a road was built from Birganj, on the Indian border, to Bhimphedi, in the foothills leading to Kathmandu, and then a ropeway was constructed for transporting small amounts of freight over the hills to the capital. In 1918, Chandra built the English College in Kathmandu, but it trained only a few members of elite families. (Dr. T. N. Upraity, the former vice-chancellor of Tribhuvan University—which is the only university in Nepal and which graduated its first Ph.D.

2. There is one curiosity in the palace that must have reflected an odd quirk in Chandra's character. Between the main dining room and a rather charming smaller room, used now by the king for receiving state guests, there is, as I was shown, a connecting antechamber lined with amusement-park mirrors that distort and distend the image of the passing visitor.

in 1968—told me, when I went to visit the university, that in his class at the English College, the class of 1945, there had been eleven students.)

All of the Rana prime ministers, Chandra included, ran Nepal as if it were a private business corporation. Any income from taxes in excess of the meager expenditures that the government made for public works and administrative expenses was kept by the Rana family, who banked it in Europe and India. The only connection that the government had with most people, who lived in isolation, often several weeks' march by foot from Kathmandu, was the tax collector. (Within the country, however, there were private principalities, like Mustang, in the west near the Tibetan border, that were allowed to function autonomously so long as the tax was collected. Mustang still has its own raja, Jigme Parbal Bista. The region was only opened to trekkers in 1992. They pay a very high fee to go there.) All opposition, or even potential opposition, was ruthlessly suppressed. Radios were forbidden to the Nepalese until 1946. Most foreign newspapers and periodicals were not allowed into the country, and when a group petitioned the government for a public library in Kathmandu in 1930, the petitioners were prosecuted for contemplating an unlawful action, and fined. There was an eight o'clock curfew in Kathmandu and a similar curfew in every substantial town in the country. Any sort of native talent in the arts or literature was discouraged and, indeed, most of the older generation of writers and artists now in Nepal have spent time either in jail or in exile. Land was held in a system of tenure and debt designed to keep the Nepalese farmer in perpetual servitude to a few large landowners—a system so intricate that even now, nearly a half-century after the fall of the Rana regime, the government still has not satisfactorily resolved the problem of redistributing the land. A few wealthy families in Kathmandu had telephones and automobiles, but the rest of the country lived in towns and villages that had remained as they were in the fifteenth century.

From Chandra Shamsher's death in 1929 until the revolution of 1950, two of his brothers, one of his sons, and a nephew became prime minister in succession. In the 1930s, secret opposition groups, including the People's Party (Praja Parishad), began forming, aided both morally and financially by King Tribhuvan, whose reign began in 1911. In 1941, the then-prime minister, Juddah Shamsher, tried to depose the king and put Crown Prince Mahendra—the present king's father—on the throne. The crown prince, who was then twenty-one, refused, in an act of great courage. After the war, the Nepali Congress Party, modeled after the Indian Congress Party, was formed in India by exiles from Nepal, and in 1947, the first of a series of strikes organized by the party began. In 1948, the Rana prime minister, Padma Shamsher, attempted some reforms, but was quickly forced to resign by his cousin Mohan Shamsher, who preferred the status quo.

In 1947, the British left India, and with their departure the traditional bond between the Rana governments and the British raj was broken. The new government of India, under Nehru, was extremely eager to promote change in Nepal. After the Communists came to power in China in 1949, it became clear that Tibet was going to be invaded. Clearly understanding the implications of having Chinese power on the borders of an unstable Nepal—after the Himalayan foothills of Nepal are crossed, going south, the terrain is completely open and merges into northern India with no natural barriers whatsoever—the Indians put strong pressure on the Ranas to modernize their government. In fact, in early 1950, Nehru stated, "If [freedom] does not come [to Nepal] forces that will ultimately disrupt freedom itself will be created and encouraged. We have accordingly advised the Government of Nepal, in all earnestness, to bring themselves into line with democratic forces that are stirring in the world today. Not to do so is not only wrong but also unwise."

In November of 1950, King Tribhuvan precipitated the events that led to the fall of the Ranas. All of the king's movements were closely guarded and any trip outside the capital could only be made with the permission of the prime minister, and then never unescorted. On November 5, the king saw the prime minister to arrange a hunting trip. What happened next is graphically described by Joshi and Rose in their book *Democratic Innovations in Nepal.*

The Rana ruler agreed and provided the necessary military escort, unaware that among the escort were several whom King Tribhuvan had already won over to his side. On the morning of November 6, King Tribhuvan and his entire family, with the exception of his four-year-old grandson Gyamendra, departed by automobile from the Royal Palace on what was ostensibly a hunting trip. The Indian embassy was located on the road the royal party was supposed to follow. Upon reaching the gates of the embassy, the king and his sons suddenly swerved through the gates and into the grounds, to the surprise and consternation of those Rana guards who had not been apprised of the king's plan. Thus the royal family took sanctuary and escaped from the Rana ruler's control. It seems probable that Prince Gyamendra was left behind to avoid suspicion about the hunting trip and to provide protection for him and the royal line in the event of mishap to the others if the plan should fail.

The Ranas attempted to entice the king out of the embassy, and when that failed they crowned his four-year-old grandson as the new king. On November 10, King Tribhuvan was flown in an Indian air force plane to New Delhi, and shortly thereafter armed rebellions broke out at several points in the Terai. In December, when the rebellion had not been contained and it had become clear that the new king was not going to be recognized by foreign governments, the Indians proposed a settlement in which King Tribhuvan was to be restored, a constituent assembly was to be brought into being for the purpose of writing a new constitution for the country, and a Rana would continue as prime minister but with greatly reduced powers. In early February of 1951, King Tribhuvan and the leaders of the Nepali Congress Party returned to Kathmandu in triumph. They were met at the airport by Mohan Shamsher, the last of the old-style Rana prime ministers. With this meeting, the Rana regime was ended, and Nepal began its struggle to reenter the modern world.

For the next four years, the king attempted to create a stable government. The coalition with the Rana prime minister failed to work and was dissolved in a few months; a chaotic period followed, during which the political power shifted back and forth between the king and the Congress Party. By March of 1955, when King Tribhuvan died in Switzerland, where he had gone for treatment of a chronic heart condition, there had been a general deterioration of the situation in the country. Inflation had decreased the value of the Nepalese rupee, and floods and droughts had brought famine to parts of the country. There were uprisings and disorders and indications of a growing Communist movement with links to the Chinese in Tibet. King Tribhuvan had been immensely popular with the Nepalese people, who revered him for the courageous stand he had taken during the Rana regimes, and for his genuinely democratic instincts. But ill health and, no doubt, personal temperament prevented him from becoming a strong central figure around whom the diverse and usually bitterly opposed political factions in the country could rally.

After Tribhuvan's death in 1955, he was succeeded by his son Mahendra, who ruled until his death in 1972. From the beginning, Mahendra made it clear that he was a strong personality to be reckoned with. Despite the disapproval of his father and the possibility that he might be jeopardizing his chances of succession, he married a Rana noblewoman in 1952, just after the revolution, when feelings against the Ranas were running extremely high. In 1955, soon after he had become king, he issued a statement in which he said, "Today marks the completion of four years of democracy in the country, but it is a matter of great shame that we cannot point to even four important achievements that were made during this period. If we say that democracy is still in its infancy, we have seen such qualities as selfishness, greed and jealousy which are not found in an infant. If we say that it has matured, unfortunately we do not see it flourishing anywhere, and, I presume, this is not hidden from anyone in the country."

The four-year period from the beginning of Mahendra's rule to the installation of the first elected ministerial government on May 27, 1959, was one of political chaos. There were ten different regimes, which oscillated in tone from conservative to liberal, but in which the king played an increasingly important role. General elections and a new constitution had been promised to the Nepalese since the revolution of 1951, and when the constitution was finally presented in 1959 it provided for a bicameral parliament, with an elected prime minister, but it also reserved for the king a wide variety of fundamental powers. Despite the political inexperience of the Nepalese, and the fact that the country appeared to have so much political division, the 1959 elections were both extremely orderly and remarkably unanimous. The Nepali Congress Party, which had been so active in fomenting the overthrow of the Ranas, won a stunning and nearly total victory. The new prime minister, B. P. Koirala, was a charismatic, thirty-nine-year-old revolutionary, an intellectual (he was widely known as a short-story writer), and, in the spirit of the Congress Party, a socialist. Despite some sporadic unrest in some of the western districts of the country and a few border incidents with China,[3] it seemed to many observers within and without Nepal that the Congress government was making slow but steady progress with the grave problems of the country. Therefore it came as a great surprise when, in December of 1960, King Mahendra suddenly, with essentially no warning, dismissed the Congress government and arrested Prime Minister Koirala. (Koirala was held in detention a few miles from Kathmandu until his release in October of 1968 by the king.) The reasons for the king's actions in 1960 have never been fully explained, but, very likely, the king saw in Koirala a growing political force that, if not checked, could erode the power of the monarchy. It is said that some of the younger Congress politicians had made it known that they regarded the monarchy as an outmoded institution. King Mahendra, unlike his predecessors under the Ranas, was a strong activist, and it is quite likely that he found it intolerable to play a role almost secondary to his prime minister.

In 1963, Nepal began experimenting with a political system known as the *panchayat*. The country was divided into seventy-five districts, comparable to counties, and fourteen zones, comparable to states. Each village unit with a population of at least two thousand elected what was known as a local panchayat—literally, a "committee of five," *panch* being the Nepali word for "five"—although the committees had, in practice, more than five members. They were responsible for local affairs such as schools and roads. At the next level were the town panchayats, which consisted of eleven members selected from the various local panchayats. Next in the hierarchy came the district panchayats, and then the zonal panchayats. At the apex of the system

3. At one point during 1960, it appeared as if the Chinese were going to make a serious territorial claim to Mount Everest, but this was settled in April of 1960 when Chou En-lai stated in a press conference in Kathmandu that the Chinese acknowledged the Nepalese sovereignty over all of the approaches to the summit from the south.

was the National Panchayat, which was located in Kathmandu. The king was able to appoint his own sixteen members to it, and there were, in addition to the representatives from the districts and zones, also representatives from special groups such as service veterans. While the National Panchayat could propose and debate legislation, it was the king who had the ultimate authority to decide whether any such proposed legislation would actually become the law of the land. It was clearly not a democratic system in the sense that we understand the term.

Moreover, in December of 1960, King Mahendra made all political parties illegal in Nepal, and several party leaders were arrested. Many were subsequently released on the condition that they refrain from party political activities. But some of them proceeded to organize underground movements—both Congress and Communist—and the whole situation might well have gotten out of hand, as it did in the spring of 1990, if events on the Nepalese frontiers had not intervened. In October of 1962, the Chinese and the Indians had a serious territorial war in Ladakh, which borders Nepal on the west. This served to remind the Nepalese of the precariousness of their own national existence. "Nepal," it has been said, "is like a fragile clay vessel wedged between two giant copper cauldrons"—China and India. While the Himalayan wall to the north is a formidable natural boundary, it is not impregnable. But the Chinese have made no historical claim to Nepal of the sort they have made to Tibet and Ladakh. There were no borders to rectify.

On the other hand, relations between India and Nepal have always been complicated and, at times, very strained. To take a recent example, in April of 1989, the government of India, led by Rajiv Gandhi, closed nineteen of its twenty-one Nepalese border-crossing points. (Nepal's southern border, with India, which is very open, has always been semitransparent to migrations of individuals.) But this involved closing points of the border used by the trucks and buses that carry most of the commerce. The stated reason for this action by the Indians had to do with a purchase in 1988 of antiaircraft guns from China by the Nepalese. This certainly was an irritant; more importantly, however, the Trade and Transit Treaty between the two countries had expired and no progress had been made toward renegotiating it. The Indians raised tariffs on Nepalese goods being exported, and curtailed the supply of petroleum products that the Nepalese could import. Nepal has no oil of its own, and so its economy was seriously affected.

These events, and their lack of resolution, are often cited as important factors leading to the revolution that took place in Nepal in the spring of 1990. But the reasons go much deeper. Indeed, there is cause for concern about Nepal's future as a viable independent political entity. After King Mahendra died in 1972, his son Birendra took over. He is the first Shah king ever to have had a western education—Eton and Harvard. People who have met him have told me that they have found him to be an amiable and well-meaning man. But they have also noted that he does not seem to be a very shrewd politician. Moreover, his western education has not really prepared him for either the byzantine maneuverings of the Nepalese court or the real day-to-day problems of what is still a largely agrarian society. There is an English-language daily newspaper—*The Rising Nepal*—published in Kathmandu. Before real freedom of the press was established in 1990, it was the only legitimate English-language newspaper in the country, and it printed what the government told it to. (It still represents the point of view of the monarchy, but now it has many competitors.) It features on its editorial pages a daily homily signed by the king. One wonders if he reads them, let alone writes them. Here is a typical example: "Democracy is more than a system of government and encompasses the utilization of fundamental rights by all citizens living a way of life sustained on democratic norms." This was addressed to a citizenry, largely illiterate, whose average income was, and still is, about a hundred fifty dollars a *year!* And who lived in a country that, at the time, had few of the basic democratic freedoms—such as that of the press.

Of the queen, I am afraid that I have not heard much that is affectionate. She is reputed to be a master of political intrigue—a quality lacking in her husband. I have one indelible memory of her. In the spring of 1987, I was in Kathmandu. It was just before the monsoon, and the city was like a sauna. I had been doing some shopping in the center of town when I suddenly found myself caught up in a sort of tidal wave of people. I asked what was happening, and was told that the king and queen were about to pass by on their way to a ceremony in one of the local temples. I managed to find a place on the sidewalk from which to watch the proceedings. First there came an army escort with sirens blaring. This was followed by a giant black limousine bearing the royal couple. I caught sight of the queen. She was in the backseat, unsmiling and magnificently dressed. There seemed to be no connection between her and the people surrounding me on the sidewalk. It was as if they occupied different planets. When the troubles started in earnest a bit later, photographs began appearing in *The Rising Nepal* of her together with poor village children, or with hospital patients. The scenes looked as if they had been painfully staged. It was too little and too late.

In 1979, King Birendra sponsored a nationwide referendum to decide between the panchayat system and a return to party politics. Whatever the real outcome of the vote, it was declared a tie and the panchayat system was retained. For the next several years there was a small, but persistent, rise in political terrorism—bombings and the like. This came as a surprise to observers of the country. As compared to India or Pakistan, modern Nepal has been an extraordinarily peaceful society. Any casual reading of, say, an Indian newspaper reveals a level of violence in that country that is truly shocking. In Nepal, even the "terrorists" seemed to go out of their way to destroy only property and not human life. That is why the events of 1990 were so surprising. They began on February 18, which was to have been celebrated as a holiday—Democracy Day—in honor of the panchayat system. Instead, there were strikes and riots, which continued for the next several weeks. People were jailed and, allegedly, brutalized. The climax came on April 6, when a crowd estimated to have been some two hundred thousand people marched up the main street of Kathmandu—the Durbar Marg—toward the Royal Palace, chanting pro-democracy slogans. Soldiers guarding the palace opened fire, and in the melee some two hundred marchers were killed. Clearly, the next step could well have been a civil war.

Fortunately for the country, the king decided to act. He dissolved his cabinet and agreed to legalize political parties. He invited the

opposition to form a new government and to write a new constitution—a task that was completed the following November. This constitution stipulates that the king cannot make any executive decisions
without consulting his elected prime minister. Free speech and
other human rights were guaranteed. That is the reason that there
has been such an exuberance of newspapers and magazines—
many of them strongly critical of the establishment. In May of 1991,
there were elections for the newly constituted parliament. The
Nepalese went a bit overboard. Some *forty* political parties were
created. Since most of the population is illiterate, these parties
distinguished themselves by symbols, such as a tree or an elephant.
All over the country slogans like VOTE FOR TREE were painted on
buildings or walls next to the symbols. They were still visible the
following fall when I returned to Nepal. The two principal con-
tenders in the election were the United Marxist Leninist Party—
which proposed both a radical redistribution of land and a
reduction of the country's dependence on foreign aid—and the
Congress, which had a much more centrist platform. In the event,
the Congress won about half the seats in the parliament, enough
to govern the country. Girija Prasad Koirala, one of B. P. Koirala's
brothers—B. P. had died—became prime minister.

To anyone with an understanding of the problems of the country,
it was clear that, while this development was very desirable, by itself
it was not going to solve anything. The most obvious dilemma—really
a disaster—the country faces is its exploding population. A 2.6 percent growth rate may not sound like much, but it means that the
population—barring a catastrophe—will double every thirty years.
One does not have to be a demographer to observe the effects this has
already had. When I first visited Nepal in 1967, it was one of the few
countries in Asia to *export* food. The exportation of rice to India from
the Terai was one of Nepal's largest foreign exchange earners. Now
the country *imports* food. When one visits a Nepalese village, the thing
that strikes one immediately is the overwhelming presence of children. They are everywhere. Very young girls walk around carrying
still-younger children on their backs. Then there are the men and
boys. What is striking about them is that they do not seem to have

much of anything to do. Underemployment and unemployment are chronic and widespread. No amount of parliamentary rhetoric can change this. These are concrete problems that must be dealt with concretely, or the country will sink deeper and deeper into poverty and chaos.

For that reason, I was not too surprised to see a disillusionment with "democracy" begin manifesting itself. In a country like Nepal, it is easy for a poor and relatively unsophisticated citizen to equate a political label with an economic one. The fact that the standard of living of a Nepalese hill farmer has not much improved since 1990 is proof to *him* that "democracy" has failed, and hence something else should be tried. Thus, in the summer of 1994, there was a no-confidence vote in the parliament and the king declared that new elections were to be held in the fall. As it happened, I was once again back in Nepal. The election campaign was in full swing and it was becoming increasingly clear that, this time, the Communists were going to win. I had two experiences that taught me a lot about the present situation. I was on my way to Tibet—a voyage I will describe at the end of this book. The first encounter took place before I left for Tibet, and the second took place after I reentered Nepal.

The first encounter was with a very intelligent and articulate taxi driver in Kathmandu. I was returning from the center of town to my hotel, which was on the periphery. The traffic was awful, so we had plenty of time to talk while he dodged pedestrians, bicyclists, and animals of all sorts, to say nothing of other vehicles. He told me that he had never had a collision, which struck me as nothing short of miraculous. As is often the case with taxi drivers in many parts of world, he began to discuss politics. He told me that although he had become disgusted with the corruption and inefficiency of the Congress Party, he would vote for them anyway. He was very worried, he said, about what might happen if the Communists won. Interestingly, I thought, his concern was not so much about the possible loss of the personal freedoms that the Nepalese had just gained. What he was really worried about was how such a Communist government would be viewed by people outside Nepal. Would it mean that foreign aid—absolutely necessary for the development of the country—

would cease? Would it mean that tourists, also now vital to the economy of the country, would stop visiting Nepal? About all I could reply was that I hoped that the Communists would not win and that if they did, the consequences would not be as bleak as he imagined. I must say my answers sounded a little lame to me and that the future did look rather uncertain.

My second encounter, a few weeks later, was totally different. The group I was with had just returned from an extensive voyage in Tibet. Its conclusion had involved a five-day trek from the extreme western border of Tibet and Nepal down to a town in Nepal—Simikot, the capital of the remote Humla district—from which we expected to be able to fly back to Kathmandu. Indeed, as it turned out, we were able to return in a giant Russian helicopter—clearly a military relic—that was flown by two Russian pilots who, I am certain, were veterans of the war in Afghanistan. I mention this because it will serve as an additional counterpoint to what I am about to describe. We had made our camp—actually on the flat roof of a building—and I wandered into the center of town. One of my favorite activities in towns like these is to go to somewhere in the center—a town square if possible—and just sit there, watching. Sooner or later something happens. In this case, after about ten minutes or so, a man— somewhere in his forties, I would guess—came and sat beside me. He was with a small group of younger boys. A teacher, I thought.

He began the conversation by asking me where I was from in serviceable, Nepalese-accented English. I told him. He asked whether the United States was a democracy. I told him that I thought so. He then said that a democracy was no good. It had not done anything for Nepal. He pulled a pamphlet, written in English, from his pocket. It was the crudest and silliest sort of Communist propaganda. He told me what wonders the Communists were going to bring to Nepal— how everyone was finally going to get his share of the land. At this point, I must confess, I began to lose patience with him. I had just come from Tibet—five days' walk to the north. I had seen what happens when a Communist regime is imposed on a country. I knew from talking to Tibetans how much they would give for an opportunity to vote for their own form of self-government. And here was a perfect fool about to *vote* a Communist regime into power. This indeed is what happened. In the elections of 1994, the Communists won, and began to govern the country. It did not take long for disillusionment to set in again. In the fall of 1995 they were voted out of power, which shows that, at present, democracy is really functioning in Nepal.

2

Fortune Has Wings

In 1970, when I was doing research for my profile of Nepal, I made a count of the number of aircraft that were then based in the country. As nearly as I could tell, there were twenty-four, of which eighteen were owned and operated by the Nepalese. Most of these planes had been given to the Nepalese by various countries. The variety of these machines, and the list of places from which they had come, was a manifestation of the fact that, at the time, Nepal was one of the few countries in the world where *all* the major powers, and many of the minor ones, were, for whatever reasons, actively engaged in constructive aid. They still are, although with somewhat altered priorities, and with some soul-searching by the Nepalese themselves. Included in my 1970 list were seven DC-3s of American origin. Five of these were operated by the Royal Nepal Airlines Corporation— RNAC—a government-controlled entity that then had a monopoly on the commercial transport of freight and passengers within the country. One of the planes belonged to the king's own Royal Air Flight, and one belonged to the Nepalese army. There was a forty-passenger Dutch Fokker Friendship turboprop then used by the RNAC for its international flights. There were two Swiss-built Pilatus Porters; one belonged to the United Nations mission in Nepal, the other to the Swiss Association for Technical Assistance. These were

STOL—short takeoff and landing—planes adaptable to extremely short fields. In fact, most of the "fields" they used—and still use—are just that—grassy pastures on which buffalo, yaks, and goats graze until the plane comes in. Anyone who has flown in and out of a variety of these swards has a favorite. Mine is the Dolpo airport—if you can call it that—at Juphal in western Nepal. This is the place into which one flies to start the trek into the Dolpo region—a fascinating and beautiful area, bordering Tibet, made famous by Peter Matthiesen's book *The Snow Leopard*. It was opened up to general trekking in 1990, and I went there a year later. Although I had been alerted to the characteristics of the Juphal airstrip in advance, the reality surpassed my expectation. The field is about four hundred ninety meters long— the bare minimum for a STOL. It slopes downward, and has a marked depression in the middle. It is situated on a mesa with mountains surrounding it and, to add to the ambience, there is a giant rock at the end. There is also a control tower, equipped with a radio to talk to planes and other airfields and a loud siren to frighten off the various beasts that graze on the sward. While we were waiting for some days for the appearance of the plane for our return flight—a common occurrence—I had several long discussions with the controller, a very intelligent and humorous man. I mentioned, in the course of these colloquies, that to ensure a prompt and punctual flight back to Kathmandu, we had actually paid to transport, on our *incoming* flight, an official of the RNAC whose sole function was to make sure that our return flight was in order. Nonetheless, and despite the best efforts of the controller, it was three days before the scheduled plane appeared. On several occasions the controller pointed out to me that without the plane, we would be facing a walk out that he estimated at three *weeks!*

To continue the 1970 list: There were two Bell helicopters and one STOL Heliocourier (made in Bedford, Massachusetts) used by the United States Agency for International Development. These were employed on all sorts of AID missions, including flying animals and fruit trees to remote farms, and keeping Peace Corps volunteers supplied with medicines. In addition to the DC-3, the king then had, as gifts, one Russian Ilyushin-14 transport (something like a DC-3), one French Alouette helicopter, one Canadian-made Twin Otter, and three Chinese-made Harvesters. Most of these planes saw rather little service, mainly because they cost too much to run. To complete this list, the army had three British twin-engine Pioneers, also STOLs, of which two had been more or less cannibalized to provide parts for the third, and one Russian MI-4 helicopter, an earlier version of the MI-17 helicopter on which we had flown in the fall of 1994. An odd addition to the local aerial scene was a Cessna owned by an outfit called the Summer Institute of Linguistics, made up of people who had apparently come to the country to translate the Bible into Nepali. The Cessna was occasionally available to climbers and hikers for charters.

Since 1970, the aviation scene has advanced dramatically, both on the ground and in the air. Kathmandu's airport, which is presently called the Tribhuvan International Airport, was originally known as Gaucher Field. Since *gaucher* means "cow pasture" in Nepali, one may imagine what the state of the art was. The field has since been extended and modernized, so that it can now accommodate the large jets that fly directly from Europe. Both RNAC and Lufthansa offer such flights. There are also flights from Kathmandu to Lhasa on China Southwest Airlines, as well as flights to Pakistan, India, and Thailand. Recently, a direct airlink between Kathmandu and Paro in Bhutan was opened. All these international flights make use of a new air-conditioned—by solar power—air terminal. There are also now competing companies such as Everest Air and Asian Airlines—the outfit that owns the Russian helicopters—that offer a variety of flights within the country. I cannot even begin to estimate the number and variety of aircraft that have entered service in Nepal since my informal survey of a quarter-century ago.

So far as anyone can confirm, an Englishman by the name of Mickey Weatherall made, in 1947, the first landing of *any* plane in Nepal. (I have heard rumors that during the Second World War, there were landings in Nepal by Allied pilots flying in and out of China.) In 1947, the country was still under the rule of the Rana family and hermetically sealed to foreigners, but some hunting parties were allowed into the Terai, and Weatherall flew into Simra, in the south, for hunting. By 1949, DC-3s were landing on the pasture that is presently the international airfield. In 1951, Indian National Airways—a now-defunct company that, despite its name, was owned by a Rana in India—inaugurated a weekly service to Kathmandu from Patna and Calcutta in northern India. In 1953, the Indian army, at a cost of $147,000, laid down a concrete airstrip over the old cow pasture. At the same time, the Indians built a remarkable road from Kathmandu to Rauxaul—on their northern border—called the Tribhuvan Rajpath. While the road, over which I have traveled several times, is not as well engineered as the so-called Freedom Highway that the Chinese built in 1967—which links Kathmandu to Tibet—it is, considering the extraordinarily tortuous mountain terrain that it crosses, a more remarkable achievement. The sixty miles or so of the road that pass through the mountains just to the south of Kathmandu are composed of an endless series of hairpin turns over steep ravines. In the summer monsoon months, many parts of the road tend to get washed away by landslides, and whenever I have traveled over it, small groups of Nepalis were, every few miles, chopping up large rocks with hammers in order to get small stones with which to fill in some of the weak spots. Despite the imperfections, the road is in constant and very heavy use by cars, buses, and trucks, and it is the main supply line connecting Kathmandu, and the adjoining territory, to India.[1] That the two roads, taken together, link India to Chinese-controlled Tibet is a fact whose geopolitical significance is lost on no one.

In May of 1958, the Royal Nepal Airlines Corporation was formed, with 51 percent of the shares under the permanent control of the government. Until 1963, when RNAC acquired the Fokker Friendship, which is pressurized, all of its commercial flights were made with the DC-3s, which are not. The acquisition of the Fokker Friendship

1. Something I had not realized until my last bus trip on this road is that the city seems to "close" at midnight. We had taken an excruciating twelve-hour chartered bus ride from the southern Nepalese border town of Nepalganj back to Kathmandu. (There had been the usual failure of plane connections.) When we arrived at the entry to the city, the gates across the road were closed. There then ensued a sort of frantic negotiation to persuade the gatekeepers, who had been sleeping, to let us through. Perhaps the fact that we were tourists—possibly money changed hands—finally persuaded them to open the gates.

for use in tourism was a very important step forward for the country. At the time, Dacca was in East Pakistan—not part of India—and when round-trip service between Dacca and Kathmandu was inaugurated in March of 1963, tourists could, for the first time, come to Nepal by air without passing through India. Of even more importance for the country's independence was the introduction by Thai Air Lines in December of 1968 of Caravelle service from Bangkok, followed by its DC-9 service in February of 1970. It is this ever-expanding air service that is largely responsible for the explosion of tourism that has taken place in the country in the last twenty-five years.

Until the overthrow of the Ranas in 1950, there were, as we have seen, essentially no foreign visitors to Nepal. The first visitors to arrive in the early 1950s were mainly alpinists. In 1950, the French climbed Annapurna—actually Annapurna I, since there exists an entire range, several of whose mountains are called Annapurna with a numerical suffix indicating how they rank in altitude compared to Annapurna I's 26,504 feet. At the time, it was the highest mountain in the world to have been climbed to its summit. The mountain is in western Nepal, and the French climbers were the first Europeans ever to visit the region. The maps, where any existed, were so poor that the climbers spent most of their time looking for the mountain. It is perhaps ironic that at present, some two-thirds of the tens of thousands of trekkers who come to Nepal trek in this region. Indeed, there are so many trailside hotels that many trekkers do not even bother to carry a tent. In 1955, Thomas Cook & Co booked the first real tourists into Nepal, a group that flew in from India while on an around-the-world tour on the ship *Caronia*.

That tourism got started in Nepal when it did was due, as much as to anyone, to an extraordinary and delightful White Russian named Boris Nikolaevich Lissanevitch. He was known in Kathmandu—he died in 1985 at the age of eighty—simply as Boris. Before the Russian Revolution, the Lissanevitch family were horse breeders for the nobility, an occupation that went rapidly out of fashion when Odessa, the family seat, was taken over by the Reds. At this time, Boris, who was in his early teens, was training to be a naval officer, a career often favored by the aristocracy; indeed, both of his brothers were naval officers. When it appeared that Odessa was going to be permanently occupied, the Lissanevitch family fled, on horseback, to Warsaw. The situation in Odessa, however, remained fluid for a considerable time during the revolution, and in one of the periods in which the Whites seemed to have regained control, the family returned. The White occupation was short-lived, and it became necessary to find some sort of cover for Boris to keep him from being interned as a former czarist military functionary. As it happened, he and his mother were staying with an aunt who was the ballet mistress of the Odessa Opera House and a noted teacher of ballet. She arranged for Boris to become registered as a member of the corps de ballet, and to make matters more convincing, he began studying ballet, which he found, to his surprise, he both liked and was gifted at. He remained in the Odessa company until 1924, when he fled to France. After some desultory employment, he joined Diaghilev's Ballet Russe. For the next four years Boris toured Europe with the Ballet Russe, but when Diaghilev died, in 1929, the company disbanded and Boris was once again on his own. For the next four years he danced with several companies in Europe, performed in a celebrated production of *The Miracle* in London with Léonide Massine—a reviewer called Boris "the personification of lithe, sinuous evil"—and married his first wife, the dancer Kira Stcherbatcheva. Kira and Boris became a well-known theatrical-dance duo, and in 1933 they were invited to tour the Far East. Their tour lasted three years and took them to India, China, Bali, Ceylon, and French Indochina. During this time, Boris developed a special fondness for Calcutta, whose clubs, racetracks, and cafés were, in the era of the British raj, among the most elegant in the Far East. But, as Boris saw it, there were two serious defects in the city's social life: There was no private club that admitted both Indians and Europeans, and there was no place to get a drink after 2 A.M. In December of 1936, with the aid of some wealthy Calcutta friends, Boris opened the "300 Club" in a palace built and abandoned by an eccentric Armenian millionaire. It was limited to exactly 300 members, Indian and European, and the bar remained open twenty-four hours a day. In addition, he imported a Russian chef, Vladimir Haletzki, from Nice to provide the cuisine. Boris once remarked to me that whenever one found a

Boeuf Stroganoff on the menu in a restaurant in India, one could be sure that the chef was someone whom Haletzki had trained at the "300." Of course, most of the Indians who belonged to the "300" were wealthy aristocrats, maharajas and the like, who could afford it, and through the club members Boris came to know the Indian establishment that functioned under the raj. In particular, he got to know those members of the Nepalese Rana family who had built homes in India, often because they had been exiled by the Rana rulers for holding antagonistic political views. He became an especially close friend of a Nepalese general, Mahabir Shamsher Bahadur Rana, who had left Nepal with a considerable fortune and had taken up residence in India. It was through General Mahabir that Boris met King Tribhuvan, who—although the nominal ruler of Nepal—was essentially a prisoner of the Ranas. Their first meeting occurred in 1944. (During the war, the "300" had been used in part as a recreation center by military personnel, pilots and others stationed in India.) By this time, it was clear to many observers, Boris included, that the days of the British in India were numbered and that, with their departure, many institutions, including social clubs for the elite, would disappear. More significantly, since it was the British presence in India and its tacit, or explicit, acceptance of the Ranas that had helped stabilize the regime, it became evident that, in the absence of the British, a revolution in Nepal might be expected. Indeed, while the king's nominal reason for being in Calcutta in 1944 was to seek medical help for a chronic heart condition, he was, in fact, using these visits to make contact with exiled Nepalese like General Mahabir, and with the Indian Congress Party, which favored a change of regime in Nepal. The "300 Club" became the medium through which these meetings were arranged, and Boris became a very close friend of the king. In 1947, India gained its independence, and by 1951, the Ranas had been overthrown and the king restored to power.

Boris had become an avid big-game hunter since first coming to Asia, and it had long been his ambition to visit Nepal and hunt in the jungles of the Terai. Under the Ranas, he had not been permitted to do so; thus, when King Tribhuvan invited him to come to Kathmandu, he readily accepted. Boris once described for me his first night in Kathmandu. Considering what has happened to the city since, it borders on fantasy. He was taken for an automobile ride in the city by the king and two of his sons. No sooner had they started driving than a leopard jumped across the path of the car and, after staring at its occupants for several seconds, fled into the suburbs. Boris said to himself, "My God, what a country!" and decided then and there to move to Kathmandu. But first he needed an occupation. Since 1946, Boris had given up the direction of the "300 Club" and had, among other things, attempted to set up a distillery in northern India. The distillery failed, but the experience convinced him that he might explore the prospects for alcohol brewing in Nepal, which up to that time had been carried on in informal family settings, free of taxation. General Mahabir had become the Nepalese minister of industry, and he saw at once in Boris's proposed distillery a chance for the government to collect some new and badly needed revenues. Boris received a license to import alcohol and acquired the exclusive legal franchise for brewing it in the Kathmandu valley.

At first, it looked as if the brewery would be a great success. But Boris had not realized that there were well over a thousand private distilleries in the valley, and that many of these were owned by influential citizens, who were not in the least pleased either by the new competition or by the prospect of taxation. Pressure was brought to bear on the government, and the matter came to a head late in 1954, when Boris's license to import alcohol was suddenly revoked. To compound matters, he was arrested for not having fulfilled the part of his contract that stipulated that he would pay the government a certain guaranteed minimum yearly tax. He protested that, to earn the money to pay the tax, he needed the alcohol that he could no longer import, but the protest was to no avail. He tried to bring suit, but the legal system in Nepal made it impossible for anyone to bring suit against the government. Thus, Boris went off to jail. He was apparently the first European to have been jailed in Nepal, at least in modern times, and hence it was not clear to anyone what should be done with him. By this time, he had become a naturalized British citizen, and at the instigation of the British embassy, he was taken out of the normal communal jail cell where he had first been put and incarcerated in the relative luxury of the tax office itself. Here he lived for six days, among the tax clerks, until he was finally transferred to a private cell; he was moved from there to the local hospital when he became ill. After two and a half months, he was released. By this time, King Mahendra had succeeded his father, after the latter's death in March of 1955. He agreed to release Boris on the condition that Boris would write a letter of apology. Boris refused, but a compromise was worked out whereby the king's secretary wrote the letter and Boris simply signed it.

Several months before this episode, Boris had begun to create the first international hotel in Nepal, the Royal, and had persuaded the government to begin issuing tourist visas. For the use of the hotel, he had leased half of a former Rana palace—hence the name. The other half was used by the Nepal Rastra ("Central") Bank for its offices. All during the period in which Boris was in jail the new hotel was being put together, largely under the direction of his wife. (In 1948, Boris and Kira had been divorced, and Boris had married a beautiful Danish girl named Inger Pheiffer, a talented artist.) Everything   knives and forks, plumbing fixtures, stoves and ovens—had to be imported or specially made. Boris was determined to serve first-rate European cuisine, a policy that meant he had either to grow the vegetables and fruits himself (he introduced the first strawberries into Nepal) or to import them from India or Singapore. Pigs were a case in point. The domestic pig could not legally be imported into Nepal because of the prevalent feeling that it was an unclean animal. But the Nepalese were very fond of wild boar. Thus, Boris imported a number of white Hampshire "wild boars" from England, which he bred and raised. These animals appeared to thrive in the valley, and Boris had a herd of some two hundred in the hills above Kathmandu. A certain number of them also used to wander around the hotel grounds, along with a large collection of dogs, birds, and squirrels, and some Himalayan brown bears that were kept in a cage. The pigs were a staple in the cuisine of the hotel, and Boris had visions of moving them to the south of Nepal, allowing them to multiply, and selling the extra meat to India. He imagined a fleet of refrigerated trucks moving south with pork, coming back north along the India–Nepal highway, and stocking the first supermarket in Nepal. Like many such visions, it never came to pass.

Two months after being let out of jail, Boris received a royal command from King Mahendra to cater his coronation, which was to take place on the second of May, 1956. There were to be several hundred invited guests, including newspapermen and photographers from all over the world. It was the first time that the coronation of a Nepalese king had been made an international event. It became a symbol of Nepal's desire to join the world community. Boris had to fly everything in from abroad, including fifty-seven cooks and one hundred fifty trained servants from India, six thousand live chickens, one thousand guinea fowl, fresh fruit from India, whiskey, soda, glasses, and several tons of ice (there was no ice plant in the country). The coronation and the royal banquet were a great success, and Boris and the hotel became established fixtures in the valley. Until the 1960s, the Royal was the only hotel with cosmopolitan standards in Nepal, and Boris built up an extensive international clientele. For a time, his guests included several ambassadors and most of the personnel from the foreign-aid missions, who lived in the hotel until their residences in Kathmandu could be built. Nearly every mountaineering expedition that passed through the country stayed at the Royal at what Boris called his lowered "expedition rate." (One often had the impression that if he had not been restrained by the female members of his entourage, Boris would have offered *everyone* an "expedition rate.") Besides feeding the expeditions, Boris used to bail out some of them from entanglements with governmental red tape. One of his prize possessions was a collection of rocks chipped out of the summits of several of the highest mountains in Nepal by climbers who had lived at the Royal.

The unconventional atmosphere at the Royal was not for everyone. The rooms were huge and somewhat cold at night. Some of them had stuffed tigers on the floor, souvenirs of Boris's days as a hunter. Boiled drinking water used to be delivered to the rooms each night in whiskey bottles that had seen service in the bar—the celebrated Yak and Yeti that was the social focal point of the valley. It was wood-paneled and featured a splendid wood-burning fireplace in the middle of the room and many comfortable chairs and couches. The plumbing in the hotel was noisy and uncertain, and the electricity a bit on the sporadic side, and the whole affair looked as if it needed rehabilitation. It closed in the early 1970s. The palace is still there. For nostalgia's sake I go and look at it each time I visit Kathmandu. It now seems to be entirely occupied by offices. On the front lawn there is a sign that says ELECTION COMMISSION.

Boris's next project was the construction of a restaurant, which he also called the Yak and Yeti. It was completed in February of 1970, and was one of the showplaces of the Kathmandu valley. For it, Boris rented part of another Rana palace—there is no shortage of them in the valley—and in it created a mixed astrological and Newari decor that stunned the eye of even the most blasé. (When I visited the site shortly before opening day, about a ton of Newari carvings lay carefully stacked on the floor of the future kitchen, waiting to be mounted on walls and archways.) The Newar arts, like the wild animals and forests in Nepal, are in danger of disappearing, since in their urge to modernize, the Nepalese have acquired a concrete fetish. Concrete has been something of a luxury in the valley—mortar costing something like ten dollars a sack. In 1974, with the help of the West Germans, the first cement factory in Nepal was constructed, on the site of a limestone quarry near the Chobar Gorge. No one, it seems, gave any serious thought as to what its environmental impact would be. To put it simply, the factory has ruined what used to be one of the loveliest and most tranquil spots in the valley. When it operates, it spews out a spume of polluted smoke, which joins the exhaust from gasoline-powered vehicles, and the smog from the rest of the factories in Kathmandu, to form a lethal cauldron—the air quality is one of the unhealthiest of any major city in the world.

To return to more innocent times. Beginning in 1967, and until the hotel closed, I used to stay there for weeks at a time. I became part of Boris's extended family. As such, I was often invited on Sunday outings. One stands out in my mind. In 1967, a large British Royal Air Force crew had come into town. They had flown in on a Beverly—a huge cargo plane. They were bringing in supplies from Singapore for some of the Gurkha military bases in the south of Nepal. As luck would have it, an air compressor in their plane failed, so they were grounded in Kathmandu for several days. The boys put up at the Royal, and Boris set about looking after their welfare. There were daily planning sessions that took place either in Boris's private apartment in the hotel—which one reached by climbing a hazardous-looking, tiny, circular metal stairway from the second floor, and which contained a remarkable collection of Nepalese and Tibetan art—or in the Yak and Yeti bar. In one of the planning sessions in the bar, Boris decided to take the boys on a picnic, and he invited me along. "We will go to Sankhu in my Land Rover," he said, "and I will show you a wall I bought"—an invitation that, needless to say, I readily accepted. Sankhu is one of the oldest towns in the valley and was, at the time, accessible only by jeep or Land Rover.

At ten the following Sunday morning, we all assembled on the lawn in front of the Royal: about fifteen airmen, two Land Rovers, an Italian staying at the hotel whom Boris had also invited (the Italian had hired the additional Land Rover for his own transportation, which, as it turned out, was very fortunate), Boris's mother-in-law (a delightful woman named Esther Scott), and one of her dogs. Boris brought out some wicker baskets from the hotel containing a splendid picnic lunch, several dozen cans of chilled beer, and a couple of bottles of imported red wine—a commodity then very difficult to come by in Nepal. Needless to say, all of this was on the house. Mrs. Scott and I, the dog, and several airmen got into Boris's Land Rover. It turned out to be a rather ancient affair that he had once driven overland from England. In fact, on the way to Sankhu its transmission gave out, and we only succeeded in getting there by being ferried in the Italian's Land Rover. At a later stage, the Italian was sent back to the hotel to summon an additional jeep to ferry us all back. Sankhu turned out to be an extraordinarily beautiful Newari village that seemed to have come right out of sixteenth-century Nepal. We picnicked near a lovely pagoda temple, many centuries old, located in a pine grove on top of a hill. After lunch, Boris took us for a walk through the village. He came to an ancient house with magnificently carved windows and wood paneling—masterpieces of Newari craftsmanship. "I bought this wall," Boris remarked happily. "The owner was going to tear it down and put up something in cement. The carvings would have been burnt, probably, so I bought the whole wall." It ended up in the Yak and Yeti restaurant.

Since 1955, when Boris persuaded the government to issue tourist visas, tourism has grown almost exponentially in Nepal. It is the number-one source of foreign exchange in the country. To give some idea of the growth: According to government figures, there were 6,179 tourists in 1962. By 1981, the number had risen to 161,669. By now, it is well over a quarter-million, although it appears to be decreasing a little, perhaps as a reaction to the deterioration of the environment in Kathmandu and elsewhere. In 1961, tourism brought in some seventy-eight thousand dollars in revenue; by 1981, the figure had risen to fifty-two *million*. It has probably doubled since then. A corollary to this is that both hotel and restaurant facilities have grown almost beyond recognition compared to what they were in the 1960s. A very recent guide to the country[2] lists four five-star hotels in Kathmandu—hotels that charge over a hundred dollars a night. Two of them, the Annapurna and the Soaltee Oberoi, were in existence when I first went to Nepal in 1967. The third, the Everest, was, until recently, managed by the Sheraton Corporation. The fourth I will come to shortly.

After the Royal closed, I shifted my headquarters for a while to the Annapurna. It was owned, like many of the other hotels at the time, by the royal family, and was managed by a Swiss. It had a cavernous lobby and a swimming pool. The rooms were small but adequate. Its truly redeeming feature was, and is, its air-conditioned coffee shop, where one can get buffalo burgers and cappuccinos. The top-of-the-line hotel in Kathmandu was, and probably still is, the Soaltee Oberoi—part of the Indian Oberoi chain of luxury hotels. It was well out of town and had four restaurants and a casino. It never occurred to me to stay there, but I did go with Boris in 1967 to attend a reception honoring the first anniversary of its opening. It was presided over by Prince Himalaya, King Mahendra's oldest brother, who was, at the moment, the acting ruler of Nepal. (King Mahendra was in Alaska

2. Choegyal, Lisa, *Nepal,* Insight Pocket Guides (London: APA Publications, 1993; distributed in the United States by Houghton Mifflin Company, Boston).

shooting bear; the crown prince, Birendra—the present king—was at Harvard studying; and the king's other brother, Basundhara, also was temporarily out of the country.) It was a gala occasion that featured a floor show (consisting of some singers imported from India, an exotic dancer, and an orchestra), and a free gift for everyone in the form of a ballpoint pen manufactured in China. To me, at the time, the provenance of this pen also seemed exotic, since the United States had no relations with China and Nepal's relations were, as usual, precarious. Now the shops in Kathmandu are flooded with Chinese-manufactured goods, to say nothing of the goods such as cameras and electronic equipment imported largely from Japan. The guests at the gala, dressed in their tuxedos and ball gowns, represented the cream of Kathmandu society: diplomatic missions, important government personalities, and the like. The atmosphere was as remote from village life in Nepal as it would have been if the reception were held in Paris or London. Since the Soaltee is located at a safe distance from the city, it resembles a luxury hotel of the sort one might find anywhere. If it were not for a few wall decorations and the Nepalese help, one might imagine that one was not in Nepal at all.

The name of the so-far unnamed five-star Kathmandu hotel—as perhaps the reader has guessed—is the Yak and Yeti. When the Royal closed, Boris had a dream of founding a new hotel that would be the jewel of Kathmandu. It would have all the conveniences of a western hotel, but would also be a showplace for Nepalese arts and crafts. It was never clear to me what Boris's actual role in this project was supposed to be. I do know that at some point, he told me that his partners had eased him out of the operation. Before that happened, Boris lived for a while in the Rana Palace—which became the new hotel, and which was where he had his Yak and Yeti restaurant. It is set in its own small park, and has, indeed, every convenience, including a color television in every room. My only experience of staying there was as a "guest" of South West China Airlines. The flight to Lhasa that some two hundred of us were meant to take from Kathmandu failed to appear on the day scheduled. So after waiting six or seven hours in the airport, we were all bused to the Yak and Yeti to spend the night. A somewhat cynical Englishman I had been talking to during the wait said that it was a particularly fortunate choice of hotel. It was so expensive, he noted, that South West China Airlines would move heaven and earth to get its flight operational the following day, to avoid paying for *two* nights for us in the hotel. He was right. That evening we were treated to a giant buffet dinner. One of the entrées, labeled by a small printed sign, caught my attention. The sign read BEEF STROGOFF (sic). I think Boris would have been much amused.

Most tourists to Nepal spend a day or so in Kathmandu, looking at the temples and the extraordinary street scene, and then pass on. Hence they are not aware of the difficulties involved in seeing most of the country. A tourist visa, which costs about forty dollars (the rates change from time to time) is obtainable at various Nepalese embassies and consulates around the world. It is also available on arrival, if you do not mind standing in a very long and slow moving line at the airport. You had better have photos and dollars available. The visa is valid for thirty days and can be extended, with only minor difficulty, for up to three months. It can be further extended for another month with considerably more difficulty—but that is that. Tourist visas are valid only for the Kathmandu valley, Pokhara—in western Nepal, within sight of the Annapurna range—and a wilderness game reserve called the Royal Chitwan National Park in the Terai. Any other travel requires special permits—usually trekking permits—that are issued by the immigration office. Typically, they cost about five dollars a day for the first four weeks, and ten dollars a day thereafter. Some regions, like Dolpo and Mustang, cost more. These permits become your passport inside the country. (Trekkers usually leave their actual passports safely locked up in their hotels in Kathmandu.) The one hundred fifty or so trekking agents in Kathmandu can take care of the formalities—otherwise these are up to you. To think that you can go trekking without these permits is a folly. There are checkpoints all over the place, and if you arrive at one without the correct documents, you will be turned back—no matter that this could mean several days' walk in the opposite direction. Even if you show up at such a checkpoint with the correct documents, you may find yourself waiting interminably for permission to pass. The soldiers who guard these obscure outposts do not have a great deal to do. Annoying trekkers relieves a good deal of the boredom. A Zen-like attitude of indifference will get you farther, faster.

What most tourists want to try to see is Mount Everest, which is about a hundred ninety miles northeast of Kathmandu. You cannot see the mountain from the town itself. But you can see it from the relatively nearby Dhulikhel Mountain Resort, although it looks disappointing—much lower than many of the closer-by mountains. What is not disappointing is the sight of the Himalayan chain at sunrise from Dhulikhel. Almost the whole chain is visible, and it bursts into reds and golds as the sun rises. There cannot a more glorious mountain view. What is also not disappointing, if the weather cooperates, is the so-called Everest flight. This is a one-hour flight operated daily, weather permitting, by the RNAC. It makes use of the Fokker Friendship, which has particularly large windows. The flight makes its way to the Everest region and circles in the general neighborhood of the mountain. It is a stunning spectacle, and the perspective makes it clear just what a gigantic mountain Everest is. To really approach the mountain requires a several-week, high-altitude trek.

Some years ago, the government set aside some one thousand square miles in the south for a game reserve, part of which became the Royal Chitwan National Park. Whole villages were moved out into other parts of the Terai. In the middle of the jungle, a hotel called Tiger Tops was built, with the financial backing of two Texas oilmen. Its jungle setting, near the Rapti River, is beautiful. One way to reach it is to fly from Kathmandu to the private Meghauly grass airstrip and then travel by elephant—a two-hour operation—through the jungle to the hotel. A rather less conventional method is to travel by river-raft from a point somewhat west of Kathmandu, eventually floating down the Narayani River into the Terai—a trip that takes three or four days. I did this in 1979, at a time when river-rafting in Nepal was still in its exploratory phase. I had received a commission from a magazine to do a kind of travel article on Nepal—an update of my earlier *New Yorker* profile. The only time available to me was midwinter, so any real high-altitude trekking was out. In any event, I thought it would be interesting to see what other sorts of adventures were available to people who might not want to trek for several weeks.

I enlisted the help of my friend Claude Jaccoux, whom the reader met in the introduction, and will meet again in the next chapter. By this time, Jaccoux had himself begun to organize trips to Nepal, and he had his own ideas of what we might explore. The first thing that surprised us upon reaching Kathmandu in late January was how nice the weather was. It was chilly at night, but clear and sunny during the day. Even then there were intimations of the traffic and pollution problems that have now come to engulf the city, but it was all still delightful. One of our treats was a lunch at Boris's new restaurant—he had by 1979 moved his operations out of the nascent hotel, and his new restaurant was simply called Boris. He had invented a drink that he called a "yak tail." It consisted of tomato juice and vodka, along with various other ingredients, which were a secret. By the time we had had two, we were beyond good and evil. Then Boris produced lunch, which featured a snipe pâté followed by *bekti*—a freshwater fish found in the Ganges. When I went to pay the check, Boris said that that was out of the question. We were his guests and no arguments. He must have done that sort of thing too often, because the restaurant later went out of business. He opened another one, also called Boris. His son now operates yet a third restaurant called Boris in the Thamel—the Tibetan quarter of Kathmandu.

Then came the river-rafting. I had never set foot in such a raft, and did not have the slightest idea of what such a trip entailed. Neither did Jaccoux. But, encouraged by the notion that my article might produce all sorts of wonderful publicity for this nascent activity, the rafting company presented the package—which consisted of supplying the raft, the two Sherpas—yes, Sherpas—who were going to steer it, the food and tents for three or four nights of camping on the banks of various rivers, and the means to transport all of this to the first river we were to float upon. The night before, the Sherpas appeared in our hotel bearing a couple of rubber bags, each slightly larger than a front-handlebar bag for a bicycle, in which they said that we were to stuff all of our worldly goods for three nights on the river. Since our final destination was Tiger Tops, our jungle outfits, such as they were, could be sent down by air; we would need very little in the way of clothes for the river. Because we had taken the elephant ride in 1967, it was agreed that this time, once we reached our final river landing, we could go to the hotel by jeep. Little did we know.

The following morning we went by Land Rover to our beach of debarkment. It was extremely early in the morning and we were dressed for the beach. So we stood shivering while the Sherpas and their assistants inflated the raft with a gasoline-powered air compressor. I used the time to study the equipment. My suspicious eyes fell on the oars. They appeared to be made of wood and were only three in number. I decided to risk looking like a total fool and asked the man who appeared to me the senior Sherpa whether *three* oars were enough. "What happens if you break an oar?" I inquired with a certain amount of timidity. "We never break oars," replied the Sherpa, putting me in my place. I assumed that the third oar, like the third eye in a Buddha, had a largely spiritual function.

The first morning on the raft was sheer bliss. The river meandered uncertainly south with a flow barely exceeding that of a discharging bathtub. The scenery was beautiful and the weather ideal. We were a total novelty and much admired and stared at by the locals as we floated by their fields. Then we hit the first serious rapid. I was not at all prepared for this. Neither, it appeared, was the Sherpa—a sort of novice-in-training—who was at the oars. We began bouncing from rock to rock like a steel ball in a pinball machine. It was a sensation that I did not like then and have never liked since. Our Sherpa helmsman seemed genuinely distressed—a posture that was significantly enhanced when one of the oars snapped like a toothpick. By this time, we had navigated the worst of the rapid, and the senior Sherpa took over. He replaced the useless oar with the spare and rowed us to shore for our first campsite. He was very apologetic about the fractured oar and said that never in all his career as a rafter—some six months, I gathered—had such a thing happened.

I am as willing to forgive and forget as the next man, especially if the apology is followed—as it was on this occasion—by one of the best dinners I have ever had—cooked on the beach. The next day we set off again, this time with the senior Sherpa at the helm. Again, we had a few hours of bliss, followed by a series of rapids of an order of magnitude more violent than those of the previous day. A second oar disintegrated. By some miracle of navigation, the Sherpa got us to shore. At this point, I called a halt to the proceedings. I had no idea of where we were, or how we were going to get to Tiger Tops, but I was not going to set foot again in that raft. I told the senior Sherpa that he should find the nearest village and return with a rescue plan. I then lay down on the beach to await events.

In about an hour, our Sherpa returned with a local who had a large empty wicker basket of the kind that Nepalese porters use. This was a good sign, since it meant that we were going to walk somewhere—we knew how to do that—and that our belongings would go in the basket. It is true that I was wearing a pair of flimsy Chinese-made tennis shoes that I had bought for the river, but they would have to serve for the trek. Our Sherpa explained the plan. We would walk down the river on a path along its banks for some indeterminate time—less than a day. Then we would find a "ferry"—some kind of commercial boat—that would take us to the place where a Chinese crew was working on the road they were building north from the Terai. We would then, he hoped, be able to hitch a ride on a Chinese truck or Jeep to the Indian border town of Bhairawa, not far from Tiger Tops. We would contact base and await further instructions. He would come with us, leaving his colleague to guard the raft. There was little point in debating the matter since it was clearly all the plan that was available.

Remarkably, all of this came to pass. The walk was a delight. On one occasion, we surprised an entire troop of monkeys doing antics on the beach. The "ferry" turned out to be a gigantic hollowed-out log that held some twenty people who came and went to various ports on the river—which by now had begun once again to resemble a bathtub. The Chinese road engineers were exactly where they were supposed to be. They were surprised to see us, but quite friendly. We hitched a ride in a large four-wheel-drive vehicle and arrived at Bhairawa at nightfall. We put up in the best hotel in town—a dreadful fleabag. However, one of the possessions I had put into my rubber bag, and hence into the porter's basket, was a small can of a very powerful insect spray. On the front of the can were line drawings of all sorts of noxious insects along with a skull and crossbones—precisely what was needed.

Our Sherpa was able to call Tiger Tops on the telephone. We were a day early, but since this was their off-season there would be no problem in accommodating us. Indeed, they would send a couple of Jeeps to town. On the Jeep trip to the Tiger Tops hotel, most of whose buildings are on stilts to keep them well above the jungle floor, I was surprised to see how close to civilization it was: When you fly in by air, you feel that you are landing in the middle of the jungle. But that proximity of nature and civilization is true of many of our own national parks as well.

Now I have to say something about the tigers. The place is not called Tiger Tops for nothing. There are tigers in the park. I am not sure how many, but I think it is substantially less than a hundred. Tigers need a huge habitat. Each family group has a very large territory whose periphery is patrolled, as I understand it, by the dominant male. He and his female of choice meet very infrequently—something that might also prolong a large number of human relationships I have observed. At Tiger Tops, a live buffalo is staked out to attract feeding tigers. When this happens, always after dark, one is summoned from the lodge to walk quietly down a jungle path and observe the tiger, who is spotlighted from above. I had been to Tiger Tops twice before, but had not seen an actual tiger. On the other hand, I had seen rhinoceroses, crocodiles, peacocks, pheasants, and barking deer, so I had not been too disappointed. But this time, upon arriving at the hotel, I discovered that a small crew of scientific tiger watchers was present. I think it was a Smithsonian Institution project. They had given the tigers collars with radio transmitters so that they could follow them and study their breeding habits, to better preserve the species. This had a bonus: The researchers *knew* when one of the tigers was in the neighborhood of the hotel and would go after the buffalo. They were able to announce that that very evening, we would see a tiger. And so we did. If you have ever seen a tiger under circumstances like this, the lines of Blake's poem, "Tyger, tyger, burning bright / In the forests of the night..." make perfect sense. It is a beautiful and haunting sight.

Of course, not all of the tourists who come to Kathmandu can afford to stay at the Soaltee, or the Yak and Yeti, or to visit Tiger Tops. In fact, there is a group of tourists who started coming to Kathmandu in the 1960s whose lack of obvious means of support eventually became a headache to the Nepalese—the hippies. There was an international hippie circuit through Asia that had its ports of call in countries such as Afghanistan, Laos, and Nepal, where drugs were both legal and readily available on the open market. In Nepal, the hippies smoked processed *ganja*—"hashish"—that sold for about forty cents a pound. *Ganja* grows wild in the Nepalese countryside, and on treks one can walk through fields and inhale a miasma that takes one back to Washington Square Park in Greenwich Village. Smoking pipes of hashish has long been an ingredient in some Nepalese and Indian religious practice, and in Kathmandu it was common to find pagoda temples in which people gathered to smoke a communal hashish pipe and listen to a guru chant, or sing together. I do not pretend to be an expert on the extent to which drugs are presently used in Nepal, but my sense of it is that this ritual use of drugs is more and more confined to a minority of the older generation. On the other hand, Nepalis of all ages are tremendous cigarette smokers. Nepal produces indigenous tobacco that is used to make a vast assortment of cigarettes, usually named after mountains or animals—Sagarmatha (the Nepali name for Everest), Lion, Annapurna, and Nanga Parbat (a mountain in Pakistan) are a few of the brand names I have noticed over the years. Many of these cigarettes are manufactured in a plant donated to the Nepalese by the Russians some years ago, at a cost of about six million dollars. Like many of the industrial-aid projects in Nepal, this one was designed to allow the Nepalese to manufacture something for which they would otherwise have had to pay foreign currency. There is just now beginning to be an awareness in the country that cigarette smoking can actually be bad for one. In retrospect, it is a pity that the Russians did not donate a factory to manufacture something else.

When we first came to Nepal, in 1967, the drug scene was still active, but was beginning to decline. It was not entirely clear at the time whether the use of drugs was or was not, strictly speaking, illegal.

If there were laws, they certainly were not being enforced. There were public places like the Tibetan Blue Restaurant, which was painted blue and run by a Tibetan, where hashish was smoked openly. There was also a commune outside Kathmandu that called itself the "LSD United Nations." For one Nepalese rupee, one could get one's passport stamped HIPPIELAND. Boris also told me that there was a young woman resident of the "United Nations" who for a small offering would display her feminine gender. Boris said that she had a considerable following among Nepalese men who, because of the communal living arrangements—more than one generation of married couples sharing a single sleeping area—rarely got to see a naked female body. In any event, for a time the "freaks," as they were known locally, were tolerated by the authorities as a sort of amusement. However, this permissive attitude changed when it began to become apparent that young Nepalis were themselves beginning to use drugs—hard drugs. Many of the citizens of "Hippieland" were deported. Now the use of drugs in Nepal is manifestly illegal, although one is sometimes approached by hustlers in the Thamel who offer to sell both hashish and/or their sisters. It is said that some of these people work for the police, and that Nepalese jails are exceedingly unpleasant. About the only thing that remains in Kathmandu from the 1960s is a street in the Thamel called "Freak Street"—that is the name on the signs and city maps. Like all the streets in the Thamel, it is densely lined with shops that sell Tibetan rugs or trekking gear or T-shirts.

Even in the 1960s there were delightful cafés and restaurants into which one could venture without having one's mind expanded by the exhaust from hashish pipes. One of my favorites was a place called the Camp. It had been founded in early 1967 by an Indian from Bombay named Ravi Chawla. He had been working for Burmah-Shell in India when, in his thirties, he decided to pack it all in and come to Nepal with his family. He opened the Camp, which served American-style breakfasts of pancakes and eggs as well as Tibetan food. Ravi had installed a hi-fi set that played classical music. He also had installed a red Moroccan-bound book called *The Camp Register* in which guests offered poems and drawings. One of my favorites went, in part:

This bloody town's a bloody cuss,
No bloody trains, no bloody bus
And only Ravi cares for us
in bloody Kathmandu.

The bloody roads are bloody bad,
The bloody hash is bloody mad
It makes the saddest bloody glad
in bloody Kathmandu.

And then:

To quench a thirst is bloody dear,
Ten bloody bob for bloody beer
And is it good?
No bloody fear,
in bloody Kathmandu.

It is now over a quarter-century since I read those lines. I wonder what has happened to the author or, for that matter, to Ravi. But the café tradition continues at places like the Rumdoodle and Mike's Breakfast. Speaking of tradition, let me recount a small adventure that Jaccoux and I had in 1979. As I have mentioned, by this time Jaccoux had come to Nepal several times as the guide and organizer of his own treks and climbs. He had gotten to know a fair number of local Nepalese entrepreneurs. One afternoon, he returned to the hotel where we were staying to announce that we were going to be escorted by one of his entrepreneur friends to a *"bouge"* where one could get *tungba. Bouge* is a French slang word for a "dive" or a "joint." Tungba, as Jaccoux explained, is a Bhutanese millet beer. For some reason that I have never understood, tungba is illegal to sell both in Nepal and in Bhutan. But, as Jaccoux had discovered, there was a sort of speakeasy somewhere in the back alleys of the Thamel where we could drink tungba. Indeed, his Nepalese contact was going to come to the hotel shortly to escort us there. I was torn between my urge for journalistic completeness and my concern that we would all be arrested and spend an indeterminate amount of time in a Nepalese jail. The former won out, and we allowed ourselves to be led through the streets of Kathmandu to an old house in a dark alley. We had to climb a ladder to get to the second floor, where there was some exchange of signals with the management. We were let into a large, dimly lit room with a number of small tables and floor cushions on which to sit. When my eyes got accustomed to the light, I made out several people on nearby cushions. They were speaking a rapid mixture of English and Nepali and, after eavesdropping for a bit, it became clear that they were Peace Corps volunteers back from the field to Kathmandu for a bit of rest and recreation. This made me feel somewhat better. The authorities, if they arrested us, would now have to deal with the full force of the U.S. government. Our Nepalese escort explained to the proprietors of the *bouge* that we wanted tungbas. Soon after, there appeared a concoction that, as I recall, was contained in a sort of gourd. We each had a gourd. The gourds were penetrated by individual straws—literally some sort of tube made of straw. The beverage was a crude beer with lumps. A fork might have helped. I sipped mine as best I could. Nothing happened, and soon we departed, leaving the Peace Corps, who were now discussing irrigation projects.

Not long ago, a mountain-climbing friend of mine told me an anecdote—a scene that he had witnessed sometime in the 1960s, when he had come to Nepal as a member of a mountaineering expedition. They had not climbed their mountain, but had returned to Kathmandu intact. Considering that something like one in ten Himalayan climbers dies in these attempts, this in itself was something of an achievement. He wanted to notify his next of kin in Colorado that he was safe and sound. The only overseas telephone or telegraph open to the general public at the time was at the main post office in Kathmandu. My friend went there to send a telegram. He found himself in a slow-moving line of like-minded expatriates of one sort or another. Just in front of him was a couple who must have been residents of Hippieland. He wore a saffron robe and earrings and had shaved his head, while she wore one of those long granny dresses and had a look of fixed and determined benevolence. They were talking, and my friend gathered from the conversation that they were in some financial distress. It had apparently been decided to telephone her parents somewhere in the United States in order to request them to send money to Nepal on an urgent basis. They, and my friend just behind them, finally got to the relevant telephone clerk. He patiently took down the information—the number, and so on—from the couple. Then he said, "We will place your call next Thursday"—in something like a week!

In this respect, Nepal has been utterly transformed in the last twenty-five years. All the major hotels in Kathmandu now have international telephone service. In fact, it is easier to call New York from one's hotel room than it is to call another number in the city—the local phone service is still suspect. One can routinely fax or e-mail to, or from, Nepal. Given this—and the glittering hotels like the Yak and Yeti, the air-conditioned tour buses, the shops in Kathmandu with all their television sets and computers in the windows, and even the international-class restaurants—it is easy for a visitor to get the impression that Nepal's prosperity might be approaching that of Switzerland. Such an impression would be totally false. Let us review a few figures. The fact that the average earned income per Nepali per year is about one hundred fifty dollars really does not tell us much: Nepal is an agrarian society. Most of the people practice some sort of agriculture or horticulture for a living, and these should be at least self-sustaining. The real question, then, is how well nourished is the population. The minimal calorie intake for survival is usually given as 2,256 calories a day. Surveys of the Nepalese population show that at least a quarter of the people live on less than 1,750 calories a day. In other words, about a quarter of the Nepalese population appears to be starving or, at least, badly undernourished.

This certainly affects both the health of the population and its life expectancy. The fact of the matter is that Nepal is not a very healthy country. A visitor must be very careful to avoid ailments such as amebic dysentery and hepatitis, which are common. Except in the best hotels in Kathmandu, which have their own treated water supply, one cannot trust any water in the country. Ice for drinks is a well-known trap; so are rapidly flowing streams, which may well be contaminated by Giardia. In the countryside, something called "bottled mineral water" is now sold; it is just the local untreated water, put into a bottle. One gets used to brushing one's teeth in tea and using iodine tablets to render the water safe to drink. In the south, malaria has come back in forms that resist the old quinine-based prophylactics. There are new ones, but, in time, these too will become less and less effective. Nonetheless, life spans in Nepal have been gradually increasing. One set of figures I saw recently listed a life span of fifty-one for women and fifty-four for men; another listed forty-eight for women and fifty-two for men. To give some sort of benchmark, in 1967—and despite the fact that, thanks to people like Sir Edmund Hillary, their medical facilities were much superior to those of the general population—the Sherpas had a life expectancy of some thirty-five years. Their life expectancy is now comparable to that of the rest of the population.

In all such surveys—life expectancy, literacy, you name it—Nepalese women always do substantially worse than men. As far as life expectancy is concerned, this is partly, but only partly, explained by the complications of childbirth. (The fertility rate is said to be some six or more live births per woman—contraception is all but unknown.) There is also the social status of women. In a typical Hindu family—90 percent of the population is Hindu—the birth of a girl-child is regarded as a catastrophe. Young girls are more poorly fed, educated, and nurtured, and this is reflected in all the statistical data about Nepal. For example, one set of figures I have seen regarding literacy gives a nationwide literacy rate for men of 22 percent, and for women, 3 percent; a more optimistic set, which may apply to the Kathmandu valley alone, gives 55 percent for men and 18 percent for women. In either case, the significance is clear.

Furthermore, women are exploited. This goes beyond the observation that in countryside farm villages, and even in cities, women seem to be working harder. It has to do with such phenomena as young girls being sold by their poverty-stricken parents into prostitution in India. A recent, and allegedly conservative, estimate by the Indian Health Organization concluded that there were something like one hundred thousand Nepalese women working in Indian brothels. *Himal,* a bimonthly magazine published in Kathmandu that is devoted to the entire Himalayan region, dedicated a whole issue to the problems of women in Nepal and the other Himalayan countries. It showed that there are the beginnings of a feminist movement in Nepal. One of the articles, by a feminist writer who lives in Kathmandu—Sujata Rana— was entitled "The Sex Worker and the Market." She wrote, "The popularity of Nepali girls in Indian brothels seems to be a combination of 'exotic' looks or origin (the mountains), fair skin and if it is to be believed, the fact that Nepali prostitutes are more willing to disrobe fully than their Indian counterparts." Rana estimates that there are now about five thousand Nepalese prostitutes working in the Kathmandu valley. Many of these women came to Kathmandu to work in the carpet or garment industries; when this did not provide a living, they turned to prostitution. As a consequence of this, and of the volume of travel in and out of the country, AIDS is beginning to be recognized as a medical problem. One account that I read said that there were about twenty-four documented cases in Nepal. It is hard to know how accurate such a figure is, but it does serve as a warning.

It is easy to say that education is the answer to many of these problems. In fact, the government does what it can to encourage girls and young women to go to school. But what should people in a country like Nepal be educated to do? We see in our own country that it is possible to develop a cadre of educated people who will never find employment in the fields in which they have been educated—theoretical physics, for example. In a developing country like Nepal, a large group of young people with education but no employment will rapidly become part of the problem rather than part of the solution. But certainly one profession that—in any future one can foresee for Nepal—cannot possibly have too many practitioners is medicine. In 1967, when I first went to Nepal, there were an estimated 220 doctors—people who practiced what we would call western medicine— in the entire country. Of these, 120 practiced in the Kathmandu valley. (There were four dental surgeons in all of Nepal.) This worked out to be one doctor for every fifty thousand Nepalis. The present figure is estimated to be one doctor for every twenty-five thousand people;

this is deceptive, however, since most parts of the country have no doctor. At the end of the last chapter I noted the fact that, after our most recent sojourn in Tibet, we had trekked into Simikot—the capital of the very remote Humla district in northwestern Nepal. This visit reminded me that in 1967, a medical emergency had occurred in the neighboring, and equally remote, Bajhang district. There appeared to be an outbreak of anthrax—a very deadly disease. One of the worries was that infected animals might be dumped into the Karnali River, thus compromising the entire drainage system for western Nepal. The only way to reach this area was—and still is—by helicopter or STOL, and the U.S. AID mission, which had such aircraft, was called to help. In fact, a team of specialists was flown in from the Centers for Disease Control in Atlanta, Georgia. It turned out, as these specialists were able to confirm, that anthrax was not involved. The people were sick with bubonic plague and the animals with rinderpest. Bubonic plague is treatable with antibiotics, and a vaccination program was carried out for the animals. In the end, both outbreaks were controlled with a minimal loss of life. I was curious how, twenty-five years later, the medical situation had evolved. When I asked people in Simikot, they told me that there had been a doctor there a few years ago, but he had left. Now there was, they said, no doctor at all. I asked what happened when people got really sick. The only reply was a shrug of the shoulders.

There is a "drug," however, whose influence on Nepalese society has been vastly more profound than any amount of hashish: foreign aid. I call it a drug because when administered, it can create a state of temporary euphoria, followed by dependence, followed by the most terrible sort of withdrawal symptoms if it is ever stopped. Everywhere one looks in Nepal, one sees the effects of foreign aid—many of them very positive. Here are a few examples. Until 1954, when a campaign to eradicate mosquitoes in the Terai was begun by the World Health Organization and U.S. AID, much of the area was essentially uninhabitable. The fifty-mile-long Rapti valley, where Tiger Tops is located, was infested with malaria-bearing mosquitoes. Ninety percent of whatever population lived there, it was estimated, had malaria. To deal with this, it was decided to break the man-mosquito-man chain of infection by spraying the interior of Terai village houses with DDT. At first, the villagers, who did understand the reasons, objected vehemently. But not for long. By March of 1967, the rate of infection had been reduced to 0.4 percent. With the help of U.S. AID, five thousand people were resettled in the valley, which now has irrigation, medical facilities, and a school system. With the aid of the World Food Program, the Nepalese government started fish farms in the Rapti valley rivers. It is true that, because of the resistance of new strains of mosquitoes to DDT, malaria has made something of a comeback. This has required the use of malathion, which is six times more expensive than DDT, to reestablish mosquito control. This, too, one supposes, is paid for out of foreign aid funds.

Or take the matter of education. Until the Ranas took over the country in 1846, education in Nepal was always associated with religious institutions. In the north, these were Buddhist monasteries; in the south, Hindu temples. Before 1768, when they were expelled, a few Christian missionaries founded schools. But during the century of Rana rule, education became the exclusive privilege of the elite. The Ranas imported English teachers for their children, and before the Second World War some English high schools were founded in Kathmandu and the larger cities in the south. The Gurkha soldiers who came back from the British army after the standard fifteen-year period of service established a few local elementary schools in the hills; even now, in remote hill towns one sometimes sees groups of children being taught, in an almost military rote drill, by an elderly ex-Gurkha soldier. After the war, the Ranas were essentially forced by the example of the expanding drive for education in India and China to provide more schools. By 1951, there were 310 primary and middle schools, eleven high schools, two colleges, one normal school, and one special technical school.

It was at this time that one of the most remarkable figures in Nepalese education—himself a kind of foreign aid—first appeared on the scene, in the form of Father Charles Moran from Chicago. Father Moran, who died a few years ago in his late eighties, had founded a Jesuit school in Patna, in northern India, in the 1930s. Several Nepalis, including members of the Rana family, attended his school, which was modeled after a typical English public school. He was therefore well known to the Ranas, and when they came under pressure in Nepal to do something about the educational system, they turned to him. This was in 1949. But Father Moran, realizing that a revolution was inevitable in Nepal, stalled accepting the invitation for a year or so, until there *was* a revolution. The new regime—the monarchy of King Tribhuvan—again asked him to come to Kathmandu, and soon after, he founded a private elementary school in Godavari, just outside the capital. There is now a high school there as well, and the elementary school has changed its name to St. Xavier's. The student body is made up almost entirely of Buddhists and Hindus. Although the school is run by the Jesuit order, there is no proselytizing, which is forbidden by the constitution of Nepal. When last I examined the statistics, there were about two hundred fifty boys—it was founded as a boys' school—who boarded in Godavari, and about an equal number of day scholars. There is a tuition charge, but many of the boys are there on scholarships, ensuring a certain diversity. The classes are conducted in English and are designed so that a boy who does well at St. Xavier's can go on to a foreign university and not be at a disadvantage. Incidentally, Father Moran was also a noted worldwide ham-radio operator. His station, 9N1MM, was always a very desirable ham address. One of the things he used to do was relay messages from Himalayan climbers to the outside world. Now, most of the large expeditions come equipped with their own satellite links.

Recently, I heard of another nongovernmental bit of foreign educational aid. The Kingdom of Mustang, which, as I have mentioned, is in western Nepal, north of the Himalayas, is, because of its proximity to Tibet—it actually borders Tibet—a sanctuary for the practice of Tibetan Buddhism. But, at least until it was opened up to trekking, it was also one of the poorest and most isolated regions in Nepal. The few people I knew who managed to get there before the general travel ban was lifted reported that the conditions of poverty exceeded almost anything they had seen in the rest of the country. Apparently, word of this—and of the fact that the religious institutions were, due to a lack of trained monks, in the process of disappearing—reached the Dalai

Lama in Dharamsala. He dispatched a mission consisting of an elderly monk, who had been born in Tibet but had fled the country, and a small retinue to travel to Mustang, something they accomplished by foot and horseback. One of their goals, which was achieved, was to select two young boys to return with them to Dharamsala to be educated as monks so that, in the future, they can serve the religious—and thus to some extent the educational—needs of their community. It was a tiny gesture—considering the needs—but a profoundly moving one.

Of course, both Father Moran and the Dalai Lama were, and are, in the business of quality education for the few—for a kind of chosen elite. In a way, this is the simplest kind of education to provide, since such a small number of very gifted students are involved. But what of the many—the masses of Nepalese boys and girls and young men and young women who do not go to these elite schools? In principle, elementary education is compulsory in Nepal for both girls and boys. But in practice, there is an acute shortage of elementary schools and schoolteachers, especially in the countryside. It is probable that no more than 20 or 30 percent of the children now go to school, although the number appears to be steadily growing. To give some idea, a 1981 survey showed that there were 10,340 primary schools in the country, as opposed to 310 in 1951, and 918 high schools, as opposed to 22. It is a common sight in the early mornings in Kathmandu to see children on their way to school. But it is an even more common sight to see children driving animals or coming into town to work.

There are also about one hundred degree "colleges" in the country, most of them liberal arts colleges granting a B.A. degree. In 1959, with the help of U.S. AID funds, Tribhuvan University was founded in Kathmandu. Since 1967, many of its six thousand undergraduates and graduate students have been attending classes in a campus constructed a few miles south of the city. I have visited this campus, and some of the other ones in the city, a number of times over the years. Shortly before the new campus opened officially, I had a long talk with Dr. T. N. Upraity, who was then the vice-chancellor. As I mentioned previously, Dr. Upraity was one of the few students to take a degree at the English College in Kathmandu. He then went to the University of Oregon for his doctorate. Even then, in 1967, Dr. Upraity was already worried about what would happen to these university graduates. A great many of them wanted to stay in Kathmandu, where—if they had been educated in the social sciences—the only career open to them was within the national government. Since political parties were then banned, even peaceful political activity was unavailable as a safety valve. This is certainly one of the factors that led to the revolution of 1990. One of the most effective foreign aid outfits in Nepal in matters of education—and, in general, in the attempt to improve the quality of life for the Nepalese—has been our Peace Corps. They have also been largely responsible for changing the perception that Nepalese once had of Americans. In 1963, an unnamed American author writing in an official publication made an attempt to assess the Nepalese impression of Americans. He noted: "A fairly large number of Nepalese have had some form of contact with Americans, mainly with tourists or those composing [sic] official missions. The general stereotype which has arisen from this acquaintance depicts them as good-hearted, generous and friendly, but basically simple people of somewhat limited perception." He went on to say, "According to all reports, volunteers of the United States Peace Corps have already had a measurable effect in improving the image of the United States."

I think it is fair to say that in 1967, the year of my first visit to Nepal, the Peace Corps volunteers *were* the image of the United States. There were so few American tourists, and such a tiny minority of them ever ventured outside of the Kathmandu valley, that if one did travel in the countryside—inevitably by foot—and it became known that one was an American, it was immediately assumed that one must be in the Peace Corps. This, of course, is no longer the case, since tens of thousands of Americans annually trek in the backcountry of Nepal. In 1967, there were something like three hundred fifty Peace Corps volunteers in Nepal. Now there are something like one hundred seventy. Then, as now, the volunteers went only where the Nepalese government asked them to go. They work in fields chosen by the Nepalese: typically, agriculture, rural construction (bridges and roads) improving the water supply, and now computer-oriented occupations. Most of these men and women live in villages in the hills or in the Terai. Many of them teach in schools, where they try to reorient the traditional educational methods. In Nepal, a person was considered educated if he, or sometimes she, could recite from memory large bodies of religious text. The volunteers now try to teach the children problem-solving skills—how to cope with unfamiliar situations. I heard of one interesting form of service—one that appealed to me especially. There was a young volunteer who had had training in mathematics. His job was to produce a modern high school mathematics textbook in Nepali—something that did not exist. Like all volunteers, he had signed up for a minimum of eighteen months, and had had an intense language course in Nepali before he came to the country. Many of the volunteers, in the course of time, learn some of the local languages as well. Some of them were of the opinion that the Nepalese schools try to teach English too soon. Many children start English in the third grade—which might be all right, except that a large number of them do not come to school speaking Nepali. They rather speak one of the local languages, such as Sherpa or Newari, so they also have to learn the national language. This probably has changed quite a bit in recent years, thanks to the radio. There are now Nepali-language radio programs heard all over the country, so that, more and more, Nepali is becoming the lingua franca of the entire nation. Indeed, Sherpas who live in Kathmandu have told me that their children are embarrassed to speak Sherpa in the city and insist on speaking Nepali.

While countries such as Switzerland, which set up yak cheese-producing factories, or Israel, which trained Nepalese paratroopers, have small-scale programs of aid in the country, the major donors have been large binational or multinational operations. Binational arrangements are made between Nepal and a single donor country, whereas multinational arrangements are between Nepal and entities such as the World Bank, the Asian Development Bank, or one of the United Nations operations, such as the World Health Organization. In 1976, the World Bank helped set up something called the Nepal Aid Group—NAG. There were so many countries trying to aid Nepal that they had begun falling over each other; one of the purposes of

NAG is to see that projects are not duplicated. At present, sixteen countries belong to NAG. The list is interesting for both whom it includes and whom it does not. In alphabetical order one has: Australia, Austria, Belgium, Canada, Denmark, France, Finland, Germany, Japan, Kuwait, the Netherlands, Sweden, Saudi Arabia, Switzerland, the United Kingdom, and the United States, along with seven multilateral agencies. Notably absent are China, India, and Russia. These three countries have been among the most important donors to Nepal. After Japan and Germany, India is presently the most important contributor. In the past, Indian aid, as I have mentioned, built the Tribhuvan Highway and Airport, as well as telecommunication and irrigation facilities. The Chinese, who in the past have given as much as 10 percent of Nepal's total donor aid, were, as we have also seen, responsible for major road-building activities. The former Soviet Union used to be a major player, but Russia has now ceased to be a significant factor. The United States was close to the top of the list until the mid-1960s.

What has all of this meant to the country, and where is it going? In the spring of 1992, *Himal* devoted an entire issue to this question. Here is a quote from an article by Ashutosh Tiwari, who is identified as "a college student interested in the Nepali economy"—parenthetically, many of the facts cited above come from Tiwari's article. He wrote:

> The year 1951 was remarkable for two events that dramatically altered Nepal's political and economic directions. The first, of course, was the end of the century-old Rana regime, stirring political consciousness that swept hill and Terai. The second was that foreign aid made its debut in January of that year.... The United States Government's gift of NRs [Nepalese rupees. I will not try to translate these figures directly into dollars. One would have to take into account inflation and the exchange rates at the different epochs. As I have mentioned, the present official exchange rate is something like forty-five NRs to the dollar. But what I will do shortly is give the figures for what percentages of development costs are provided by foreign aid. Those are the numbers that are really startling] 22,000, provided under President Harry Truman's Point Four

*programme, was the first droplet of foreign aid, which was soon
followed by grants and technical assistance programmes from India
and others. For a country that had been heretofore rigidly isolation-
ist, Nepal decided that it liked the taste of aid, and opened the faucet
wider. For whatever good it might have done, foreign aid has since
come to stay, in a flurry of donor dollars, marks, yen and pounds.
According to an unofficial estimate made by a member of the
National Planning Commission (NPC), the total aid (including
loans) that Nepal has gathered since 1951 to 1990 from both foreign
governments and international banks, stands at a stunning current-
price figure of around NRs 85,000 million.*

This is roughly two billion dollars, of which half is in loans. In other
words, in a country where the annual income is about one hundred
fifty dollars per person, each Nepali's share of the national debt is
about sixty dollars, and getting larger.

But these numbers do not really tell us what it would mean to Nepal if
this aid were suddenly to evaporate. According to the most recent figures I
can find, at least 60 percent of Nepal's development program is being paid
for by foreign donors. Here is Tiwari again—and his point of view is rather
widely shared, at least among the more politically sophisticated sectors of
the population, in Nepal: "Critics charge that foreign aid, on the whole, has
not helped Nepal, if one takes development to mean reduction of poverty.
Claiming that relatively only a few groups in Nepal, particularly elites in
Kathmandu, have benefitted from aid, they point out that there is a larger
percent of poor people today in the country than ever before. They further
attack foreign-funded development projects as being riddled with ineffi-
cient management, poor planning, unattainable objectives, high overhead
expense, and a staff more interested in perks than productivity." An American observer recently stated this point of view succinctly when he remarked
that Nepal was "undernourished and overadvised."

This raises the obvious question—which Tiwari goes on to discuss:

*Should Nepal turn off the aid tap altogether? The repercussions,
according to Mahesh Banskota, an economist at ICIMOD [These
initials are an acronym for the International Centre for Integrated
Mountain Development. This is an entity based in Kathmandu that*

was set up some ten years ago, and funded by countries such as the United States and Switzerland, as well as local governments, to study problems common to all the Indian subcontinental mountain regions. It has run into problems of conflicting national interests, but it has produced some useful studies], are equally alarming. Eighteen percent of Nepal's educational activities, 26 percent of social programmes, 47 percent of health-related work and about 50 percent of irrigation schemes will stop immediately. Can Nepal afford to lose those sectors? So mired is Nepal in foreign aid over the last four decades that kicking it off altogether does not yield any more benefits.

The title of this chapter, "Fortune Has Wings," is the same title that I used for the chapter in the first incarnation of this book, and it covered the same general area—the development of modern Nepal. It is a slogan I had come across in 1967 on the blackboard in one of the schools that Sir Edmund Hillary had created for the Sherpas of the Everest region. It was part of an English lesson. (One of the other slogans was GOD BLESS OUR KING.) At the time I wrote this chapter, I wondered whether the children in that school had any idea of how their futures—their "fortunes"—would depend on "wings." "Wings" was for me a kind of metaphor for foreign aid. At the time, the notion of Nepal being "mired" in foreign aid would have seemed absurd to me. Everywhere one looked there were projects crying out to be done.

Moreover, there seemed to be no impediments to the future. As I have mentioned, Nepal was a food-exporting country, selling wheat, rice, and millet—thousands of metric tons—to India. From this point of view, the population appeared to be in balance with the food resources. At the time, about a third of Nepal was covered by forest— sal, sisau, semal, khair, karma, and ansa trees grew in the south, while in the Himalayan regions in the north there were forests of rhododendrons and junipers. I remember camping in such a forest on a high pass in the Annapurna region one night when it snowed. The next morning, we found snow-leopard tracks near our tents. When I revisited this place twenty years later, in the 1980s, the forest was gone—cut down—and what had been our isolated campsite was now a "forest" of small hotels, restaurants, and lodges, and a couple of trekker tent cities. There is almost no place in Nepal where one can now find a real forest.

This degradation of Nepal's environment—which has been accompanied by a growing gap between the rich and the poor—has also had profound effects on the character of the people. In 1967, the one thing that visitors agreed about the country—apart from its incredible natural beauty—was how extraordinarily nice the Nepalese were. There seemed to be a kind of harmony between the evironment and the character of the people who inhabited it. One still finds this—if one gets as far as possible away from the centers of development. There are still some places in Nepal that are so remote as to be completely unspoiled—but not many. Recently, I came across a kind of warning published by the U.S. Embassy in Kathmandu. It read in part: "While Nepalese are generally friendly and present no threat to trekkers, the number of violent incidents in recent years against trekkers has unfortunately increased. Crime, while still low by Western standards, does exist on the trails [to say nothing of the cities]. Westerners have been the victims of murder and violent assaults. All the victims have been travelling alone or as a couple. The general motive seems to have been robbery, even though the possessions of some of the victims were insignificant by American standards." (The writer of this does not seem to have had the experience of being asked by a maid in a hotel room whether she can have permission to take, for herself, a used razor blade out of a wastepaper basket; or of being asked by a child in a Nepalese village for a broken shoelace about to be thoughtlessly thrown away.) Then there was a series of cautionary recommendations to "help you enjoy your trek." After these were concluded, there was a coda that read, "The embassy recommends that you do not take night buses in Nepal. There have been serious problems recently with bandits holding up such buses."

If someone had read me this paragraph in 1967, taking out the references to place, and asked me to guess which country was being referred to, the last country in the world I would have chosen was Nepal. The Nepalese have made a Faustian bargain with development and, having supped with the Devil, they will have to figure out how to leave his table. We cannot, and should not, do it for them.

3

Some Walk-Going

Prologue

The next two chapters can be thought of as a unit. They both concern trekking in the same area—the Sherpa country on, and around, Mount Everest. It will be noted that I did not say they both concerned the *same trek*. The two treks, one taken in the fall of 1967 and the other in the fall of 1983, were so different in ambience that if I had not taken both of them myself I would not have recognized the description of the second from the first, and vice versa. The following simple set of facts tells all. During our 1967 trek, which lasted thirty-seven days, the only other trekkers we saw were a family of Americans, who turned out to be Peace Corps volunteers on vacation from teaching school in the Terai,[1] and a small handful of other westerners also on vacation from various duties in the country. In 1983, there were some twenty *thousand* trekkers in the same general region during the same general period. In order to render this duality, I have divided the material into two different chapters. The first deals with the history of Everest and the Sherpas, and our 1967 trek, while the second deals

1. They told me, incidentally, that one of the problems they faced in the classroom was poisonous snakes getting in through windows and the like. They said that they had learned to leave this matter to the children, who knew how to deal with it.

with what we found in 1983. I will not continually interrupt the narrative of the first chapter with comments that will be made, generally by example, in the second. However, I will make some changes in the narrative of the earlier trek so that, for example, I do not give the impression that some of the dead are still living.

Some Walk-Going, 1967

In many ways, Ila Tsering, whom I first met in 1967, was a typical Sherpa. Like all Sherpas, he was short (five foot three, about the Nepalese average for men), dark, and Mongolian-looking. (In Tibetan, *Sherpa* means "man from the east"—*shar* is the word for "east"—but no one knows what "the east" refers to, exactly. Several centuries ago, it is thought, the Sherpa tribe migrated south into Nepal and northern India from Tibet. As for the Tibetans themselves, they look astonishingly like our Native Americans. This may not be too surprising, since many scholars claim that the precursors of the Natives of North and South America migrated in prehistoric times from Asia, across what is now the Bering Strait adjoining Alaska and Siberia, into the Americas.) Like most Sherpa men, Ila wore his hair short. (Tibetan men wear *their* hair extremely long, like a woman's, and some tie it up in coils with bright ribbons.) Like most Sherpas, Ila was married to one woman (both polygamy and polyandry, though forbidden by Nepalese law, are practiced by a few Sherpas, the most common arrangement being the marriage of a woman to two brothers) and had a fairly large family—three boys and a girl. As was true of many Sherpa families, there was a history of tuberculosis in Ila's— his wife had the disease until it was arrested by the arrival of modern medicine in his community. Like most Sherpas of the time—now many live in Kathmandu—Ila lived in the Solu-Khumbu region of Nepal. Solu and Khumbu are contiguous districts in the northeast, next to Mount Everest. Solu, the more southerly, is in the "lowlands"—its villages are at about nine thousand feet. In Khumbu, the villages are at eleven or twelve thousand feet, and the yak pastures, where the Sherpa herders live in the summer, are as high as seventeen thousand feet, which is almost two thousand feet higher than Mont Blanc, the highest mountain in western Europe. Ila, and his family, lived in Namche Bazar, the district capital of Khumbu, which is at about twelve thousand feet. Like most Sherpas, Ila was multilingual. His mother tongue, Sherpa, is closely related to Tibetan but has no written form, so Tibetan serves as the written language. Spoken Sherpa and spoken Tibetan are sufficiently different that I have seen Sherpas and Tibetans choose English as their preferred common spoken language. But Ila spoke and wrote Nepali as well as Tibetan. Sherpas now generally speak Nepali, and—if they have had the advantage of formal schooling—read and write it. Ila also spoke Hindustani—a mixture of Hindi and Urdu. Like many modern Sherpas, Ila understood English and spoke it with a charming accent and a rather astonishing turn of phrase. (There does not seem to be any sound in Sherpa equivalent to the English "f," so *fruit* comes out "prut," and *breakfast*, "birkpass.") Like all Sherpas, Ila practiced Lamaistic Buddhism, his religious life being guided by the lamas who live and study in the monasteries in Solu-Khumbu. The spiritual leader of the Lamaistic Buddhists is the Dalai Lama. For the Sherpas of Khumbu, his spiritual representative is the abbot of the monastery in Thyangboche, a few miles from Namche Bazar. In addition, the Sherpas are animists—they believe in a complex set of spirits and deities who live in the streams, trees, and high mountains of Solu-Khumbu.

What then distinguished Ila from most Sherpas, who were farmers, herders, or traders—now one might add hotel-keepers—was his occupation, which he referred to as "some walk-going." Before 1965, when the government of Nepal temporarily banned all mountaineering expeditions in the country because their number had become unmanageable, along with their irresponsibility about crossing the border into Tibet, inflaming the Chinese, Ila's "walk-going" took him with English, Japanese, Indian, and American climbing teams. His function was what he called "carrying go." There is carrying and there is carrying; Ila's version consisted of transporting food and other supplies to very high altitudes over very difficult mountain terrain. Technically, Ila was a "tiger." The

British, who discovered the extraordinary physical and human virtues of the Sherpas in the course of their first Everest expeditions in the 1920s, gave the nickname "tiger" to those Sherpas who carried to the highest elevations or who showed special courage. It soon became a custom of the Himalayan Club of Darjeeling—the Indian hill station east of Nepal from which many early assaults on the peaks were mounted—to make formal "tiger" awards to outstanding Sherpas. In the 1950s, a Himalayan Society was formed in Nepal and became, for a while, a kind of Sherpa union. The closest thing to a union now is an entity called the Trekking Workers' Association of Nepal, but it does not seem to be extremely effective. There is also a group called the Nepal Mountaineering Association. It runs a mountaineering school in Manang in the Annapurna region of western Nepal. This school provides technical mountaineering instruction for Sherpas. The instruction is given by professional European mountain guides. When I paid a visit to the school in the mid-1980s, the teachers were French Chamonix guides. The fact that a Sherpa has attended this school, and has a certificate from it, is probably the best assurance available that such a Sherpa is qualified to do technical mountaineering. But most treks involve trail-walking—albeit, sometimes quite difficult trail-walking—for which the training at the school is largely irrelevant. What matters here is the character and reliability of the Sherpa, which is best ascertained by consulting people he has previously worked for, or by having confidence in the trekking agency that employs him. Some agencies employ their Sherpas on a year-round basis to be certain that they will have, during the trekking and climbing seasons in the fall and spring, the "best" Sherpas available. I will shortly explain how we managed to employ Ila. On an organized trek the head Sherpa—the so-called *sirdar*—will hire and, indeed, pay the porters and any other Sherpas he may need to hire.

In 1967, the Himalayan Society set the rates for "carrying." For a porter, it was about twenty-five rupees a day—then about a dollar. For Ila's work, it was at least twice as much. Porters, who simply carry loads, are men, and occasionally women, who come from the hill tribes of central Nepal. Their principal occupation is subsistence farming. To supplement their meager income, they hire out as porters.

It should be understood that portering for treks and expeditions is only a small fraction of the load-carrying work that these men and women do. In the hills of Nepal, there are no motorable roads, and it is unlikely that there ever will be. The terrain is too difficult, and the economic payoff too limited. Almost everything that is sold in every shop in everyone of these remote hill villages has been brought there on the back of a porter. The rest comes in by plane or helicopter. One of the worries, incidentally, about the introduction of large helicopters for transporting freight into these hill villages is that porters may become extraneous, and this source of supplemental income disappear. But that is for the future.

What a porter can carry, and the terrain over which it is carried, defies my comprehension. A grown, male, Nepalese porter routinely carries at least eighty-five kilograms—nearly two hundred pounds. These loads are, as a rule, placed in wicker baskets with a strap that comes across the forehead, called a *namlo*. I have seen extremely strong western climbers unable to lift off the ground—let alone carry—such a basket. I have tried it myself, and could not make one budge. To get better traction on the steep, slippery trails, porters usually go barefoot, or wear sandals. The soles of their feet become thicker than the soles of most shoes. Nonetheless, the feet of porters are continually subject to injury. If, when you trek in Nepal, you happen to have a doctor in your group, he or she will be spending evenings bandaging the feet of porters. The present top wage for a porter is about one hundred fifty rupees a day—about three dollars. It is hard to know what to say about this wage. Compared to the annual average per capita income in Nepal, it is perhaps reasonable; compared to what these men and women actually do, it is absurd. What has struck me on every trek or climb I have been on in Nepal is how kind and decent these people are. Every trekker and every climber in Nepal owes the success of his or her expedition to porters. Without them, none of us would ever have gotten anywhere.

Back to Ila Tsering. While he took part in many expeditions, throughout the Himalayas, his most outstanding work was probably done with the American expedition to Mount Everest in 1963. (The paucity of climbing expeditions during those years is reflected in the fact that one can speak of "the American expedition to Mount Everest in 1963." On my visit to the same area twenty years later, there were *three hundred* climbers in the Everest base camp. If one had asked for "the American expedition," no one would have had the slightest idea of where to direct one. I was reminded of the fact that when someone went looking for Edward Whymper, the Englishman who in 1865 first climbed the Matterhorn, in the town of Cervinia, on the Italian side of the mountain, all he had to do is to ask for the "Englishman." Try that today!) On March 23, 1963, Ila was with a group that was caught in an avalanche on the lower slopes of Everest; an American climber, Jake Breitenbach, was killed, and a Sherpa, Ang Pema, was badly injured. Ila carried Ang Pema down to the base camp on his back. There, the remaining members of the expedition debated whether or not to continue, and decided to go on. The subsequent success of the expedition was due, at least in part, to the fact that the Sherpas were willing to carry on after the accident. On May 1, James Whitaker and a Sherpa, Nawang Gombu, of Darjeeling, made it to the top. On May 21, Ila and four other Sherpas carried supplies to an altitude of 27,250 feet on the west ridge of Everest—less than two thousand feet below the summit, and higher than all but a handful of mountains in the world—in support of two successful American assaults, each by a different route. For his work on Everest (before the final push, Ila was reported to have said, "All smart Sherpas down sick. Only crazy Sherpas up here"), Ila was selected—along with four other Sherpas, two from Solu-Khumbu and two from Darjeeling—to visit the United States, with the aid of a grant from the state department's Bureau of Educational and Cultural Affairs. On the way, Ila stopped in Switzerland long enough to climb the Matterhorn, which he found pretty tame. On July 8, 1963, President Kennedy presented the Hubbard Medal of the National Geographic Society to the American members of the expedition, and to the Sherpas as well. Hanging in Ila's house in Namche Bazar was a delightful picture showing the president bending down to put the medal's ribbon around Ila's neck. Both men are grinning broadly.

After the climbing ban of 1965, the expeditionary Sherpas of Solu-Khumbu fell on relatively hard times, because there was no expeditionary work for them. Their situation would have been incomparably worse if it had not been for a retired British army officer, Lieutenant Colonel James Owen Merion Roberts, formerly of Second King Edward VII's Own Gurkha Rifles. Roberts, who is now in his late seventies, had been climbing in the Himalayas for years, and had served as the transportation officer for the 1963 American Everest expedition. (This was not exactly a sinecure, since the expedition required nine hundred porters to move its equipment from Kathmandu to the base of Everest, a distance of more than two hundred miles through some of the most rugged terrain on earth.) There is probably no one in the world who knows the Himalayas better than Roberts; in addition, he served as military attaché to the British Embassy in Kathmandu from 1958 to 1961, which gave him considerable familiarity with the intricacies of Nepalese governmental administration. He speaks both Nepali and Hindi. In 1965, Roberts, who then lived in Kathmandu—he now lives near Pokhara in western Nepal, and raises pheasants in an attempt to preserve the local species—founded an outfit that he called Mountain Travel. (At present, what was Roberts's original company, which is still located in Kathmandu, is called Tiger Mountain; its independent, California-based spin-off is called Mountain Travel.) Roberts's idea was to organize and outfit small trekking expeditions into the backcountry of Nepal for people who were willing to hike and camp but might not know how to get along in a strange, and fairly wild, country, with an incomprehensible language. His first clients were three American ladies, aged fifty-six, sixty-two, and sixty-four, from the Midwest. They were clearly in splendid shape, because in the company of three Sherpas and nine porters, all supplied by Roberts, they made the trek from Kathmandu to Namche Bazar and back—a dogleg route of 190 miles each way, as the crow flies—in a little over a month, and apparently enjoyed the trip thoroughly. (The distance as seen by the crow is not a very relevant measure of this trip, however, since so much of it is nearly vertical; some of the passes rise to nearly twelve thousand feet.) At present, Roberts's old company handles several hundred trekkers a year and employs the equivalent of several major expeditions' worth of Sherpas as guides and cooks, as well as a few hundred porters. It also provides the logistical support for many mountaineering expeditions as well as trips into Tibet. These trips can last from a couple of weeks to well over a month, with a range of prices that depend on the trip—a hundred dollars a day and up. For this, Tiger Mountain, and the other trekking companies in Kathmandu, supply food, tents, and sleeping bags, along with sufficient personnel to carry the equipment and cook the food. All the trekker must supply is his or her personal gear and what Roberts once called in one of his brochures "feet in good, hard shape."

Ila Tsering was one of Lieutenant Colonel Roberts's sirdars. It was in this capacity that I came to know him. He was the sirdar for the thirty-seven-day trek I made in 1967 with Claude Jaccoux and his then-wife, Michele, into Solu-Khumbu. Jaccoux, although he had been a professional climber for over a decade, had never been to the Himalayas. Neither had Michele. (And neither had I.) She was a member of the French national ski team, but skiing in the Himalayas was then unknown. Now, a few brave souls have skied off of summits such as that of Mount Everest. My trip was a fulfillment of a childhood dream—to see Mount Everest. Its history, and the almost legendary tales surrounding the attempts to climb it, had always fascinated me.

Mount Everest was a "British mountain," thanks to Edmund Hillary and Tenzing Norgay, who climbed it in 1953, and the history of British attempts dating back to the 1920s. But the British were nearly beaten by two Swiss expeditions in 1952, and if they had failed, a very strong French group had been given permission by the Nepalese government to attempt the mountain the following year. As we have seen, until 1950 almost no foreigners had been allowed into Nepal, but when the ban was lifted, the government started selling climbing rights to its mountains, which included eight of the ten highest in the world. The fee was arranged according to altitude. Up to 1965, when all climbing in Nepal was temporarily banned, the eight highest—Everest (29,022 feet), Kanchenjunga (28,208), Lhotse (27,923), Makalu (27,824), Dhaulagiri (26,810), Cho Oyu (26,750), Manaslu (26,640), and Annapurna I (26,504)—cost 4,800 Nepalese rupees, then about seven hundred dollars, apiece. The rest of the mountains above 25,000 feet cost 3,200 rupees each; mountains below 25,000 feet cost 1,600—

then less than two hundred fifty dollars. This last category presented some ambiguities of interpretation, because northern Nepal abounds in "hills" and glacial passes that range in altitude from eighteen to twenty thousand feet but, in their contexts, hardly seem like real mountains at all. By now, all of the "eight-thousanders"—the peaks over 8,000 meters, or about 26,250 feet—have been climbed. But any traveler in northern Nepal comes across mountains—often stunning mountains, in the twenty-thousand-foot range—that have no names on the map and very likely have never been climbed, or even attempted.

In 1969, the Nepalese government lifted the climbing ban they had imposed in 1965. The Tourism Act of 1978 and the Mountaineering Expedition Regulation of 1979 set new terms and conditions for climbing expeditions. For example, expeditions were required to carry life insurance for the Sherpas and the other personnel working for them—something like eight thousand dollars for work above 6,000 meters. They were also required to "provide equal opportunity to climb the summit for those persons who have reached the last camp." This was surely a reference to people like Ila Tsering, who carried supplies to such camps, but then might not have been invited to join the summit teams. It is interesting that nearly all the climbing reports one sees now from Nepal include Sherpa summit climbers and, needless to say, Sherpa casualties.

The money that climbing in Nepal costs has also been steadily increasing. At least one reason—obviously, the Nepalese want to earn as much as possible from this activity—is an attempt to control the degradation of the Himalayan environment. Once tourism got started in Nepal, the Nepalese—really by default—got into the business of mass tourism. I will later show how this contrasts to Bhutan and Tibet. Clearly, to charge a fee of $250 to climb a typical Himalayan peak, or even $700 to climb Everest, was to say that, from an economic point of view, the mountain was open to anyone—hence the three hundred climbers who were in the Everest base camp region in the fall of 1983. (Over five hundred climbers have by now reached the top, with fatalities exceeding one hundred twenty-five.) Presently, the Nepalese seem to have realized that this was a mistake: There are just too many people on these mountains. Very recently, they raised the fee for climbing Everest to $50,000, for an expedition that can have no more than ten climbers. Two more can be added, with special permission, for an additional $5,000 apiece. Other prices have been raised correspondingly. At the low-altitude end, the Nepalese have designated a selection of peaks in the six-thousand-meter range—new ones get added from time to time—that are called "trekking peaks." These cost in the two- to three-hundred-dollar range, and are open to trekking groups that have applied for them. It should be made clear that, even though they are called "trekking peaks," they are serious business, usually requiring at least one high-altitude camp and some level of technical mountaineering skill—and often a great deal of it. To give some idea of the risks involved, in the fall of 1994, *eleven* climbers were killed in a single accident on the 6,091-meter Pisang Peak in western Nepal—one of the designated trekking peaks. The temptation for a trekking agency to offer the bagging of a trekking peak as part of its agenda is considerable. Before embarking on one of these excursions, one should make sure one has a very clear idea of what one is getting into, or one may not get out of it in one piece.

It was the British who "discovered" Mount Everest. In 1852—at least according to the legend—a Bengali, Radnath Sikhdar, who was working as a statistician for the British survey of India, supposedly rushed into the office of Sir Andrew Waugh, the surveyor general, and announced, "Sir, I have discovered the highest mountain in the world!" How Mr. Sikhdar could possibly have known this defies explanation, but in any case the mountain he had in mind had been listed in the survey as Peak XV. No altitude was given. It was not until 1865 that Sir Andrew formally named it for his predecessor, Sir George Everest. The first altitude given for the peak, in 1852, was 29,002 feet; on the basis of later measurements (in 1907 and 1921–22), this was raised to 29,145 feet; but it shrank back to 29,028 feet—8,848 meters— as a result of a survey made in 1955 under the auspices of the Indian government and confirmed in 1974. In 1987, much consternation was caused by new satellite measurements of both Everest and K-2, which is on the border between Pakistan and China, that purported to show that the latter was higher than the former. But these measurements seem to have been wrong. A 1992 measurement with a rayon laser, using several points of triangulation as well as satellites, reconfirmed the 29,028 figure. But there is a nuance. There appear to be about six feet of snow at the summit. Hence, if one takes away the snow, the summit rocks are at 29,022 feet—all of which goes to show that it is not easy to measure precisely the height of a mountain.

Of course, the Tibetans and Sherpas who lived near the base of Everest were aware of its existence long before the British arrived in India. Indeed, the Tibetan name for Everest is Chomolungma, which has been translated as "Goddess Mother of the World," or "Goddess Mother of the Snows." But big as it is, Everest is one of the most difficult mountains in the world to get a good view of. (K-2 is even harder.) As I have mentioned, it is not visible from the Kathmandu valley, and if one looks at it from the hilly vantage points nearby, it does not seem like much. In fact, if one does not know exactly where to look, one can easily miss it altogether. It is no wonder that the Nepalese thought several other peaks were higher. (In some books on Nepal written before 1850, Dhaulagiri, in western Nepal, was said to be the highest mountain in the world.) Because Nepal was completely closed to expeditions before 1950, the southern flank of the mountain, which lies in Nepal, remained unexplored until it was visited briefly in that year by a small British-American party. As for the northern approaches to the peak, Tibet, too, was closed to Westerners during the nineteenth century, but in 1904, Sir Francis Younghusband arrived with a contingent of British troops and forcibly opened up diplomatic and trade relations with Tibet. Still, it was not until 1921 that a British reconnaissance party made its way to the Rongbuk valley on the northern, Tibetan, side of the mountain. In 1922 and 1924, British parties engaged in two absolutely extraordinary attempts to climb the mountain from the Tibetan side. A member of both parties was George Leigh-Mallory. (It was Mallory who, at a lecture in Philadelphia, replied "because it is there" to a question about why he wanted to climb Everest.) Since first coming to Everest, in 1921, Mallory had become enslaved by the mountain. E. F. Norton, a climber with the 1924 party, wrote of him: "The conquest of the mountain became an obsession with him, and for weeks and months he devoted his whole time and energy to it, incessantly working at plans and details of organization; and when it came to business he expended on it every ounce of his unrivalled physical energy."

Reading the accounts of these pioneering attempts, one is constantly struck by the almost completely casual and innocent heroism of the participants. Almost all were public school men (Mallory, indeed, taught at Charterhouse), and, when not otherwise occupied, could be found in small tents at various altitudes reading aloud to one another from *The Spirit of Man, Hamlet,* or *King Lear.* As Mallory wrote in his account of the 1922 expedition, "On another occasion, I had the good fortune to open my Shakespeare at the very place where Hamlet addresses the ghost. 'Angels and Ministers of Grace defend us,' I began, and the theme was so congenial that we stumbled on enthusiastically, reading parts in turn through half the play." This reading of the Bard took place at twenty-one thousand feet, above the Rongbuk glacier, and shortly thereafter Mallory and a companion managed, without oxygen, to climb to twenty-seven thousand feet— just two thousand feet short of the summit. A second team, using oxygen, got a little higher, but a third attempt on the mountain peak ended in disaster when seven Sherpas were killed in an avalanche. This expedition marked the first use of oxygen (which the Sherpas called "English air") in climbing, and it also marked the first appearance of Sherpas in a mountaineering expedition. In 1924, the British were back en masse, with 350 porters and twelve climbers. Mallory was now thirty-seven, which seems to be a prime age for Himalayan climbing. (Young climbers usually lack the kind of temperament required to slog away day after day, often with little or no progress, on a Himalayan giant.) On June 4, E. F. Norton and T. H. Somervell reached over twenty-eight thousand feet without oxygen. On June 7, Mallory started up with a young companion, Andrew Irvine. They were followed by N. F. Odell, the expedition geologist (who, incidentally, discovered marine fossils high on the mountain, showing its suboceanic origins). Odell had not come on the expedition primarily as a climber, but in its early stages he had shown himself to be so strong that he had been given the task of following Mallory and Irvine, one camp behind, to offer them whatever support they needed. On June 7, Odell, who was in Camp V, at a little over twenty five thousand feet, received a note from Mallory—carried down from Camp VI by some Sherpas—that ended, "Perfect weather for the job!" The next morning, Odell started up after Mallory and Irvine, and his record of what he saw remains one of the most celebrated passages in all alpine literature:

At about 26,000 feet, I climbed a little crag, which could possibly have been circumvented but which I decided to tackle direct, more perhaps as a test of my condition, than for any other reason. There was scarcely 100 feet of it, and as I reached the top there was a sudden clearing of the atmosphere above me. I noticed far away, on a snow slope leading up to what seemed to me to be the last step but one from the base of the final pyramid, a tiny object moving and approaching the rock step. A second object followed, and then the first climbed to the top of the step. As I stood intently watching this dramatic appearance, the scene became enveloped in cloud once more. . . .

This was the last time that Mallory and Irvine were ever seen. Odell continued up alone—and in a driving blizzard—to over twenty-seven thousand feet, in the vain hope of finding them. But there was no trace. Nine years later, on the next expedition to the mountain—also British—Mallory's ice ax was recovered at a point not far above the place from which Odell had been watching. How did it get there? Did the men get to the top and fall upon their descent, or were they lost in the snows before reaching the summit? No one knows.

In the 1930s, the British mounted four Everest expeditions from Tibet, the last one in 1938. All were stopped a thousand feet or so from the summit. One of the climbers who took part in both the 1935 and 1938 expeditions was Eric Shipton. Shipton, who died some years ago, was one of the greatest expeditionary climbers who ever lived. The route by which the British ultimately climbed the mountain in 1953 was first mapped out in 1951 by a group led by Shipton—which included Hillary—from Nepal. In the 1970s, I had a chance to spend an evening talking to Shipton. I was extremely curious to know whether he thought Mallory and Irvine had climbed the mountain in

1924. He told me that he was not sure, but he was more sure that, summit or no, they had fallen upon their descent. He explained to me that the part of the route that they were on had outward-sloping slabs of rock— very likely snow- and ice-covered. Descending them would have been like trying to come down an icy roof. Moreover, he said that in 1938 he had stood—deliberately—at exactly the spot from which Odell thought he had seen the two men. Shipton said—and, indeed, he showed me a picture—that above him in the distance were two specks that looked like climbers. When he got closer, he discovered that they were rocks. He thought that this was what Odell might have seen.

In 1933, the British sent two small planes over the summit of Everest, and for the first time the Nepalese approaches to the mountain were photographed. In 1934, a rather bizarre and somewhat pathetic English mystic named Maurice Wilson made a solo attempt on the mountain in order to publicize some of his theories, which included the notion that if a man were to go without food for three weeks, he would emerge in a state like a newborn child but with the benefit of all the experience of his past life. Wilson had never been on a mountain, but he somehow got the idea that if he could succeed in climbing Everest alone, it would help establish his theories. At first, he planned to crash a small plane as high as possible on the mountain and make the rest of the trip on foot. He got as far as Purnea in India, where his plane was confiscated, and then walked the rest of the way—about two hundred miles—to Darjeeling. There he trained for months and arranged with some Sherpas to be taken, disguised as a Tibetan, to the base of Everest. He, of course, had no permission to climb, but he made a favorable impression on the head lama of the monastery in Rongbuk, with whom he had many discussions. In May of 1934, he started for the summit, and died of exposure in his tent somewhere above twenty-one thousand feet. His body and diary were found by the British expedition of 1935.

Himalayan climbing was suspended during the Second World War, and it was not until 1950 that expeditions to Everest were resumed. (In 1947, there was another solo attempt, by a Canadian, E. L. Denman, who also disguised himself as a Tibetan and who was accompanied by none other than Tenzing. They retreated safely from a point a little above the spot where Maurice Wilson had died.) By then, the political situation had completely altered: Tibet was closed, and Nepal open. In 1950, a small Anglo-American group made the first trek by westerners into Namche Bazar. The next year, Shipton led an exploration of the whole southern flank of Everest, mapping the general outlines of what became the climbing route up its south face. In 1952, the Swiss got permission to try the mountain, and again approached it via Namche Bazar. The party succeeded in forcing the great icefall—one of the most dangerous parts of the mountain—that leads from the Khumbu Glacier to the Western Cwm, a glacial valley that Mallory had seen from the north in 1921 and given a Welsh name in honor of the fact that he had done his first climbing in Wales. In late May, Tenzing and Raymond Lambert, a famous Swiss guide from Geneva, reached a point that was a little more than a thousand feet below the summit. The Swiss were back in the fall of 1952, and once again Tenzing and Lambert were stopped, at about the same point. Then it was the turn of the British. This was the year of the coronation of Queen Elizabeth II, so that nothing was to stand in the way of this expedition. Shipton, who was supposed to have led it, was replaced by Sir John Hunt, a military man. Indeed, the expedition was organized almost like a military campaign—the logistics put together like clockwork. Shipton always did his climbing either alone or with a small group of friends. But Hunt's logistics worked, and on May 29, 1953, Hillary and Tenzing reached the top, following the Swiss route as far as it went. In the snows of the summit, Tenzing buried a little red-and-blue pencil, given to him by his daughter Nima, as an offering to Chomolungma, the Goddess Mother. This was Tenzing's seventh Everest expedition. Hillary's reactions were a little more down to earth. Upon returning to base camp, his first remark to the waiting John Hunt was, "Well, we knocked the bastard off!"

Ever since the Swiss traversed Nepal from Kathmandu to Namche Bazar, those expeditions that have walked from Kathmandu have used some variant of the Swiss route. (Now one can save a few days of trekking by driving as far as Jiri, where there is a Swiss dairy project. In the next chapter, I will discuss how at present most trekkers and climbers really get to Namche Bazar.) In 1967, in the absence of any real guidebooks, the existence of this route was very valuable, since the Swiss had written it up in a book called *Avant Premièrs à l'Everest*. The book was sufficiently detailed that one could use it as a sort of guide. Reading it, I was forcibly struck by the decisive role of the monsoon in determining when one can travel in Nepal. The monsoon comes to Nepal in early June and leaves, as a rule, by mid-September. It is caused by the fact that during the early summer, the thin, dry air above the Tibetan plain rises, creating an enormous low-pressure system to the north of Nepal that draws up moist air from the Bay of Bengal. This moist air is wrung dry as it rises to cross the Himalayan barrier, with the result that to the north of the mountains the land is essentially a desert, while to the south it is something of a tropical paradise. During the monsoon, travel by foot is all but impossible. The dirt trails, often exceedingly steep, become as slippery as ice, and the rivers are swollen with rain and with water from the melting snows of the Himalayas. The trek from Kathmandu to Namche—and, indeed, all east–west travel in Nepal—involves crossing the innumerable rivers that flow south from Tibet. The bridges, if they exist at all, often consist of a few logs thrown across the stream. During the monsoon, the logs are carried away, and the bridge has to be rebuilt the following fall; it is quite rare to find a bridge that is high enough and strong enough to resist the monsoon waters. A third difficulty of traveling during the monsoon is the insects, snakes, and, above all, leeches that abound in the tropical countryside during the summer. While a leech bite does not usually cause any serious trouble, there is nothing more revolting. The leeches of Nepal are, on the average, about an inch long. After a rain, they line the foliage along a muddy trail and sway back and forth until a person or an animal passes. Sometimes they drop down from leaves above the trail, but most often they climb into one's shoes and lodge themselves between one's toes. It is useless, and even somewhat dangerous, to pull off a leech, since this causes a wound that tends to ulcerate. (One accepted method is to apply heat from a match or a cigarette to the leech so that it detaches itself. Shortly I will describe another.) As a rule, leech bites do not hurt, so one is unaware of having been bitten until one discovers that one's clothes are covered with blood. Traveling over leech-infested terrain is no picnic.

All Everest expeditions have had to reckon with the monsoon. There are two possible strategies: to arrive at the base of the mountain in the late spring and climb until the monsoon strikes, or to arrive in the fall, just after the monsoon, and climb until the winter snows set in, during late November. In 1952, the Swiss tried both, and after reading their account of the trek to Everest in the early fall, before the monsoon had blown itself out—Lambert severely sprained his ankle when he slipped on a wet trail, and the leader of the expedition, Dr. Gabriel Chevalley, acquired a seriously infected ankle from a leech bite—I decided that, whatever else, we should avoid the bad weather. What with one thing and another, the earliest we could make the trek was late September, a schedule that worked out very well for Jaccoux, since it fell exactly between his climbing and his skiing seasons. Sometime in April, I wrote to Roberts, and a few weeks later I got back a cheerful, businesslike reply on Mountain Travel stationery, which had printed across the bottom PACK A SUITCASE AND TAKE OFF FOR MOUNT EVEREST—rather as if it were a stroll in the park. Roberts indicated that a trek to Everest might well be organized for late September, when, with luck, the monsoon would have ended. Roberts was booked up months in advance, so, monsoon or no, we accepted the dates he proposed and began making arrangements for the trip.

Among other things, Roberts sent his clients a detailed list of things to bring and medical precautions to take. Among the latter was a formidable set of suggested vaccinations, including typhoid, tetanus, cholera, smallpox, polio, and gamma globulin, to prevent hepatitis A. (The 1995 list adds the series for hepatitis B and A, as well as vaccinations against meningococcal meningitis, diphtheria, and, sometimes, rabies. Most people no longer take either the smallpox or the cholera immunization. If one is planning to travel in the Terai, a malaria prophylaxis is essential.) During the spring, I involved myself in an all but endless series of visits to my doctor for shots, and I assumed, naively, that the Jaccoux were similarly engaged. The French, although they invented vaccination, do not appear to believe in it. When I arrived in Europe in early June, the Jaccoux announced that they were going to take the bare minimum—cholera and small-pox—then required to enter the country, and *tant pis pour les autres.*

Despite my fervent arguments about the terrible dangers they were exposing themselves to, they stuck to their intentions, and, I must confess, got through the trek in splendid health. However, they did pay a visit to Dr. Guy de Haynin, the chief surgeon at the hospital in Mulhouse, who had been the expedition doctor for one of the French expeditions to Nepal and, the summer before, the doctor for a French expedition to the Peruvian Andes of which Jaccoux had been a member. In fact, Jaccoux had served as de Haynin's medical assistant during the Peruvian expedition. Dr. de Haynin, in a gesture of great kindness, supplied us with a complete pharmacy, suitable for every medical situation we might come up against, short of major surgery. Fortunately, as it turned out, most of the huge array of medicines that we took along came back unused.

Of much more relevance was the matter of clothing. From the Swiss account, it was clear that, during the course of our trek, the climate was going to change from tropical to arctic. We planned to wind up somewhere near, or above, the base camp of the British 1953 Everest expedition, which is at 17,800 feet, and from all accounts we could expect extreme cold, high winds, and snow. On the other hand, during the first week or so of the trek we would be passing through tropical jungles, and our main problem would be avoiding heat prostration. Shorts, bathing suits, and parasols would solve the heat and sun problems, but the cold was something else. The Jaccoux taught skiing and, as Michele said when we were discussing the matter, *"Nous, on connaît le froid."* Following their advice and a clothing list supplied by Roberts, I ended up taking along—working from the inside, out—long thermal underwear, two wool shirts and a pair of heavy climbing pants, two heavy sweaters, two windproof, light nylon jackets, a heavy down jacket, two wool hats, a pair of wool gloves, a pair of leather gloves, a pair of enormous mittens, hiking shoes and climbing shoes, several pairs of extra-heavy wool socks, and a track suit, which Jaccoux had suggested would make a good pair of pajamas. (One memorable evening, when we were camped in our tents in the snow at sixteen thousand feet, I wore almost all of this, and Michele claimed that she had on seven layers.) In addition, we took three cameras and enough film for several thousand pictures, a portable electric razor, a sewing kit for the Jaccoux, a portable radio (which broke down almost immediately), Malraux's *Anti-memoires* for the Jaccoux, two months' supply of Galoise cigarettes (at the time both Jaccoux smoked) and an equivalent quantity of pipe tobacco (at the time I smoked), two decks of cards, two small ice axes and a coil of light nylon climbing rope, and several boxes of laundry soap. I had also purchased twelve cans of the best Swiss insecticide, and twelve cans of insect repellent, as well as several thousand chlorine tablets for purifying the drinking water. Upon a last-minute inspiration, we stocked up with vitamin C tablets, on the grounds that there might not be much available in the way of fresh fruit. Actually, we had fruit of some sort almost every day.

After a summer of vigorous training of one kind or another in the French Alps, we found ourselves, by the end of September, flying over the flooded rice paddies of northern India, across the Himalayan foothills, past the great snow-covered peaks of western Nepal, and down into the valley of Kathmandu—surely one of the most spectacular flights in the world. Roberts had sent a Land Rover to meet us at the airport, and later, once we had settled in, dropped by the Hotel Royal, where we were staying, to say hello and to introduce us to Ila Tsering. Roberts turned out to be a courtly, soft-spoken man with a slight limp that, apparently, did not impede his walking or climbing. He had the air of someone who had spent a great deal of his life out of doors. I asked him if he thought the monsoon was over, and he said that it had not rained for two days, which was a good sign. He told us that the leeches had been particularly bad during this monsoon, but added, "I shouldn't think that you will have much trouble if the rain holds off." While this conversation was going on, Ila stood silent, studying us. I suppose he was wondering what sort of people he was about to spend the next five weeks with. After Roberts left, Ila came to our rooms to see how our equipment was arranged. We had been instructed to have everything packed in plastic bags, which, in turn, would be put into the wicker baskets to be carried by the porters. Each of us had been allowed about thirty pounds of gear, plus whatever we wanted to carry for ourselves. When Ila saw the climbing rope and ice axes, he remarked, "Climbing something?" with a cheerful laugh that seemed to indicate that he did not take the prospect very seriously. We had it vaguely in mind, following a suggestion of Roberts, to climb part of a shoulder of Pumori, a seven-thousand-meter mountain, across from Everest, from which Shipton had mapped the original Everest climbing route.

We then had a couple of days to explore Kathmandu. I will never forget our first night. It was warm and, as it happened, the Nepalese were celebrating the festival of Tihar—the autumn festival of light. The houses—the tiny wooden houses—were decorated with oil lamps, so that the entire city appeared to glow with a flickering illumination. There was at that time in Kathmandu almost no vehicular circulation: The entire city was a kind of pedestrian mall. As we wandered from street to street, we kept changing centuries, often finding streets that seemed out of the Middle Ages. We wandered into pagoda temples to listen to people chant. There were almost no other tourists. The whole experience was enchanting and unreal.

Early in the morning of September 30, we piled our gear into one of Roberts's Land Rovers and left Kathmandu on the first lap of the route to Everest. For the first thirty miles, we were able to take advantage of the Chinese-built road running from Kathmandu to the Tibetan border and beyond. At the time, foreigners were only allowed to travel the sixty miles that led to the frontier town of Kodari. For our purposes, we just wanted to travel the first thirty miles, to a point called Dolalghat, which is at the junction of the Indrawatti and Sun Kosi Rivers. At Dolalghat, the rivers are crossed by a bridge—also built by the Chinese—a magnificent structure that, as someone with a somewhat mordant sense of humor said at the time, was "just wide enough for two tanks and a motorcycle." (I heard that when the bridge was completed, the American ambassador asked the king what he would do if he discovered that the Chinese were starting to use it to invade Nepal. "Then I would inform you," the king is alleged to have replied.) The Land Rover stopped and let us out in front of an open shed on the near side of the bridge. Clustered around the shed was a large assortment of people of various races—Tibetans, Sherpas, Tamangs, and Newars. It took several minutes before it dawned on me that most of them were connected with our trek. When I finally got them sorted out, our roll included three Sherpas, in addition to

Ila; six Tibetans, who, it later turned out, were "high-altitude porters," with considerable experience on expeditions and absolutely unbelievable resistance to the cold (among them a mother and a daughter, who, like most Tibetan and Sherpa women, were capable of carrying almost as much as the men, and who had walked from Solu-Khumbu to Kathmandu and there done a good deal of shopping, the results of which they were taking back home); and a group of eight to ten (it varied from day to day) Tamang porters, members of a tribal group that lives in the high hills near Kathmandu and speaks a Tibeto-Burman language, which is distinct from either Sherpa or Tibetan. The Newars apparently owned the shed, which served as a kind of open-air refreshment stand. We tried to keep out of the way while Ila began the task of putting various possessions of ours into various wicker baskets. There was a total chaos of people and animals. (It turned out that we were taking along some live chickens.) For a while we stood in the sun, but it beat down with such a leaden, tropical intensity that we soon moved into the limited shade afforded by the shed. Jaccoux had had the inspiration of buying three Indian parasols in the market the day before, and, in addition, we had brought along two sun helmets (Michele preferred a bandanna), all of which were indispensable. After a half-hour or so our caravan was organized, and we crossed the bridge and started up a nearby trail that turned east, away from the road.

The tone the trek was to take for the next two weeks was set right at the beginning—up and down. We began at once what Roberts referred to in his notes for Everest trekkers as a "long and rather tiring climb to over 6,000 feet." To be sure, in comparison with any of the training walks I had taken in the Alps, this should have been a bagatelle, and still more so for Jaccoux. But the trail was steep and the heat overbearing. Perspiration streamed down our faces, and at one point, as we passed a little village, Michele bought a length of cotton cloth, out of which she made a sari to take the place of the jeans she had been wearing. The trail was jammed with people. We saw men, women, and children carrying sacks of grain, reams of paper and cloth, long bundles of bamboo poles, salt, and animals too small to be herded. The beginning of our trek coincided with the ten-day Dassain festival, which celebrates the victory of the goddess Durga over the buffalo-headed demon Mahissasoor. Animals are brought from the countryside to Kathmandu for sacrifice, and many of the animals we saw—chickens, goats, and buffalo—were on their way to the city for that purpose. At one point, I met a man who spoke excellent English and said he was a doctor out on a call in one of the villages—a rare sight in the countryside. The doctor asked where we were going, and when I told him that we were on our way to Namche Bazar and the base of Everest, he looked at me as if I were slightly daft and suggested renting a helicopter.

After walking for a couple of hours, we came upon a large pipal tree under which the residents of a nearby village had constructed stone blocks just high enough so that anyone carrying a load could set it down by backing into the block and leaving the basket, or whatever, on the top. It was a delightfully shady spot, and we joined a dozen or so Nepalese who were resting in the shadows. By this time, although we had walked only a few miles, the heat had become so intense that every step in the sun was a major effort, and we were grateful when Ila announced that we would make an early halt and camp close to a spring by some nearby rice fields. We crossed the fields, which were wet and green from the rain of the recent monsoon, and got ready for our first night on the trail. This involved a routine that we maintained for the next five weeks. First, the tents were taken out. We had two light green tents—one for the Jaccoux and one for me. They were carried by a Tibetan with an extraordinary face, rich with humor and deeply lined. Michele nicknamed him *"l'Indien"* because of his remarkable resemblance to a Native American chief. (The Indian had a marvelous sense of balance, which he demonstrated later by carrying me on his back, like a child, across some thin planks that spanned a monsoon-swollen river. I had started out across the planks but had not liked their looks, and climbed back to solid ground. Before I knew what was happening, the Indian had hoisted me onto his back and was trotting across the narrow, swaying boards with the agility of an acrobat, setting me down gently in the grass on the other side.) At our nightly camps, there would then be a general flurry of activity, usually accompanied by singing, while the tents were rolled out and set up.

Another porter—also a Tibetan, whom Michele called *"le Chanteur"*—always led the singing, which consisted of some eerie, haunting, and terribly sad-sounding songs of Tibet. Meanwhile, two of the Sherpas, a cook and an assistant cook—Nepalese treks have a certain chic—would start a fire to boil water for tea. Initially, we had some misgivings about the water, and Michele was allotted the job of discreetly keeping an eye on the cooking, to make sure that everything was washed or boiled. However, after a few meals it became clear that the Sherpas were absolutely scrupulous about all hygienic matters connected with us, although they themselves drank water of every description without treating it and without giving it a second thought. Apparently they had learned that a trekker is a delicate creature who must be treated with extreme care if he or she is to be kept moving.

As soon as the water came to a boil, tea would be served—really a light meal consisting of biscuits, sardines, cheese, peanut butter and jam, and sometimes Sherpa bread, a rich concoction made of millet and nuts. We were then free to do what we liked until dinner, which was served between five-thirty and six. During the interval, we washed, mended clothes, and read, and sometimes Jaccoux conducted a little clinic for any of the porters or Sherpas who were ailing—mainly from sore throats and infected blisters acquired from walking barefoot, both of which responded very rapidly to antibiotics. We also had a chance to study the scenery. What we saw the first afternoon was typical of the Himalayan foothills in early fall. Everywhere we looked, there were rich fields of green set in terraces that climbed the hills. The earth was carpeted with flowers in explosive tropical colors. We could make out neat-looking villages of stone houses, often painted white and pink, some with wooden roofs, some with thatch, and some with slate. The Nepalese in the countryside have a keen sense of color and are fond of brightly decorative flower gardens. Since our campsite afforded a view to the north, we could see the great Himalayan range—a sort of distant white wall, the summits so high that we often confused them with clouds. Jaccoux wrote in his diary that first night, *"Sentiment de Paradis."*

Dinner was always our gala meal. If it was warm enough, as it was on the first nights of our trek, we would eat outside, instead of in our tents, in the light of a candle or a kerosene lamp. (In the tropics, the sun appears to set all at once, and by five-thirty or six it was night.) The first course was inevitably soup—usually powdered, but sometimes fresh chicken soup made from the remains of one of the birds the Sherpas had cooked. As we wandered through the villages, Ila would call out to any of the local women who might have some fresh food to sell, *"Hey didi! Macha? Kukra? Phool? Phal?"* ("Hello lady! Fish? Chicken? Eggs? Fruit?"), and sometimes he was successful. If not, we ate rice and peas mixed with onions, or sometimes canned sausages or spaghetti. Later, when we got into Sherpa country, we were treated to some of the Sherpa specialties, such as *mo-mo*—a delicious spiced dough wrapped around chopped mutton or goat and then fried crisp. Dessert was fruit—fresh tropical bananas, mangoes, or mandarins if they were available, or, if not, canned fruit from India. It was a thoroughly nourishing and adequate diet, but as the weeks wore on, we began getting odd cravings for different tastes—Jaccoux had visions of *boudin* (baked blood pudding with apples), Michele of red wine, and I of ice cream. (We never managed to consume enough sugar to restore the energy that we expended walking ten or so miles a day—up and down—and when we returned to *chez* Boris in Kathmandu, thin as rakes, we fell like vultures upon every rich dessert we could lay our hands on.) By the end of the dinner, the Sherpas had put candles in our tents, and I was generally so tired that it was no trouble to fall asleep at seven or seven-thirty, while the Jaccoux read or played endless games of cards.

At our first camp, Ila suggested an early start the next day to escape the sun, so we agreed to get up at six-thirty, and to drink a light tea in order to skip breakfast and get under way as quickly as possible. As the days went on, our rising time grew earlier and earlier; in our eagerness to avoid the heat, we were usually on the trail well before six. Our second day was eventful in that, on the one hand, Jaccoux was bitten by a leech, and, on the other, a new and remarkable Sherpa personality was revealed to us. The leech bite was completely unexpected. We had been bathing in a warm, azure jungle stream and had left our shoes on the bank. When Jaccoux started to put his shoes back on, he noticed that blood was flowing from between his toes. He removed a grisly-looking black leech by touching it with a cigarette ember—the classic method—applied alcohol, and put his shoes back on. Neither Michele nor I had been bitten, but it was a signal to watch out. As for the Sherpa, his name was Ang Dorje, and he was Ila's assistant. He had the broad, sad, wise face of a circus clown, and as I got to know him better, I realized that he was one of the kindest people I had ever met. On the first day, a chronically weak ankle had been giving me a good deal of trouble, and I had used my parasol as a kind of crutch, which had not done much good. The following morning, when Ang Dorje appeared at my tent with tea, he was carrying a long stick that he had carved more or less into the form of a ski pole. "Horse," he said, giving it to me. From that day on, Ang Dorje and I and the "horse" were inseparable. Nothing was ever said, but whenever I was limping along the trail behind the rest of the group, I would notice Ang Dorje sitting on a rock a little way ahead of me and staring off into space, as if taking a rest. His resting places were always at a point where the trail forked or where it was rough or slippery, and as I reached them, he would materialize at my side discreetly, as if he had just happened to be there, by accident. It was never very clear to me how much English he understood. We carried on long conversations in which he taught me Sherpa words in exchange for their English equivalents, and I was confident that he followed everything I said. However, one very cold night we were camped in a small, windy, wooden cabin not far from Everest. Sherpas do not have chimneys in their houses; they leave the doors open to let out the smoke. This cabin did have a chimney, but the Sherpa domestic habits prevailed. I gave Ang Dorje a long and feeling discourse on how comfortable it would be in our cabin if the door were kept closed and the heat kept in, and he nodded sagely. Then he left the cabin, only to return a few minutes later leaving the door open, and he asked, as he pointed to it, "What English word this?" With the English instruction they were even then receiving, the younger generation of Nepalis would have known. English was already being disseminated to children. This I had discovered to my advantage. One day, I was moving along the trail alone; the Jaccoux had raced ahead, Ang Dorje had gone off for something, and the porters were far behind. Without paying much attention to where I was going, I found myself in a scrub jungle where the trail, as far as I could make out, completely disappeared. After wandering around aimlessly for half an hour or so, I began to get really worried that I was lost. To add to the general tone of things, the sun was setting, and I had just been bitten by a leech. At this point, a small Nepalese boy appeared from nowhere. He was carrying a large kukri and looked to be about ten. I began to gesticulate in the general direction of Tibet and to babble, "Sherpas, sahibs? Sherpas, sahibs?" in some desperation. He looked at me calmly and, in splendidly articulated English, said, "Where are you going?" Considerably abashed, I allowed myself to be led off in the direction of our party.

The days rolled on in a succession of jungle valleys, mountains, ridges, and rivers, and as we approached the high mountains, the valleys grew steeper, the ridges higher, and the rivers swifter and colder. Each morning, Ang Dorje would arrive at my tent with tea and an outline of the day's activities—"Some down going—go river, river, birkpass, up—go steep road." In our new routine, we had breakfast in midmorning, and it became the other substantial meal of the day, with eggs, pancakes, toast, and coffee. It was meant to last until teatime. When we camped in towns, the children—who had had almost no opportunities to see westerners—would come and surround our tents and stare at us. At times, a man or a woman would come to us to ask for medicine for a child (if there was one English word that all the Nepalis in the countryside then knew, it was medicine), and Jaccoux would try to find something in our pharmacy that would do some good. Once, he told a mother whose baby was suffering with infected sores to wash the child with soap. She said that she did not have the money to buy soap, which cost a rupee and probably represented a substantial part of a day's wages. We gave her several bars of our soap.

The Swiss route that we were taking was, in general, so arranged that all the camps were on high ground, which is dry and hence relatively free of jungle fauna. Sometimes, though, we found it convenient to complete a stage and a half in one day, especially if the following day featured an especially severe climb. (We would time our descent for the late afternoon so as to be able to climb in the very early cool morning.) Hence, one night we camped in a tropical jungle near

a stream. That night Ila displayed his talents as a barber. Michele had
been talking with Ila about his activities during the monsoon season
and had learned about the barbering. Jaccoux is celebrated in
Chamonix for his long, elegant blond plumage, and it was out of the
question that he would submit to have any of it removed by a barber
of unverified skills. On the other hand, I had forgotten to get a haircut
before leaving France, and my hair was beginning to curl down over
my neck—an annoyance in the heat. So I became a willing victim. I
was seated on a rubber poncho, and Ila went to work with a pair of
scissors under the watchful gaze of our entire expeditionary force.
Amid murmurs of general approval, Ila proceeded to remove most of
my mop, leaving a sort of crew cut. When it was over, Michele
commented, "*Ça te va,*" and that was that.

We decided to celebrate the event with a small toast with our
expeditionary cognac, purchased in the New Delhi airport. One of the
two bottles was brought out, and we settled back to contemplate the
tropical night. Suddenly something came hurtling out of the jungle,
ran past our tents, and jumped out at me. I leaped up in the air and
emitted a bloodcurdling yelp, which brought Sherpas running from
all directions. Ila, who had seen our visitor disappear into the jungle,
said, "Eats snakes," from which I concluded it must have been a
mongoose. It dawned on me that if it had, it might well have been in
search of its dinner. Jaccoux, armed with a long stick, led a thorough
search of the tents, but failed to turn up anything.

The next morning, as we walked through the jungle, we saw huge,
silver-gray, gibbonlike monkeys swinging from tree to tree. Michele
and I were bitten by leeches, and after my bite we made a major
scientific discovery. The leech had been removed by applying a cigarette to it—the Sherpas favored salt—and was lying in the grass, still
moving. We still had more or less intact our twelve cans of insect
repellent, which had turned out, if anything, to attract the Himalayan
flies, and which I had suggested we chuck into the nearest ravine since
the cans were taking up space. Before doing this, however, we decided
to spray the leech with the insect repellent to see what would happen.
Instantly it curled up into a ball and died. We now had a first-rate
antileech weapon, and during the next several days, until we reached

the high mountain country, one of us always walked with an aerosol can of insect repellent at the ready.

After a week, we reached the important Hindu village of Those, which had a large school and an ancient ironworks, one of the few then functioning in Nepal. The village was located just on the frontier of Sherpa country; in fact, after leaving it, we crossed an abrupt nine-thousand-foot pass, and, as if by magic, the character of the countryside, the people, and even the architecture was transformed. With the Chinese invasion of Tibet, there had come a sharp change in the Sherpas' attitude toward Nepal. Until the invasion, they did not really regard themselves as Nepalese. ("Nepalese," to them, referred to the inhabitants of the Kathmandu valley.) However, when the Chinese smashed the monasteries and religious shrines in Tibet and broke down the whole traditional structure of Tibetan society, the Sherpas began to turn toward their own government. In most Sherpa homes, one saw, side by side, portraits of the Dalai Lama and the king of Nepal. The older generation of Sherpas had a deep-seated fear of the Chinese after what happened in Tibet; indeed, when I once visited an old lama in a small monastery south of Namche, he insisted on lifting up my sunglasses and looking at my eyes—to be sure that I was not Chinese—before he would talk to me.

The Himalayan ridges divide Nepal into small sections, and the ruggedness of the terrain keeps the different populations almost intact. We were now in Buddhist territory. The people had a definite Mongolian look, and the countryside was dotted with *chorten* (or *stupas,* to use the Sanskrit word)—monuments in the shape of the contemplating Buddha. There were also numerous *mani* mounds (*mani* means "prayer" in Tibetan), usually erected in the middle of the trail and covered with carved stones on which the sacred formula OM MANI PADME HUM was etched again and again. Sherpas passing a mani always leave it on their right, so that if they come back by the same trail they will have made a full circle around it, in deference to the full circle of the wheel of life. On each ridge, now sprinkled with snow, there was a cluster of prayer flags printed with religious messages. The houses had wooden shutters that could be closed against the winter winds. (Glass was then almost unknown in the Nepalese countryside.) We had definitely left the tropical jungles and the rice fields of the Himalayan foothills, and the cold nights told us that we were approaching the high mountains. We crossed a pass nearly twelve thousand feet high and felt the first effects of the thin air, which made us a little dizzy and short of breath. Coming down through some lovely pine forests, we reached the village of Junbesi—one of the largest and most attractive villages in the district of Solu. We had now been walking ten days, and although we had seen a number of high mountains, Everest remained hidden behind the nearby hills. Ila promised us that if the sky was clear, we might catch a glimpse of the mountain from a high ridge beyond Junbesi. The next morning, we churned up the ridge, and from it got a stunning view of the Himalayan wall near Everest, but the Goddess Mother herself lay hidden in the clouds. Ang Dorje flapped his arms and blew in a gallant attempt to disperse them, but after a half-hour or so we gave up and continued along the trail to a campsite above the Dudh Kosi, the river that drains the whole south of the Everest range.

We intended to follow the Dudh Kosi valley up into the mountains, but first we had to cross the river and go through some low, damp fields. It had rained the night before—a last trace of the monsoon—and the trail was muddy, slippery, and alive with leeches. I have never seen anything like it. Leeches were everywhere—on our shoes, our legs, our arms. I was bitten four times in ten minutes, and the legs of a porter in front of me were streaming with blood. We kept spraying ourselves with insect repellent, but every time we stopped to do this, more leeches attacked us. Finally, Ila said, "Now quickly go!" and, all but running, we raced to higher ground. When we stopped, we were all thoroughly shaken. It was at this point that we began to wonder if it would be possible to make our return trip by air. As it happened, every morning at about eight or so, when the sun began to beat down and we were starting up a hill, we had been hearing the sound of a small plane passing overhead. "Swiss people," Ila had said. "Lukla going." Lukla (at 9,200 feet) is a small village above the Dudh Kosi valley; a few years prior to our trek, Edmund Hillary had carved a small grass airstrip out of a field on a hillside there. There were then no regular flights to Lukla, but from time to time Mountain Travel had been able to charter one or another of the STOL planes that were based in Kathmandu. It had been our original idea to walk to Namche and then fly out from Lukla, but we had abandoned this plan when it began to appear that it would be difficult, if not impossible, to arrange a charter. Given the leeches, however, we thought we might take another crack at it. (As it turned out, the monsoon was over for good in a few days, and people who traveled our route a week or so later told us that it had been completely dry, with not a leech in sight.)

Our hopes were raised a few hours later. I found the Jaccoux talking, in French, to a Sherpa on the trail. The Sherpa explained that he had learned French in Montpellier, where he had gone to study the prospects for viticulture in the Kathmandu valley. He had flown into Lukla in the morning to spend the Dassain holiday with his parents, who lived in the region, and his plane, he said, had returned to Kathmandu empty. A bit later, as we pushed along a wooded trail leading up the Dudh Kosi, we met a British Gurkha officer who had been in Namche on a holiday to see Everest, and he told us that behind him on the trail was a party of four—an Australian forester working in Nepal in the forest conservation program, and three British ladies whom he was escorting. They had booked a plane out of Lukla in a day or so, the Gurkha told us, and he could speak to the pilot to see if something might be arranged for us. After a few hours, we ran into the Australian and the three ladies, all looking fit and sunburned, and the forester said that he would be glad to talk to the pilot, and that we could expect to get a radio message at Dr. McKinnon's in a day or so. From reading Roberts's notes, I knew there was a New Zealand doctor named John McKinnon who ran a small hospital—also set up by Hillary—in the Sherpa village of Khumjung, in the hills beyond Namche. The notes also mentioned a radio at the hospital, and our whole aviation scheme seemed to be falling into line. Little did we know.

That night, we camped by a pair of excellent wooden bridges built in 1964—again by Hillary—across the Dudh Kosi and its adjoining tributary, the Bhote Kosi. The bridges made an enormous contribution to the life of the Sherpas, since Namche is the trading center for the whole area and could now be reached from the lowlands by a relatively convenient trail; previously, crossing the rivers had been a major, risky operation. Our camp was on the Dudh Kosi itself, and from it no mountains could be seen at all, since they were blocked by the huge cliffs etched out by the river. However, the next day, given clear skies, we were promised a full and dramatic view of Everest and its satellites. By now, the winter weather pattern was beginning to settle in, which meant bright, clear skies in the morning, followed by a clouding-over in the afternoon, and sometimes snow in the evening. To be as sure as possible of getting a good view, we left at the crack of dawn the next day. We were now over ten thousand feet—the lowest altitude we would be at for the next three weeks, but still sufficiently high that we could not move too fast on the stiff uphill trudge toward Namche. As we climbed slowly, mountains began revealing them-selves in all directions, and soon we were surrounded by great snow-covered peaks. Every now and again, we would stop while Jaccoux took out his map and compass and tried to identify some of the mountains, to make sure that we were not overlooking Everest. Up ahead, we saw a level place in the steep trail and an array of prayer flags near a mani—a sure sign that there was a special view of the peaks. When we reached the mani, we looked to the north, up the valley, and fell into a stunned silence. First, like the brim of a glistening crown, we saw the massive ice wall of Nuptse, perhaps ten miles away. Soaring above it was a black, majestic pyramid, seamed with snow; from its top a plume of white floated off into space. It was Everest, and it looked like the Queen of the World. We stood fixed to the spot for nearly an hour with all the Sherpas and Tibetans seated around us. Finally, Ang Dorje said, "Beautiful. Now Namche go," and we started up the trail, which swung off o the left, hiding the mountains.

Ila had gone on ahead the night before to spend the evening with his family in Namche, and before we reached the village, we were met by a lively-looking young boy who Ang Dorje said was Ila's son. Soon after, Namche itself appeared from around a bend. It was set in a horseshoe-shaped arena and clung to the side of an enormous gorge that dropped down into the Bhote Kosi. There were about eighty stone houses in the village, and also a police checkpoint. Our trail led directly into the police station, where Ila was waiting, along with a couple of sleepy-looking Nepalese constables dressed in khaki. We had to hand over our trekking permits, and then there was a lengthy pause while they were passed around, commented on, and noted in various books. Next, we were taken to visit the district governor of Khumbu, a distinguished-looking former Nepalese army officer named Colonel Bista. The colonel greeted us in his pajamas and bathrobe and invited us to have morning tea with him while we explained where we had come from and where we planned to go. "If there is something I can do for you, let me know," he added—an offer for which we were soon grateful. In the meanwhile, Ila had set up our tents on a hillside a little above the town, and because it was clouding over and beginning to snow, we retired inside them.

During the afternoon, an almost endless series of Tibetans stopped by to sell scrolls, rings, beads, bracelets, silver cups, and prayer wheels. We had just seen off the last vendor, and broken out what was left of the remaining bottle of cognac, when a figure appeared outside our tent in the now driving snow. I peered out and saw a rather elegant looking young man wearing white pajamalike pants, a somewhat oversized army overcoat, and brightly colored wool gloves. Before I had a chance to say anything, he invited himself into the tent and introduced himself as Sub-Inspector Rana of the Nepalese police. The name rang a bell. A few days before, we had met on the trail a young Swiss who had come to Namche without a trekking permit and had spent the better part of two weeks trying to arrange for one by telegraph. During this period, he passed a good deal of time discussing life and literature with Sub-Inspector Rana, whom he had come to regard as something of a cultural oasis and bon vivant. "Rana has a garden in which he grows six kinds of vegetables," the Swiss had told us.

We offered Rana a seat on one of the sleeping bags and a beaker of cognac.

"*Merzi, madame,*" he said to Michele, whose nationality he had apparently learned from studying our entry in the official book. "Do you pronounce it '*merzi*'?" he asked, and Michele spent five minutes repeating *merci* over and over, until Rana's pronunciation was about right.

"You are an American," he said to me, and added, "I admire your John Steinbeck and your Agatha Christie," helping himself to another bit of brandy. In this general vein the conversation flowed along until dinnertime, when we invited Rana to share our meal—which consisted mainly of rice, peas, and onions. "I admire your onions, madame," he informed Michele, who was staring gloomily at the now-empty cognac bottle. We had told Rana that we planned to go see Dr. McKinnon the next day, and he offered to join us, provided that the police station was in "perfect order" in the morning.

The next morning there was no Rana, so, assuming that the police station had not been in the best order, we left for Khumjung and the McKinnons. Khumjung is a typical high Sherpa village. It is at 12,300 feet and consists of a large number of sturdy-looking stone houses set among yak pens and potato fields. The walk from Namche to Khumjung is surely one of the most beautiful in the world. On it, one sees another group of the satellites of Everest, especially Ama Dablam. While Everest impresses one with its size, Ama Dablam, which is only 22,350 feet, impresses one with its elegance. It is a perfectly shaped mountain—a sort of ice Matterhorn—with steep faces of delicately fluted ice. It was climbed in 1961 by a mixed New Zealand–American group. The sole American in the party, the late Barry Bishop, who, a few years after, climbed Everest, and whom I met in Nepal, told me that Ama Dablam is a much more difficult climb than Everest even though it is much lower.

Leaving the fields and the yak pens, we followed a series of neat paths up to a modern building—the Khumjung hospital. The McKinnons, who were then both in their twenties, turned out to be an extremely cordial and attractive couple. He said that he had first come to Nepal with Hillary in 1964, when he was still a student, to climb and to help build the bridges. He fell in love with the country, and two years later, when Hillary succeeded in building a hospital with funds raised through his speaking tours in New Zealand and with private contributions, McKinnon volunteered to be its first doctor, a post he held until 1968, when he returned to practice in New Zealand. As the hospital's first doctor, he was an ideal choice. He and his wife Diane, who taught English in one of the Hillary schools (from

1961 up to the time of our visit, Hillary, with the aid of the local villagers, had built six schools in the Solu-Khumbu area), succeeded in immersing themselves in the life of the community. Some time later, Mrs. McKinnon took us to visit one of the Sherpa schools. It was a two-room affair in a modern Quonset hut–like structure. The "headmaster" was a multilingual Sherpa from Darjeeling. Although it was November, the school was about to close for a long winter recess, since many of the pupils were about to leave for the lowlands with their parents, who had second homes in the lower valleys, where the winters are less severe. The major school term was in the spring or summer. The children, perhaps a hundred of them of various ages, were engaged in their English lessons, reciting in loud choruses. This is the place where I saw on the wall the motto FORTUNE HAS WINGS— and wondered if the children had any idea of how important "wings," in the form of the airplane, would be in their futures.

Being a doctor in Solu-Khumbu was not a passive matter, since at the time the Sherpas had had relatively little experience with modern medicine, and were inclined to put their faith in spirit mediums and magic potions. McKinnon had to prove that modern medicine was more effective than looking into the silver mirror of a spirit medium, and to do so he had to put in many miles of walking over very steep terrain to visit his patients, since Sherpas who feel that they are really sick prefer to stay in their own houses to die. Treatment was free. The most persistent problems at the time were tuberculosis and goiter. Goiter, brought on by a lack of iodine in the diet, was common throughout the Himalayas, because such iodine as there was in the soil was removed by erosion and not replaced by the rains, which are iodine-free, the mountains being so far from the sea. Now, the use of iodized salt, which has to be imported since Nepal has no salt of its own, is obligatory, but at the time this program had not yet been implemented. Hence whole villages in Solu-Khumbu were afflicted with the disease and, what was worse, there was a high incidence of cretinism among the children. (There is a high correlation rate between parents with goiter and cretinous children. Indeed, this phenomenon was noted in Alpine valleys by Whymper, inspiring him to quote from the missionary hymn when describing them—"Where

every prospect pleases and only man is vile"—a thought that often
went through my mind when passing through some of the Solu-
Khumbu villages. Whymper came to understand the cause—a lack of
iodine in the diet. Michele, who had grown up in the Alps, remembered being taken to the seashore as a child for a sort of "iodine cure.")
Until the diet could be changed, McKinnon attempted to treat his
patients with iodine tablets and iodized oil. There was a problem
knowing just how large a dose to administer, and he had conducted
a series of experiments to find out. I nearly gave him a fit when I
innocently announced that we had been dispensing iodine on our
walk. What I meant was that we had been treating cuts with liquid
iodine. He had understood that we had been handing out tablets.

Tuberculosis is a much more complicated matter. It is hard to
detect in the early stages, unless a Sherpa is willing to come to
Khumjung for an X ray or, at least, a skin test. Moreover, the treatment, while very effective, is lengthy. No Sherpa could afford to spend
a year or so in a hospital. McKinnon worked out a program that
allowed Sherpas with tuberculosis to live in a wing of the hospital for
three months—with their families if necessary—and then return to
their villages. In each village, he trained two people to act as nurses.
They were able to administer the necessary shots twice a week, and
they knew enough about the symptoms to recognize if someone
appeared to need help. In Namche, I met one of McKinnon's
"nurses," who turned out to be a very intelligent fifteen-year-old boy.
He was, among other things, responsible for treating Ila's wife. In
addition, McKinnon gave all the children in the area skin tests and
smallpox vaccinations. Even as late as 1963, when the American
Everest expedition had passed through Solu-Khumbu, whole villages
were being ravaged by smallpox epidemics. It was at about that time
that Hillary started the vaccination program, which saved many lives
and which McKinnon carried on.

During the monsoon, the McKinnons hardly ever saw any Europeans, and such rare mail as they got was carried to the hospital by
porters. During the winter, many Sherpas head south. It is not uncommon for a Sherpa family to have as many as three houses—one
in the high mountains, one in a village like Khumjung, and a third

down below, where it is relatively warm in the winter. Now the winter home may well be in Kathmandu. McKinnon told me that he did not miss either his mail or his visitors, since he and his wife shared the social life of the Sherpas—the weddings, the naming ceremonies (a baby is named by its grandparents in a lively ceremony in which a good deal of *chang,* the local beer made of corn or rice, is drunk), and the funerals. (Sherpas cremate their dead, as do the Hindus of southern Nepal. The Hindus preserve part of a bone and bury it in one of the sacred rivers beside which cremations take place.) McKinnon was also engaged in a potato experiment. The potato is the cornerstone of the Sherpa diet, although, oddly enough, it seems to be a relatively new arrival in Solu-Khumbu. Christoph von Furer-Haimendorf, a noted anthropologist, made a lifetime study of the Sherpas. In his book *The Sherpas of Nepal,* he noted that "it is certain that the potato was not known in the Himalayas until comparatively recently and the two most likely sources of its spread into Eastern Nepal are the gardens of European settlers in Darjeeling and the garden of the British residency in Kathmandu." This would make the potato something over a hundred years old in Solu-Khumbu, and Furer-Haimendorf connects this dating to the time when the monasteries were built in Solu-Khumbu. There have been monasteries in Tibet for centuries, but the monasteries in Solu-Khumbu are quite new. The thought is that they were built, and the monks allowed to withdraw from the population, after the introduction of the potato gave the Sherpas enough food that everyone was not required to scratch crops from the rather meager soil. The traditional Sherpa "method" of growing potatoes was to throw the plants into the ground and hope for the best. McKinnon took a plot of land belonging to the hospital and cultivated half of it using careful agricultural methods, and half of it Sherpa-style. What he found, perhaps not surprisingly, was that on the careful half he grew twice as many potatoes as on the Sherpa half, and that the potatoes were larger and freer of blight. He hoped the lesson was beginning to sink in.

Among the letters that McKinnon had received in the last delivery from Lukla before our arrival was one from Mountain Travel saying that space was available on a flight to Kathmandu on the second of

November—in about two and a half weeks—for three people. How-ever, we learned to our dismay that McKinnon had no radio—one had been ordered but had not arrived—so that we had no way of communicating with Kathmandu. McKinnon said that our only chance was to persuade the authorities in Namche to send a wire to Mountain Travel on the police wireless, and to pray that it got there. Leaving Khumjung, we walked back to Namche to look for Sub-Inspector Rana in the hope that we could convince him to send the wire. We stopped by the police station; it was manned by a lone constable who, from time to time, jumped from his desk to chase an errant goat out of Rana's vegetable garden.

In due time, Rana was found. *"Bonsoir, madame,"* he said to Michele, bowing, kissing her hand, and apologizing for not appearing in the morning. We explained our plight, and after thinking the matter over he said, "I would, of course, like to help you. But it would be very courteous if first you were to talk to Colonel Bista. If he signs the telegram, then I would be honored to send it by our very wireless."

Colonel Bista was engaged in the nightly volleyball game that took place between the police and the soldiers in Namche, and we had to wait a half-hour or so before we could see him. I had, in the meanwhile, written out a telegram, which the colonel, when he was free, read very carefully, offering a few suggestions for its amplification, remarking that it was the Dassain holiday in Kathmandu and he was not sure how soon it would be delivered. In any case, we had done what we could, and the next day we were off to the base of Everest with the understanding that if an answer ever came through, it would be sent up by runner.

That morning, the Tibetan porters showed up early. They were dressed in heavy clothes, and instead of the Chinese-made basketball shoes that they had been wearing since leaving Kathmandu, they now wore wonderfully colorful, heavy cloth boots with thick soles. Ila appeared with some expedition gear, including a down-filled sleeping bag, that he had used with an Indian expedition at an altitude of twenty-six thousand feet on Everest. "Next days, some cold," he said. The evenings had already been "some cold," and we were putting on more and more clothes to keep from freezing. However, the day of our departure was bright and warm, and we set out for the Thyangboche monastery, the home of the reincarnated lama who is the religious leader of the Sherpas of Solu-Khumbu. It was a beautiful walk, with Everest and all of her satellites in full view, and in a few hours we struggled up the steep hill—12,600 feet high—where the monastery was, and into a nearby cabin built by an Indian expedition for use by Everest trekkers and climbers. It was drafty, but Hillary—leave it to Hillary—had constructed a splendid wood-burning stove in the living room that kept everything warm as long as one continued to feed it and kept the cabin doors shut. (This was the cabin where I had my linguistic exchange with Ang Dorje.) The walls were covered with signatures of members of former Everest expeditions and trekkers who had spent the night there. For us, it was the first time in more than two weeks that we had slept in any sort of a building, and we were happy for the change. Ila had promised us a visit to the head lama before we started off into the mountains, and for that purpose he had bought three white ceremonial scarves, which we were meant to present to the lama; in return, he would give each of us one of his own scarves.

The head lama of Thyangboche was chosen for his role while still a small child. He came from a Sherpa family in Namche, and when he was very young he had begun to talk about his "home" in Thyangboche, where he had never been. The monks of Thyangboche, hearing of this, obtained some of the clothes of their head lama, who had just died, and mixed them with objects not belonging to the lama. The child, who was then four, picked out the clothes of the old monk. He was immediately heralded as the reincarnation of the old lama and brought to Thyangboche to study. When he was sixteen, he was sent to Tibet for more study, and in 1956, he came back to Thyangboche as its abbot. When I first met him he was in his early thirties. I was immediately impressed by him. He spoke no English, but his brother did, and he acted as our interpreter when Ila's English failed. The abbot's apartment was simple, but he had many modern devices—a radio, a camera, a watch—that had been given to him over the years by people on expeditions. Apart from study, religious ceremonies, and running the affairs of the monastery—the monks depend partly on donations and partly on a certain amount of commerce they carry on in the community and, when possible, in Tibet—the abbot's main interest was in flowers. He had a small hothouse, which he and his brother had built to protect his flowers during the winter. Friends sent him seeds from all over the world, and he had a book filled with all of the seed envelopes, along with the names of the donors. The abbot accepted our scarves, and took three of his own and touched them to his forehead as a blessing. While this was happening, Ila stood beaming. It was obviously a ceremony that meant a great deal to him, and he later told me that he would not go into the high mountains without the blessing of the abbot.

One of the things that I discussed with the abbot was the yeti—the legendary abominable snowman. It is safe to say that no reliable western observer has ever seen one, although some curious, bearlike tracks have been photographed on the remote glaciers near Everest, and elsewhere in the Himalayas. On the other hand, the yeti does play a persistent role in the mythology of the region. Sometimes it is given semihuman characteristics, sometimes it is said to carry people off, but most often it is said to look like a bear, or perhaps some sort of simian. The abbot had never seen one, but he told us that when the snows were very heavy around the monastery some of the other abbots claimed to have seen such a creature. (Among the Sherpas, it is usually a distant cousin or an uncle, now passed on, who once saw one.) He told us that in one of the monasteries down the valley there was a scalp, and a bone from a hand, that were claimed by the local authorities to be from a yeti. At this point, the abbot smiled and pointed to a chair that was obviously covered by a goatskin and said, through his brother, "It is the same kind of yeti as this." Later, we visited the monastery itself, and for a small donation, the ancient abbot produced the objects in question. Ang Dorje, who, I gathered, did not have a very high opinion of the yeti question in general, donned what was presumably a goat scalp, and we took his picture with great solemnity. Most of the other Sherpas seemed to take the whole thing as a joke, so we did not learn anything more about the yeti than we had known before we went to Nepal.

We left Thyangboche and headed north. The villages became cruder and cruder, and the terrain more barren. The tree line in Nepal is very high, and we were now at nearly fourteen thousand feet—the altitude of a good-size Swiss Alp—and it was still grazing land for yaks. Wood was scarce, so we used dried yak dung for fuel. It made an excellent smokeless, odorless fire. On the trail we passed yak caravans being driven down for the winter. The yak is a great, shaggy beast, but incredibly timid; it will all but climb a vertical bank to get out of one's way on the trail. (I did once encounter an aggressive yak. Not far from Thyangboche, I was walking along peacefully when I heard several people croaking *"Ee-yuk, Ee-yuk"*—a series of sounds that Sherpas make if there are yaks around. Above the general din I heard Michele yelling, *"Attention,* Jeremy—*un yak fou!"* I looked up and found myself staring into the eyes of a rather malicious looking brown yak that was attached by a string to a Sherpa who was trying to restrain it. It lowered its horns, and I went up a rock embankment in very great haste, and stayed there until the animal was led away. A few nights later, I had a somewhat different encounter with a yak. We were camped in one of their pastures. Sometime after midnight, I was awakened by the sensation of cold air and snow on my face. I looked up and, to my surprise, could see the stars rather than the top of my tent. Indeed, it was being towed in the general direction of Tibet by a yak who had gotten entangled in the ropes holding it down and was now making off with it. With the aid of the Sherpas we managed to recover the tent and restore order.) The Sherpas have great affection for yaks. (One night, we heard some piercing cries not far from our camp, and I at once thought of a leopard, since I had read in a book on the British Everest expedition that its camp had been visited by one after dark. Moreover, Jaccoux claimed that he could make out a pair of glittering eyes off in the scrub. But when I asked a Sherpa what kind of animal is was, he replied, "Doesn't eat yaks," which seemed to settle the matter. It was probably a small wildcat of some kind.) Being Buddhist, the Sherpas will not, in general, kill any animal, but if a yak should happen to drop dead, or if someone else should kill it, they are delighted to eat the meat. Sherpas are profoundly religious, but not dogmatic. As Buddhists, their greatest concern is to add to their *sonam*—the budget of moral credit that a Buddhist accumulates in order to escape the cycle of birth and rebirth. For example, a rich man can increase it by having a temple built for the community. There were, and are, some very wealthy Sherpas in Solu-Khumbu. Namche Bazar was the great trading station on the way to Tibet, and before 1950 enormous yak trains passed through the town en route to the Nangpa La, a nineteen-thousand-foot pass leading to Tibet. From Tibet Sherpas got salt, copperware (all the cooking utensils in Solu-Khumbu were of copper—and very beautiful, too—although now they have been supplanted by tin and aluminum objects, usually of Chinese manufacture), and animals, for which they traded rice, carried up from the lowlands, and dyes, among other things. We were told of one trader who came back from Tibet with a profit of eighty thousand Nepalese rupees—over three thousand dollars, a fortune in local terms—from the sale of one yak train's worth of goods. He was having a small temple built in Namche, and while we were there, we watched the famous Sherpa artist Kapa Kalden in the process of decorating the interior and the huge prayer wheel. One can also lose *sonam*. In his book on the Sherpas, Furer-Haimendorf gives a list of some of the sins that can lead to loss of *sonam*. It is an extraordinary list, and it gives an idea of why people who have come to know the Sherpas are so fond of them. Among the items are the following:

1. To threaten children or make them cry is sin, whatever the reason.
2. To fell trees is sin, though on occasion it is inevitable; even to pick flowers is sin, and it is sinful to set fire to the forest.
3. To marry a girl who is unwilling is sin both for the husband and for her parents, who arranged for the marriage.
4. To talk ill of someone behind his back is sin, particularly if what one tells about him is not true.

We camped in some deserted yak pens in Pheriche, a summer village, now abandoned, since the yaks had gone below. The nights were now desperately cold. As long as the sun was up, it was quite comfortable, but as soon as the shadows began to creep over the ground, the temperature plummeted to near zero, and we made a dash for the tents, to put on every ounce of warm clothing we had brought along. It was much too cold to bathe, and Jaccoux said that it would be inadvisable even to wash, since the dry air was so dehydrating that we risked being severely burned and chapped by the sun. By now, we were all beginning to feel the effects of the altitude—headaches and dizziness. The streams that led down from the Khumbu Glacier—the glacier that comes down from the sides of Everest—were frozen, and we crossed them gingerly. Our next, and highest, camp was at seventeen thousand feet—higher than the summit of Mont Blanc—and the three of us were beginning to feel truly worn-down by the altitude and the cold. We were merely a mile or two from the Tibetan border. This was the only place in Nepal where the government then allowed one to get that close to the border, since the way is blocked by the Everest range. It would take a full-scale expedition to cross it. However, we could see some of the peaks in Tibet and also the Lho La and the Shangri La. *La* is the Tibetan word for "pass," and Shangri La is an impressive but bleak-looking pass that leads into Tibet.

We now began to see for ourselves what Sherpas and Tibetans are capable of doing on high-altitude climbing expeditions. While we were literally trembling with cold and fatigue, Ang Dorje was wandering around happily in a light shirt and tennis shoes with no socks. I asked Ila if the altitude ever bothered him, and he said, "Twenty-six thousand feet, some headache getting." At sixteen thousand feet my head felt like a melon. The next day we climbed the Kala Pattar. By any standard it is a *montagne à vache*—a gentle, grassy slope with a few rocks on top. But the summit is over eighteen thousand feet. I found climbing it tough going. I seemed to be held back by a sort of invisible wall, and every time I moved, I felt as if I were hauling a ton of bricks. From the summit we got an incredible view of Everest and the Khumbu Glacier. Everest was perhaps a mile away, but the summit was still two miles above us. It now began to snow—the first sign of winter. We abandonded any idea we had had of going higher and hurried down. In passing, we had a chance to look at the memorial tablet that the American expedition on which Ila served had erected to Jake Breitenbach, the climber who had been killed on the Khumbu

ice fall. (In 1970 his remains were discovered on the Khumbu Glacier.) When we got back to our tents, it was snowing heavily. I was so
tired that when Jaccoux handed me a headache pill I just stood there
holding it, not knowing what to do with it. I somehow got back to my
tent and lay gasping on my sleeping bag. After a few minutes, the head
of Ang Dorje appeared in the tent. "Soup ready," he announced, and
in came a tray of warm tomato soup and crackers. He stood there while
I ate it, to make sure that I was all right, and then left.

We still had plans to do more climbing and hiking, but the snow
was coming down in thick gusts, and we were really exhausted by the
altitude. So the next morning, we began the trip back. On the first day,
we passed a huge lake, ice blue, that nestled against the mountains.
"In summer, many yaks," Ang Dorje told us. When we got a little
farther down, we were met by a runner from McKinnon bearing a
letter from Mountain Travel that had just arrived. The office had
received both our telegram and a personal message from the Australian forester. We could take the plane on the second of November.

That was a few days away. We spent our time at Thyangboche, with
the McKinnons, and some in Namche. In Namche, a crestfallen Sub
Inspector Rana told us that while we were gone a yak had gotten into his
garden with the six kinds of vegetables and had eaten every last one of
them. Ang Dorje, Ila and a small group of our Tibetan porters were
hurrying on foot back to Kathmandu to meet some new trekkers, whom
they were taking to western Nepal, near Annapurna. To make sure that
we didn't get into any trouble, and were fed periodically, Mountain
Travel had assigned two young Sherpas to take us to the airstrip in
Lukla—a day's walk from Namche—and to look after us until the plane
came. They were eighteen, and at first, I was worried about how two
young boys would fare as cooks as guides. There was no need for concern.
Both of them had been on expeditions since they were fourteen, both had
gone to the Hillary schools, and they spoke excellent English. They were
dressed in Western-style blue jeans, and when we left Namche for Lukla,
one of them was carrying a transistor radio on which he listened to music
from Radio Nepal and India.

For the next three days, we camped next to the tiny airfield which
we pretty much had to ourselves. The boys turned out to be fine cooks,

and we feasted on pancakes and chapattis-unleavened bread. Each morning at sunrise, the Swiss plane came in to leave off people. It was not yet our turn, and the pilot informed us rather tersely that we would have to wait until it was. One morning, the passengers turned out to be the German ambassador to Nepal and the United Nations High Commissioner for Refugees; they had come up to look at some Tibetan refugee villages. Another morning, a U.S. AID heliocopter came floating in with a passenger who said that he had been sent by the Smithstonian Institution to collect Tibetan manuscripts.[2] At eight-forty every morning we got the English-language news broadcast from Kathmandu. Otherwise, we sat around, somewhat bored, waiting for our plane. Finally, on November 2, as scheduled, it came in over the mountains. After the plane took off, we could see unfolding beneath us the whole route that we had walked the previous month. There were tiny trails that we had climbed up and down, over steep ridges and through terraced fields and jungles. Here and there we could spot a familiar village clinging to the mountainside, and to the north we could see the great white mountains, with the clouds hovering near their summits. As I looked at them, I thought of a Nepalese legend that tells how they came to Nepal. In the beginning, the mountains, which were the oldest children of the god Prajapati, all had wings, and they flew about the world as they liked. However, Indra, the god of rain, wished to bring the waters to the people of Nepal. So he cut the wings from the mountains, which then fell to earth and could no longer fly. The wings became clouds, and still cling to the mountains. So, wherever there are mountains there are clouds, and water from their rain nourishes the earth beneath.

2. I recall at the time being somewhat skeptical of this explanation. There was a good deal of CIA activity in Nepal, some of it in support of a guerilla movement that I will discuss in the chapters on Tibet. It was also reported that the Chinese had made some probes over the high passes near Everest. It would not surprise me if a place like Thyangboche was also an observation point and that this flight was connected with that activity.

4

Some Walk-Going, 1983

Friday, October 21: Roissy, France

It is 6 A.M. I have been at the Charles de Gaulle Airport for about half an hour. There is no one else in sight. Nothing is open. But now a trim-looking young woman wearing jeans has gotten out of a taxi. She has a rucksack and an ice ax, and is dragging a large duffel bag. I do not recognize her, but, given the ice ax, the duffel bag, and the rucksack, she must be one of us. She comes over and, as I suspected, she is part of a group of thirty-five of us who are about to go trekking in the Everest region of Nepal with Claude Jaccoux Voyages—an entity created by Jaccoux in the 1970s. Our experience in Nepal in 1967 gave Jaccoux the taste for exotic travel. Over the years, he and I have done a good deal of it together: overland from France to Pakistan in a Land Rover; Kilimanjaro; and, among others, a 1979 trip to Nepal. This will be my fourth trip to Nepal and Jaccoux's nineteenth. He has been back to Solu-Khumbu many times since 1967 and has told me about some of the changes there. I haven't been back and I am anxious to see for myself. One of the changes, obviously, is that we are a group of *thirty five!*

Jaccoux and I have been corresponding about this trip for several months. In one of his letters, written last July, he informed me that we will divide into two groups, "one strong and the other weaker." He added, with not-atypical irony, *"J'imagine que tu te battras pour être dans les forts!"* Be *that* as it may, he also sent along a day-by-day program of the proposed trek. The first thing that struck my wary eye upon reading it was the fact that we would be camped out for sixteen days at altitudes greater than eleven thousand feet. I also noticed that the "weak" would cross something called the Cho La at an altitude of about eighteen thousand feet, for which exercise crampons and an ice ax were advised. God knows what the "strong" would be doing. In preparation for all of this, I spent the summer tromping up and down a myriad of assorted Rockies near Aspen. But I have now been out of the high mountains for nearly two months, and I have been assured by assorted experts that whatever conditioning I received during the summer is now totally worthless. *Tant pis.*

The blue-jeaned young woman, it turns out, is a medical secretary from Strasbourg. This, she says, is her first *grand voyage*. She seems very nervous, so nervous that she cannot eat the croissants we have ordered for breakfast at the airport cafeteria, which is now open. It seems from what she tells me that there are essentially two independent groups of us. One will be led by Jaccoux and the other by a mountain guide from Marseilles named Guy Abert, whom I have never met. The young woman has climbed in Chamonix with Abert and will be part of his group. By this time, the Lufthansa counter, where all of us are meeting, seems alive with people carrying ice axes, rucksacks, and duffel bags. In addition to the thirty-five in our combined groups, there is another contingent of about the same number from an organization called Nouvelles Frontières. They all look about sixteen and are, they say, also headed for the Everest region.

Jaccoux arrives. We had dinner last night but apart from that I have not seen him in two years. He turned fifty last May. I am fifty-three. He and Michele, who are divorced, have a daughter, Claire, who is married to a young filmmaker. They, in turn, had a daughter a year ago, making Jaccoux a grandfather. He is the most physically fit grandfather I know. He looks about the same as he did ten or fifteen years ago. His blondish brown hair seems unchanged and as copious as ever. From time to time he has written me about some mountaineering accident or other that he has had, but of those there is no apparent trace. He has been guiding all summer and has just come back from trekking in Ladakh in northern India. To boot, he has given up smoking. He is obviously ready to go. I, on the other hand, have made a private decision to do the strict minimum on this trek. If I can get through *that* I will be well satisfied.

We will fly to Frankfurt, change planes, fly to New Delhi, and fly to Kathmandu. The duffel bags and rucksacks are loaded, and we are on our way.

Saturday, October 22: Kathmandu

Before we left Paris I asked Jaccoux how long it would take to get to Kathmandu. He said about twenty-four hours. I thought he was crazy. How could it possibly take twenty-four hours of flying to get anywhere? He was wrong. It took twenty-seven hours. From Frankfurt to Karachi was seven hours in the air, followed by about two hours on the ground while mechanics tried to figure out how to restuff an emergency slide that had somehow inflated and flown out one of the doors back into the plane. Since there was no way to do it, they finally cut the slide off. It then took two hours to fly from Karachi to New Delhi, where we arrived at 3 A.M. local time. Jaccoux dealt with all of this in his usual way. He took some kind of sleeping pill, one probably strong enough to use during major surgery. He then covered his eyes with a blue eyeshade and was out of business until we reached New Delhi. Here we will wait in one of the waiting rooms in the airport until morning, when our flight leaves for Kathmandu.

It is now close to seven—the flight leaves at seven-thirty—but Jaccoux has made the ominous discovery that Royal Nepal Airlines has never heard of us. This is the height of the trekking season in Nepal, and flights are booked and even overbooked months in advance. I run into a pair of Americans who say they have been in the New Delhi airport for two days trying to get on a flight to Kathmandu. It does not look good. The Royal Nepal Airlines flight has gone its way and I have resigned myself to what seems to be the inevitable when a mysterious Indian stranger appears and informs Jaccoux that we are set to go on the Air India flight that leaves at nine-thirty. How *that* was arranged, God knows. When we leave, the sun is shining. It is a bright, clear day, which means that we will get a marvelous view of the western part of the Himalayan chain—Annapurna, Dhaulagiri, and the rest. Old hands on this flight know that one wants to be on the left side of the plane when going up to Kathmandu. The mountains are on the left. I am on the right side but, by bobbing and weaving, I can still see them, and they still take my breath away.

Landing in Kathmandu always has a kind of magic-carpet quality for me. From the air, the city, with its pagoda temples, looks like something out of a fairy tale. It is just after the monsoon and the fields are an incandescent green. Usually, this mood is rapidly dispelled by an interminable wait to clear customs. But this time the procedure goes rapidly, and the thirty-five of us get on a chartered bus that takes us to our hotel. By the time we get there, it is close to 1 P.M. Our plans are now somewhat ambiguous. This has to do with the way trekking has evolved since we first visited the country. Most of those trekkers who now travel in the Everest region simply do not want to spend the thirteen days it takes to walk there from Kathmandu. In many ways, this is a pity. One misses the intimate contact with the Nepalese countryside. Also, one misses the acclimatization process. To take the plane to Lukla, which is what most trekkers now do, means to be at high altitude almost at once. Many people have great difficulty making this transition, and it can ruin the pleasure of the trek. It can also be quite dangerous. In fact, climbing expeditions often still make the walk simply to get into condition and acclimatize to altitude gradually. But the reality is that trekking around Everest, and indeed in most of the country, now depends on the airplane. That has created all kinds of problems, which Jaccoux, once checked into the hotel, has gone off to deal with.

The first problem is to find us a plane. The basic plane that is available is the Canadian-built Twin Otter, of which the airline has two.[1] This plane will hold about sixteen trekkers and climbers plus their gear. The flights begin operating at about seven in the morn-

1. As the reader has discovered by reading chapter 2, the airplane situation in Nepal has evolved since 1983. There are more choices. But none of the basics has changed. Getting to and from Lukla during the trekking season is still a nightmare.

ing—if there is no ground fog in Kathmandu. Often there is ground fog, which does not burn off until perhaps nine or ten. The flights then operate until noon, when, very often, clouds begin closing in on Lukla. Visibility is absolutely essential in these mountain flights. One of the local pilots once said to me, "If in Nepal you encounter a cloud, it usually has rocks in it." This means that there is a narrow time frame in which the Lukla flights—which take about forty minutes—can operate. On a good day, between the two Twin Otters, there might be four flights to Lukla; on a *very* good day, six. Some eighty trekkers can be ferried to Lukla on a good day. Our group alone, which was one of dozens in Kathmandu all wanting to go to Everest, consisted of thirty-five.

Jaccoux, like all foreign tour operators in Nepal, works with a Nepalese trekking and mountaineering organization. All of these organizations, if they are substantial, have people stationed at the airports in Kathmandu, Lukla, and other trekking designations during the season. Their full-time job is to get their agencies' clients onto airplanes. Someone who simply shows up in the airport wanting to fly to, say, Lukla, will usually be out of luck. Hence, the first thing that Jaccoux does when getting to Kathmandu is go to his agency to see when his group can expect to leave. On this occasion, he warns us that it could be as early as the next morning at seven, so we had better get our gear in order. Privately, I hope this will not happen, since I am tired from the flight from Europe. Also, I would welcome a few days to look around Kathmandu again. But I spend the afternoon arranging my things so that I will be set to leave the next morning. I am relieved when Jaccoux shows up in the early evening to announce that there is no space for us on the next morning's flight, so we have the day off. Finally, I can get to bed.

Sunday, October 23: Kathmandu

This has been a very pleasant day off. I have spent much of it in the Thamel—the Tibetan quarter—cruising the shops and the bookstores. There are now a number of English-language bookstores, some of which have fairly advanced physics and mathematics books in their windows. Nepal is producing a young generation of scientists and engineers. In one of the bookstores, I asked if they still had my old book on Nepal—*The Wildest Dreams of Kew*—which, at least in 1979, one could get in Kathmandu in a British edition. The proprietor expressed great regret that it was no longer available. He said that I should write a new one. "It will sell like a hotcake," he assured me.

Finally, I get back to the hotel, in time to get ready for a party I have been invited to this evening. There is a note from Jaccoux saying that we will not go tomorrow, and that the Abert group has not gotten off either. They will try tomorrow. But the party is a great success. Kathmandu has always attracted pretty and adventuresome women from all over the world, and many of them seem to be here this evening. Boris is also here. He tells me he is now seventy-eight. He looks fine. His Yak and Yeti restaurant was closed, he informs me, but he expects to open another new one in a few weeks. He does not seem much changed and it is very good to see him. My old friend Elizabeth Hawley, one of the world's greatest experts on Himalayan mountaineering lore, tells me that, prior to the fall of 1983, 135 different people from about thirty expeditions had climbed Mount Everest. She would know, since part of her job as a Reuters correspondent is to provide all of the mountaineering news from Nepal. She also tells me that as of just ten days ago, there has been electricity in Namche Bazar, provided by a small hydroelectric generating project. Electricity in Namche—it is a different world. There are several people at the party from different trekking agencies, and from them I hear an amusing tale. A few years ago, in one of their promotional stunts, the Canadian Club people buried a case of whiskey somewhere near the high pass that we are scheduled to cross. However, as a joke, a second group, which included a couple of Sherpas, dug up the case and reburied it father north on the Shangri La—an even higher pass, at nineteen thousand feet. As far as anyone knows, the case is still up there waiting for some hardy soul to dig it up. The second group offered it back to Canadian Club for a "ransom," but was refused. I get to bed after midnight.

Monday, October 24: Kathmandu

Last night—or really early this morning—there was a violent thunder and lightning storm in Kathmandu. In all the times I have been here I have never seen lightning. I ask Jaccoux if he remembers having seen lightning in these mountains, and he does not. Thunder over the Himalayas is very impressive and a little frightening. This morning, one can see a good deal of fresh snow. But the day is clear, and the Abert group is able to fly to Lukla. Perhaps our day will come.

Tuesday, October 25: Kathmandu

One of the Twin Otters has broken down, so there will be no flight for us today. Jaccoux has arranged a bus trip for our group to the Dashinkali. About twelve miles from Kathmandu, in the countryside, a shrine is dedicated to the Hindu goddess Kali—the terrifying goddess of death. At this particular shrine, animal sacrifice is still practiced. I have, to put it mildly, no fondness for animal sacrifice, but the drive is one of the loveliest short excursions one can make from Kathmandu, so I go along. Besides, I have been so busy wandering around Kathmandu that I have not really spent any time with our group, and it seems to me a good idea to get to know some of the people I am going to be trekking with—assuming we ever get to Lukla. I get down to the lobby of the hotel around seven and it is a polyglot mass of trekkers, some coming, some going. There is gear everywhere. Some of these people are going to western Nepal by bus, so at least they are not in competition for the spaces to Lukla.

As our chartered bus leaves Kathmandu for the Dashinkali, the road begins to climb, and soon we have new and wonderful views of the Himalayas. We arrive at midmorning. The atmosphere is that mixture of the sacred and the mundane that often seems to attend Nepalese religious ceremonies. When we get out of our bus we are inundated by beggars and hawkers of every persuasion. The business of children asking for things is something that seems to be of fairly recent origin here.

Jaccoux reminds me of something that I have forgotten from our 1967 trip. He was struck by his observation that the only place we visited where children asked for things such as "bonbons" was the ancient and very interesting town of Kirtipur, in the Kathmandu valley. He was so taken by this anomaly that he looked into the matter; he discovered that there had been an American film crew there the previous summer that had distributed candy to the children. By the time we got there, a few months later, the children assumed that any foreigner might give them candy. By now, however, the phenomenon of children asking for money, or candy, or pens—and often very aggressively—is pervasive and exceedingly unpleasant.

I strike up an extensive conversation with a lively kid who speaks English extremely well. He is selling lucky charms. He tells me, "Business is good luck—no business bad luck." I ask him how old he is and he says, "Fifteen." I ask him if he is married and he says, "Yes." I ask if he has any children and he says, "Five." He adds, with a huge, mischievous grin, "And after one more year I want to marry a French girl." Of these we have a goodly supply in our group, but when I mention his interest to them there are no takers. I ask him how to say, "I don't have any money" in Nepali. He tells me that the phrase is *Paisa chhaina*. He makes me pronounce it several times until I get it right. He then tries to sell me a charm. I say, *"Paisa chhaina."* He looks a little dumbfounded until he realizes that he has been hoisted by his own petard. He then breaks into irrepressible giggles. I buy two charms. I wear them both on the way back to the hotel just in case they might have an effect on the airplanes.

Wednesday, October 26: Kathmandu

Today we got as far as the airport. We woke up at four-forty-five to be ready to leave with our gear at six. Two flights for Lukla were listed, the first leaving about seven. Last night we almost gave up. Jaccoux said he could not be optimistic about our getting out at any specific time in the near future. He said we might consider another trek—to Langtang, which is due north of Kathmandu and for which no airplanes are involved, for example. We talked it over and decided that we would stick to our original plan and to try to go to Everest. The airport appeared to be a total chaos of trekkers and Nepalis trying to get to various places. Somehow, out of all of this, Jaccoux managed to get six members of our group onto flights to Lukla. They were called one at a time by name. Someone said that it was a little like the Last Judgment. At ten-thirty-one, according to my watch, there was the sound of loud hammering. Someone said, "They are fixing the plane." At ten-forty, those of us who had not been summoned gave up and came back to the hotel.

Thursday, October 27: Namche Bazar

Dear Lord, what a day! The hotel was instructed to wake us at four-forty-five—like yesterday—but for some reason they phone us at three-forty-five. By five, we are ready to leave for the airport. A special flight has been arranged for seven o'clock, for those of us who did not get off yesterday. By the time the dust settles and we are loaded on with our gear, it is seven-thirty. I manage to get a front seat, just behind the pilots. Both of them are Nepalese, although the pilot has on his black bag a decal that says, in English, NO MORE MR. NICE GUY. While the flight from New Delhi to Kathmandu is beautiful, this is surely the most spectacular mountain flight in the world. One flies close to the eastern range of the Himalayas. As one goes east, the peaks get higher, culminating in the spectacular mountains around Everest—Lhotse, which at 27,923 feet is the fourth-highest mountain in the world; and, a little farther away, Makalu, which at 27,824 feet is the fifth-highest; along with an almost uncountable panoply of snow-and-ice-covered summits of every imaginable shape and size. It is hard to make a choice of direction in which to look. From the air, the field at Lukla looks like a postage stamp. It is still a grass-and-dirt field, and it is so small that the pilots must land uphill in order to stop their planes. Conversely, they take off downhill over a precipice that leads down at least a thousand feet to the Dudh Kosi River. It is not flying for the faint-hearted.

When I was last here, in 1967, Lukla consisted of a field perched above a small Sherpa village. There was, needless to say, no tower, no airport hotel, nothing—just a field. The present Lukla has everything the previous one lacked. In fact, it now calls itself the Lukla International Airport. There are innumerable small, innlike hotels of uncertain quality, as well as a very substantial and comfortable hotel—the Sherpa Cooperative Hotel—with hot and cold running water. What next!

After we land, the first order of business is to rearrange our gear. We have worn our heaviest clothing on the plane so that it would not be weighed with our baggage. The weight limits on these flights are strict. At nine thousand feet—Lukla's altitude—it is pretty snappy at eight-thirty in the morning, but not cold enough to justify wearing all that gear. We begin by locating our Sherpas and porters, some of whom are at Lukla and some of whom have gone ahead with the first six members of our group, who came in yesterday. That done, we have breakfast—eggs and chapatis—and coffee and tea. Then Jaccoux explains the facts of life. The original plan that Jaccoux worked out in France assumed that we would be in Lukla on Monday. It is now Thursday, which means that we have lost three days. If we want to complete the full program, some of the schedule will have to be revised. In particular, instead of walking from Lukla to Namche in two days—the original plan—we will try to get to Namche today. This means, first, descending more than six hundred feet, to a place upriver called Phakding—which was to have been our first campsite—then climbing up to about twelve thousand feet, which is the altitude of Namche. The entire exercise will take a minimum of eight hours. We all agree that, under the circumstances, it is the thing to try, and we set off at our various paces.

While still in Kathmandu, I purchased a wonderful new guidebook to Nepal written by two professors at the Tribhuvan University in Kirtipur—Trilok Chandra Majupuria and Indra Majupuria. What I like about this guide is its candor and accuracy. I am also very fond of its writing style, which captures the cadences of the way Nepalis often speak English. There is a paragraph entitled "While Trekking" that I have, more or less, committed to memory, and whose advice I intend to follow. It reads: "By plane or bus you can reach your departure point for trekking. A new feeling can be experienced. Departure time should be usually early in the morning. Fix porters ahead of your schedule. Usually they are quite punctual. During trekking you should see that it is very important to maintain your trekking rhythms. It should be generally 300m (984 feet) per hour on an upward slope and 400–600m (1,312-1,968 feet) per hour for a downward slope." The Majupurias do not say so, but this must refer to changes in altitude. If not, it seems incredibly slow to me.

In a definitive book on the effects of high altitude, *Going High*, the noted American climber and doctor Charles Houston suggests the following schedule. Take one "day" to reach five thousand feet. (He does not say what a "day" is, but six to eight hours is a normal-to-heavy trekking day.) Then, says Houston, take one day for each two thousand feet of altitude changes, up to ten thousand feet. Thereafter, take one day for each seven hundred to one thousand feet. This pace is much slower than the one the Majupurias recommend, and it makes a good deal more sense to me.

It is quite clear to me that our trek to Namche is going to violate both of these limits.

The Majupurias go on to say:

Do not walk fast on the trail as it is harmful. Do not mind if any members of your group walks fast, you should be slow and steady at your normal pace. Porters like to walk quickly and stop frequently. Let them do so or ask them to keep pace with you, but you maintain your rhythm. Experience shows that you should not move very straight as it is tiresome. Another hint given by porters is that your pace should be crisscross. These hints will not make you feel tired during the trail. In the next morning, the sirdar or chief porter [the sirdar is most definitely *not* the chief porter; he is not generally a porter at all] *gets up early and offers you hot tea or coffee which can be repeated if you want. Early hours begin with washing and cleaning. Take breakfast, pack up things and start trekking. It is advised that trekking should be done generally for 3 hours in the morning and 3 hours in the afternoon. During the mid-day, relaxing is suggested. Take care during the trek you should eat more. During trekking keep some distance with your friends otherwise you may discuss your own things. Enjoy the trail with your eyes and ears. In the evening you can write in your diary if you want. Porters like to halt about 10–10:30 A.M. as they do not eat breakfast. They fill their plate with rice or* tsampa *[barley flour] and eat a good quantity. Smoke a* bidi *[a small cigar] or cigarette and become ready for the rest of the day's march. During the day you may want to have a wash in the sun or you may do so in the evening at your halting place or may not do so at all. There are several tea shops along the trail where you can enjoy hot tea. It is better to halt several times during the day as you have to get acclimatized and develop the habits. A camping site should be near the water and near a place which gives a good view. . . .*

Apart from smoking the bidi, it all seems like fine advice to me. On the way down from Lukla, however, there is not much opportunity for "crisscross." Jaccoux tells me that this part of the trail has been made into a kind of "superhighway," because there is so much traffic—human and animal—to and from Lukla. Indeed, every few minutes one meets up with trekkers, Sherpas, or trains of various beasts of burden. There are still no wheeled vehicles here, and it is difficult for me to imagine that there ever will be. Apart from everything else, there is the risk that any vehicular road might be wiped out by a flood. Indeed, in September of 1977, an avalanche fell from Ama Dablam—that magnificent, 22,350-foot, Matterhorn-like mountain north of Namche. The avalanche fell into a lake that feeds the Dudh Kosi River. It created a thirty-foot wave in the river that washed away part of the trail we are walking on—including seven bridges. The devastation seems to have been repaired, and if Jaccoux had not told me about it, I do not think I would have noticed anything.

As we walk, we pass a number of small hotels, tea shops, and restaurants. Some of the hotels advertise hot showers. All of this is completely new to me—none of it was here in 1967. Around noon, we stop for lunch, and after lunch come to the small Sherpa community of Jorsale, part of which was wiped out in the 1977 flood. Just beyond Jorsale is the entrance to what is known as Sagarmatha National Park—Sagarmatha being the Nepali name for Everest. This park, which was created in 1976 and encompasses an area of 1,243 square kilometers, contains all the high mountains in the Everest region. It was created to preserve the area, because the number of trekkers and climbers had simply become too large, and their effects on the environment too destructive, to let matters continue without some kind of regulation.

At the entrance to the park, one is stopped by a uniformed park official. One must show one's trekking permit, which bears one's photograph and passport number, and states the precise region that can be visited and for how long. Our trekking permits are good for about three weeks. They also state that "He/She must, however, keep twenty-five miles off the northern borders of Nepal." One then pays a fee of sixty rupees—about two and a half dollars—for an entry permit that allows one to stay in the park for the duration of one's trekking permit. (However, there is a very high fee—on the order of a hundred dollars—for using a video camera.) This permit, a pink paper, has on its back the park rules, and from it one can get a pretty clear idea of the kind of concerns that led to the creation of the park. Rules 2 and 3 are particularly instructive. Rule 2 reads: *"Trekking is an acceptable challenge. But* please do not litter, dispose it properly. Please do not remove anything from the park. Please do not damage plant. Please do not disturb wildlife. Please do not carry arms and explosives. Please do not scale any mountain without proper permission. Please do not scale any sacred peaks of any elevation. Please keep all the time to the main trek routes."

I was told in Kathmandu that, since the creation of the park, there has been a resurgence of wildlife in the region, which suggests that hunting must have taken place there before these rules went into effect. Wolves, snow leopards, various kinds of deer, and pheasants are coming back. The wolves have created a problem for the Sherpas, who now must protect their yaks more carefully.

Rule 3 reads: "Be self-sufficient in your fuel supply before entering the Park. Buying fuel wood from local people or removing any wood materials from the forest is illegal. This will apply to your guides, cooks and porters also."

This rule has to do with the fact that, between the trekkers and the local people, the forests in Sherpa country, and indeed in much of Nepal, were simply being cut away. A corollary of this was a dramatic increase in land erosion. In a sense, the Himalayas are being washed into the Indian Ocean. There are attempts at reforestation all over Nepal, but it is not clear that these do, or can, keep up with the destruction of the forests. It was pointed out to me in Kathmandu that, while these regulations against using wood for fires in the park are obeyed by trekking companies—for example, we were packing in with us large cans of kerosene—they are not being obeyed by the local people, who have little or no contact with the park officials. Indeed, as I passed some of the little hotels and restaurants along the trail, I noticed stacks of firewood, and, from time to time, I came across Sherpas carrying baskets of wood. If this continues, soon all the accessible forests will be gone.

Not far beyond Jorsale, the Dudh Kosi and Bhote Kosi Rivers join. The trail bisects the distance between the two rivers and ascends about two thousand feet to Namche. It is quite a pull, and by the time I get to Namche it is dark. Because of the brand-new electric lights, I have no trouble finding my way around the town. I am surprised to find it crammed with shops, restaurants, and little hotels. The houses seem about the same—classic stone Sherpa construction—but what is new are the glass windows. They were almost nonexistent in 1967. While I wander around the main street I run into a couple of members of our group, and they show me where we are camped—in a small field behind one of the hotels. That night we have a cheerful dinner in our communal "mess tent," which we top off with a few generous libations of the expedition whiskey.

Friday, October 28: Kunde

In the Jaccoux itinerary, this day's activity has been advertised as a *"Journée d'acclimitation,"* which I would freely translate as a day in which Jaccoux intends to train the balloons off of us. It has been a fairly cold night, and I am sure that it is going to get colder. The Sherpas wake us at seven-thirty—rather late for a trekking morning— and by the time we get going, it is nine-thirty. The object of the exercise is to hike to Kunde, a lovely Sherpa village about a thousand feet higher than Namche, and then climb a 14,500-foot peak behind the village. This will presumably enable Jaccoux to see what kind of shape everybody is in. Our group ranges in age from a sixty-year-old man— who works for the French railways but whose hobbies are climbing and skiing, in which he engages every week all year long—to a fellow in his twenties who works for the French space program and also climbs and hikes. In between are several young women whom I would estimate to be in their early thirties. One is an ophthalmologist who practices in Lyons. She has spent a year practicing in general medicine in Africa. She will be our trek doctor. Two of the other women are nurses, so medically we should be all right. There is a smattering of engineers, as well as an electronics technician from the physics laboratory in Orsay. Nearly all of these people—about half men and half women—are either dedicated climbers, or have been on treks with Jaccoux before, or both. I seem to be the second-oldest, and I intend to try not to slow things down.

The walk to Kunde is stunningly beautiful. One has the first views of the magnificent Ama Dablam. A sign not far from Namche warns trekkers about the effects of altitude, pointing out that one trekker in a thousand in the Everest region dies from altitude-related disorders. In fact, we heard that, the night before, a seventy-four-year-old trekker died following a heart attack at the Thyangboche monastery, which is at nearly thirteen thousand feet. I discussed this with Jaccoux, and asked him why more people did not get into serious altitude problems when they climbed Mont Blanc, which is at an altitude of 15,771 feet. People simply come off the street in Chamonix and successfully climb Mont Blanc. Jaccoux thought the reason was that, when one climbs Mont Blanc, one spends at most one night at high altitude—something like twelve thousand five hundred feet. One climbs the mountain early the next morning and, as a rule, is back in Chamonix by the afternoon. On the other hand, the Everest trekker spends at least two weeks at altitudes well over twelve thousand feet and is often camping at altitudes substantially higher than that of Mont Blanc. The body either adapts to this, or it breaks down. Jaccoux noted, "It's too bad that the most beautiful trek in Nepal is also the most dangerous."

The trail, which is as wide as a jeep road, leads over a pass at about thirteen thousand feet and then down into Kunde. Our first stop is the Hillary hospital that we visited in 1967, when John McKinnon was its doctor. He is now back in New Zealand, practicing—we correspond from time to time—and I am curious to see how his projects are faring sixteen years later—especially his work on the iodine problem, which had then caused so much goiter and cretinism.

The hospital is in a neat rectangular building with a magnificent view of the mountains. There is a long stone terrace in front of it, and our group pulls up to it while we go in search of whoever might be inside. I knock on the door and an amiable-looking, bearded young man appears, identifying himself as Keith Buswell, the present New Zealand doctor. I tell him of my friendship with the McKinnons. He says that, in fact, John McKinnon will be visiting the hospital in a few weeks, so we will just miss each other. Buswell tells me that he has only been in Kunde for two months, but is planning on staying for two years. I ask him about the iodine matter, and he tells me the problem has essentially been solved. There have been, as far as he knows, no recent cases of cretinous children born to parents with goiter. The therapeutic technique that was successfully used was injections of iodine—at least initially. (The Sherpas more or less refuse to eat iodized salt.) Then an odd thing happened. Sherpas, like most farmers on the Indian subcontinent, use human waste as fertilizer. This waste now contains iodine in sufficient quantities— it appears—to iodize crops such as the potato, the staple of the Sherpa diet. The net result is that in one way or another, the iodine problem has been solved.

Buswell also sees relatively few cases of tuberculosis, which was another of McKinnon's major problems; those he does see, he can treat. Smallpox, which used to ravage entire villages, has long since been eradicated by inoculation. Buswell tells me that the Sherpa lifespan is now longer than that of the general Nepalese population, in substantial part due to the better medical care Sherpas get. In the general population, there is something like one doctor per twenty-five thousand Nepalese. On the other hand, Buswell was treating a population of, at most, a few thousand. It is estimated that some twenty thousand Sherpas live in the *entire* Solu-Khumbu region. However, many of these people live several days' walk from Kunde, which is in Khumbu, and probably do not get to the hospital.

Our medical women want to see what the operating room looks like, and Buswell gives us a tour. They ask him if he can perform complicated childbirths—cesareans, for example. He says that he can, but that Sherpa women, if it is at all possible, want to have their babies at home. When we go outside to join the rest of the group it turns out that another of our women has a problem that she wants to discuss with Dr. Buswell. She speaks only French, so I act as interpreter. She has a thyroid condition, for which she has been taking medication. But the previous night she broke the bottle and lost the medicine. Our doctor and Buswell confer, again with me acting as interpreter, to figure out how to replace her medicine. It turns out that this is possible from the medicine in the hospital. We insist on paying both for the medicine—which Buswell wants to give us for free—and the established trekkers' consulting fee, which is a hundred rupees (some five dollars). The hospital needs this money and we are glad to donate it. As we leave, Buswell asks us not to give any candy to the Sherpa kids. "It's bad for their teeth," he says, "and there is no dentist in the region."

We climb our peak with me bringing up the rear. By the time we get back to our camp in Namche it is dark. I manage to take a hot shower—the last for a while—using a nearby hotel's primitive system, in which hot water is poured into a bucket, from which a pipe feeds it into the shower when one opened a valve. It may be crude, but it feels wonderful. I am asleep by seven-thirty.

Saturday, October 29: The Phortse Bridge

At 6 A.M., as expected, the Sherpas wake us for tea. There is a good deal of packing to do. Jaccoux ran into someone who told him that he had been over our high pass in basketball shoes, which must mean that there is less snow up there than usual. In any case, I am jettisoning my crampons. One less thing to carry. I have, on the other hand, rented an ancient ice ax in Namche. It has a wooden handle, which makes it something out of the dark ages of mountaineering. But it looks perfectly adequate to me. On this part of the trip, the heavy loads are to be carried by beasts—yaks, or *dzopchuks*, or whatever they are. By the time the animals are loaded, it is nine-thirty. Then our first stop is the police station just above Namche, for the inevitable trekking-permit check. That having been done, we move out on the trail, heading north and a bit east.

I am hoping we might get a glimpse of the now-defunct Hotel Everest View.[2] It is located near Kunde at an altitude of some thirteen thousand feet. The idea was to provide a luxury accommodation for people who might want to fly in for a day or so; there was a STOL airstrip at nearby Shyangboche. The hotel was constructed by some Japanese entrepreneurs.

In 1979, we visited an equally remarkable establishment. It was in a beautiful Sherpa village called Phaplu, which is a little south of the Everest region, and is at nine thousand feet—a veritable "lowland." It, too, was a luxury hotel that had been constructed by a then–twenty-four-year-old Sherpa named Rinzi Lama. He came from an extremely wealthy and distinguished Sherpa family. Rinzi called his hotel the Hostellerie des Sherpas. He had studied the hotel business in Italy. At the time we met him, he spoke Sherpa, Tibetan, Nepali, Hindi, English, and Italian. His uncle represented essentially the entire Sherpa community in the national parliament, and his family had made what amounted to a fortune, in local terms, by trading in Tibet. The hotel cost Rinzi about thirty-five thousand dollars to build—an enormous sum for Nepal. He built the whole thing using local labor. It had magnificent, Tibetan-style decorations, and chandeliers with electric lights, which he ran from a special generator since there was no other electric power in Phaplu. It had a sign in front which read—and I preserve the original spelling:

"Hostellerie Des Sherpa"
Really Just Two &1/2 Hours From Junbesi Through The
Beautiful Coniferous
&Rhododendrons Along The Terribly Romantic River Valley
In The Sherpa Village of Phaplu
Approximately (Ft.8000 Mt.2400 Telecommunications-
Airstrip, Medical Facilities) *Middle of January 1976*
Opening of Surprising, Exciting&Unimaginable
"Hostellerie Des Sherpa"

2. The hotel reopened in 1990. As of this writing, the cost is $135 per person, per night, per room. Oxygen is extra.

Unique&Excpetional Hotel Capable of Arousing Full of
Amicable Feelings Built & Decorated in Smartest Sherpa
&Tibetan Style Six Luxirious Bed Rooms for Romantic Ex-
plorers
Attach Bathroom *With Running Hot & Cold Water Bathtub*
Shower Watertap W.C. & Heater in Each Room & Bathroom
Plus
Six Three Beds in Each Warm Room For Expert Trekkers
Hygenic &Clean Environment
Laundry Work
Delicious International Cusines
Mysterious Bar in Candle Light
Crazy Music in Discotheque
Six Gentle Horses for Quite Ride But Sorry No Daily
Newspaper & Any Drug
"Hostellerie Des Sherpa"
Unbelievable Discovery
For Your Holiday's Relax& Enjoyment,*For*
Acclamatisation of Your Trekking & Expeditions
Trust Us: Please Come to Have Drinks Together
All the Prices Are Very Fair
Waiting Your Pleasureable Visit

Sincerely, Rinzi Pasang Lama,
G.Manager

It was a marvelous place in a superb setting, but it failed, since the
only way to get there—apart from walking for a week—was to fly to
the STOL airstrip in Phaplu in a very small plane. Given the pressure
on airline service—especially during the trekking season—it was
simply not possible to guarantee transportation there. We had visited
in January, when there are essentially no trekkers.

Our trail, as it turns out, does not go by the Everest View, but
follows the classic route to Everest, the same route that we took in
1967. But after lunch we will branch away from it and head into what

is, at least for me, terra incognita. We are on our way to the Gokyo valley near the base of Cho Oyu, a magnificent, 26,750-foot mountain on the Tibetan border. This is an area that was completely closed to us in 1967. We begin by heading up a steep trail to the top of a ridge at 12,900 feet. (Jaccoux has brought along a very accurate altimeter—good up to 26,000 feet—from which he reads off the altitudes.) I am resting at a large chorten on the top of a ridge—the usual site—when along comes one of our Sherpani, as Sherpa women are called, following one of our beasts, which she massages from time to time with a stick to indicate who is in charge. She has a beautiful, strong, Asiatic face—a lovely-looking young woman. She must be carrying at least forty pounds in a woven basket on her back. She is wearing a long black dress, typical of Sherpa women, with a decorative necklace, also typical. The dress comes down to the well-worn pair of blue basketball shoes on her feet. These shoes are a symbol of the new Sherpa prosperity that trekking has brought. In 1967, the Sherpas and Sherpanis—except those who were going to high altitudes on snow—largely went barefoot on trails like this.

The Sherpani smells of smoke—not disagreeably. There are not many chimneys in the houses in Solu-Khumbu. There were not many in 1967, and there still are not. Smoke from the interior fires used for cooking and warmth pervades Sherpa houses. The place of honor in a Sherpa house is next to the fire, which—considering the temperatures inside these houses—is not very surprising.

As she walks along, the Sherpani sings a mournful, wordless song over and over. I am very fond of the melody and wish I had enough of an ear that I could sing it too. From time to time she says something like "eeuk-eeuk" to her beast. She and her beast are walking at a delightfully slow pace, so I tag along. She occasionally meets a girlfriend on the trail and they have a giggly chat. The only thing I can think of asking when we are walking along together is "Yak?", pointing to the beast. *"Dzopchuk,"* she says, giving the beast an affectionate tap on the rump. That about exhausts my Sherpa, and she does not know any English. We pad along the trail in our separate linguistic spaces. I wonder if she ever fantasizes about marrying a trekker or a climber. I know of two cases where it happened. In 1979, the American climber Annie Whitehouse married the Sherpa Yeshi Tenzing. Tenzing had been a cook, and Annie Whitehouse one of the climbers, on an all-women's expedition to Annapurna the year before. Then, a few years ago, a Colorado climber—a friend of mutual friends—married a Sherpani from Namche. It was, I am told, tough sledding for them at first, since neither spoke the other's language. Furthermore, the woman's family ostracized her for marrying outside the Sherpa community. The marriage did not go well and ended in divorce, although she remains in the United States.

The Sherpani, her beast, and I pull into a beautiful campsite near a bridge that crosses the Dudh Kosi River. A few hundred feet above the bridge is the village of Phortse, which at 12,600 feet is said to be the highest year-round community in all of Nepal. I can tell, as the sun sets, that it is going to be a cold night.

Sunday, October 30: Luza

As I suspected, it *was* one cold night. Perhaps it is old age, but I cannot seem to get myself warm enough at night, even when I am wearing everything I can think of. The hot tea I had in my canteen to drink during the night has frozen solid—iced tea—and it remains half-frozen for the whole day. On the other hand, there has not been a cloud in the sky since we got here. In 1967, at just about the same date, it snowed nearly every day until we gave up.

The cold and the altitude are beginning to get on people's nerves. One of our married couples has been fighting all morning. She seems somewhat stronger than he does—or, at least, in better shape. And she is rubbing it in. The great French guide Armand Charlet refused to take married couples climbing together because he was afraid that this sort of thing might happen. The nice thing about a trek like this is that, by choosing one's pace, one can walk by oneself, or at least with compatible people. I have been walking by myself when suddenly there is the first spectacular view of Cho Oyu at the head of the valley. This is clearly *its* valley. The mountain, which was first climbed in 1954 by an Austrian group, looks like a giant, snowy armchair. It is said to be the "easiest" of the eight-thousand-meter mountains. Lots of luck—it has killed its share of climbers. The trail leads straight to our next stop, the tiny "summer village"—a village that the Sherpas inhabit only in the summertime, because of its altitude, and its inaccessibility in other seasons—of Luza, which is at 14,100 feet.

When we arrive at Luza in the late afternoon, the Abert group is already here, having spent a rest day. We have not seen the Abert group since it left Kathmandu for Lukla last Monday. Today has been a perfect fall day—cold, but sunny and clear, with extraordinary views of Cho Oyu. We arrive at the campsite as the sun is beginning to set, and it is already quite cold. No sooner have we arrived than Abert finds Jaccoux and tells him that one of his party is missing. It turns out to be the young medical secretary from Strasbourg with whom I shared a croissant in the Charles de Gaulle Airport, and who told me that this was to be her first *grand voyage*.

She apparently went for a walk by herself and never came back. This is potentially a very serious matter, because she is not equipped to spend the night out in the subfreezing temperatures that are rapidly enveloping us. Exposure at high altitudes can turn a minor mishap into a fatal one. Jaccoux immediately organizes a search party, consisting of himself, Abert, our doctor, and a Sherpa or two. We lend them the extra equipment they might need, such as flashlights. In an hour or so they are back. The worst has happened. They found the young woman dead. She apparently died in a fall, but how it happened no one can say. Her body was brought back and is put into a small tent, by itself. I participate in drawing up, with the aid of our doctor, the formal death certificate, which has to be in English. I realize, for the first time, how few words are needed to describe the cause of death. The fewer the better, our doctor says. We are faced with the question of what to do next. Here, the division of the expedition into two groups plays a role. Some people from the Abert group, with whom she was trekking, want to stop the trek right here. To our group, she is a stranger; I may be the only one who talked to her. Furthermore, it was not even clear in practical terms what it would mean to stop the trek. We are two weeks, by foot, from Kathmandu, and, given the premium on flight space from Lukla, to return before our scheduled day would mean either waiting for up to ten days in Lukla, or walking back to Kathmandu. The only thing that makes any sense is to continue.

Abert took it upon himself to stay with the body of the young woman; to make whatever arrangements he could to notify her family, via the French embassy in Kathmandu; and, if possible—and if the family wished—to bring the body back to France. It was at this point that we learned something about Nepal that I, at least, had not known. Despite the urging of the embassy, and despite the family's willingness to pay for the transport down from Solu-Khumbu by air, no plane could be chartered for the purpose of transporting a dead body. In Nepal, planes are only for the living. (One can see the logic of this from the point of view of a very poor country, with very few planes.) On this matter there was no possibility of compromise. Hence, it fell upon Abert to arrange with the local lamas to give the young woman a proper Buddhist funeral. Since the Sherpas cremate their dead, the young woman was cremated.

The sight of the small tent in which the young woman's body lay until the funeral has remained vividly in my memory ever since.

Monday, October 31: Gokyo

After a fitful night's sleep, I get up with a sore throat. I take a gram of vitamin C and a tetracycline pill and decide that I am "cured." I have now evolved a trail philosophy: Since I like to walk slowly, I start out before most of the group; this way, I and they end up at the same place at about the same time. The trail goes up sharply for a bit, and then moseys off in the general direction of Cho Oyu. After about three hours, I encounter some of our Sherpas in what looks like a yak pen. They tell me that this is where we will have lunch. There is nothing to do but lie in the sun and wait, which is fine with me.

Next to come into view is Jaccoux, who has evidently moved up the trail like a deer. He informs me that not far behind him is a beautiful American woman—not part of our group—who is trekking by herself, since her boyfriend, it seems, has ditched her. Jaccoux is usually reluctant to speak English, but when it is a matter of a pretty girl, he is willing to make the effort. Not long after we have this conversation, there in fact *is* a very pretty woman walking by herself. I say hello and invite her to join us for lunch. She has not had a square meal for days, and is glad to accept. Despite the fact that her boyfriend left her, she is determined to make use of the remaining three weeks on her trekking permit. She is gutsy to be trekking by herself.

After lunch, she goes her way and we go ours. The upper Gokyo valley is one of the most beautiful places I have ever seen. It culminates at the tiny village of Gokyo itself, which is on the shore of a magnificent blue-green mountain lake. The thought occurs to me that, if this place were only ten thousand feet lower, it might become the Lake Tahoe of Asia. At 15,800, we will be camping tonight 29 feet higher than the summit of Mont Blanc.

Tuesday, November 1: Below the Cho La

Jaccoux has once again told us the facts of life. The first and determining fact is that we do not have enough porters. We do have the *dzopchuks,* but there is no way that these animals are going to get over the Cho La. It comes down to this: The *dzopchuks* and the Sherpanis will go back down the Gokyo valley and then back up, by the normal trekking route, to the village of Lobuche, which is at about 16,200 feet. It is a long way around the mountain and it will take them fully two days. Our Sherpas can carry enough tents that we can sleep four to a tent for a couple of nights. There should be just enough food. We will have to carry everything else—sleeping bags and the rest. This means that, for the hardest day of the trek, we will be carrying about double our usual load. The alternative is to go with the *dzopchuks* to Lobuche. Three of the group—including the bickering married couple—decide to do just that. They have had enough of the altitude.

We head down the Gokyo valley trail and, at a place that the Sherpas have no trouble picking out, turn east. A little climbing brings us to the lower tongue of the Ngozumba Glacier, which, if one followed it north, would eventually lead, at least judging from the map, to the summit of Cho Oyu. From the map, it looks like we cannot be any farther than twenty-five miles from the Tibetan border. This part of the glacier is slippery but not very icy. It is a morass, but the Sherpas seem to know where they are going. There are occasional cairns in the ice, showing that we are on the right track. Without much trouble, we cross the glacier, and find ourselves on a high sward just below the pass. From here, the pass looks difficult but not impossible. Tomorrow will tell the tale.

Wednesday, November 2: The Cho La

There has not been much of a chance to sleep—crowded as we are in our tents. Everyone seems to have spent much of the night reading by flashlight. I brought a couple of light paperback books for occasions like this. One of them happens to be a collection of essays by Camus entitled *The Myth of Sisyphus*. Well, if the Brits could read Shakespeare on Mount Everest, I am entitled to read Camus under the Cho La. The title essay ends, "The struggle itself towards the heights is enough to fill a man's heart. One must imagine Sisyphus happy." We do not seem to know any of the details of the route that Sisyphus followed up his underworld mountain when he endlessly pushed the stone to the summit, but if it was like the route up Cho La, it is difficult for *me* to imagine that he was happy. The terrain on the way up is not technically difficult; there is certainly no need for a rope. But it is steep, and it is composed of that kind of unstable rock on which one takes two steps up, and slides one step back down. All of this is at an altitude of over seventeen thousand feet. The only virtue of any of this is that it has enabled me to get to know, a little bit, one of our Sherpas.

This has not been easy. Unlike on our 1967 trip—three of us together with a small number of Sherpas for several weeks—we are now seventeen, with about the same number of Sherpas. The sirdar seems to be a very nice man, but he is so unassuming and soft-spoken that I have never even found out his name. There are just too many of us for anyone to get to know anyone else. On the climb to the top of the Cho La, I am, as usual, bringing up the rear. The oldest Sherpa, a man named Tashi, seems to have been given the job of seeing to it that I keep going. He says, every once in a while, "Now slowly going, slowly going." I grin at him and he grins back. He offers to carry my pack, but I tell him that that is not necessary. He cannot be much taller than five foot three. He has a wizened face and is as tough as nails. He reminds me of Ang Dorje, my friend from 1967. Poor Ang

Dorje. I inquired after him in Kathmandu at his old trekking agency. They told me that he had died—apparently from the effects of alcoholism. Sherpas do drink quite a bit—*chang* (beer) and *rakshi* (a local eau-de-vie and very potent). They are also happy to drink anything their employers offer them. When their life span was about thirty-five years, there was not enough time for degenerative diseases such as those associated with alcoholism to declare themselves. Now there is. Sherpas, like the rest of the Nepalese population, are beginning to die of diseases of the "rich," such as heart attacks and cancer.

In any event, I am moving steadily—if slowly—upward, with the snow-covered summit of the pass getting ever closer. It is horribly tiring work, and I am constantly having to sit down and catch my breath. But things do not seem, at least to me, impossible, or even desperate. I look up and see Jaccoux coming back down in my direction. That is indeed odd. The last time I saw him was at breakfast, when he gave all of us something like a Mars bar, to give us an extra shot of glucose to get us over the pass. When he arrives above me, I am sitting down on a small rock, and he tells me to come up where he is. I tell him that I am perfectly satisfied with my rock and don't see any reason to go up to his. He says the reason is that he is going to take my pack. There is no arguing about this. He puts it on and remarks that it seems incredibly light to him. Thanks. He also remarks that I look my fifty-three years. Thanks again. It is true that I have not shaved in several days, and have a sort of white beard. It is also true that the various sunblocks that I have been using do not seem to have worked: My nose is peeling, and the rest of my face is multicolored. I am trying to think of something equally insulting to say to him when I notice that we have reached the snowy summit. I also notice that the woman who had the thyroid problem is being, more or less, carried by two Sherpas. After she has been seated for a while, she seems recovered. The rest of the group are sprawled out variously eating lunch in the bright sunshine. It is a magnificent place and, if I were not so beat, I would enjoy it a lot more.

After lunch, Jaccoux gives me some kind of glucose pill, and we head off on a wide track in the snow in a fairly gentle downward direction. The track becomes steeper. Here is where crampons would come in handy. I begin to slide and Jaccoux takes an arm, and in this somewhat ungainly fashion, we get off the snow and ice and onto a rocky trail. After a while, Jaccoux points to where we are eventually going—a place called Dzonghila, at 15,900 feet. The trail has now broadened, and since there is no way I can break anything, Jaccoux takes off for the camp at his usual pace. This leaves me alone in a vast valley with the sun beginning to set. I am very tired but I like the solitude. From time to time I look back to where we have come from. From here, our path looks vertical. Going at my own slow pace, I manage to get to our camp just after the sun has set. I am asleep by eight. It has been a very long, tough day.

Thursday, November 3: Lobuche

This has been a relatively easy day, which is just as well, because I am beat. This is the eighth day that we have been at this without a rest. Our original schedule called for a couple of rest days, but we lost them when we had our problems catching a plane to Lukla. The woman with the thyroid condition, and her husband, have gone back down toward Namche. The three people who left two days ago have also gone down. That leaves eleven of the original sixteen—plus, of course, Jaccoux. Lobuche, at 16,200 feet, was the highest place we camped in 1967. It was a pretty grim place then, consisting of a few yak pens and, as I recall, one stone building with no windows and no doors. The town is now on the main trekking route to the Everest base camp. It is crawling with trekkers of every size, shape, and nationality. There are a few small hotels, which sell, among other things, beer at fifty-five rupees—at current exchange rates, more than two dollars a bottle. Considering where we are, it seems like a bargain. I hear an American say, "We saw a lot of mountains from the ridge, but I don't know what they are." Dear Lord! Everest cannot be much more than five miles from here.

Friday, November 4: Pheriche

Some of the group have gone off to climb the Kala Patar. Having done it in 1967, I have decided that I do not need to do it again, especially since we do not plan to camp tonight at Lobuche, but quite a bit farther down the valley, at Pheriche. The Kala Patar people are not expected to get into camp until nine, or so, tonight. I loaf a bit in the sun during the morning and then follow our *dzopchuks*—which have now rejoined us—down to Pheriche. At just under fourteen thousand feet, Pheriche is practically in the lowlands. It is a substantial village, and it has in it one of the most interesting institutions to have been constructed here since 1967, namely, the Trekkers' Aid Post. So far as I can make out, this was the idea of a Peace Corps volunteer named John Skow. It began in 1973 in which Skow lived in Pheriche during the trekking season—the middle of September to the first week in December—and, with the support of several of the large trekking agencies, he performed various services for trekkers. However, in 1975, a hundred thousand dollars was raised to build a small hospital—one that could service the local community, but whose main function would be to give medical support to trekkers and climbers. By this time enough people had gotten into serious trouble with the altitude that the idea was welcome. The hospital's first doctor was a man named Peter Hackett, who later became the director of high-altitude research in the Department of High Altitude Studies of the University of Alaska in Anchorage. In the first year of its operation, Hackett's newly constructed hospital had 436 trekker patient visits and 503 Sherpa patient visits. The Sherpas are treated free and the trekkers are charged.

The hospital, largely funded by a nonprofit organization called the Himalayan Rescue Association, is located in a compact stone building. It normally has two doctors on duty. When I call, one of them—a British doctor named Patrick O'Sullivan—is out in the field. As part of their job, the doctors visit places like Gokyo from time to time to see if anyone up there is in trouble. The doctor present is a thirty-two-year-old, bearded American from Iowa named Tony Waickman. He is in the process of making a chocolate cake, since O'Sullivan is soon to leave and Waickman wants to give him a farewell dinner. He tells me that his own medical specialty is cardiology—which must be useful, considering some of the trouble his prospective patients are likely to get into. He says that the physicians serve the hospital on an unpaid, voluntary basis and, in fact, are in Nepal only on tourist and trekking visas. He says that they have seen as many as fifteen hundred—fifteen *hundred*—trekker patients in a season, with ailments ranging from skin diseases to pulmonary edema—a severe and often fatal form of altitude sickness. He, and everyone else I have spoken to, agrees that there is only one really effective thing to do about altitude sickness—get the patient down to lower altitudes. The "miracle cure" is to lose a couple of thousand feet of altitude—not always easy. Barring that, the best things one can do include injecting diuretics, which cause the body to lose fluid—the buildup of fluid in the brain and lungs being the dangerous element of edema—or giving the patient oxygen.[3] But there is no substitute for getting down. Waickman tells me that the one thing the doctors will not do is mountain rescue. He says, "If their friends can't save them, they will die." However, not long before this discussion, he had been able to help an injured climber on Ama Dablam who was close to the base of the mountain. He tells me that when he finishes his stint in Pheriche, he intends to go back to Thailand, where he was working in a refugee camp. He strikes me as a very impressive young man.

By the time I leave the hospital it is dark. The group that climbed the Kala Patar begins coming in around nine. They tell me that they are glad to have done it—*once*.

Saturday, November 5: Chukung

From Pheriche, we head back toward Tibet in a northeasterly direction, up the valley of the Imja Kola River. This valley was also off-limits to us in 1967—too close to the border. I have read and heard

3. Sometime after our visit, I learned about the so-called "Gamow bag." This is a kind of portable pressure chamber that was invented by Igor Gamow, the son of the late, remarkable, Russian-born physicist George Gamow. These bags can be collapsed into a carrying case not much larger than a sleeping bag. The patient is placed inside, and the bag is manually inflated, creating some of the elements of lower altitudes. Even a relatively short stay in the bag can relieve some of the emergency symptoms of high-altitude sickness. In my opinion, no high-altitude trek in a remote area should be conducted without one of these bags—which can be rented in Kathmandu. That a trek should also carry emergency oxygen goes without saying.

from friends that it is one of the most spectacular places in all of Nepal. This becomes apparent once we climb a ridge that separates Pheriche from the higher village of Dingboche. At this point, we begin to see the mountains that flank the valley. On our right is Ama Dablam, so close that we can almost touch it. We look through binoculars for an expedition climbing the mountain while we were here, but we cannot find them. On our left is the south face of Nuptse, as well as Lhotse. In front of us is a whole array of snow-covered peaks, some of them with fluted walls that look as if they have been carved by a sculptor. Of the south face, the great Tyrollean climber Reinhold Messner—who has climbed all the eight-thousand-meter mountains, including Everest more than once—has stated that it is not for climbers of this century—maybe the next. It towers some ten thousand feet above the valley and is absolutely sheer and swept with avalanches. It is beautiful to look at—from the safety of the grassy valley.

We get to Chukung—a small summer village, at 15,500 feet—in midafternoon. Jaccoux announces that tomorrow we will split into two groups. There will be a climbing group, which he and Abert will lead, that will try Island Peak, a twenty-thousand-foot, fairly difficult "trekker's peak." The other group will be a hiking group that can try a nearby ridge at 16,500 feet. I announce that I am planning to constitute a third group. I have been walking for nine days, without a rest, at high altitude, and I am taking tomorrow off. Jaccoux makes some slightly disparaging sound, but I have made up my mind.

Sunday, November 6: Chukung

A delightful day. I have a late breakfast in the sun and watch the ridge group go off. Our Sherpanis are doing their laundry in a nearby stream and I decide to wash a couple of shirts. I hang them on my tent to dry. When I look at them an hour later they are frozen stiff. At noon Jaccoux and Abert leave for the base camp of Island Peak. They have found three takers from among us, plus the faithful Tashi, who is carrying the expedition tent. They disappear up a melancholy-looking ridge. I read and think and watch the snow blow off the summits of the great mountains until the sun sets. A big dinner, a glass of the expeditionary cognac, and early to bed.

Monday, November 7: Dingboche

We are on our way out. It will take a few days to get to Namche and Lukla, but that is our general direction. The first stop is Dingboche, a large Sherpa village about a thousand feet lower than Chukung. Here we will regroup. When we leave Chukung, the Island Peak people have not yet come back. It is an easy downhill walk to Dingboche, and we arrive in the afternoon. The Sherpas have set up camp at the lower end of the village. Across the way there is a local restaurant—a pleasant, somewhat primitive place, in which the cooking is done inside over an open fire. The large restaurant is full of Sherpas and the odd trekker drinking beer or rakshi. It has gotten very cold outside, and it is nice to be in here. We order some potatoes, which are fried in yak butter and taste fine. Near the fire is the dried carcass of some unidentifiable animal. From time to time, the Sherpani who is doing the cooking cuts off a piece and cooks it. I decide I will pass on that one. After the potatoes, we wander back to the camp. Our sirdar is here, and, since he has nothing else to do, I decide to ask him a question about Sherpas that has been exercising me. I have never seen a Sherpa wearing glasses (apart from glacier goggles). I had asked our ophthalmologist about this, and she said that she had noticed it also. Her conjecture was that the nearsighted Sherpas fall down cliffs as children and are thereby weeded out of the population. Since the life expectancies are in the early fifties, the farsighted ones never need corrective glasses. Besides, the population hardly reads anyway. I ask the sirdar. This takes a good deal of doing, since his English is not very good; for a while, he thinks I am complaining about my own glasses, which I wear all the time. When we succeed in communicating he laughs and says Sherpas only need glasses "if some snow coming." As far as he is concerned, this settles the matter.

The first of the Island Peak group to come down is Abert. He says that only Jaccoux got to the top, and that no one else got very far. Pretty soon Jaccoux comes along, saying they had a cold and miserable night at base camp. It appears as if Tashi performed heroically getting water for everyone. Jaccoux says the final summit wall was quite steep, and consisted of loose snow over ice—a rather dangerous business. Pretty soon everyone else returns, and we have a huge dinner to celebrate. In the middle of it, a runner comes up from Pheriche with a note for Jaccoux. The woman with the thyroid condition is in the hospital at Pheriche and will be there for several days. From the note it is not clear what has happened, but Jaccoux and our doctor will head to Pheriche the first thing next morning.

Thursday, November 9: Thyangboche

We have had a bad night. A yak has been loose near our tents, and it was so cold that no one felt like getting out of their sleeping bags and chasing it away. It snorted around the tents all night, making it all but impossible to stay asleep. To boot, this morning the Sherpanis, who always come to the tents with the morning tea, got us up at six. There is no reason to be up this early. There is no sun, and it is so cold that one has to eat breakfast with one's heavy gloves on. The group looks a little beat. It is time to be getting down.

We are now back on the standard trekking route. The lower we get, the lusher the scenery becomes. It is as if life is flowing back into everything. It is odd to feel this way, since we are still above twelve thousand feet; here, though, a couple thousand feet can transform the vegetation. We stop at a small village for lunch. While we are sitting in the restaurant, a couple of trekkers dressed as if they just stepped out of the L. L. Bean catalog arrive and demand lunch in a hurry. A couple of nights at fifteen thousand feet will calm them down. Jaccoux appears with our doctor. It turns out that the woman in the Pheriche hospital had phlebitis, a blood clot in her leg, probably altitude-related. This is a life-threatening condition, if it is not treated. It is very likely that the hospital in Pheriche saved her life. She is now out of danger and will be helicoptered back to Kathmandu as soon as a helicopter can be flown up to Pheriche—which, I gather, can take forty-eight hours (and costs several thousand dollars). Jaccoux, like many people who organize difficult trips to out-of-the-way places, insists that all of his clients obtain the form of medical insurance that pays for this kind of thing, as well as for emergency repatriation. It will pay for her helicopter flight.

Our destination for the day is the monastery at Thyangboche. I read recently that a committee is at work trying to select a new version of the Seven Wonders of the World. If I were on that committee, I would vote for Thyangboche. The monastery rests—almost floats—on a kind of mesa at 12,600 feet. The mesa is fringed by fir trees and rhododendrons. The gilded main temple was rebuilt after it was destroyed by an earthquake in 1934. This is the spiritual center of the whole Solu-Khumbu region—the religious center for the twenty thousand Sherpas who live there. Its spiritual leader is still Nawang Tenzing Zang-Po—the reincarnated head lama, or *rimpoche,* we met in 1967. I still have the white scarf he blessed by touching it to his forehead. He has written a small booklet on the monastery. This is what he says about the view: "To the east is Ama Dablam, to the south is Tamserku, to the north Taweche. To the northwest is the mountain god Khumbila, to the northeast Everest. The Emja River flows in the north, Dudh Kosi in the west, a small river in the east, and Nakding River in the south. In the lower areas there is thick forest, in the middle areas the forest is thinner, and in some places there is none at all. In the higher areas there is very thin forest. In summer and spring there are many flowers, and the smell is lovely. Everyone likes this place which is called Tengboche. . . ."

My great fear is that all the trekkers might have ruined the place. I am extremely happy to find that this is not so. In 1967, the only structure that was extraneous to the monastery was the small wooden shed that Hillary had built for trekkers and climbers. We signed one of the walls, along with every other expedition that had come through. The shed is still there, but it is locked, so I cannot go inside to look for our names on the wall. But now, in addition to the shed, there is a handsome trekkers' lodge, built by a New Zealand group as part of the Sagarmatha National Park facilities. The sense is very present now that this place is a treasure that must and will be preserved. There are a couple of restaurants that are innocent enough as not to spoil anything. In one of them I ask if the rimpoche is here at present. I thought that I would try to see him. I am told that he is away and, in fact, is engaged in some kind of negotiations to see if there is any way of bringing the Dalai Lama back to Tibet. I am also told that this very evening there is to be a special service in the monastery connected with the new moon. We decide to go.

The interior of the monastery, where the thirty-five monks live, is open to visitors. The *gompa*—the monastery building—is three stories high. In the first story is the main temple. Although electricity is anticipated, the gompa's principal illumination still comes from a gas lamp that casts strange shadows. The center of the temple is an open square, and it is surrounded by wooden benches. The exterior benches are for visitors, and we are invited to sit on them. Shoes must be removed before entering the sanctuary and, since the floor is stone, one's feet soon become extremely cold. Monks move in and out of the room in no apparent order. It is very difficult to understand what is happening. An elderly monk consults a book from time to time, and a musician brings out a huge conch shell, while another prepares a gong. Some of the younger monks come in and are instructed to take some special hats out of a case. To me, the hats look like lunar crescents. The whole ceremony takes at least an hour to prepare. Finally, the musicians begin to play, and the monks walk around the square carrying various sacred objects, some of which they place on an altar. They also light oil lamps and drink something out of small beakers. I find it very interesting but completely incomprehensible. One has the feeling of making contact with a past that we have all but lost touch with. I cannot decide if this is good or bad. The ceremony is over. We file out and go silently back to our tents.

Wednesday, November 10: Namche

The Sherpanis wake us at five. This is their last day, and they must be eager to get home. A bit later, the sound of horns can be heard from the monastery. I think the festival is still going on. As soon as the sun comes up, we begin the relatively easy walk to Namche. We have lunch on the way and arrive in midafternoon. I decide to do a little shopping, and to try to find my old friends, Ila Tsering and Ang Dorje.

Namche is crawling with shops. In some ways it is sort of a mess: too many people crowded into too small a space. I buy a long-sleeved cotton sweater and a few other things, since I have just about run out of even marginally clean clothes. I then try to locate Ila Tsering. I ask in a shop in which the Sherpani seems to speak good English. English is now commercially advantageous here, and many more people speak it than in 1967. She says there is no *Ila* Tsering, but there is an *Ulla* Tsering. Perhaps they are one and the same. This Ulla, according to her, is an "old man." I explain that my friend "Ila" was a sirdar and had been a great climber. Yes, yes, her Ulla and my Ila are one and the same, but now he is an old man whose business is "some yaks." I make a rapid calculation and conclude that Ila is probably a year or so younger than I am. In any case, I get directions to his house. Then I ask about Ang Dorje. She has never heard of Ang Dorje. But she sends a Sherpa to show me the way to Ila's. It is a large house, but it seems empty. We find someone who tells us that Ila has gone to Lukla with a train of yaks to bring in some trekkers. Since we are going to Lukla tomorrow, perhaps I will meet him there.

Thursday, November 11: Lukla

Before I begin the long walk to Lukla, I take a hot shower—my first in two weeks. It is marvelous. On the way to Lukla, I keep trying to spot Ila. I pass several yak trains coming in the opposite direction. One of them is led by a man who looks vaguely familiar, but he does not seem to recognize me, and we pass in silence. The walk to Lukla takes me about eight hours. When I get here, the sun has set. I pass various stores, and in front of the Royal Nepal Airlines office I hear a trekker say that he is number eighty-nine on the waiting list for a flight back to Kathmandu. There are trekkers everywhere. I head for our camp, which is just above the Sherpa Cooperative Hotel. I have privately decided that if we are stuck in Lukla for several days, I will take a room there. I have had about enough of tents and cold water. I meet our sirdar, and he tells me that I must have crossed Ila going the other way. It must have been the man who looked a little familiar. We simply did not recognize each other. Sixteen years is a long time.

Tonight we have a sort of feast in which we roast goat meat—which is terrible. We give the Sherpas presents. I give Tashi a shirt and a pair of down slippers. He is the only one of the Sherpas I have gotten to know at all. We and the Sherpas drink to each other's health, and then I spend what I hope will be my last night for a while in a tent.

Friday, November 12: Airborne

When I wake up, clouds have begun to gather over the mountains. The weather is changing. The sirdar says, "Some snow Khumbu side." There are four scheduled flights in and out today. Really three scheduled, plus ours—the last—a special flight for our group. (The Abert people got out yesterday.) At seven, we bring our gear up to the field. The clouds lift and the first flight comes in at about eight. Trekkers come and go. I meet an American woman who has been leading trekking groups for many years. I ask her how the Sherpas have changed. She tells me that the young ones do not know the Sherpa dances anymore. She quotes something someone said to her: "The Sherpas are going to become part of the modern world. They can't be kept up here in cages like animals in a zoo just to preserve them." That is certainly right, but one only hopes that much of what is so valuable in that society will be saved.

Two more planes come in, bringing more trekkers. Then, finally, our plane arrives. As it takes off and then gains altitude, I can see Everest—the Goddess Mother. A plume of snow is blowing from her summit.

Epilogue

On January 19, 1989, the main building and the courtyard of the Thyangboche monastery caught fire and burned down. Some of the religious artifacts and old manuscripts were saved, but most were lost in the fire. The previous April, electricity had come to Thyangboche, and it seems that an electric heater was to blame for the fire. A monk unfamiliar with its use had placed it too close to flammable materials. It was thought that such electric heat—from a hydroelectric generator—might save firewood. But even this seems to have been misguided. People simply stayed up later and burned even more wood, since the electric heaters were inadequate. An international campaign was launched to raise money to rebuild the monastery. It succeeded. Reconstruction began in April of 1990; the new gompa was dedicated in September of 1993. It is said to be at least as beautiful as the previous one, which, it will be recalled, had been reconstructed after the earthquake of 1934.

Finally, I *did* get to see Ila Tsering—a few years after this trek and in the unlikely location of Aspen, Colorado. One of Ila's sons had come to the United States—sponsored by some of the people who had trekked with Ila—to begin a course of studies that would eventually lead to his becoming a doctor (something that has now happened). The same people helped Ila come here, to visit his son and to travel around the country. In the course of this, he passed through Aspen, where I spend my summers. I wish that the visit had been more successful. Ila seemed very much older than I thought he would, and he also seemed quite dazed by all the sights and sounds of this strange place. I did my best to make him feel welcome, but he seemed lost and disoriented. Perhaps he was already sick with the cancer that killed him a year or so later. In any event, I will always be grateful to him for introducing me to his wonderful homeland.

5

Nepal Again

In the fall of 1986, I returned to Nepal to trek with Jaccoux around the Annapurna range—a trek of some two hundred miles, lasting about a month. It is one of the most beautiful treks in Nepal, and also one of the most popular. Air transport is not the problem here since one can, and we did, make the trip to western Nepal by bus. The problem is that there is essentially one circuit, which must serve both for the trekkers and for all of the local commerce, which is transported on the backs of either animals or people. Two-thirds of the trekkers in Nepal—perhaps twenty thousand individuals—travel all, or at least part, of this circuit in any given year. The effects of this on the environment and the spiritual values of the people have been dramatic—and sometimes devastating.

Certainly trekkers bring in money, some of which does go to raising the standard of living of the local people.[1] The fact that the life

---

1. An interesting question has been raised about the economic balance sheet of the luxury hotels in Kathmandu and elsewhere. To provide accommodations at a standard that this category of visitor demands requires facilities that cannot be manufactured in Nepal. This includes everything from bathroom fixtures to the color television sets one finds in every room. These must be imported, and must be paid for in foreign currency. One wonders, therefore, if this loss of foreign currency is made up by the foreign currency that enters the country when tourists pay for these accommodations. I simply do not know.

expectancy of the Nepalese has increased by at least ten years since my first visit in 1967 is testimony to that. But at what cost? Here are a couple of examples.

While I did not get to reunite with Ila Tsering in 1983, I did make contact with one of his sons in 1986. As I mentioned in the last chapter, one of his sons had gone to the United States, begin his medical training. Another, I learned, was a monk in the Thyangboche monastery. The third was in the trekking business in Kathmandu. I went to see him. He told me that he could see the decline of traditional Sherpa values in his own family. His children did not want to speak Sherpa, since Nepali was the language of Kathmandu, where they lived. The only time he returned to Namche was in the summer, when the tourists were gone—the monsoon season. Then, he and the other Sherpa families got together to sing Sherpa songs. I wondered if his children joined in.

Speaking of children, the begging and the demand for money by children and young people on the traditional trekking routes has now become infernal. But the changes are deeper than that. When I first went to Nepal, the local people seemed genuinely pleased that one had come from so far away just to see them and their country. This is no longer so. To give a personal example: On the last day of our Annapurna trek, I was walking along the shore of a lovely lake on my way to the town of Pokhara. I was immensely happy. We had just completed a long and difficult walk of some two hundred miles, and were about to go home. It had been a beautiful trip—one of the most beautiful I had ever been on. I was walking along the path in a state of grace. From the other direction came two young Nepalese men dressed sort of like "Teddy boys." I have no idea who they were. When they got close to me on the trail, one of them threw something at me—a piece of dirt, or something like that. I went ballistic. It was a violation of everything that I loved about Nepal. It was completely unprovoked—absolutely gratuitous. I was carrying an ice ax, and I was sorely tempted to use it. But then I asked myself how I would feel if a part of a country that I loved were invaded by an army of foreigners—all of whom had material goods that I could never hope to possess. Perhaps I would throw something, too.

In any event, it was during this 1986 trek that I began thinking my future treks in Nepal would have to be far enough off the beaten track that the number of other trekkers would be at a minimum. Indeed, in the 1990s, I completed two such treks—the first to the remote Dolpo region in western Nepal about which Peter Matthiessen had written his classic book, *The Snow Leopard*. This was in 1992, just after the area was opened, and was again an adventure with Jaccoux. We did not take the standard trekking route and did not see a single foreigner until we were on our way out. It brought me back to 1967. This region is now open to general trekking, but perhaps its remoteness will help preserve it. Then, in the fall of 1994, again with Jaccoux, I trekked from the Tibetan border down into the even more remote western district of Humla. I will describe this in a later chapter. But again, there were no foreigners whatsoever. So, for those who want to do so, it is still possible to find the wonderful ambience of the old Nepal.

But, while I was touring the Annapurnas in 1986, I kept running into people, mostly young, who had just returned from Tibet and who told me that traveling in Tibet, as far as they were concerned, was the same kind of pure adventure that traveling in Nepal had been in the early days of tourism. I had had a lifelong interest in Tibet, but with the Chinese occupation, I had given up any idea of actually going there. In fact, I had not realized that in 1985, the Chinese had begun issuing tourist visas for border crossings into Tibet from Nepal, an enterprise that got under way in earnest in 1986. Suddenly, here were all these people on the trail around the Annapurnas, fresh back from Tibet. When I returned to Kathmandu I decided to look into the matter. The more I did, the more I became intrigued about the prospects of visiting Tibet. There was, however, a practical problem. How could I possibly swing two trips to this part of the world in a single year—financially and in every other way? With no good answer, I returned to New York.

Then an extraordinary thing happened. In the late fall of 1986, I learned that I had been selected as one of the five winners of the Britannica Award for 1987, an award then given out by the Encyclopaedia Britannica for the "dissemination of learning"; in my case, for writing about science for the general public. Apart from a gold medal and a handsome monetary prize, the award contained a remarkable provision. The awardee was to give a lecture on any subject of his or her choosing, anywhere in the world, the expenses to be paid and the arrangements to be made by the Britannica. Immediately, a wild plan began to emerge in my mind. I would give my lecture at the Tribhuvan University in Kathmandu and use the occasion to go on to Tibet.

My first thought was that the people at the Britannica would consider the idea of lecturing in Kathmandu absolutely mad. On the contrary; nothing could have pleased them more. Here was the dissemination of knowledge on the grand scale. My second thought was that the officials at the Tribhuvan University would consider the idea of giving a lecture there on the history of modern cosmology—my putative subject—equally mad. On the contrary, nothing could have pleased *them* more. In fact, that very spring there was going to be a series of celebrations in Kathmandu to commemorate the fortieth year of United States–Nepalese relations, and my lecture would fit in with the rest of the events. Thus it was that in April of 1987 I found myself once again on my way to Nepal.

This trip was a very revealing one for me. In the first place, I had never been in the country in the premonsoon season. The leaden humidity and saunalike temperatures, at least during the day, sap one's energy. I cannot imagine how the business of the country gets done. In the second place, I made contact with the scientific establishment of Nepal. In 1967, I do not believe there *was* a scientific establishment. I recall suggesting to Dr. Upraity, the then-vice-chancellor of Tribhuvan University, that it might be a nice idea to hold an international physics conference in Nepal, since so many physicists climb and hike in the mountains. He told me that that might be nice sometime in the future, but that for the present, there was so little context that he didn't see that the local people could get anything out of such a conference. In fact, it took until the spring of 1989 before the first such conference was held. By the 1980s, an active group of physicists in the country created the Nepal Physical Society. Their goal was—given the very difficult economic conditions—to broaden the education of young people in physics and to try to make it relevant to the practical problems of the country. They publish a journal, and in one of the issues I ran across an article by Professor S. R. Chalise entitled, "The Growth of Physics in Nepal." Professor Chalise wrote, "We scientists of a poor country like Nepal, must always bear in mind that all our knowledge and talent must be directed to improve the lot of the common man. Science and technology must not be utilized to make life comfortable for a small minority. It is therefore very important that scientists take interest in the national issues, be involved in the total development process and direct their activities to those areas which will convince both the policy makers as well as the masses of their utility."

While I was in Kathmandu, an episode occurred that demonstrated, at least to me, how far along this scientific program had come. The incident began when it was alleged that some powdered milk sent from Poland to Bangladesh after the Chernobyl nuclear reactor accident contained dangerously high levels of radiation. The rumor then spread that this powdered milk had come to Nepal from Bangladesh. This caused a panic. Without powdered milk, there simply was not enough milk to meet Nepal's needs. Hence, people stopped using milk: a nutritional disaster in a country like Nepal, where so many people simply cannot get enough to eat. In 1982, King Birendra had established the Royal Nepal Academy of Science and Technology (RONAST), of which he is the chancellor. The function of RONAST is to coordinate all of the scientific development within the country. It has the capacity to mobilize scientists in Nepal to address an important matter such as—in this case—the determination of the radioactive content of milk. This was done. On April 29, 1987, *The Rising Nepal*, Kathmandu's English-language daily newspaper, commented in an editorial:

> *The government has done well to take into control all powder milk that has already arrived in the market and it has made clear that the milk will be released only when it is proven in tests that it is wholesome and safe for consumption. In order to conduct tests competently, a high level committee consisting of senior scientists and doctors has been set up by RONAST to ascertain the radioactivity level of milk and other foodstuffs and the panel is expected to*

submit its report within a week. It is very important that the maximum radioactivity level safe for the Nepalese people be determined; the level appropriate to any other country may not be proper to the Nepalese people [perhaps because of their low standard of nutrition] and hence the crucial need to independently ascertain the acceptable limits for the Nepalese taking into consideration all relevant factors. Second, the tests ought to be conducted in such a manner that no misunderstandings may develop among the consuming public. Since tests are conducted to determine the safety level, no compromise of any kind should be entertained and they should be such as to inspire the people.

By the time I left Nepal in May, the tests had been carried out, and it had been determined that no radioactive milk powder had been imported into Nepal. All of this work was performed by the country's indigenous scientists; this in a country that, until 1957, did not even have a university.

I gave two lectures while I was in Nepal. The first one, on the history of modern cosmology, the official Britannica Award lecture, was given in the the large lecture hall on the main campus of Tribhuvan University in Kirtipur. One can see the Himalayan range through the windows of the lecture hall. *Le tout Kathmandu* was there. I was very pleased to see such old friends as Father Moran, then in his eighties, but looking ageless. We discussed how much we both missed Boris. The lecture was a very formal affair, with the pomp that is special to elite social functions in that part of the world. I was given three lengthy welcoming speeches and a "concluding few words from the chair," delivered by Dr. Ratna Shumshere J. B. Rana, the vice-chancellor of RONAST, who congratulated me on my citations from the Upanishads. An Indian colleague of mine had been kind enough to point out some passages in the scripture that seemed to intimate the Big Bang cosmology.

The ambience of the second lecture was totally different and more familiar. The physics professors asked if I would give an informal lecture for students and faculty of physics, at the Amrit Science Campus in Kathmandu. This campus is located in the Thamel—the

Tibetan quarter. It is in a large, nondescript bulding, on a busy, extremely noisy, traffic-burdened street. I must have passed this building a hundred times without ever realizing what it was. The first problem I faced was deciding what to lecture on and at what level. I had been given several issues of the *Journal of the Nepal Physical Society,* and had noticed several popular articles on both cosmology and elementary particle physics—my specialities. I finally decided to lecture on something that would be an amplification of one of the articles I had read, and to make the level match that of the article. The inside of the building, when I got there the afternoon of my lecture, turned out to be a warren of ancient-looking classrooms and teaching laboratories. I was very moved watching a roomful of young Nepalese men and women making measurements designed to reveal some of the properties of light. They were so absorbed, like young science students everywhere, although with a minuscule fraction of the facilities taken for granted in our colleges and even high schools. As I watched them at work and during my lecture, I kept thinking of how far the country had come, but also how far it had to go.

All this took place on Thursday afternoon, April 30. On the morning of the first of May, I was on my way to Lhasa.

Nepalese village; the distinctive stupa is at right.

Ila Tsering, the author, Michele and Jaccoux at the summit of Kala Patar, Nepal. Mount Everest appears in the background.

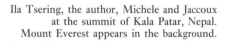

Ila Tsering and Claude Jaccoux at the summit of Kala Patar, Nepal.

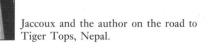

Jaccoux and the author on the road to Tiger Tops, Nepal.

Bernstein

Monks board a Royal Nepal Airlines plane.

Author crossing a typical Nepalese bridge.

Jaccoux

The author and Michele on the trail toward Everest. Nepal.

Jaccoux

The north face of Everest (at right), from Tibet.

Lamas dancing, Shigatse.

Lama dancing in lion mask, Shigatse, Tibet.

Pilgrims at the summit of
Drolma La, Tibet. Prayer flags
can be seen behind them.

The author searching his packs
at the airfield in Dolpo, Tibet.

The Potala Palace, Tibet.

Palace of the Gu–je Kings, en route to Kailas.

Tibetan ferryman, crossing the river
Yarlung Tsangpo.

Bhutanese and pack pony with Chomo Lhari.

George Bogle in formal Bhutanese clothes given to him by the Deb Raja, in an oil painting c. 1775 by Tilly Kettle.

Bernstein

Bhutanese boy.

Bernstein

Archery competition among
Bhutanese soldiers.

Bernstein

The road to Kailas.

Bernstein

Kailas.

Part Two

TIBET

6

The Past

When Alexandra David-Neel died in her home in Digne, France, on September 8, 1969, she was just six weeks short of her 101st birthday. Her father, Louis David, a French radical journalist, born in 1812, who had been forced into exile in Belgium, had not married until the age of forty. He then married a twenty-year-old Belgian school-teacher, Alexandrine Borghmans, and their only child, Alexandra, was born sixteen years later. The marriage was not a happy one and, as a child, Alexandra frequently thought of running away from her parents' home. Many years later she wrote, "Ever since I was five years old, a tiny precocious child of Paris, I wished to move out of the narrow limits in which, like all children my age, I was then kept. I craved to go beyond the garden gate, to follow the road that passed it by, and to set out for the Unknown. But, strangely enough, the 'Unknown' fancied by my baby mind always turned out to be a solitary spot where I could sit alone, with no one near, and as the road toward it was closed to me I sought solitude behind any bush, any mound of sand, that I could find in the garden, or wherever else my nurse took me."

She continued, "Later on, I never asked my parents for any gifts except books on travel, maps, and the privilege of being taken abroad during my school holidays. When a girl, I could remain for hours near a railway line, fascinated by the glittering rails and fancying many lands toward which they led. But again, my imagination did not evoke towns, buildings, gay crowds, or stately pageants; I dreamed of wild hills, immense deserted steppes and impassable landscapes of glaciers."

When Alexandra was five, her family moved from Paris to Brussels, where she spent the next fifteen years. She was enrolled in the Bois Fleuri, a Carmelite convent school. In 1889, after a brief sojourn in England, she returned to Brussels and took up the study of voice. Even as a young teenager she had shown signs of vocal ability. Not long afterward she left home for good, moving to Paris, where she found inexpensive lodgings in the Latin Quarter with a local branch of the Theosophical Society. It was at this time that she found what became her true vocation, in the Musée Guimet in Paris, a museum devoted to the Far East. She spent hours in a small reading room, near a statue of the Buddha, poring over books about the Orient. In her early twenties, she inherited a small amount of money from a grandmother, which she used to finance her first trip to Asia, a long sea voyage to India and Ceylon. The money spent, and with no prospects of financial aid from her family, she returned to Paris to earn her living. She was now a respected, well-trained singer, and for a period of several years around the turn of the century, she sang both opera and operetta, even traveling to Indochina with a comic opera touring company. In 1900, she found herself in Tunis, where she met her future husband, a distant cousin named Philippe-François Neel, a thirty-nine-year-old railway engineer who worked in North Africa. They were married in 1904 but, although they remained married until his death in 1941, they barely saw each other. Nonetheless, Alexandria regarded "Mouchy"—her nickname for her husband—as her closest friend and staunchest supporter.

Almost from her wedding day, Alexandra made it clear that she did not intend to have a conventional marriage. There is no indication that she and Philippe ever had sexual relations. A recent biography, *Forbidden Journey,* written by Barbara and Michael Foster, credits Alexandra with a vivid sex life, including premarital relations with Philippe. I remain skeptical. I do not think the Fosters make a convincing case. While Philippe continued to support her financially to some degree, she began an independent career as a journalist, living mostly in Paris and London, occasionally giving lectures in comparative literature. Soon after they were married, Philippe offered her a trip back to Asia, but it was not until 1911 that she finally went. The trip lasted fourteen years. At that time the thirteenth Dalai Lama (the present Dalai Lama is the fourteenth) had, for political reasons, sought temporary refuge with the British in India, and Alexandra got the notion that she would travel to Darjeeling to interview him for a French publication. As it happened, the thirty-seven-year-old thirteenth Dalai Lama was a man of considerable sophistication who, unlike his predecessors, had had a good deal of contact with Europeans. Thus, Alexandra became the first western woman ever to be granted a private audience with any Dalai Lama. This interview, and the circumstances surrounding it, transformed her life. She loved the atmosphere of the Himalayan frontier towns like Darjeeling, and she met a wide range of people, including, for the first time, Tibetans. She was greatly taken by the snow-covered mountains that float above these towns like some sort of distant promise. The Dalai Lama was very impressed by her general knowledge of Buddhist doctrine, and his final piece of advice to her was to learn Tibetan.

At about this time she also met, and favorably impressed, Sidkeong Tulka, the crown prince of Sikkim, who invited her to visit Gangtok, the Sikkimese capital, a several days' horseback ride. The prince was also a lama, and the two of them spent hours discussing the nuances of Tibetan Buddhism. After a brief and not very happy sojourn in Benares, she accepted the prince's offer of a small apartment in a monastery near Gangtok. Here she acquired a Tibetan tutor and, at age forty-four, began her study of Tibetan, a language she became fluent in. In 1914, after the death of his father, Sidkeong became ruler of Sikkim. He gave Alexandra carte blanche to wander as she pleased in his country, accompanied only by an interpreter. She did manage to acquire, as an additional companion, a fifteen-year-old Sikkimese boy, who had entered one of the monasteries as a novice. His name was Yongden and, from 1914 until his death in 1955, he traveled with her constantly. Indeed, in 1925, the uncharacteristically recalcitrant Philippe agreed to sign papers that made Yongden their adopted son. Not long after she had taken on Yongden as part of her retinue, she decided to visit Tibet. By this time, the thirteenth Dalai Lama had returned to Lhasa, the capital city, and Tibet had, characteristically, once again closed its borders to foreigners. For Alexandra, a large part of the appeal of visiting it lay in the fact that, for a foreigner, and especially for a woman, Tibet was forbidden terrain.

In 1916, Alexandra made her first visit. She, Yongden, and a monk she had hired to serve as a guide, all on horseback and accompanied by baggage-laden mules, crossed the Sikkimese border into Tibet, with no permission, and proceeded to the second-largest city in the country, Shigatse, some five hundred miles southwest of Lhasa. Then, as now, Shigatse was the seat of the Tashi, or Panchen, Lama. In the Tibetan hierarchy, at least until the Chinese occupied the country in 1959, the Dalai Lama was the supreme secular as well as religious authority, while the Panchen Lama was meant to be Tibet's spiritual symbol. Traditionally, he presided over the monastery of Tashilhunpo near Shigatse; "a mass of white buildings," wrote Neel, "crowned with golden roofs that reflected the last dim rays of the sun." The Panchen Lama, as well as his mother, received Alexandra most cordially, and after hours of talk with him she was awarded the red robe of a graduate lama—a considerable honor. Afterward, she decided to return to India, where she received the unpleasant news that she was being fined and expelled from the country for having illegally crossed the border into Tibet. This made her all the more determined to visit Lhasa, but now the only route open to her was through China. In 1917, she arrived in Beijing with Yongden and set out on a seven-month, two-thousand-mile journey to the Kumbum monastery in Mongolia, where she and Yongden spent the next three years. She then began a series of nomadic trips along the frontiers of Tibet, until, in 1923, at the age of fifty-five, she began the adventure of her life—a journey to Lhasa.

Alexandra David-Neel's great travel book, *My Journey to Lhasa,* was written in English, despite the fact that her mother tongue was French, and first published in 1927 by Harper and Brothers. This must certainly have been a reflection of the favorable royalty terms that she extracted from an American, as opposed to a European, publisher. In a biographical sketch in the book *On Top of the World,* about women explorers in Tibet, Luree Miller reported that after Neel had passed her hundredth birthday, her English publisher, John Robinson, paid her a visit in her home in France. Miller wrote, "He expected to find a wise old woman meditating and preparing for her death. Instead he found a canny bargainer familiar with every clause and percentage of her contracts. She wanted to negotiate with him to forgo the royalties on the translations of her books and get instead a big advance immediately." And this when she was a *hundred!*

Photographs of her in her late eighties show her as a formidable white-haired lady. An earlier photo, taken during her stay in Tibet and entitled, *Madame Alexandra David-Neel as the guest of the Tashi Lama's mother at the private dwelling of the Tashi Lama in the Tashil-hunpo's Monastery,* shows Alexandra in a robe and a Tibetan hat, with what appear to be wings on it, towering over the Tashi Lama's mother and staring at the camera with grim determination. Another, entitled *Madame Alexandra David-Neel with two Tibetan ladies,* shows her again robed but wearing an enormous Tibetan good-luck necklace. The "ladies" are wearing costumes that pale by comparison. My favorite shows Alexandra and Yongden in robes, Yongden wearing eyeglasses—rare in that part of the world—with a pleasant, intelligent-looking face, while Alexandra reveals a trace of a smile.

Her 1923–1924 trip to Lhasa with Yongden all but defies comprehension. Their route, a giant, looping detour away from the direct caravan route from Beijing to Lhasa, began in the Gobi Desert. For seven months, they traveled southwest, until they reached the Tibetan border. It was there that the *real* trip began. Up to this point, there had been no need for disguise, and Alexandra and Yongden had been able to use porters. Now, however, they were proposing to enter Tibet, moving westward toward Lhasa, for which they had no permission. Alexandra's notion was that they should travel away from the trade routes, disguised as a pilgrim lama—Yongden–and his Tibetan mother. To this end, she and Yongden

> *... discarded the only pieces of spare clothing we had kept. Nothing was now left to us except the clothes we were wearing. We had not even a blanket, although we knew that, during winter, we should have to cross high, snowy ranges, passes of over 18,000 feet. ... We*

had only one aluminum pot, which was our kettle, teapot and saucepan, all in one. There was also one lama wooden bowl for Yongden, an aluminum bowl for myself, two spoons, and a Chinese travelling case containing one long knife and chopsticks, which could be hung by the belt. That was all. We did not intend to indulge in refined cooking. Our meals were to be those of the common Tibetan travellers: that is to say, tsampa [a barley flour, which is the staple of the Tibetan diet] mixed with buttered tea, or eaten nearly dry, kneaded with butter. When circumstances would allow, we would make soup. Forks were useless with such a diet, and even our two cheap spoons could not be produced freely, as they were of a foreign pattern such as only affluent Tibetans possess. Arjopas [pilgrims traveling on foot and often begging their food], as we pretended to be, have none.

Alexandra attempted to disguise herself. She wore a hairpiece made out of jet black yak hair and, "in order to match that color I rubbed a wet stick of Chinese ink on my own brown hair. I hung large earrings on my ears, and they altered my appearance. Finally I powdered my face with a mixture of cocoa and crushed charcoal to obtain a dark complexion. The 'make-up' was rather strange, but suppliers to the theatrical trade, from whom I could have obtained better ingredients, have not yet opened branches in the Tibetan wilds!" Hidden away beneath her robes, she carried a small compass, some maps, a watch, some gold and silver, and a revolver. Alexandra would certainly have used the latter if necessary—the Tibetan trade routes were swarming with bandits. On an earlier trip, she had not hesitated to break up a fight involving armed men, using a bullwhip. But displaying any of these things would have immediately revealed that she was a *philing,* "foreigner," and the news would very quickly have reached the authorities, who would have thrown her out of the country—or worse.

When possible, Alexandra and Yongden traveled at night to avoid people. Sometimes, to beg food—they were afraid to buy any, since they were supposed to be moneyless pilgrims—they were forced to spend the night in villages. This experience gave Alexandra a unique insight into the way common Tibetans lived, but it had its drawbacks. As she wrote, "In a country where everything is done in public, down to the most intimate personal acts, I was forced to affect peculiar local customs which embarrassed me terribly."

One local custom that she practiced was something that she had learned in her years in the monastery. Known as *thumo reskiang,* it is the apparent ability of Tibetan mystics to control their body temperature through a kind of special meditation, and, in particular, to will themselves into feeling warm. She wrote that, during one winter, while living at thirteen thousand feet, she deliberately spent five months dressed in nothing but a thin cotton garment, practicing the thumo discipline. On one bitterly cold night during their trip, Alexandra and Yongden discovered that the flint and steel they had been using to make fires had gotten wet and useless. Alexandra sent Yongden to collect twigs and dried yak dung, a common fuel in Tibet, while she put herself into a thumo trance with the wet flint and steel next to her body. By the time Yongden returned, she wrote, she had dried the fire-lighting materials and had a small fire going. In her book, and in a sequel, *Magic and Mystery in Tibet,* these matters are described straightforwardly, with no apologies to the skeptical.

As far as I am concerned, the greatest mystery of all was her ability to travel for hundreds of miles on foot, and in the dead of winter, in this most austere land. Once one sets foot on the Tibetan plateau, it is difficult to find anyplace that is much less than ten thousand feet in altitude. Lhasa is at 11,830 feet, and Shigatse at 12,800 feet. Today, one can drive in a matter of hours from the Nepalese border, a few thousand feet above sea level, to a sixteen-thousand-foot-high plateau from which a vast sweep of the Himalayan range, rising to the summit of Mount Everest, can be seen to the south. Most of Tibet is above fifteen thousand feet. Winds sweep across the lunar surface of this great plain and, at first sight, one's impression is that nothing can possibly grow there. Nonetheless, great herds of yak and sheep roam these plains, along with the odd enormous jackrabbit loping along, and one is led to wonder whether these remarkable animals have found a way of metabolizing rocks. It was not difficult to keep unwanted foreigners out of Tibet: All one had to do was to deny them permission to buy food in the widely spaced villages where any was available. In this sere and naked land, in the dead of winter, Alexandra and Yongden marched day after day west toward Lhasa.

In the late winter of 1924, some four months after they had entered Tibet, they got their first view of the Potala, the fortress-cathedral home of the Dalai Lama, then the administrative nerve center of Tibet. The massive structure, set high on a hill, seems to float in midair. Alexandra became the first European woman to see it. She wrote, "As we advanced the Potala grew larger and larger. Now we could discern the elegant outlines of its many golden roofs. They glittered in the blue sky, sparks seeming to spring from their sharp upturned corners, as if the whole castle, the glory of Tibet, had been crowned with flames." She decided that she would continue with her disguise to try to explore Lhasa. As she wrote,

I was in Lhasa. No doubt I could be proud of my victory, but the struggle, with cunning and trickery as weapons, was not yet over. I was in Lhasa and now the problem was to stay there. Although I had endeavored to reach the Tibetan capital rather because I had been challenged than out of any real desire to see it, now that I stood on the forbidden ground at the cost of so much hardship and danger, I meant to enjoy myself in all possible ways. I should really have felt ashamed of myself had I been caught, locked up somewhere, and taken back to the border, having only had a superficial and brief glance at the exterior of the palaces and temples. This should not be! No! I would climb to the top of the Potala itself; I would visit the most famous shrines in the vicinity of Lhasa, and I would witness the religious ceremonies, the races, and the pageants of the New Year festival. [The Tibetan new year usually begins in February, although some years it begins in March. Of the vagaries of the Tibetan calendar, more later.] *All sights, all things which are Lhasa's own beauty and peculiarity would have to be seen by the lone woman explorer who had had the nerve to come to them from afar, the first of her sex. It was my well-won reward after the trials on the road and the vexations by which for several years various officials had*

endeavored to prevent my wanderings in Tibet. This time I intended
that nobody should deprive me of it.

For two months, Alexandra and Yongden wandered undetected
around Lhasa and its environs. She then decided that she would
leave the country, traveling southward into British India. Since the
Tibetan authorities had little interest in people *leaving* Lhasa, she
left it in style: riding horseback, accompanied by Yongden and a
servant. In August of 1924, she arrived at the town of Gyantse, then
the third largest in Tibet and, for reasons I will explain later, the
headquarters of a resident British trade agent. The usual trade
route from Tibet to India passed through Gyantse. The astonished
British Resident, David Macdonald, received her and gave her
permission to stay in the mission's rest house. Although Macdonald
was disappointed that Alexandra was not more forthcoming with
details of her trip—she was saving the better anecdotes for her
book—he was gracious enough to provide her with a brief hand-
written document:

To all Whom it May Concern

> *This is to certify that Madame Alexandra David-Neel visited*
> *at Gyantse while she came through Lhasa from Eastern Tibet.*
> *D. Macdonald 21/8/24*
> *British Trade Agent*
> *Yatung, Tibet*

After a sojourn in Sikkim and India, Alexandra decided to return
to France with the intention of resuming—in some sense or other—
her marriage with Philippe. However, he balked at the idea of her
moving in with him with her vast collection of books on Asia, to say
nothing of Yongden, and after a brief reunion in France he returned
to Africa. They never made any further attempt to live together,
although Philippe generously provided money for her, to say nothing
of storing her Tibetan artifacts, until in 1927, with his help, she
purchased a house on a hill in the south of France near Digne. She
named it Samten Dzong, Tibetan for "Fortress of Meditation," and

lived in it, when she was in France, for the rest of her life, sharing it with Yongden until his death in 1955. Her books and articles brought her fame, which she enjoyed immensely. She remained tough, lucid, and shrewd into her hundredth year. It was typical of her that, when she was eighty, she made a deal with the community of Digne, agreeing to bequeath to it the posthumous royalties on her books, provided the community would exempt her from taxes for the rest of her life. It was unlikely that anyone expected her to live for another twenty years.

While Alexandra David-Neel was the first western woman to enter Lhasa, she was not the first western woman to enter Tibet. Luree Miller's book, *On Top of the World,* describes the exploration of Tibet in the late nineteenth and early twentieth centuries by women. In 1872, Elizabeth Sarah Mazuchelli—"Nina"—the wife of a British army chaplain stationed in India, was carried in a device called a Barielly dandy, a sort of portable armchair, in the general direction of Tibet, followed by her reluctant husband, Francis. In *My Journey to Lhasa,* Alexandra makes no mention of her predecessors, including the redoubtable Annie Taylor, who in 1892 became the first European woman to actually enter Tibet. Annie Taylor was an English-born missionary stationed in China. In 1887, she made her way to the Kumbum monastery in Mongolia, the very place where, thirty years later, Alexandra was to spend three years studying. Taylor presented a large number of biblical text cards, written in Tibetan, to the bemused monks.

During her sojourn at Kumbum, Annie acquired a liking for the Tibetans who were studying there, and gradually she conceived a plan to bring the Word to the interior of Tibet—that is, to travel to Lhasa. Like Alexandra David-Neel, Annie took on a young boy, a Tibetan from Lhasa named Pontso, who became her traveling companion for the next twenty years. Luree Miller reported that, one evening in March of 1891, while Annie was in Darjeeling, she heard a voice commanding her to go to China, as a preliminary to entering Tibet. In time she assembled a group of five Asians, including Pontso, and six horses, and this unlikely caravan set off from Tauchau in China a year later to make a dash for Lhasa. Within days, they were beset by robbers, who made off with nearly everything, including four of the horses and two of the Asians. Nonetheless, she continued, sleeping in the open. On Christmas Day, 1892, she reported in her diary that she had stumbled upon an old campsite with plenty of yak dung for fuel. She wrote, "We are resting in our pleasant hiding place. A nice Christmas Day, the sun shining brightly. I had fellowship in spirit with friends all over the world. Quite safe here with Jesus." However, on January 3, 1893, she was arrested and ordered to leave the country by the same route that she had used when entering. As it happened, she was then only three days' march from Lhasa. Arguing that, if she were forced to repeat her march without an escort, she would die on the road, she managed to persuade the authorities to give her ten soldiers to accompany her for eleven days, after which she was on her own. In April, she arrived back in China, having made a thirteen-hundred-mile round trip in seven months. Eventually, Annie Taylor settled in Gangtok, the capital of Sikkim, always with an eye to returning to Tibet. But sometime after 1907—the precise date is not known—she returned to England and, historically speaking, vanished.

Besides their extraordinary courage and stamina, these women had in common the notion that they were visiting, or attempting to visit, a proper country, Tibet, with a well-defined boundary and government. The historical chronology of how this came about is made somewhat complicated by the peculiarities of dates in the traditional Tibetan calendar. Tibetans employ a lunar calendar, which would in theory assign to each month 29 ½ days. Since the solar year contains 365 ¼ days, each lunar year—twelve lunar months—is 11 days too short. To make up for this, every three years the Tibetans added a month. However, like a wild card in a poker game, the extra month could be placed anywhere in the Tibetan calendar year, the position being determined by an astrological forecast indicating which spot would bring luck. Actually, even this is a slight oversimplification. In practice, Tibetans round off the lunar month to exactly thirty days, but then they go ahead and add the extra month every three years anyway. To make up the difference, certain days of the month—again decided by the official astrologer—are simply eliminated, or, if some days are thought to be particularly fortunate, they may be doubled. At the end of each year, the official astrologer presents the calendar for the following year. Until then, there is no future calendar. The new year begins in February, except in those years that begin following an added month, when the year begins in March. Hence, when modern historical writers on Tibet indicate that some event occurred in, say, April of A.D. 619, it gives one pause.

The days of the Tibetan week—seven in number—are named after the sun, the moon, and the five visible planets: Mars, Mercury, Jupiter, Venus, and Saturn. *Sa* is the Tibetan word for "planet," and the seven days are thus named, in order: *Sa Nyima, Sa Da-wa, Sa Mik-mar, Sa Lhak-pa, Sa Phur-bu, Sa Pa-sang, and Sa Pen-pa.* Until the eleventh century, a twelve-year calendar cycle was used, each year being named after one of the following animals: mouse, ox, tiger, hare, dragon, serpent, horse, sheep, ape, bird, dog, and hog. In the year A.D. 1027— one hopes the historians have made the correct conversion—the Tibetans began a sixty-year cycle, as advocated in the Kalacakra-Tan-tra—a Sanskrit religious text that was translated into Tibetan in that year. To make up the sixty-year cycle, the twelve animals are com-bined with five elements: wood, fire, earth, iron, and water. Thus, the years have colorful names like Fire-Mouse or Iron-Ape. Tibetan historical documents contain phrases like "On the thirteenth day of the eighth month of the Water-Tiger year. . . ." One is reminded of what Alfonso X of Castile said when the notion of planetary epicycles was explained to him: "If the Lord Almighty had consulted me before embarking upon the Creation, I should have recommended some-thing simpler."

Assuming the historians have calculated the conversion correctly, the first date in modern Tibetan history is A.D. 617, the year that Songtsen Gampo, who can be regarded as the founder of the modern Tibetan state, was born. Prior to that, there had lived a homogeneous race of people with black hair, brown eyes, and brown skin, and often strongly resembling Native Americans, in a land that was variously called Bod (by the Tibetans), Bhot (by the Indians), Tobet (by the Mongols), and Tufan (by the Chinese). They practiced a shamanistic religion called Bon (pronounced *Po*), one of whose symbols was a reversed swastika, which can still be found as a decoration in some of the monasteries. They spoke a Tibeto-Burman language, with roots in both Chinese and Thai, that had no written counterpart. The country, a collection of fiefdoms, had no national capital. It was apparently not uncommon for the son of a local ruler to take over for his father at age thirteen. One would imagine that the average life span of these people was in the late twenties or early thirties.

Apparently, Songtsen Gampo became ruler of his local domain at thirteen. He must have been a remarkable man. He succeeded in unifying Tibet, and established Lhasa as its national capital. He sent one of his ministers, Thon-mi Sam-bhota, to India to devise a script to use for written Tibetan. A version of Kashmiri Sanskrit was chosen and remains in use. People who try to learn Tibetan say that it is difficult to make the oral and written languages correspond, because the language is so unphonetic. This surely has to do with the artificial way in which the written language was grafted onto the spoken one.[1] Thon-mi Sam-bhota also brought back Buddhism from India and Nepal and this, eventually, was grafted onto Bon, to produce the special form of Tantric Buddhism still practiced in Tibet.

Songtsen Gampo had at least two wives, one Nepalese, one Chinese. These wives, who have become canonized in the Buddhist tradition as the Green and White Taras, are credited with completing his conversion to Buddhism. The Chinese wife—the White Tara—was, according to Tibetan historians, a sort of war prize. During much of its early history, Tibet more than held its own militarily against its

1. My own knowledge of Tibetan, meager as it is, has been acquired by reading such books as *A Cultural History of Tibet*, by David Snellgrove and Hugh M. Richardson. I have therefore tried to adopt the spelling of Tibetan words as they are used in this book. To give some notion of what is involved, the letters *g, d, b, m, r, s*, and *l*, and the apostrophe ('), can appear at the beginning of words and are not pronounced. Thus, as an example, the systemization of the Buddhist texts that was done around the fourteenth century, which can be transliterated into English as *bs Tan'-gyur*, or "Translation of the Treatises," is pronounced *Tenjur*. (Incidentally, the same word is, to take another source, transliterated as *Tengyur* in Victor Chan's *Tibetan Handbook*. Looking up these terms in various texts can send the mind reeling.) Alexandra David-Neel used the spelling *thumo* for yogic power to raise one's body temperature. The word is pronounced *tumo*. In my next life, I would like to return as a master of the Tibetan language. In this one, I beg the indulgence of readers more knowledgeable than I for inconsistencies in these transliterated spellings.

neighbors, including China and Nepal. According to tradition, both wives brought, as part of their marriage dowries, statues of the Buddha, and each was given a newly constructed temple, built around her statue. The White Tara's temple was built in Lhasa over a small lake that the Tibetans filled in with logs and earth. This temple, now known as the Jokhang, still stands, having been restored many times, most recently after its desecration in the late 1960s by the Red Guard in the course of China's Cultural Revolution. At this point, a visitor to the Jokhang would be hard put to say which of the statues and frescoes are the originals and which are total or partial restorations. Many Tibetans say that the statue given to Songtsen Gampo by the White Tara still stands in its original form. This statue, in the heart of the Jokhang, is the most sacred object of Tibetan Buddhism.

After the death of Songtsen Gampo, his descendants ruled until the end of the ninth century, when Tibet became a chaos of local chiefs and religious leaders, each with his own domain. In the early thirteenth century, the Mongols came to dominate Tibet. The Tibetans, separately or united, were no match for the Mongols, and in 1207 they worked out an arrangement with Genghis Khan according to which they agreed to pay a certain amount of tribute to him, in return for being left alone. This agreement was honored until Genghis Khan's death twenty years later, after which the Tibetans stopped paying ransom. In 1240, however, Godan, the grandson of Genghis, amassed an army, which invaded Tibet, looting several towns and villages. Then Godan did a very strange thing, as recounted by the Tibetan diplomat and historian Tsepon W. D. Shakabpa in his book *Tibet: A Political History*. Godan decided that he needed instruction in the Buddhist doctrine, and, having learned that the most religiously learned man in Tibet was Kunga Gyaltsen, the abbot of the Sakya monastery in eastern Tibet, he wrote the following remarkable letter, translated and quoted in Mr. Shakabpa's book. It reads:

> I, the most powerful and prosperous Prince Godan, wish to inform the Sakya Pandita, Kunga Gyaltsen, that we need a lama to advise my ignorant people on how to conduct themselves morally and spiritually.
>
> I need someone to pray for the welfare of my deceased parents, to

whom I am deeply grateful.

I have been pondering this problem for some time, and after much consideration, have decided that you are the only person suitable for the task. As you are the only lama I have chosen, I will not accept any excuse on account of your age or the rigors of the journey.

The Lord Buddha gave his life for all living beings. Would you not therefore, be denying your faith, if you tried to avoid this duty of yours? It would, of course, be easy for me to send a large body of troops to bring you here; but in so doing, harm and unhappiness might be brought to many innocent living beings. In the interest of the Buddha's faith and the welfare of all living creatures, I suggest you come to us immediately.

As a favor to you, I shall be very kind to those monks who are now living on the west side of the sun. . . .

This was hardly an offer that the Sakya Pandita was in a position to refuse. And so he became religious tutor to Godan. As Mr. Shakabpa put it, "Sakya Pandita instructed Godan in the teachings of the Buddha and even persuaded him from throwing large numbers of Chinese into the nearby river," a method used by the Mongols to keep down the population. With the Sakya Pandita, there began a relationship between the Mongol rulers and certain lamas of Tibet, who were provided protection and patronage as a reward for religious counseling. It was just this relationship that became the foundation of the Tibetan theocratic state. Kublai Khan, Godan's son, provided civil muscle for the theocratic rule of the Sakya Pandita's nephew, Phagpa, and the matter was formalized in the late sixteenth century when Altan Khan created the institution of the Dalai Lama. The great monastery of Tashilhunpo, near Shigatse, was founded in 1447 by a monk named Gedun Truppa. It eventually housed three thousand monks. After Gedun Truppa died, his successor, Gedun Gyatso, who was born a year after Gedun Truppa's death, was chosen because he was thought to be Gedun Truppa's reincarnation. The notion of successive religious figures being reincarnations of their predecessors is a tenet of Tibetan Buddhism that appears to have evolved from the Bon belief in divine kingship. The abbots of certain important monasteries in Tibet, as well as certain monasteries in Nepal and elsewhere, are taken to be reincarnations.

When Gedun Gyatso died, he, in turn, was succeeded by a reincarnation named Sonam Gyatso. Sonam Gyatso became the religious tutor to Altan Khan and, indeed, converted the khan to Buddhism. Out of gratitude, the khan in 1578 conferred the title of Tale (Dalai), Mongolian for "Ocean," implying that Sonam Gyatso's knowledge was as deep as the ocean. Since Sonam Gyatso was the third incarnation of Gedun Truppa, he became, therefore, the third Dalai Lama. The present Dalai Lama, Tenzin Gyatso, is the fourteenth. When referring to any of his predecessors, the present Dalai Lama uses the term, "The previous body."

For the third and fourth Dalai Lamas, the title was little more than an honorific. This changed with the revelation of the fifth—the Great Fifth, as he is known—Lozang Gyatso, in 1622. The Mongol ruler then was Gushri Khan, and on the fifth day of the fourth month of the Water-Horse year—corresponding to year 2186 after the death of Buddha, that is, A.D. 1642—in a ceremony in Shigatse, he conferred the spiritual and temporal power to rule Tibet onto the Dalai Lama, who then designated Lhasa as his capital. Three years later, the Great Fifth ordered the beginning of the construction of the Potala, his palace, one of the architectural marvels of the world. (It was rumored to be scheduled for destruction by the Red Guard, but, again according to rumor, was saved by the intervention of Chou En-lai and the regular Chinese army.)

The Potala is really two palaces—the White Palace, completed during the Great Fifth's lifetime, and the Red Palace, completed after his death. The whole structure encompasses over a thousand rooms. Its thirteen stories are set on a hill that rises a thousand feet above Lhasa. As Alexandra David-Neel discovered, and as anyone who has ever visited Lhasa can confirm, it is the first thing one sees as one approaches the city, and it is visible from everywhere in Lhasa. The remains of eight Dalai Lamas are entombed there in golden stupas, or rounded tombs. The stupa of the Great Fifth rises more than three stories. It is built of sandalwood and covered with over eight thousand pounds of gold.

The Dalai Lama's rule is not hereditary in the usual sense of the term. Dalai Lamas belong to the Gelugpa, or "Yellow Hat" (as opposed to the "Red Hat"), Buddhist sect, in which the lamas are celibate. A Dalai Lama can come from any segment of Tibetan society. The present Dalai Lama, who was born in 1935, came, for example, from a peasant family from the Amdo region of Tibet, which is now part of the Chinese province of Tsinghai. The selection process by which Dalai Lamas are chosen is mysterious. Heinrich Harrer, the Austrian alpinist who was interned by the British in India just before the Second World War, and who escaped by walking into Tibet—and later wrote his classic *Seven Years in Tibet*—became a kind of tutor to the present Dalai Lama. He asked the Dalai Lama how he had been discovered. The Dalai Lama himself, Harrer reported, did not remember the event, but he put Harrer in touch with the then–commander-in-chief of the Tibetan army, Dzaza Kunsangtse. Kunsangtse recalled that, before the thirteenth Dalai Lama, the present Dalai Lama's predecessor, died in 1933, he gave "intimations" regarding his rebirth. Harrer wrote, "After his death, the body sat in state in the Potala in traditional Buddha-posture looking towards the south. One morning it was noticed that his head was turned to the east. The State Oracle was straightway consulted, and while in his trance the monk Oracle threw a white scarf in the direction of the rising sun. But for two years nothing more definite was indicated." In the meanwhile, Tibet was ruled by a regent who had been appointed by the previous Dalai Lama.

Indeed, this was a common practice. It had been recognized that a Dalai Lama, a child, would be unable to govern for many years, so that an interregnum regent would be necessary. In fact, during much of the recent history of Tibet, the country has been really ruled by a regent. As Hugh M. Richardson (Richardson served for nine years in Lhasa as the head of the British mission, until the takeover by the Chinese) points out in his book *Tibet and Its History,* during the 120 years between the death of the seventh Dalai Lama in 1757 and the birth of the thirteenth Dalai Lama in 1876, actual authority was held by a Dalai Lama for only 7 years. During this period, only the eighth Dalai Lama reached maturity—the others dying mysteriously before they could take power from the regent—and the eighth Dalai Lama effectively abdicated to his regent.

It was the responsibility of the regent to locate the reincarnate of the thirteenth Dalai Lama. He went on a pilgrimage to a lake, and on its surface, he reported, saw a vision of a three-storied monastery near which stood, in Harrer's words, "a little Chinese peasant house with carved gables." It is a misconception that the reincarnate must have been born at the instant of the Dalai Lama's death. Indeed, in principle, years may pass. In this case, the serious search did not begin until 1937, four years after the death of the thirteenth Dalai Lama. By this time, the matter had become the urgent concern of the entire country, since without a Dalai Lama Tibetans then, as now, felt bereft of divine protection. One of the search parties went to Amdo and there found the house with the carved gables near a three-storied monastery with golden roofs. What happened next was described by Harrer: "Full of excitement [the search party] dressed themselves in the clothes of their servants. This maneuver is customary during these searches, for persons dressed as high officials attract too much attention and find it hard to get in touch with the people. The servants, dressed in the garments of their masters, were taken to the best rooms while the disguised monks went into the kitchen, where it was likely they would find the children of the house."

Harrer went on:

As soon as they entered the house, they felt sure they would find the Holy Child in it, and they waited tensely to see what would happen. And sure enough, a two-year-old boy came running to meet them and seized the skirts of the Lama, who wore around his neck the rosary of the thirteenth Dalai Lama. Unabashed the child cried, "Sera Lama, Sera Lama!" It was already a matter of wonder that the infant recognized a lama in the garb of a servant and that he said that he came from the Monastery of Sera—which was the case. Then the boy grasped the rosary and tugged at it till the Lama gave it to him; thereupon he hung it around his own neck. The noble searchers found it hard not to throw themselves on the ground before the child, as they no longer had any doubt. They had found the Incarnation.

For reasons involving the intricate question of Chinese "suzerainty" over Tibet, which I will discuss later, that part of the Amdo
region had a Chinese governor whose permission had to be sought
before the emigration of the child was allowed. The Chinese governor
charged the Tibetan government the equivalent of $92,600, an enor-
mous sum by Tibetan standards, to allow the departure of the child.
It was only after he was well within Tibetan territory that it was
publicly announced that the fourteenth Dalai Lama had been discovered. The actual coronation of the child as a Dalai Lama, with full
administrative and religious authority, did not take place until 1940.
In the meanwhile, the young incarnate had impressed everyone with
his intelligence and serene religious vocation. In this sense, he was
quite a contrast to the successor of the Great Fifth, the sixth Dalai
Lama, who was known as a poet and a womanizer and whose poems
arc still recited and sung in Tibet.

Alexandra David-Neel notwithstanding, Tibet seems to have attracted few westerners. Even Marco Polo never visited Tibet. The first
known western visitor was a religious missionary, the Jesuit John
Grueber, who arrived in 1661. He was followed by the Capuchins,
Father Giuseppe d'Ascoli and François de Tours, who arrived in the
capital in 1707. The Capuchins established a mission, which was
closed in 1745. They left behind a bell inscribed TE DEUM LAUDAMUS,
which hung for at least two centuries in the Jokhang palace above the
passageway leading to the White Tara's statue of the Buddha. The
bell seems to have disappeared. I made a considerable effort to find it
when I visited the Jokhang in May of 1987. One of the older monks
identified a bell, which indeed looked very different from the other
bells hanging in the passageway. Much to the amusement of a line of
Tibetans waiting to worship at the statue, I clambered around with a
flashlight, trying, unsuccessfully, to find the Latin inscription. Heinrich Harrer, in the successor volume to *Seven Years in Tibet, Return to
Tibet,* reports that he, too, made an attempt to find the bell, and was
told that it was locked up with other historical relics. One hopes that
it is safe.

By the eighteenth century, with the firm implantation in India of
the British East India Company—the "United Company of Mer-

chants trading in the East Indies," to give it its full name—it was inevitable that some contact would be made between the Tibetans and the British. This occurred thanks to the Panchen Lama. The institution of the Panchen Lama was established by the fifth Dalai Lama, the Great Fifth. He had a beloved teacher, Lobzang Chokyi Gyaltsen, whom he appointed to be the abbot of the Tashilhunpo monastery near Shigatse. Additionally, he pronounced that this abbot would continue to undergo reincarnation, with the title of Panchen Lama. The Panchen Lamas were meant to occupy themselves with things of the spirit. The Dalai Lama, as both spiritual and temporal leader of the country, could not devote himself fully to spiritual contemplation and study, while the Panchen, free of earthly cares, could. Since the Dalai Lamas after the Great Fifth rarely ruled the country, the Panchen Lama became a second (or third, if one counts the regent) center of political power. The Panchen often became, and still is, a tool of the Chinese in their attempts to reduce the authority of the Dalai Lama, and to widen their influence in Tibet. Indeed, the most recent Panchen Lama, who died in 1989 under suspicious circumstances—which I will discuss later—lived in Beijing, visiting Tibet from time to time. Some Tibetans regarded him as a quisling who sold out his country to the Chinese, while others gave him credit for engineering whatever occasional liberalization there has been in Tibet since the occupation.

On March 29, 1774, Warren Hastings, the governor-general of Bengal, received a remarkable letter from the Panchen Lama. Hastings had just sent a small army in pursuit of some Bhutanis who had attempted to unseat the raja of Cooch Behar in Bengal. Having discharged its duty, the army had continued moving northward, into the Bhutanese hills close to the Tibetan border. At that point, the Panchen Lama wrote,

Having been informed by travellers from your quarter of your exalted fame and reputation, my heart, like the blossom of spring, abounds with gaiety, gladness and joy; praise that the star of your fortune is in its ascension; praise that happiness and ease are the surrounding attendants of myself and family. Neither to molest nor persecute is my aim; it is even characteristic of my sect to deprive ourselves of the necessary refreshment of sleep, should an injury be done to a single individual. But in justice and humanity I am informed you far surpass us. May you ever adorn the seat of justice and power, that mankind under the shadow of your bosom, enjoy the blessings of happiness and ease.

Contrast this with the Panchen's remarks about the ruler of Bhutan, one Deb Judhur: "As he is of a rude and ignorant race (Past times are not destitute of instances of the like misconduct, which his own avarice tempted him to commit.) it is not unlikely that he has now renewed those instances; and the ravages and plunder which he may have committed of the skirts of Bengal and Bahar provinces have given you provocation to send your vindictive army against him."

Cutting through the rhetoric, it is clear that the Bhutanese had been thoroughly alarmed by the use of British power and had appealed to the Tibetans to use their diplomacy to bring an end to the hostilities before they got out of hand. This served Tibetan interests, since it established a dependency on the part of Bhutan, and it also kept the British army out of Tibet. However, to Governor-General Hastings, the Panchen's unexpected letter seemed a wonderful opportunity both to expand trade into new terrain, and to learn about a remote and hitherto unknown country, Tibet. Indeed, it had been thought for some time that Tibet might prove a useful route to China. There now came into the scene one of those wonderful figures who make reading about the history of this part of the world such a delight, namely George Bogle.

Bogle was born in Scotland in 1746 and, at age twenty-three, went to India, where he joined the British East India Company. Bogle seems to have made a favorable impression on everyone he came into contact with, including Hastings, who assigned to him the task of traveling to Tibet to open diplomatic relations with the Panchen Lama. Bogle was just twenty-eight when his expedition set off for Shigatse on the thirteenth of May, 1774. Bogle's account of the expedition, along with a biography of Bogle, and other items, can be found in a book called *Narratives of the Mission of George Bogle to Tibet,* edited by Clements R. Markham and published in 1879. The book is now a collector's item, but I had the good fortune of coming across a copy in a private library in Kathmandu. (There is now a facsimile edition, published in India.) All the quotations here are from that edition. Mr. Markham reproduced the *private* commission Bogle received from Hastings, which shows the extent of Hastings's fascination with Tibet. In it, he asked Bogle to do the following:

1. To send one or more pair of the animals called tus, which produce the shawl wool. If by dooley, chairs, or any other contrivance they can be secured from the fatigues and hazards of the way, the expense is to be no objection.

2. To send one or more pair of the cattle [yaks] which bear what are called cowtails.

3. To send me carefully packed some fresh ripe walnuts for seed, or an entire plant, if it can be transported; and any other curious or valuable seeds or plants, the rhubarb and gensing especially.

4. Any curiosities, whether natural productions, manufactured paintings, or what else may be acceptable to persons of taste in England. Animals only that may be useful, unless any that may be remarkably curious.

5. In your inquiries concerning the people, the form of their government, and the mode of collecting their revenue, are points principally meriting your attention.

6. To keep a diary, inserting whatever passes before your observation which shall be characteristic of the people, the country, the climate, or the road, their manners, customs, buildings, cookery, etc., or interesting to the trade of this country, carrying with you a pencil and a pocket-book for the purpose of minuting short notes of every fact or remark as it occurs, and putting them in order at your leisure, while they are fresh in your memory.

7. To inquire what countries lie between Lhasa and Siberia, and what communication there is between them. The same with regard to China and Kashmir.

8. To ascertain the value of their trade with Bengal by their gold and silver coins, and to send me samples of both.

9. Every nation excels others in some particular art or science. To find out this excellence of the Bhutanese.

10. To inform yourself of the course and navigation of the Brahmaputra River, and of the state of the countries through which it runs.

Bogle, it appears, took to heart Hastings's injunction to take a notebook, and his *Narratives* were the result. As a few entries will show, they are a delight.

Of polyandry, then widely practiced, he noted: "The elder brother marries a woman, and she becomes the wife of the whole family. They club together in matrimony as merchants do in trade. Nor is this joint concern often productive of jealousy among the partners. They are little addicted to jealousy. Disputes indeed sometimes arise about the children of the marriage; but they are settled either by a comparison of the features of the child with those of its several fathers, or left to the determination of the mother."

Of the oracles, he noted, "The Tibetans have great faith in fortune telling, which indeed seems to be common to all mankind, except our European philosophers, who are too wise to believe in anything."

He marveled, as has every traveler to Tibet, at the forbearance of the Tibetan people. "They have none of the markets, fairs, churches, and weddings of England; they have none of the skipping and dancing of France; they have none of the devotion of the lower people in other Roman Catholic countries; they have none of the bathings, bracelets, etc., of the Bengali; and yet I know not how it comes to pass, but they seem to bear it all without murmuring." It is clear from this entry that, despite Bogle's keen sense of observation, the role of religion in Tibet was beyond him. Indeed, he wrote, "The religion of the Lamas is somehow connected with that of the Hindus, though I will not pretend to say how."

Nevertheless, Bogle got on famously with the Panchen Lama and his family. This seems to have led to one of the most remarkable elements in the whole episode. It would appear that while in Shigatse, Bogle *married* one of the Panchen Lama's sisters. I say, "it would appear," because one can search the entire 1879 edition of the *Narratives* in vain to find any reference to this singular event. The source is Richardson's book, *Tibet and Its History,* which states, "In 1775 [Bogle] reached Tashilhunpo and, before long, had won the friendship of the Third Panchen Lama and had cultivated a close intimacy with his family. He married a Tibetan lady, described [by whom Richardson does not say] as a sister of the Panchen Lama, by whom he had two daughters. The girls were later educated at Bogle's ancestral home in Lanarkshire and there each married a Scottish husband. All reference to Bogle's Tibetan wife seems to have been suppressed when his papers were edited for publication; but his descendants, of whom several survive in Britain, now look back to that ancestry with pride." Bogle, whose career seemed so promising, died of a fever in Bengal in 1781. He was only thirty-four.

It is in Bogle's narratives that we also find the first intimation of the "Great Game," an expression that seems to have first appeared in print in Kay's *History of the War in Afghanistan* (1843), referring to the sometimes clandestine and sometimes overt power struggle among the Russians, the British, and—at least in Tibet—the Chinese for the right to have the dominant influence in Central Asia. Bogle first ran across it when he tried to get permission to visit Lhasa. The Panchen was willing, but he did not have the authority to issue such a permission. The Dalai Lama had not reached his majority, so the nominal head of the country was the regent. But it was Bogle's impression that the regent could do nothing without the permission of the Chinese emperor's representatives in Lhasa, the so-called Ambans, usually two in number. Bogle wrote, "Two Chinese viceroys, with a guard of a thousand soldiers, are stationed in Lhasa, and are changed every three years. The Emperor of China is acknowledged as the sovereign of the country; the appointment to the first offices in the state is made by his order, and, in all measures of consequence, reference is first had to the court of Peking; but the internal government of the country is committed entirely to natives; the Chinese in general are confined to the capital, no tribute is exacted, and the people of Tibet, except at Lhasa, hardly feel the weight of a foreign yoke."

The early eighteenth century had been a period of civil unrest in Tibet, and in 1720, the Manchu emperor K'ang Hsi had sent a strong force to Lhasa to restore order. It was he who created the institution of the Ambans. From that time until the full Chinese takeover in 1959, the issue of Tibetan independence from China—or lack of it—was a constant source of irritation between the two countries. Compounding the irritation was Tibet's stormy relationship with its southern neighbor, Nepal. In the eighteenth century, after the Gurkha kings succeeded in unifying Nepal by force, they turned their attention northward, and invaded Tibet. In 1788, they were met by a mixed Tibetan and Chinese army, and were finally defeated in 1792. The fact that Chinese soldiers had helped to defeat the Gurkhas became one of the principal arguments used by the Chinese that Tibet was not an independent state. Indeed, as Bogle noted, all the foreign affairs of Tibet were then decided by the Ambans. In particular, the Ambans concluded that the British might have had a hand in the Gurkha invasion, and decided to seal off Tibet from foreign influence. In return, the Chinese would defend the country if and when it was invaded. This "patron-lama" relationship remained viable so long as the Chinese had the power to fulfill their side of the equation.

But in 1854, the Gurkhas again invaded Tibet, in force, and this time the Chinese were unable to come to the aid of the Tibetans. The Tibetans were forced to conclude a humiliating treaty with the Nepalese in 1856, the second clause of which indicated that the Nepalese had decided to take over the role of the Chinese. It read, "The States of Gorkha and Tibet have both respected the Emperor of China up to the present time. The country of Tibet is merely the shrine or place of worship of the Lama, for which reason the Gorkha Government will in future give all assistance that may be in its power to the Government of Tibet, if the troops of any other

'Raja' invade that country." Treaty or no, the Nepalese did not lift a finger when, in 1903, Tibet was invaded by the British—and indeed, the invading force consisted largely of mercenary Gurkhas.

In the half-century between these two events, Tibet acquired its reputation as a land of mystery. The only systematic exploration of the country was made clandestinely by a group of Indians in the employ of the Survey of India. These spies became known collectively as the Pundits, and the first of them, Nain Singh, entered Tibet in 1866. Their job was to map the country. They used a variety of methods to keep track of the miles. Nain Singh, for example, had a rosary that looked like the traditional Tibetan rosary, with its 108 beads, except that in Singh's case the number had been rounded off to an even 100, which he used to count off distances. Others used such devices as compasses hidden in prayer wheels. The Pundits got as far as Lhasa, where their glimpses of the Tibetan capital seemed to add to its intrigue.

The fullest, and certainly the most savorous, account of the 1903 British invasion is to be found in Peter Fleming's book *Bayonets to Lhasa*. The key player in this inning of the Great Game was Lord Curzon, the man who in 1899 became the viceroy of India. As Fleming pointed out, Curzon's attitudes, if not formed on the playing fields of Eton, were formed in its debating society. As a schoolboy, he participated in a debate on the question "Are we justified in regarding with equanimity the advance of Russia towards our Indian frontier?" In the debating society's minute book, he summarized his position: "The policy of Russia was a most ambitious and aggressive one. It dated its origin from the time of Peter the Great by whom the scheme or conquest had been first made. He did not imagine for a moment that the Russians would actually invade India, and were they to do so, we need have no fear for the result; but . . . a great question of diplomacy might arise in Europe in which the interests of England were opposed to those of Russia. It might then suit Russia to send out an army to watch our Indian frontier. In such a case as this England's right hand would obviously be tied back." The notion that the sinister hand of Russia could be perceived constantly at work in Tibet formed an important part of Curzon's thinking throughout his tenure in India.

Friction between the British and the Tibetans was caused by the poorly demarcated frontier between Sikkim and Tibet. Indeed, the Tibetans did not accept that the British had any right to sovereignty over Sikkim. Curzon attempted to communicate with the thirteenth Dalai Lama by letter on these matters and, much to his exasperation, the letters came back with every indication that they had never been read, at least not by the Dalai Lama. One can only wonder what the history of this part of the world would have been like if the Dalai Lama had humored the British by entering into a correspondence over a remote boundary in a region that was frequented only by the occasional yak herder. Curzon's anger at what he regarded as both a personal and an official slight was compounded by the matter of Aharamba-Agyan-Dorjieff, a Russian monk of Mongolian origin, who had somehow gotten himself into the good graces of the Dalai Lama and became a sort of representative of the Tibetan government in St. Petersburg—to what end, if any, was never entirely clear. As far as Curzon was concerned, the comings and goings of Dorjieff were proof that the Russians were expanding their influence into Tibet. Curzon was now looking for an excuse to send an armed mission into Tibet, and he soon found one.

In November of 1903, some Nepalese yak herders wandered into Tibetan territory and were confronted by a party of armed Tibetans, who proceeded to scare off the yaks with rattles. This inspired Curzon to send the following telegram to his superiors in London: "*Tibetan Affairs. An overt act of hostility has taken place. Tibetan troops having, as we are now informed, attacked Nepalese yaks on the frontier and carried off many of them.*" This, in turn, inspired the Home Office to issue the following directive:

> *In view of the recent conduct of the Tibetans, His Majesty's Government feel that it would be impossible not to take action, and they accordingly sanction the advance of the Mission to Gyantse. They are, however, clearly of the opinion that this step should not be allowed to lead to occupation or to permanent intervention in Tibetan affairs in any form. The advance should be made for the*

sole purpose of obtaining satisfaction, and as soon as reparation is obtained a withdrawal should be effected. While His Majesty's Government consider the proposed action to be necessary, they are not prepared to establish a permanent mission in Tibet, and the question of enforcing trade facilities in that country must be considered in the light of the decision conveyed in this telegram.

Fleming commented, "Although it laid down firmly what the Government of India was *not* to do, this directive was both vague and inconsequent in its more positive aspects. What was meant by 'obtaining satisfaction' and 'obtaining reparation'? What was meant by 'enforcing trade facilities'? Taken literally, these expressions seemed to imply that a diplomatic mission with a specific purpose was now regarded in London as a punitive expedition with undefined objectives."

In the event, the man chosen by Curzon to lead this ambiguously construed expedition was Francis Edward Younghusband. Younghusband, who was born in 1863, had the Indian subcontinent and Central Asia in his bones. He, his father, four uncles, and two brothers were all to serve in the Indian army. But Younghusband was an explorer as well as a soldier and, by 1893, when he was stationed as political officer in Chitral, on the northwestern frontier between what was then India and Afghanistan, he made several overland trips to Central Asia. While in Chitral, he had met Curzon, who was also a great traveler. Additionally, he encountered and favorably impressed the Honorable Charles Granville Bruce—known as "Bruiser"—a Gurkha officer who had the notion of teaching mountain warfare to the Gurkhas, something that was to come in useful in Tibet. Bruce and Younghusband found that they had a common interest in mountain climbing and, indeed, they teamed up to climb the Ispero Zorn near Chitral. They also discussed—at least in the abstract—climbing Mount Everest. Nothing was to come of this for some thirty years. After his service in Chitral, Younghusband's career, which alternated between journalism and diplomacy, never really got anywhere—until 1903, when a telegram from Curzon summoned him to Simla to organize the mission to Tibet.

The Younghusband mission was a mismatch; the feudal and antique Tibetans wanted only to be left alone, while the full weight of the British Empire, with all its ambiguous goals and motivations, stood behind Younghusband. The unfairness of it seems to have impressed the British public. Fleming reproduced a cartoon from the November 25, 1903, edition of *Punch* that shows a fully armed British lion confronting a goatlike animal dressed in a headpiece. The caption reads:

Forced Favours

THE GRAND LAMA OF TIBET.	"Now then, what's your business?"
BRITISH LION.	"I've come to bring you the blessings of free trade."
THE GRAND LAMA.	"I'm a protectionist. Don't want 'em."
BRITISH LION.	"Well, you've got to have 'em!"

Fleming also reproduced a paragraph taken from the *Report on the Supply and Transport Arrangements with the Late Tibet Mission Force.* It speaks volumes.

Animals	Number Employed	Casualties
Mules	7,096	910
Bullocks	5,324	910
Camels	6	6
Buffaloes	138	137
Riding Ponies	185	24
Pack Ponies	1,372	899
Nepalese Yaks	2,953	2,922
Tibetan Yaks	1,513	1,192
Ekka Ponies	1,111	277

In addition, the expedition employed some ten thousand porters or coolies, of whom eighty-eight died. The expedition began with about eleven hundred soldiers with weapons, especially Maxim machine guns, which ultimately were the tools of conquest. At the frontier between Sikkim and Tibet, Younghusband encountered the first of many Tibetan emissaries whose messages were all essentially the same: The British should go back to India. Younghusband's invariable answer was that, while he had no intention of resorting to force unless attacked, he did have every intention of pressing on to Tibet. The expedition wintered in a village called Tuna, and in March of 1904, headed for Gyantse via a nearby village called Guru. It was here that the first armed skirmish took place. The Tibetans, with their antiquated arms, vastly outnumbered the British, and they more or less sat in the middle of the road and refused to budge. The British decided to disarm them. Fleming described the situation:

It is, as the world has learnt to its cost since 1904, difficult to disarm by mutual agreement; to disarm men without mutual agreement is possible only when they recognize that they have no alternative but to lay down their weapons. The Tibetan army had no alternative but did not recognize the fact. It had never seen a machine gun before; it understood only dimly how frightful was the menace of the Lee Metfords trained silently on the confined space, roughly an acre in extent, in which it was corralled; and the superstitious peasants in its ranks were sustained by a sort of half-faith in the charms, spells and other mumbo-jumbo which were supposed to render them invulnerable. They were in a death trap, but they did not know it.

The inevitable happened—the hand-to-hand skirmishing turned to slaughter. The Tibetans simply turned their backs and walked slowly to cover while they were mowed down like so many game birds. Nearly half of the original army of fifteen hundred were massacred.

Younghusband sincerely hoped that this lesson would be absorbed by the Tibetans, and that the army could now march on to Lhasa unmolested. What they were to do when they got there was not entirely clear. But in April the mission reached Gyantse, which had been its original authorized destination. The Tibetans were unwilling to discuss any of the diplomatic matters that had exercised the British until the latter left Tibet, which of course the British were unwilling to do. The Tibetans massed what remained of their army on a high pass that blocked the way to Lhasa and, although Younghusband had no authority to go beyond Gyantse, the decision was made to clear the pass. Before this maneuver could take place, the Tibetans made an ill-advised surprise attack on the British positions in Gyantse—with the same result as the slaughter at Guru. A general stalemate followed, which lasted until July, when a reinforced British column successfully stormed the great fort at Gyantse. The road to Lhasa now lay open. The question of what to demand once the army reached the Tibetan capital now took on considerable urgency.

The debate hinged on whether or not the British should demand from the Tibetans the right to station a British agent permanently in Lhasa. Younghusband categorically favored this, and Curzon agreed. However, by this time the Russians—who, it turned out, despite the comings and goings of the mysterious Dorjieff, had never been a factor in Tibet—had begun to be seriously concerned about the British incursion. They had been given general assurances that, barring the unforeseen, the British intended to leave Tibet with no agent in place. These views were relayed to Curzon. In the meanwhile, Younghusband and his army had reached Lhasa. The first official person he encountered was the Chinese Amban, Yu-t'ai. Yu-t'ai entered the British camp "preceded by ten unarmed servants clad in lavender-blue, edged and patterned with black velvet. Immediately behind them came forty men-at-arms similarly dressed in cardinal and black, bearing lances, scythe-headed poles, tridents and banners; after them came the secretaries and servants." He thought he could use the British presence in Lhasa to restore Chinese prestige, which at the time was at a low ebb. So he acted as a go-between for the British and Tibetan authorities.

By this time, the thirteenth Dalai Lama—the very one who, a few years later, would be urging Alexandra David-Neel to study Tibetan—had departed Lhasa with Dorjieff for Outer Mongolia, leaving the regent behind to negotiate on his behalf. On the seventh of September, a day that the Tibetan oracles had decided was propitious, a treaty between Tibet and Britain was signed in the Potala. Most of the clauses had to do with trade and were perfectly innocuous. However, to the main treaty Younghusband had attached a separate signed agreement. It gave the British agent at Gyantse the right to visit Lhasa "to consult with high Chinese and Tibetan officials on such commercial matters of importance as he has found impossible to settle at Gyantse." In other words, Younghusband had succeeded, or so he thought, in sneaking his agent in through the back door. This did not pass unperceived by Whitehall and, by the following October, Younghusband's career in the foreign service was essentially over, and he had been publicly reprimanded. He was given a sort of sinecure in Kashmir and, in 1910, resigned from service with the government of India. He turned his interest to religion, and to the Royal Geographical Society, whose president he became after the First World War. In this post, he helped advance the cause of climbing Mount Everest. He died in 1942 at the age of seventy-nine.

The aftereffects of the Younghusband mission were complex, and many analysts argue that they determined Tibet's future. Article 9 of the treaty Younghusband signed with the Tibetans stated that "Tibet was to have no dealings of any kind with any Foreign Power without Britain's consent." The Chinese later used this clause, along with the fact that the Amban had acted as a sort of middleman in the negotiations, to argue that Tibet was not an independent country. Both the British and the Tibetans recognized that China had what was termed "suzerainty" over Tibet. This term was never defined in any treaty signed by all parties. Curzon expressed the British view in a letter written in 1903: "We regard Chinese suzerainty over Tibet as a constitutional fiction—a political affectation which has only been maintained because of its convenience to both parties."

In 1910, the Chinese invaded Tibet. The Dalai Lama, who had returned to Lhasa from Outer Mongolia, fled to British India, using the same route that his successor would take in 1959. The Dalai Lama was welcomed in the border town of Yatung by the British trade agent, David Macdonald, who had been with Younghusband in 1904 and who was to welcome Alexandra David-Neel twenty years later. From there, the Dalai Lama proceeded to Calcutta, where he was graciously received by the viceroy. Meanwhile, the Chinese attempted, as they would again in 1959, to replace the Dalai Lama with the Panchen Lama. Then, as now, the Tibetan people would not accept the change.

In 1911, Sun Yat-sen led the revolution in China that overthrew the Manchu emperor, and the Tibetans successfully rebelled against the Chinese occupation. In 1913, the Dalai Lama returned to Lhasa. He initiated wide-ranging reforms in the feudal land system, which many Tibetans regarded as unfair. In his own way, he attempted to bring Tibet gently into the modern world. (For example, he introduced both postage stamps and paper money to the country.) He never forgot his cordial treatment at the hands of the British and, when the Great War broke out in 1914—and despite the fact that Tibet was still fighting the Chinese in the east—the Dalai Lama offered a thousand of his best troops to help the British. The political officer of Sikkim responded to the offer, noting that "the British Government was deeply touched and grateful to His Holiness, the Dalai Lama, for his offer to send one thousand Tibetan troops, to support the British Government. Please inform His Holiness that the British Government will seek the support of Tibet whenever the need arises." As Tsepon Shakabpa wrote in *Tibet: A Political History,* "The Dalai Lama took the Political Officer's letter at face value and, in spite of his preoccupation with the troubled areas of Kham [a region in eastern Tibet whose inhabitants often rebelled against central authority], kept one thousand of his best troops in readiness for helping Britain 'whenever the need arises.'" When the war ended, the troops were still in Lhasa, waiting to be called.

7

The Present

M y interest in Tibet goes back to my childhood. In 1941, when I
was eleven, my father gave me the then newly published book
High Conquest, by James Ramsey Ullman. It is a history of mountaineering, written in the grandly romantic style that was characteristic of
much of the writing about mountain climbing before the Second
World War. With the drier eyes of middle age, I can see all its flaws,
but to an eleven-year-old, with a vivid imagination, it was wonderful.
The tenth chapter is called "Summit of the World: The Fight for
Everest." It described the unsuccessful attempts to climb Everest—all
of them from the Tibet side—that had been made prior to the writing
of the book. Each expedition began in the Indian hill town of Darjeeling, then toiled through the jungles of Sikkim and then upward onto
the Tibetan plateau. Seen by a flying crow, the distance is only a
hundred miles, but the terrain is so broken up by peaks and gorges
that the actual walking distance is three times that. Ullman described
the progress of the first expedition, in 1921, which—like all rest, until
the 1950s—was basically British. He wrote:

> *Day after day they pushed northward and westward across as savage
> country as exists anywhere on the earth's surface—through sand-
> storms and raging, glacial torrents, across vast boulder-strewn plains*

and passes 20,000 feet above the sea. At night they camped under stars or enjoyed the primitive hospitality of Buddhist monasteries and village headmen. Their passports from the Tibetan authorities in Lhasa assured them kindly and courteous treatment, but the announcement of the purpose of their journey elicited only dubious shaking of heads and a solemn turning of prayer wheels. To those devout and superstitious orientals, Everest was more than a mountain. Chomolungma, they called it—Goddess-Mother-of-the World. It was sacrilege, they believed, for mere mortals even to approach it.

Then came a paragraph that stuck with me for decades and, even as a child, gave me the desire to visit Tibet. Ullman wrote:

At last in June, the expedition arrived at the Great Rongbuk Monastery, where an isolated colony of priests and hermits dwelt, some twenty miles due north of Everest. And from here, at last, they saw their mountain head on in its titanic majesty—the first white men ever to have a close-up view of the summit of the world. "We paused," wrote Mallory, "in sheer astonishment. The sight of it banished every thought; we asked no questions and made no comment, but simply looked. . . ." At the end of the valley and above the glacier Everest rises, not so much a peak as a prodigious mountain mass. There is no complication for the eye. The highest of the world's mountains, it seems, has to make but a single gesture of magnificence to be lord of all, vast in unchallenged and isolated supremacy. To the discerning eye other mountains are visible, giants between 23,000 and 26,000 feet high. Not one of their slender heads even reaches their chief's shoulder; beside Everest they escape notice— such is the pre-eminence of the greatest.

Ullman was very good at this sort of thing. What he omitted was to explain how the British—the only foreigners to do so—had gotten permission to enter Tibet at all, let alone to try to climb Everest. This, as we have seen, can be traced to the sequence of events beginning with Younghusband's expedition to Lhasa.

Younghusband had actually been considering the possibility of climbing Mount Everest, as I have mentioned, as early as 1893, so it was not surprising that, on his return from Lhasa, in 1904, he sent a small reconnaissance party to look at Everest. One of its members, Captain C. G. Rawling, having seen the mountain from a distance of sixty miles, even suggested a possible climbing route on it. Curzon also believed that the mountain was climbable and that it should be climbed by an Englishman. He favored tackling the mountain from the Nepalese side (later Mallory, who looked over a ridge onto the Nepalese face, argued—incorrectly, as it turned out—that it was unclimbable from that side), and offered to ask the Nepalese authorities for permission. That did not come until after the Rana regime in Nepal was overthrown, in 1950, and Tibet was definitively closed.

After Curzon left his post as viceroy of India, the British Everest efforts in Tibet were held up for several years because the secretary of state for India, John Morley, decided that any incursions by the British into Tibet would be contrary to a British-Russian understanding concerning the neutrality of that country. Hence, he blocked all attempts to obtain permission to climb Everest from the Tibetans. After the Russian Revolution, the British decided that they no longer had an obligation to the Russians to stay out of Tibet; hence, the Dalai Lama was approached for permission to mount an expedition to explore the Everest region. The British did not know how to get to the base of the mountain, let alone what the climbing routes might be. In 1921, the first British expedition entered Tibet, armed with the following document signed by the regent and addressed to anyone the expeditionary party happened to come across:

> *You are to bear in mind that a party of Sahibs are coming to see Cho-mo-lung-ma mountain and they will evince great friendship towards the Tibetans. On the request of the Great Minister Bell* [Charles Bell was the political officer in Sikkim who had welcomed the Dalai Lama when he fled Tibet] *a passport has been issued requiring you and all officials and subjects of the Tibetan Government to supply transport, e.g., riding ponies, pack animals and coolies as required by the Sahibs, the rates for which should be*

fixed to mutual satisfaction. Any other assistance that the Sahibs might require either by day or by night, on the march or during halts, should be faithfully given, and their requirements about transport or anything else should be promptly attended to. All the people of the country, wherever the Sahibs may happen to come, should render all necessary assistance in the best possible way, in order to maintain friendly relations between the British and Tibetan governments.

In the 1921 expedition, Mallory represented the new generation of Himalayan climbers—those who were beginning to replace the many British climbers killed or wounded during the war. His letters to his wife and various friends give a vivid description of the Tibet he was discovering. One of them will have familiar overtones to anyone who has traveled in the Tibetan countryside. He wrote to his wife: "But in the evening light the country can be beautiful, snow mountains and all: the harshness becomes subdued; shadows soften the hillsides; there is a blending of lines and folds until the last light, so that one comes to bless the absolute bareness, feeling that here is pure beauty of form, a kind of ultimate harmony."

Then he added—and this also will be only too familiar to the Tibetan traveler—"Our great enemy, of course, is the wind. On the best of days it is absolutely calm in the early morning, chilly at first and as the sun gets up quite hot. (The sun is always *scorching* and threatens to take one's skin off.) Any time between 10:00 and 12:00, the wind gets up—a dry, dusty, unceasing wind, with all the unpleasantness of an east wind at home. Towards evening it becomes very cold, and we have frost at nights. . . . The real problem for comfort now is to get the tents pitched so as to have some shelter when the day's destination is reached."[1]

The 1921 party did not try to climb the mountain. But they made a complete exploration of its lower extremities and discovered what, the following year, became the climbing route via the East Rongbuk Glacier. The leader of that expedition was the very Brigadier General

---

1. A fuller account of these letters and the early Everest expeditions can be found in the fine book on the mountain, *Everest,* written by Walt Unsworth.

Charles G. "Bruiser" Bruce who had discussed with Younghusband the possibility of climbing Everest in 1893. The 1922 expedition did not climb the mountain to its summit, but they set a new altitude record in climbing—27,235 feet. The 1922 expedition also experienced the first fatalities on the mountain: Seven porters were killed in an avalanche. This was followed by the 1924 expedition on which Mallory and his protégé, Andrew Irvine, disappeared into the mists on their way to the summit. Because of the publicity surrounding the accident—or at least so was the claim, the Dalai Lama withheld permission to the British to climb the mountain until 1933, when, as I have noted, Mallory's ice ax was recovered. There were British expeditions in 1935, 1936, and 1938, but none of them got as high as their predecessors.

In a curious way, the political history of Tibet since the 1920s is reflected in the climbing history of Mount Everest. As I have explained, that the British got permission at all to attempt the mountain from the Tibetan side was due to the close relationship that the thirteenth Dalai Lama had with British officials such as Charles Bell. That permission to enter Tibet was withheld for nine years—from 1924 to 1933—is also, perversely, related to the same relationship. While the thirteenth Dalai Lama, like his predecessors, was in theory the absolute ruler of Tibet, he had also to take into account the attitudes in the monasteries. Before the 1959 Chinese occupation of Tibet, it has been estimated, there were between a quarter- and a half-million people—mostly men—in some six thousand monasteries, in a Tibet that had a total population of less than two million. This was a constituency that a Dalai Lama, himself a product of the monastic system, could not ignore. In addition, there was the Tibetan National Assembly—led by the regent, often a man much older than the Dalai Lama—whose views could not be ignored, either. These people tended to be very conservative, and this limited the Dalai Lama's ability to modernize Tibet. In addition, he was strongly criticized for his close relationship with the British. It was in response to this criticism, and not to the deaths of Mallory and Irvine, that he closed the borders to British climbing expeditions until 1933. At that time, a far greater concern developed: the deteriorating relations with

China and Nepal, both of which seemed to have territorial ambitions in Tibet. Against these, the British could serve as a useful counterweight. Hence, from 1933 until the Second World War, the British received regular permission to climb Everest—despite the thirteenth Dalai Lama's death, at age fifty-eight, in 1933.

The last prewar British expedition was in 1938. Even if one knew nothing about modern Tibetan history except that the next climbing expedition from the Tibetan side, which was in 1960, was Chinese, it would not be difficult to infer what had happened to Tibet between 1938 and 1960. To sort out the legalistic aspects of the Chinese occupation of Tibet would be like solving Rubik's Cube. It would also be sadly irrelevant. Depending on the year under discussion, one can "prove" that parts of Tibet legally belong to Nepal, and vice versa; that parts of Tibet legally belong to China, and vice versa. Be that as it may, it is clear that, from 1911 to 1940, Tibet was a de facto independent, self-governing country. In 1914, the British had tried to normalize the situation by convening the so-called Simla Conference with China and Tibet. The British representative, Sir Henry McMahon, attempted to resolve the Chinese-Tibetan impasse over territorial claims by introducing the notion of "Inner" and "Outer" Tibet. Outer Tibet was the traditional Tibet, including Lhasa, which was to have been self-governing, subject to the vague constraint of Chinese "suzerainty"; while Inner Tibet, which bordered both China and Burma, and was Tibetan in the sense that it had a substantial Tibetan population, but which had Chinese governors, would continue to have them. The Chinese refused to sign the Simla convention, which left the British and Tibetans free to negotiate Tibet's boundaries. McMahon drew up a boundary—the McMahon Line—which ran along the crest of the Himalayas, and separated Tibet from the northeastern corner of India. This boundary was not recognized by the Chinese. Until 1933, the Chinese were kept out of most of Tibet—Outer Tibet, including Lhasa. However, in 1933 the Chinese asked permission to send a delegation to the funeral of the thirteenth Dalai Lama. This permission was granted, and the attending Chinese delegation never left. They installed a wireless radio. The British then installed a wireless, over Chinese objections, arguing that if the Chinese would remove *their* wireless, the British would do likewise. Both wirelesses remained in place. It was during this period that the British had almost carte blanche permission to try to climb Everest.

If there was one thing the Chinese Nationalists and Communists agreed on, it was the annexation of Tibet. In 1947, Chiang Kai-shek put forth the theory that the Hans, Mongols, Manchus, Tibetans, and Tungans were all parts of a single Chinese race. (The Chinese Communists would, of course, add the Taiwanese.) During the Second World War, the Tibetans had maintained a posture of neutrality, which was compromised when Chiang Kai-shek attempted to build roads across Tibetan territory over Tibetan objections. There were troop movements on both sides, but the Chinese, who were heavily engaged in fighting the Japanese, backed off, avoiding an actual confrontation.

It is important to understand, when discussing Tibetan resistance, that there were at least two kinds of armed forces in Tibet. Some of the monasteries had their own armies. Indeed, these constituted the major military force in the country. In addition, the government had its own army, which it was never able to build up since the monasteries did not want to see their own military importance diminished. In addition, the so-called Khampas—the tribal residents of the province of Kham in eastern Tibet—had their own army, if one wants to call it that. Khampas, at least Khampa men, are easily recognized. They wear high boots, and their long hair, done up with a swirling flash of red yarn, makes them seem taller than they actually are. They walk with the confident swagger of cowboys in the Old West. They are also a pretty wild bunch and, during much of Tibetan history, made their living as bandits preying on caravans of traders. They were never very enthusiastic about the central government in Lhasa, although concerning religious matters, they were devoted to the Dalai Lama.

The central government, under the Dalai Lama, was feudal. Tibetan society was divided into serfs and nobles and, in theory, the state owned all of the land. Large parcels were given to the monasteries and to individual landowners, however, and these were worked by the peasantry in return for small parcels of land for personal use. Social mobility came through the monastic orders. The Dalai Lamas, for example, frequently came from peasant stock, as did many of the other religious leaders. It also has to be stated that, in enforcing its mandate, the theocratic state could be brutal. Until the thirteenth Dalai Lama put a stop to it, serious crimes were punished by dismemberment, and a traitor to the state could lose his eyes. One of the places in the Potala palace that visitors are not shown is the so-called Cave of Scorpions, in which enemies of the state were interned, and from which few emerged. Even after the Dalai Lama's mandate against mutilation as a punishment, flogging, which could lead to death, was still practiced. This kind of medieval feudalism led some observers of Tibetan society to feel that the Tibetans would be better off without their central government altogether. For example, Alexandra David-Neel—who, since she was traveling in the disguise of a mendicant pilgrim, and since she knew the language perfectly, probably got to know the ordinary Tibetan of the 1920s as well as any foreign observer—wrote in her book *My Journey to Lhasa*, "Tibetans have lost much in parting with China. Their sham independence profits only a clique of court officials. Most of those who rebelled against the far-off and relaxed Chinese rule regret it nowadays, when taxes, statute labor, and the arrogant plundering of the national soldiery greatly exceed the extortions of their former masters." Alexandra lived, as I have noted, past her hundredth year—until 1969. By that time, whatever pretense there had been of "far-off and relaxed Chinese rule" had turned into a nightmare. What Alexandra could not have imagined is that the Chinese would attempt to cut the heart and soul out of Tibetan life by destroying its religion.

On the seventh of October, 1950, the Chinese army, supported by some Khampa irregulars, invaded eastern Tibet, while a second force of Chinese launched an invasion from the west. Since 1947, when the British had granted independence to India, the Indians had taken over the British treaty responsibilities to Tibet, including those of the Simla convention. Hence, the Indian government made an appeal to the Chinese to respect the independence of Tibet. They were told, in no uncertain terms, that the invasion of Tibet was a purely internal Chinese matter. On November 11, 1950, Tsepon Shakabpa—the author of *Tibet: A Political History,* but then an official of the Tibetan government—cabled the following appeal to the United Nations: "The armed invasion of Tibet for the incorporation of Tibet in communist China through sheer physical force is a clear case of aggression. As long as the people of Tibet are compelled by force to become part of China against their will and consent, the present invasion of Tibet will be the grossest instance of the violation of the weak by the strong. We therefore appeal through you to the nations of the world to intercede on our behalf and restrain Chinese aggression."

The government of El Salvador attempted to raise the matter of the invasion of Tibet before the secretary-general, but got nowhere. Every major power, including Britain and the United States, supported an adjournment of the question, and it was not debated for the next nine years, by which time there was nothing left to debate. After the appeal to the United Nations failed, the Dalai Lama, who was then sixteen and—although the normal age was eighteen—had been invested with the full powers of his office, was moved from Lhasa to a spot close to the Indian border. (In 1959, he finally fled to India.) The idea was that, so long as the Dalai Lama remained out of Chinese custody, there was some chance he could at least exercise a moral influence over the affairs of the country. It is for this reason—staying out of Chinese hands—that, despite his personal feelings for his homeland, the Dalai Lama has, so far, refused to return to Tibet. On May 23, 1951, a Tibetan delegation in Beijing signed, under duress, a treaty with the Chinese that, if its provisions had actually been adhered to by the Chinese, might have made the occupation of Tibet bearable. The treaty, a seventeen-point Agreement on Measures for the Peaceful Liberation of Tibet, opened with a prologue that rewrote the history of the country. However, the treaty itself—if it was ever meant seriously—contained several provisions that would have ensured the continuation of something like traditional Tibetan life.

It is unclear whether the Chinese ever intended to abide by this treaty. In the beginning, the Tibetans thought so, and the Dalai Lama returned to Lhasa on August 17, 1951. He made an attempt at land reform that was, curiously, opposed by the Chinese. Perhaps this was part of their plan: Despite a clause in the agreement stating that the central authorities would not alter "the existing political system" in Tibet, the attempt to reduce the Dalai Lama's authority began almost at once. Although, at first, the Chinese took no direct action against the monasteries—that would come later—they made little secret of their contempt for the religious side of Tibetan life, which Mao Tse-tung referred to as "poison." What transformed the situation was the havoc the Chinese wreaked on the fragile Tibetan economy. As anyone who has ever visited the country can testify, the opportunities for agriculture in Tibet are very limited. While there are more than thirty-two million acres of grazing land there are not much more than a half-million acres of arable land. Most of Tibet is desert, with a population of something like one person per square kilometer. While the Tibetan diet, which consisted largely of barley *(tsampa),* often taken in thick tea—with occasional yak meat—was spartan, there was no starvation in the country. The population and the food resources were in a delicate equilibrium. This was destroyed when the Chinese began moving in thousands—indeed, hundreds of thousands—of troops and settlers from heartland China—Han Chinese—and taking food resources from the Tibetans to feed them. This was the beginning of widespread starvation in Tibet. In addition, the Chinese began a program of road building—strategic roads to enable rapid movement of troops—and many Tibetans, a number of whom lost their lives in the process, were pressed into construction gangs. Some of the country's gold and silver reserves were "borrowed" by China and shipped out of Tibet. By 1954, much of the road building was completed, and the occupation began in earnest with a shameful Indo-Chinese pact—a pact to which no Tibetan was a party—agreeing that Tibet was an integral part of China, thus removing any external constraints, moral or otherwise, on Chinese behavior in the country.

By the spring of 1956, in response to ever-tightening Communist control, including the execution of some lamas, serious armed resistance arose in eastern Tibet. The Khampas, some of whom had fought with the Chinese, now began a campaign of sabotage and guerilla warfare. As H. M. Richardson pointed out in his book *Tibet and Its History,* this led to terrible reprisals. He quoted from a report published in 1960 by the International Commission of Jurists:

*Eye-witnesses have described how monks and laymen were tortured
and many killed, often in barbarous ways* [the Dalai Lama, in his
book *My Land and My People,* written in 1962, reported that
some were "beaten to death, crucified, burned alive, drowned,
vivisected, starved, strangled, hanged, scalded, buried alive, dis-
emboweled and beheaded"]: *women raped and others publicly
humiliated; venerated Lamas subjected to brutal and disgusting
degradations; other monks and Lamas compelled to break their
religious vows; men and boys deported or put to forced labor in
harsh conditions; boys and girls taken from their homes, ostensibly for education in China; children incited to abuse and to beat
their parents; private property seized, monasteries damaged by
gunfire; and sacred images, books and relics carried off or publicly destroyed.*

All of this incited the Khampas to even fiercer guerilla activities, and
by February of 1957, Mao Tse-tung, Richardson reported, "announced
that Tibet was not yet ready for reforms and that their introduction would
be postponed for at last five years." All of this only stiffened the Tibetan
will to resist, and in the autumn of 1958 the guerillas wiped out a Chinese
garrison with some three thousand men.

Four kilometers west of the Potala palace is a park. In this park, the
seventh Dalai Lama, in 1755, began construction of a summer palace—the Norbu Lingka ("Precious Jewel Island"). Each spring, he
and subsequent Dalai Lamas were carried in gilded, curtained palan-
quins—or rode mules—from the Potala to the Norbu Lingka. It was
a great occasion, with a long procession of lamas and nobles as well
as a "police" guard of specially chosen, very tall monks armed with
long, thin saplings, which they used to clear the crowd from the path
of the Dalai Lama. During her illicit visit to Lhasa in 1924, Alexandra
David-Neel witnessed that year's parade. She wrote, "At intervals,
somebody ran along shouting orders. The arrival of the Dalai Lama
was announced. All, women included, had to take their hats off, and
those who delayed were soon acquainted with one or another of the
lamaist policemen's weapons. Thanks to my short stature, I escaped
thumps and thrashings during the hours I stood there. When danger

threatened, I always managed to find shelter among a group of tall Tibetans who acted as a protecting roof over my head."

She continued, "The [thirteenth] Dalai Lama passed at last, riding a beautiful black mule, and accompanied by a few ecclesiastical dignitaries, all like himself dressed in religious robes—dark red, yellow, and gold brocades, half covered by the dark red toga. They wore Mongolian round hats of yellow brocade edged with fur. The Commander-in-chief rode before them, while some horse guards clad in khaki led the van and brought up the rear."

In early March of 1959, the fourteenth Dalai Lama made his accustomed pilgrimage to the Norbu Lingka. On the ninth of March, he received an invitation from the Chinese commander in Lhasa to come to the Chinese barracks to witness some sort of cultural perform-ance, but to come without his usual escort. Whatever the motive of the Chinese commander, once the people of Lhasa heard about this invitation, they concluded that the Chinese intended to seize the Dalai Lama. During the next few days some thirty thousand people gathered in front of the Norbu Lingka to prevent the Chinese from entering it. On the seventeenth of March, the Chinese fired two shells into the grounds of the palace, and that night the Dalai Lama left, in secret, for India, and an era of Tibetan history came to an end. For two days, neither the Chinese nor the Tibetans surrounding the palace knew that the Dalai Lama was gone. During the day of the nineteenth, the Chinese began shelling the Norbu Lingka—the shells reaching closer and closer to the palace buildings. Then, that evening, it was an-nounced that the Dalai Lama had fled. With this news, the thousands of Tibetans who had been guarding the palace turned their anger onto the Chinese garrisons themselves, and in the resulting melee, several thousand Tibetans were killed or taken prisoner.

With the flight of the Dalai Lama to India, the Chinese established a military government, backed up by as many as a half-million troops. (It is very difficult to know how many Chinese troops and special police units are presently stationed in Tibet. Some estimates give the number at about a million. Since only some two million Tibetans remain, one can gauge what this means in the life of the country. Any traveler in Tibet—especially in the south, near the frontier with India, where there has been continuing tension—has the constant sense of being immersed in a vast military infrastructure. One drives along for hours in what seems to be an absolutely empty space, only to discover in the middle of nowhere the telltale radar tower of some remote military air base.) The Dalai Lama stated, in 1959: "Wherever I am, accompanied by my government, the Tibetan people recognize us as the government of Tibet." In this spirit, the matter of Tibet was debated in the United Nations in the fall of 1959. It was one of those surrealistic UN debates with which we are now only too familiar. Like most of them, this one resulted in a vaporous statement endorsing human rights. It passed by forty-five votes to nine, with twenty-six abstentions. Among the abstainers were India, Nepal, and Great Britain.

For the next three decades, the Chinese attempted to destroy the traditional culture of Tibet. In our century, there has been so much cultural destruction that one has almost become numb to it. Although it is impossible to compare one such act to another, there is, in my view, something especially grotesque about what the Chinese have done in Tibet. The Tibetans were, and are, a basically kindly people, living largely for the rewards, and perhaps the sorrows, of the next life. There were essentially no radios, no cars, and no electricity, and to this day there is no railroad. Some 48 percent of the population were nomadic herders living in small, self-contained units in black yak-hair tents, which can still be seen dotting the Tibetan countryside. These people had virtually no contact with modern technology at all. Like most Tibetans, the nomads were illiterate. What they, like all Tibetans, wanted most of all was to be left alone to practice their religious life—which, for Tibetans, is everything. The noted Tibetologist Giuseppe Tucci, in his book *Tibet: Land of Snows,* written in 1967—Tucci had been visiting the country regularly since 1927—described the confrontation of this antique way of life with Chinese Communism as well as anyone has. He wrote:

> *Deep religiousness, capable of mystical raptures, but pervaded too by magical* Angst, *and expressed in varying symbols—genial or grotesque, tranquil or obscene, often hard to understand in their apparent strangeness—precisely on account of these contradictions*

cannot long, I fear, withstand the new ideas forced upon it by foreign domination. The encounter between Marxist rationalism and the Tibetan's ingenuous blend of myth, fantasy and magic brings two entirely different conceptions face to face: an inflexible abstract scheme, all figure and duties, on the one hand, and on the other the fundamental anarchy of invisible presences that control us but which we can dominate if we know their secret. Facts on the one side; imagination on the other. The life of man confined within time and space, in the service of a community which seeks economic and social betterment at the cost of individual freedom, with the new ideology; affirmation of the personality through its dialogue with the transcendent world of the divine, belittling of the real in comparison with the invisible, transcendence overriding time and space, with the Tibetan spiritual tradition.

He concluded, "Millennia of religious experience, supported by the innate archetypes of the Tibetan spirit, are hard to root out; but the very complications of a great deal of Lamaism, the bizarreness of some of its symbols, cannot long, I think, resist the disenchanted cold-bloodedness of the new principles." What Tucci did not know—what no one outside of Tibet really knew—was that, by the time that these words were written in 1967, as a manifestation of the Chinese Cultural Revolution, only some ten out of a total of 6,254 monasteries in Tibet had escaped total or partial destruction. Among the monasteries that had been totally destroyed was the great Rongbuk monastery at the base of Mount Everest, where the seven prewar British climbing expeditions to Everest had sought and received the blessing of the abbot.

Although I had been on several occasions a few miles from the Tibetan border, in the winter of 1979 Jaccoux and I actually went to the border itself. We hired a taxi in Kathmandu and took the five-hour drive to the border along what is known locally as the Chinese Road. This is the same road that we had taken as far Dolalghat in 1967, the year the road had been completed, to start our trek to Everest. Indeed, we passed the very place where I remembered we had crossed the bridge and begun our walk. I could see the trail winding off in the general direction of the high mountains. But this time, we followed the road to the frontier checkpost in Kodari. From there, the so-called Friendship Bridge spans the Sun Kosi River (the Po Chu in Tibet) over to Tibet. We could see, on a distant hill, the Tibetan border town of Zhangmu (Khasa to the Nepalese) and the Chinese soldiers who patrolled the border. By 1979, organized guerilla activity in Tibet had stopped. From 1959, when the Dalai Lama fled to India, until the 1972 Kissinger-Nixon visit to China, the Khampas, aided by the CIA in some murky operations, continued to fight the Chinese. In fact, a number of Khampas had been flown—from where exactly I am not sure, and neither were they—to Camp Hale in Colorado for training. Camp Hale, where the famed Tenth Mountain Division of the United States Army had trained in the Second World War, is nestled in the high mountains of Colorado. The terrain bears a family resemblance to that of the area in which the Khampas were going to operate in Tibet. They were then returned to the field to continue their guerilla warfare against the Chinese, entering and leaving Tibet from places in western Nepal such as Mustang. But one of the conditions that the Chinese laid down for diplomatic relations with the United States in 1972 was that we stop aiding the Khampas. At the same time, they put pressure on the Nepalese to disarm those Khampas who were operating out of western Nepal. It took the Nepalese army, and a good deal of bloodshed, to disarm them. Some ended up in Nepalese jails. With this, organized resistance to the Chinese in Tibet came to an end.

To someone like myself, who had followed both the climbing history of Mount Everest and the political history of Tibet, it was clear that something had happened in Tibet when, in 1980, it was announced that a *Japanese* climber, Yasuo Kato, had climbed Everest from the Tibetan side. Since 1964, the Chinese had designated Tibet an "autonomous republic." As part of its "autonomy," it had a Chinese military governor, General Ron Rong. It was under his administration that many of the atrocities had been carried out. But three years after Mao's 1976 death, he was dismissed in disgrace and replaced by another military man, Yin Fatang. Yin Fatang began something of a program of liberalization. Part of this program was the development of tourism in Tibet. The first tourists I encountered who had been to Tibet in the early 1980s had gone there as part of various package tours to China. These tours had now begun to include brief flying visits to Lhasa. Chengdu—the capital of Sichuan province in China, adjacent to eastern Tibet—a city of over a million people, is accessible from all the major cities in China, and it is a two-hour flight from Chengdu to the airport that serves Lhasa—indeed, the only civilian airport in the country—at Gonggar, some fifty miles by road from the city. Chengdu is 413 feet above sea level, while Lhasa is at an altitude of some twelve thousand feet, which means that the average tourist who arrived in the city this way, breathless, was probably not in much of a position to do a great deal of sightseeing. As fascinated as I was with Tibet, this kind of visit did not appeal to me at all. I decided that if there was not another way of visiting the country, I was simply not going to go there.

However, in 1985, there was a dramatic change in the situation. The Chinese announced that they would now issue visas to tourists to cross the border into Tibet from Kodari, the very border town that Jaccoux and I had visited by taxi in 1979. This opened up the remarkable prospect of driving from Kathmandu to Lhasa, and back, with a side trip to the base of Mount Everest, which is, in a manner of speaking, along the way. The road to Lhasa is blocked by snow during the fall and winter—the average altitude is close to fifteen thousand feet—so tourist travel really began in earnest in the spring and summer of 1986. In fact, in April of 1986, an Australian, Michael Buckley, and an Englishman, Robert Strauss, published *Tibet: A Travel Survival Kit,* a delightfully irreverent travel guide written, one gathers, for the young, marginally solvent traveler who is willing to try a bit of anything. Here, for example, is their review of the Tasty Restaurant in Lhasa:

> *The Tasty Restaurant . . . is a lively place with the usual system where you go into the kitchen to chose ingredients from bowls of scallions, garlic, peanuts, green beans, tinned bamboo slices, eggs, diced yak meat, tinned mushrooms and greens. [Nearly all of this, the authors pointed out, had been trucked from China.] A large meal will cost about Y3. [Three yuans. The yuan is the basic unit of*

Chinese, and hence Tibetan, money. There were, at the time—the system has now been abolished—two kinds of money used in China: renminbi, the common street currency, and FEC, Foreign Exchange Certificates—which were, at least theoretically, the only money that a foreign visitor to Tibet was allowed to use. Now one can change, for example, dollars directly into yuan, at an exchange rate of something like thirty cents per yuan.] The dumplings are good if they are fresh. Tea is brought round to tables.

This sounds promising, but the authors went on:

The one problem with this place . . . is that you eat your meal amidst what can only be described as a circus. Beggars scrounge the scraps which are scraped into bowls—some of them are obviously pilgrims from remote places who have made it to Lhasa but run out of funds. Kids beg for pens by making a scribbling motion in the palm which becomes obnoxious when thrust between your chopsticks and your face. Meanwhile cripples will hunch over your table intent on swiping an empty beer bottle to get the deposit back, whilst beneath the table, snapping away between your feet, are dogs of all shapes and sizes. Once you've finished though you can have fun watching the others react under attack.

Quite.

The authors also included a section on visiting the Everest region, which, needless to say, caught my eye. I was struck by the fact that, with a suitable four-wheel-drive vehicle, one could drive up to the base camp. In fact, *base camp* was defined, as far as I could make out, as the last place one *could* drive to. This, the guidebook noted, was some seven miles closer to the mountain than the old Rongbuk monastery, and was at an altitude of something over seventeen thousand feet. One would still be quite far from the mountain, and the guidebook went on to say, "From here on, you need proper mountaineering equipment. You would be most unwise to proceed any further unless you're in tip-top shape, have mountaineering experience, and know what you are getting into. Without a guide or a medic you could get into serious trouble, and no one is about to rescue you." Since going beyond base camp was the very thing I had in mind, if I ever managed to get to Tibet, I decided that I had better talk to someone who might tell me how to go about arranging such an expedition.

As I have mentioned, over the years Lieutenant Colonel Roberts's old Mountain Travel has metamorphosed into the large adventure-travel company that is called Tiger Mountain. But still active in the company is my old friend Elizabeth Hawley, whom I first met in 1967 in Nepal, where she has lived since the early 1960s. There is no one who knows more about Himalayan climbing than "Liz" Hawley—who reports on such matters for much of the world's press. She is one of the shareholding directors of Tiger Mountain. So when I was in Kathmandu in the fall of 1986, I asked her if there was a way in which I could drive from Kathmandu to Lhasa, visiting as much of the intervening countryside as possible, and the trek to the base of Everest from the Tibetan side. In short order, she produced a mimeographed itinerary under the Tiger Mountain logo entitled 16 DAY LHASA/EVEREST BASE CAMP. It was one of a spectrum of trips to Tibet that Tiger Mountain had been offering since the summer of 1986—a spectrum that ranged from fairly simple overland sight-seeing tours to fantastic, month-long expeditions that go overland all the way from Kathmandu through western Tibet, finally emerging in the Karakoram range in Pakistan. The sixteen-day Lhasa/Base Camp trip looked perfect for me, since it involved some days of camping and trekking in the Everest region as well as several days in Lhasa. With the various side trips in Tibet, the whole excursion would cover nearly two thousand miles. The only problem, apart from the cost, which was considerable, was that Tiger Mountain required a minimum of five people to make the trip. I returned to the United States and set about trying to recruit at least one volunteer for the trip, while the people in Kathmandu began doing likewise. Our tentative departure date was to be the first of May, 1987.

During the winter, I began receiving various communications from Tiger Mountain. The first one, under the rubric PREPARING FOR TIBET/CHINA, began, "Tibet is an uncomfortable, remote and hard destination. It also offers glimpses into one of the most fascinating, old civilizations and one of the most dramatic mountain lands. It is truly one of the last frontiers for discovery and exploration. All trips are of expeditionary nature but if you travel with an open mind Tibet will be a truly unique and rewarding experience."

Under FOOD AND BEVERAGES, I came across the following: "Please note that the Chinese meals in Tibet are of a much lower standard than elsewhere in China and often served cold. On the 12 and 15-day Lhasa tours the meals served are generally good except in Xegar but on treks/expeditions and particularly at the end of long drives expect rough and ready meals. It is advisable to bring items such as cheese, crackers, some favourite canned food, nuts and chocolates. Now that we will have Sherpas for support on 'treks' and most 'expeditions' who will be providing and preparing the food when away from hotels, we are happy that food standards will improve considerably."

The fact that we would have Sherpas was certainly *very* good news. Besides their other virtues—among them being able to produce excellent meals under conditions in which their clients can barely eat them—they are, as I have mentioned, of Tibetan origin. The Dalai Lama is their spiritual leader and, for them, a trip to Lhasa is also a religious pilgrimage. Another piece of good news was that I had found a recruit: Bil Dunaway. Dunaway was, at the time, the owner and publisher of the *Aspen Times,* in Aspen, Colorado, and used to own *Climbing Magazine.* He has climbed mountains all over the world— he was one of the original members of the Tenth Mountain Division, and once showed me Camp Hale, where the Khampas trained. He has been a downhill ski and automobile racer, and each Saturday for over a decade, we have hiked and climbed together in the mountains around Aspen. Surprisingly—considering his interests—Dunaway had never seen the Himalayas. The trip would be a pilgrimage for him, too. By February, we were informed that Tiger Mountain had found at least three additional recruits, so the trip was on.

But the cost was formidable. The authors of *Tibet: A Travel Survival Kit* estimated that, living on the cheap, one could get around Tibet for ten dollars a day, not counting Lhasa, which is considerably more expensive. However, once one gets into the matter of organized tours and expeditions, all of which must use the services of the China Tibet Tourism General Corporation, a government organization that started operating in 1985, and that has a monopoly on these matters, prices jump exponentially. It was possible to find tours that went, more or less, directly from Kathmandu to Lhasa by bus, or, if one was lucky, by Land Cruiser—a four-wheel-drive vehicle that seats five or six and can negotiate the Tibetan "highways," which are almost never paved. The most direct route is 1,004 kilometers (about six hundred twenty miles) long and can be completed in three days of *very* hard driving. Round-trip economy tours were being advertised in the newspapers in Kathmandu for something less than eight hundred dollars. If one wanted to combine this with an expedition to the Everest base camp, however, the price jumped exponentially again. Tiger Mountain, which is generally regarded as the top-of-the-line operator for expeditions like this, uses a sliding price scale that depends on the number of people involved. For five people—that is, five tourists, the accompanying staff being enormous—the price in 1987 for the Lhasa/Everest trip was $3,257 each, falling to $2,273 when fifteen or more tourists were involved. (The 1995 prices are comparable.) When the Chinese opened the Nepalese border to tourists in 1985, it was only to tourists who were with an organized tour. One of their motivations must have been the realization that, with an organized tour, one could control the *minimum* people pay. The readers of *Tibet: A Travel Survival Kit,* who are encouraged to hitchhike—something that is only marginally legal and extremely difficult (it usually involves an under-the-table payment to a truck driver, since there is essentially no public transport in the country)—are not likely to leave in Tibet a large package of foreign exchange—an immensely valuable commodity to the Chinese. As the authors of the *Survival Kit* remarked wryly, "Tibet once held claim to being the most expensive destination in the world to visit. In the Victorian era the price was probably death—meted out by either the elements or by bandits; by the 1980s the price was reduced to a group tour arm and a leg." In 1986, the Chinese began issuing visas for *individuals* to cross the Nepal-Tibet border, but in May of 1987, they thought better of this; at present, only tours can cross from Nepal to Tibet. The people at Tiger Mountain told me that the base price the Chinese charged them for such a tour was so high that, as far as they were concerned, running trips to Tibet was practically a nonprofit service.

Toward the middle of April, I headed back to Kathmandu. I managed to squeeze the necessary time away from my lecturing duties in the city to prepare for the trip. The preparation included a formal "briefing." Since Tiger Mountain was founded by an ex–Gurkha officer and has various ex-military people working for it, a certain amount of soldiering terminology is used in its operations. Thus, on Wednesday, the twenty-ninth of April, at fifteen hundred hours sharp, we were all instructed to appear at Tiger Mountain headquarters, just outside Kathmandu. By this time, Dunaway had arrived from Aspen, but neither of us had met the rest of the group. At the briefing, we were greeted by what seemed to be a small platoon of people. There were our three cotravelers, who turned out to be young American petroleum engineers. Two of them worked in Saudi Arabia, the third in London. All three had been on several treks in Nepal and looked bearded and hardy. There were four Sherpas, unbearded and *very* hardy. In addition, Tiger Mountain's office manager, Sonam Gyalpo, was to go with us. That was a fortunate piece of news, since Sonam is a Tibetan, born in Kalimpang, in West Bengal, where his parents, until the Chinese takeover in 1959, engaged in trade with Tibet. (*Sonam*, the Tibetan word for "merit," is a common Tibetan and Sherpa first name.)

Sonam's family is a microcosmic illustration of the extraordinary ability of Tibetans to land on their feet in adversity. His older brother, for example, somehow managed to go to the University of Hawaii, where he studied computer science. At the time of our visit, he was living in Vienna and working as a systems analyst; he had married an Austrian. Sonam's mother tongue was Tibetan, but his English was absolutely fluent.

To round out our group was a very droll ex–British army helicopter pilot named Garry Daintry. Daintry specialized in ironman feats like multiday bicycle rides through deserts. He was coming along to get an idea if it would be possible to organize bicycle tours in Tibet.

The briefing lasted for about an hour and several salient points stuck in my mind. First and foremost, there was the matter of the landslides. The region had been drenched with unusual premonsoon rains. This had resulted in two landslides near the Tibetan border, which had cut off the border town of Zhangmu from the roads that led to it from both Tibet and Nepal. Under the best of circumstances, we should have driven in a Nepalese bus to the Friendship Bridge, where we would have been met by a Chinese bus—no foreign cars are allowed in Tibet—which would have taken us up the fifteen-hundred-foot rise to Zhangmu and then, the next day, onward in the general direction of Lhasa. As things stood, however, we were going to be dropped at the border, where we would hire porters for the two-hour walk up to Zhangmu. The next day, we would hire more porters, who would take us under the second, more recent landslide, and on to where the Chinese bus would, it was hoped, be waiting. This brings up the matter of Chinese drivers and Tibetan hotels—at least as they were in 1987.

I learned at the briefing that there was only one hotel in Tibet that had running hot water—the Holiday Inn in Lhasa. (Now there are several; I will discuss this development in the next chapter.) Most of the rest of the hotels offered cold-water taps and outdoor latrines. Since we were going to use tents for the Everest base camp portion of our trip anyway, it struck me that, from every point of view, we would be much better off sleeping in our tents, away from civilization, than in a dubious hotel. The group agreed, and it was decided, or so we thought, that until we reached Lhasa we would camp out. That discussion brought up the matter of the Chinese drivers.

At the time, the China Tibet Tourism General Corporation employed only Chinese drivers for its buses and Land Cruisers. This too has changed. But in 1987, it reflected the secondary role that Tibetans played, and still play, in tourism within their own country. Both then and now, the key to any overland trip in Tibet is the performance of the drivers. We were warned that the Chinese drivers could be impossible. In particular, since they did not like camping, they were quite capable, we were told, despite any previous understandings, of depositing their passengers in the nearest hotel—whatever its quality. Finally, there was a laconic caution from Sonam. "With all the changes," he said, "don't expect Tibet to look like what you have seen in the pictures." With that, we were told to have our gear ready in the lobbies of our various hotels Friday morning at seven, when we would be picked up by a minibus. On Thursday, I made a few last-minute purchases in Kathmandu and, when the bus arrived on Friday, I was ready to go.

The ride to Kodari was the one that I had made with Jaccoux nearly a decade earlier—by taxi. There was one evident change: the number of children. The small towns on the way seemed to be bursting with children—a disaster in the making. Halfway to Kodari, the rickety bus broke down—par for the course—and was put back together skillfully by the driver and his assistant—also par for the course. With the delay, we arrived in Kodari in the early afternoon—that is, early afternoon in *Nepal.* It turned out that all of China, including Tibet, was on one time—Beijing time—which meant that the minute we stepped across the border, it would be three hours and fifteen minutes *later.* One consequence of this inane arrangement was that, for the next sixteen days, we would get up in the pitch black and go to bed long before the sun had set. But now our problem was to get to the Zhangmu hotel—a stiff, two-hour climb, sharply uphill—where we were to meet our Chinese guide and begin the next part of our trip, which, in theory, was to take us to our first campsite.

This part of Tibet is quite low—some six thousand feet above sea level—and the hills are forested with pines. The trail up to Zhangmu, which was boulder-strewn—during workdays, the Chinese had been blasting above the trail in an effort to reopen the road, and some of the debris had come down on the trail—was a living stream of porters carrying everything from pieces of plywood to wool—mainly yak, sheep, and goat. Yak wool is very strong and a bit coarse for sweaters. It used to be widely used in the West for Santa Claus beards. Much of it goes into the manufacture of "Tibetan" carpets—although, if one is not careful, one will purchase what is called a Tibetan carpet but is actually woven in Nepal, of wool imported from places like New Zealand. Fortunately for us, our arrival in Tibet coincided with May Day—a holiday—so that the Chinese were not blasting, and we could make the climb to the border checkpost without worrying about rocks coming down on our heads. Huffing and puffing, I arrived at the border station.

We had all been issued Chinese visas. (The visa form included the odd entry, "Religion and political party.") We showed these to the border guard, a Chinese soldier. In the briefing, we had been warned that at the border we would have to declare all of our watches and camera equipment, down to the last lens, and that we had better have the same items with us when we left Tibet. With all the formalities, we arrived at the Zhangmu Hotel about four o'clock Nepalese time— seven-fifteen local time. The lobby was a semimodern, cavernous place. I got a momentary feeling of homesickness when I looked over the registration desk to see an array of clocks, one of which was, more or less, set to New York time. Our Chinese guide was waiting for us, a diminutive, pink-cheeked, eighteen-year-old woman named Kun. She was, or so we thought, to lead us under the second landslide and up to the road where the Chinese bus and an accompanying truck would be waiting for us. The truck was crucial, since it would be carrying all of our tents and other camping equipment, as well as our food. Without the truck, there would be no camping. "Unfortunately," Kun began in her musically accented but very serviceable English—I would learn that bad news always began with "Unfortunately"—"the truck is broken down." Freely translated, this meant that there was no truck and that, very likely, there had never been a truck. Put somewhat differently, what this meant was that, until we headed for Everest in the Land Cruisers—nearly ten days hence—we would be sleeping in the dreaded Tibetan hotels. This one was a multilevel warren, dimly lit, but basically clean. There was no running hot water—as was to have been expected—and the dining room was some floors below where we were to sleep. The only utensils on the tables were porcelain spoons for the soup, and chopsticks. Since I stubbornly refuse to use the latter, I navigated an indifferent Chinese meal with the former. By seven o'clock Nepalese time—ten-fifteen local—and in broad daylight, I was fast asleep.

We had been warned that the next day would be brutal. It began about 6 A.M.—three in the morning, Nepalese time—in the pitch darkness. We staggered around the hotel using our flashlights and, after breakfast, headed out in the direction of the landslide. Whatever a typical Tibetan village may be, Zhangmu is not it. The population looked to me as if all the races of Central Asia had been put into an urn, shaken up, and drawn out at random. Since Zhangmu is low and relatively tropical, people seemed to be living almost out of doors. The odd snow-covered mountain that one could see through the trees formed a striking contrast to the hodgepodge squalor of the town. The place is set on the side of a steep hill—ergo, the landslides—and to get out of it, one had to walk up a series of terraces to what had been the road. At one point, this road simply disappeared. The beginning of the slide was signaled by a display of white prayer flags—something Tibetans put up to attract favorable attention from the gods. In the middle of the slide was the shell of what once must have been a substantial building. (On our return visit to Zhangmu, on the way out of Tibet, I saw a boulder the size of a Volkswagen detach itself and, in a series of explosive rebounds, move down in the general direction of the slide. That sort of thing must have been what did the building in.) Because of the recent rains, the middle of the slide was oozy mud that seemed to suck at one's feet as one tried to move, as quickly as possible, to the other side, once again signaled by prayer flags. Then, it was steeply uphill for about an hour to where the road was still in one piece.

With the landslide, this roadhead had become the terminus for all the traffic moving from Tibet to Nepal, and vice versa. There were buses and trucks everywhere. Since the Chinese had not yet placed a ban on individual travelers—that would come at the end of May—there were all sorts of people wandering from bus to bus trying to hitch rides. In the general chaos, we located our bus—a new and comfortable-looking Mitsubishi, with a Chinese crew of two. With all our gear, we fitted in snugly but comfortably. Our first destination was Shigatse, Tibet's second city, the home of the Panchen Lama on the rare occasions when he visited Tibet from China. We had been told that it would take about twelve hours to get there—a distance of a little over three hundred miles. There was nothing for it but to settle in and watch the scenery go by.

For the first few hours, the scenery was perfectly spectacular. The road is perched on the side of a profound gorge that has cut, like a knife, through the Himalayas. Waterfalls cascade down its sides from somewhere in the distant snows. In the eighteen miles from Zhangmu to the nearest Tibetan town, Nyalam, where we were to have camped, the road rises five thousand feet. Nyalam is at 12,300 feet, which was about as low as we would be until we left Tibet. The road is dirt and gravel, but it is a marvel of construction. One can see why it cost a good many Tibetan lives to build. It hangs over the Po Chu River like a tightrope. Beyond Nyalam, we were on the Tibetan plateau, and would remain there for the rest of the trip. Today it was not at its best. Although, generally speaking, Tibet is dry—it averages about eighteen inches of precipitation a year—the unusual April rains in Nepal had produced dark, menacing skies over the Tibetan desert. We had been promised spectacular views of the mountains, including Everest and Shisha Pagma, the only one of the thirteen eight-thousand-meter mountains entirely in Tibet. But where the mountains should have been there were only clouds. However, on our return trip, the skies were clear, and the mountain scene was mind-boggling. Out of the hazy green-and-brown Tibetan desert the mountains rose like giant, surreal icebergs. The vision was so astonishing that one expected it to vanish like a dream.

Once on the plateau, the road wound on inexorably. I tried to imagine Alexandra David-Neel walking day after day in this semidesert, in the winter, and failed. We could see the odd black nomad's tent dotting the landscape, and the inevitable collection of grazing animals—grazing on what, I could not imagine. My thought was, How could anyone—Chinese or any other—*control* this country? and just as I was thinking this, we came to a military checkpost near Xegar. Since we had all the necessary documents and were part of a tour, passing this post should have been routine. However, Kun, our young guide, began what seemed to be a cheerful flirtation with some of the soldiers at the post. One of them had a batch of pistols on a wire—which we presumed were unloaded. Kun was offered one, and she began pointing it at various of us and pulling the trigger playfully. To put it mildly, we were not amused. Even less amused was an American I met a few days later who had been on a similar tour. At the same checkpoint, his teenage guide was given a pistol with *live* ammunition to shoot. After she had scattered a few shots around, the American had

had enough, and picked her up bodily and put her back into the bus while she protested, "This is my country and I can do anything I like." When they got to Lhasa, he and his companions complained, and they were given another guide. The Chinese must have become aware of a growing number of tourist complaints about their guides and drivers, because, while we were in Tibet, an item came over the news saying that a certain number of them had been summoned to Beijing for "autocriticism." Now it has become possible to insist that one's guides and drivers be Tibetan—as I was to discover on my most recent trip, which I will describe in the next chapter.

After playing with the guns for a while, Kun seemed ready to get back onto the bus. She then asked us if we would "mind" giving a Chinese soldier a ride to Shigatse. There was little room and, very shortly, the one soldier became two soldiers. Before we had a chance to complain, Kun said, "Unfortunately, we have no choice." Someone in the group remarked that, if we were not careful, the soldiers could simply commandeer the bus and leave us at the checkpoint. They got on, young and unsmiling, with their gear, which included the brace of pistols and a guitar. Nothing was heard from them for the rest of the trip. Hour after hour went by until the sun began to set. Our list of things to bring on the trip had included dust masks, and now we could see why. Dust seemed to come into the bus from all sides, even with the windows closed. We all put our masks on, giving everyone an oddly surgical look. To add to the general ambience, the bus driver apparently had only one tape, which he played over and over again. It included, among other things, the theme music from the film *Love Story*. As far as I was concerned, it was a new and much more effective version of the ancient Chinese water torture. Finally, not long before midnight, we pulled into the Shigatse Hotel, were fed a lukewarm midnight meal, and were sent to bed with no warm shower.

Shigatse, a town of some forty thousand Tibetans, and at least as many Chinese soldiers, is a microcosm of everything that has happened to Tibet since the Chinese takeover. It is, in the first place, the home of the Panchen Lamas. At the time of our visit, the latest of the Panchen Lamas was still alive, but was living in China. That unfortunate soul had at first proclaimed the Chinese occupation to be a "wonderful" thing for Tibet. But after having been asked to denounce the Dalai Lama, and refusing, he was brought to trial and beaten into a state where he was once again able to see the merits of the occupation. In January of 1989, he came to Shigatse for a visit. By all accounts he was in excellent health. But on the twenty-ninth of January, the Chinese authorities suddenly announced that the fifty-one-year-old Panchen had died of a "heart attack." There must have been an epidemic, because the Chinese also announced that his two parents had died of heart attacks at about the same time. In May of 1995, the Dalai Lama announced that a six-year-old boy from a remote district of Tibet had been identified as the reincarnate. However, in early November, the Chinese announced that the boy, Choekyi Nima was unacceptable to them. Indeed, he seems to have disappeared along with his parents. Seventy-five senior Tibetan monks were summoned to Beijing to choose among three boys the Chinese had selected. The final choice was made by drawing lots from a golden urn. It is also clear that this was basically a political act by the Chinese—an attempt to further weaken the Dalai Lama's authority. It was also clearly a sort of dress rehearsal for what would happen when the Dalai Lama died. This is the latest, and perhaps final, chapter in the power struggle between the Dalai Lama, the Panchen Lama, and the Chinese.

The previous Panchen Lama's status with the Tibetan people was, perhaps, best reflected in the matter of the pictures. Before coming to Tibet, we were told to go into the bazaars in Kathmandu and get as many photographs of the Dalai Lama as we could lay our hands on. Among us we must have had well over a hundred—many too few. All Tibetans, it seems, know how to say something that sounds like "Dalai Lama pichu," meaning that they want a photograph of the Dalai Lama. By the time we left, all our pictures were gone—and we could have given away ten times the number we did. No one ever asked us for a picture of the Panchen Lama.

Then there was the city of Shigatse itself. The Tibetan quarter, if one can identify it, is near the entrance of the Tashilhunpo monastery. But it is completely dwarfed by the ugly Chinese city that surrounds it. The whole thing looks like a military camp, with concrete-block house after concrete-block house, most of them with ugly tin roofs.

Apart from the Tashilhunpo and the ruins of an old fort demolished in the Cultural Revolution, I could not find a single redeeming bit of architecture. To boot—and this is common in Tibet—people in the city ride their bicycles (the common mode of transportation) wearing surgical masks to protect themselves from the dust that blows in from the surrounding plains. The Friendship Store—the local department store—is depressing in another way. It is filled with ill-made objects such as plastic toy tractors, which I got the impression that Tibetan children could not afford to buy. They would stand staring at them until someone kicked them out of the store. I did not have the heart to buy anything.

The Tashilhunpo is a microcosm of what has happened to the monasteries. As with all monasteries in Tibet, its affairs are run by the Bureau of Religious Affairs. This Chinese-dominated governmental bureau decides how much money shall be allocated to the restoration of any monastery. The Tashilhunpo suffered considerable destruction during the Cultural Revolution but, perhaps because of its association with the Panchen Lama, it now seems fairly well restored. The Bureau of Religious Affairs also decides how many monks there will be, and what they will do. Very few monks are now allowed to practice a purely contemplative life. The rest work—in monastic farms, for example— so as not to become—the Chinese term—"parasites." In the monasteries I visited, I made a point of asking how many monks were present now and how many there had been before. I came to the conclusion that the current numbers must be about a tenth of those from before the Chinese occupation. In the Tashilhunpo, where there had once been some four or five thousand monks, there were then around seven hundred. The Bureau of Religious Affairs also sets the price of admission to the monasteries and, above all, the price of photographing the rooms. In the more famous monasteries, this can be as much as ten dollars a room. For most visitors to Tibet, the monasteries are the principal attraction.

None of us was sorry, the next morning, to leave the Shigatse Hotel. The meals and cold water apart, there was the matter of the keys, which is tied to the general question of service in these provincial hotels. Maybe it was part of the communal spirit, of which I have inordinately little, but none of us was allowed to have his own room keys. If one of us locked his door by setting the latch, then to get back into the room he had to persuade one of the women at the service desk on his floor, if he could find her, to let him back in. She carryied the keys to all the rooms on the floor on a giant ring. She was annoyed, and we were annoyed, at going through this ritual several times a day. Why we could not have our own keys was never explained.

From Shigatse to Lhasa is only some two hundred miles, but we expected to be all day at it and we were. There are two routes, each involving crossing passes of over sixteen thousand feet. The northern route, which we would take on our return trip, goes through some spectacular mountain scenery and links up with the road to central China. The southern route, which we took on our way to Lhasa, goes by Lake Yamdrok, which is the third-largest lake in Tibet. On a sunny day it looks like a turquoise scorpion. On this overcast and cold day, the lake was seabird gray. Like all the lakes I have seen in Tibet, it did not have a single boat on it. Our route also went through the town of Gyantse, which is linked to India by way of Sikkim. It will be recalled that the storming of the fort in Gyantse on July 6, 1904, by the Younghusband mission, was the key to opening the way to Lhasa for the British. Beyond Gyantse, our route would be identical to theirs.

It is only about sixty miles from Shigatse to Gyantse, but when we got there, Kun announced, "Boys, we will have a half-hour to see the monastery and the fort." The "boys," who ranged in age from their midthirties to their midsixties, made it quite plain that they intended to spend as much time as they wanted examining these monuments. Kun went off in a teenage sulk, and we spent an hour or so looking at Kumbum—a house of worship consisting of many interlocking chapels, with their striking, and often demonic, decorations, which one can see as one works one's way up to the gilded roof.

As we drove around Lake Yamdrok, we encountered a bicycle tour, supported by its own flotilla of vehicles, wending its way painfully in the direction of Shigatse. By late afternoon, the desert had given way to cultivated land and the road had become, miraculously, paved. It was clear that we were nearing Lhasa. Lhasa is set in a kind of amphitheater of mountains and, from a distance, has just the aura of mystery and romance one hopes from it. First, one sees the gilded roofs of neighboring monasteries, and then—fulfilling every expectation—the haunting vision of the Potala itself. It is only when one begins driving through the city that the reality becomes apparent. The Chinese have turned Lhasa into a lumpen, dreary provincial capital. In 1987, the time of my first visit, it was estimated to have had a population of about one hundred fifty thousand civilians, the vast majority of whom were Chinese. At present, the number is estimated to be between three and four hundred thousand, of which 20 to 30 percent are Tibetan. The large migration into Lhasa from China occurred after 1992, when controls on internal movement within China were relaxed. Most of the immigrants are from the neighboring Chinese province of Sichuan, but some 20 to 30 percent are Muslims from the northwestern provinces of China, who came to Tibet with the idea of improving their economic lot. Only some 10 or 15 percent of the shops and businesses in Lhasa are thought to be owned by Tibetans. Of course, these Chinese population numbers do not include either the military or the governmental sector—almost entirely Chinese. The Tibetans are gradually being marginalized in their own capital city.

It is interesting that the sense of disappointment one feels upon first setting foot in Lhasa seems to be common to all its foreign visitors—even Alexandra David-Neel. In their own irreverent way, the authors of the *Survival Kit* commented, "If you are disappointed with Lhasa, or feel cheated of the mystique you had expected, you won't be the first. The eccentric English traveller Manning delivered his verdict in 1812, and it still rings true, while he found the Potala extraordinary, he found the rest of the place a dump. In 1904, the invading English under Younghusband found their triumphal march impeded by piles of refuse, stagnant pools of water, open sewers and various rabid animals foraging for putrid scraps of food. . . ." In 1949, Lowell Thomas Jr., on a visit to Tibet (at the invitation of the Dalai Lama), wrote: "Nothing is known of modern plumbing. Refuse piles up on all corners . . . once a year these offal heaps are transferred to the fields to stimulate crops. The odors are not entirely pleasant. The nobles hold scented handkerchiefs to their noses as they ride along . . . dead animals are tossed in refuse piles to be fought over and devoured by the city's scavengers—thousands of mangy dogs and ravens!"

This less than a half-century ago. The feeling one has now is, I think, quite different. Just as the British brought, at the end of a bayonet, free trade to Lhasa, whether the Tibetans wanted it or not, the Chinese have brought, at the end of a bayonet, some of the trappings of modernity to Lhasa—including a much higher level of sanitation—whether the Tibetans want it or not. But at what cost?

In its own way as remarkable as the Potala is the Holiday Inn in Lhasa. Here we were, four days without a hot shower, dust-clad arrivals from the Tibetan desert, finding ourselves in front of a hyper-modern structure claiming to have 486 twin-bedded guest rooms, each with a color TV, its own bathroom—with hot and cold running water—and its own key; two restaurants; a bar lounge with a string quartet whose limited but nicely played repertoire included Mozart and Beethoven; and enough bottled oxygen to supply the needs of any guest who was having trouble breathing. It was almost too much to credit, especially when one was informed that the film to be shown that very evening on the TV would be *The Sound of Music*, in English, with Chinese subtitles. The hotel, I learned, had been built in 1985, and opened in September of that year under the name Lhasa Hotel. The first six months were so disastrous, in terms of tourist complaints, that the Chinese decided to enter into a ten-year management agreement with Holiday Inns. The name was officially changed to the Lhasa Holiday Inn on August 8, 1987. The manager on my visit was Swiss and, apart from him, three other Europeans ran the hotel. The staff varied in size from 580 during the winter, which is the low season, to about a thousand in the summer, at the height of the tourist season. Forty-seven of the staff were from Beijing and the rest were local people. The two main problems facing the management were training and English. In a country in which some 50 percent of the population is nomadic, sleeping in a bed, western-style—let alone making one—is exotic. All of this had to be taught.

English is a much deeper matter, and goes to the heart of what the Chinese occupation of Tibet is all about. At present, children learn Tibetan and Chinese in grade school. All the elementary school texts that I saw were in Chinese. If a child goes on to high school, he or she also learns English. I have never visited any of these schools, but the quality is said to be poor. I would have to compare them with the schools that I have visited in India and Nepal to know what this means. In 1987, all of the secondary education was given in Chinese, which meant that any Tibetan who did not want to be educated in Chinese could also not learn English. My sense is that, in the seven years since my two visits, more Tibetans have learned English. Nonetheless, I would have to say that Tibet is the most linguistically alien country I have ever visited. Even in Nepal, one can get along quite well, except in very remote regions, with English. A visitor to Tibet would do well to have a phrase book at the ready. We were very fortunate on both visits to have Tibetan-speaking people with us. In this respect, the Sherpas, it turns out, do not really count. The Sherpa and Tibetan languages have, by now, diverged to such an extent that our Sherpas spoke English with our Tibetans. Almost none of the Chinese people we encountered spoke any Tibetan at all.

For those visitors to Lhasa who stayed there, the Lhasa Holiday Inn was like an island. There are now a few more western-style hotels. But in 1987, one found that strangers in the hotel tended to go out of their way to be friendly. Take the case of the Parmesan cheese. After a couple of forays into the formal buffet in the main dining room, I had taken to eating in the coffee shop where the menu featured such items as "spaghetti Bolognese." The "spaghetti" was, I think, made out of barley, and had neither the consistency nor the taste of the "real" thing. I put "real" in quotation marks, because it may well have tasted like the item that Marco Polo brought back from China when he introduced pasta to Europe. In any event, I grew quite fond of it, and had it several nights for dinner. One night, while I was eating my spaghetti, I heard a female voice from a nearby table asking me if I would like some Parmesan cheese. I said, "Certainly," and an attractive blond woman, who had finished eating and was in the process of leaving, stood up and fished out of an enormous cloth purse one of those little green cans of Kraft Parmesan cheese with the small holes on top. She came over to my table, carefully shook a ration of cheese onto my spaghetti, and walked out with a smile. I never saw her again. Perhaps she was one of the people who answered a notice on the hotel bulletin board asking if anyone wanted to join an overland horseback trip to Chengdu—a mere fourteen hundred miles from Lhasa. Or perhaps she joined one of the overland tours back to Kathmandu, or Everest, similarly advertised.

Kun, bless her heart, managed to come up with what she called "the Number One Bus in Tibet." It was a beautiful black Japanese-made bus that was going to trundle us around Lhasa while we visited the sights. She also taught us to chant in unison a Chinese phrase that sounds something like *toddley-ba,* and means, she explained, "We are all here." Each morning we boarded the Number One Bus for our daily tour and chanted in unison, "Toddley-ba." The next few days went by in a haze of Buddhas, lamas, and yak butter. In every monastery, there are rows of perpetually burning votive lamps—often the only source of illumination—filled with yak butter. Burning yak butter has a characteristic penetrating smell that permeates one's clothes. My down jacket still exudes a light miasma of yak butter, which, I think, it will have forever.

When visiting a monastery—or other historical building in Tibet—one is sometimes not clear whether one is visiting a shrine or a museum. However, it is clear that the Dalai Lama's former summer palace, the Norbu Lingka, is a museum. It must have been lovely when its gardens were carefully tended, and people lived there. When I saw it, the grounds looked shabby and threadbare, and the pitiful zoo, with its huge and remorseful caged black bear, was an eyesore. The buildings were well preserved, gaily decorated, but very cold. The only thing that moved me was the young fourteenth Dalai Lama's room, from which he must have heard the sound of the two Chinese shells that exploded near his palace in March of 1959. One wonders if he was listening to the Phillips Victrola that still sits intact in the room. I noticed that there was an old RCA "His Master's Voice" record on it, with the title *Tibetan Songs.* When he fled, the Victrola and the records were left behind.

The Potala presents itself more as a museum than as a shrine. The monks who attend it, if they are monks, seem more concerned that one pay one's photography fee—here, some ten dollars a room—than anything else. The *stupas*—tombs—of the Dalai Lamas were to me very affecting. They are meant to overawe, with their tons of gold, but I kept thinking, Where will the fourteenth Dalai Lama be buried? Will he return to Tibet only in death, or will death be a continuation of his exile?

The Jokhang, on the other hand, is definitely a shrine. It is at the Jokhang—the most sacred site in all of Lamaistic Buddhism—that one sees firsthand the powerful, deeply profound attachment that Tibetans have to their religion. All the years of Chinese occupation do not seem to have made a dent in that. In front of the temple, the Chinese have cleared away from the old Tibetan quarter, which used to surround the Jokhang on all sides, a sort of modern square—almost a mall—lined with a few dreary Friendship Stores. But the pilgrims who come from all over Tibet to worship at the Jokhang have converted this into a kind of religious park. One reads about people prostrating themselves and loco-moting on all fours, sometimes for days, to reach holy sites like the Jokhang. And, in front of the Jokhang, one finds groups of pilgrims prostrating themselves. When one makes the traditional clockwise tour of the exterior of the Jokhang, through what is known as the Barkhor—the "Eight Corners," Lhasa's fantastic outdoor Tibetan bazaar—one finds people circumnavigating the building on their hands and knees. On my visit in 1987, I also saw pairs of Chinese soldiers, arms linked, walking ostentatiously around the Barkhor counterclockwise—the wrong way. In the next chapter I will describe my visit of 1994, which left a somewhat different impression.

It is interesting to watch the course of one's own mind in the presence of so much nearly incomprehensible religious symbolism. Over the next few weeks we each, at various times, arrived at a state of saturation that we came to refer to—no disrespect intended—as being "Buddha'd out." I became Buddha'd out one afternoon in the Drepung monastery, a few miles west of Lhasa. The Drepung, which was founded in 1416, was once the largest and richest monastery in Tibet. It its heyday, it housed ten thousand monks. On the occasion of my visit it had about four hundred, most of whom worked in the nearby orchard. It is a maze of chapels, festooned with Buddhas and labyrinthine murals. One does find the odd monk reading and chanting from one of the flat, often wood-bound, texts that fill the libraries of these monasteries. I had listened to one of these monks—a wonderfully serene looking elderly man, whose mouth seemed largely untroubled by teeth—chant for about ten minutes when I realized that I had become Buddha'd out. I decided that the only cure for this pitiable state of mind would be to find out the meaning of what this good man was actually chanting—even just a tiny bit of it. I enlisted the help of our Tibetan leader from Tiger Mountain, Sonam Gyalpo, and one of the Sherpas. We approached the kindly-looking monk. I explained through my interpreters that I wanted to know what just a single page said. The monk studied me carefully then said, through my interpreters, that I would not be able to understand it. This was too much. In my Buddha'd-out state I heard myself saying, "Try me. I understand the quantum theory; Bell's theorem; the Everett many-worlds interpretation; the Einstein, Podolsky, and Rosen experiment. Just try me." I do not know how this was translated into Tibetan, but the monk did agree to chant a single page. Sonam and the Sherpa listened intently, their faces falling unhappily as the chant proceeded. At the end, they had to confess that they had not understood a single word either. I decided that they were in the situation of a Reform Jew from a Manhattan congregation who goes to Brooklyn and asks one of the Hasidim to chant from the Talmud. I felt a great deal better about the whole thing, and was prepared to visit our final monastery in Lhasa, the Sera.

On our way to the Sera monastery, on the outskirts of Lhasa, we passed the new athletic field and stadium built by the Chinese. No one could recall the stadium's having actually been used for anything. Perhaps it can be used for the *lungom-pa*—the Tibetan mystics who used to put themselves into a kind of trance and then run at high speed, sixty miles or so at a clip, across the Tibetan plateau. Alexandra David-Neel, on her walk to Lhasa, reported having encountered one from time to time. The Sera monastery is noted as a site for what are called "sky burials." In Tibet, because of a shortage of fuel, cremation is for the rich. In his introduction to his translation of the *Bardo Thodol*—the Tibetan Book of the Dead—the text that is read to a dying Tibetan to prepare him or her for the forty-nine days of Bardo, the state after death in which the next life is approached, W. Y. Evans Wentz described the Tibetan attitude toward burial. He wrote, "Tibetans generally object to earth burial, for they believe that when a corpse is interred, the spirit of the deceased, upon seeing it, attempts to re-enter it, and that if the attempt is successful a vampire results, whereas cremation, or other methods of quickly dissipating the elements of the dead body, prevent vampirism."[2] Since cremation is not commonly practiced, a low caste of Tibetans called *domdens* reduce the dead body into morsels, which are then eaten by birds of prey: vultures, ravens, and kites. There is an isolated rock formation, close to the monastery and not open to visitors, where this ceremony is practiced at dawn. When we got to the Sera, it was midmorning, and the only trace of whatever ceremony might have taken place earlier was the wheeling of a few isolated birds. It was an eerie sight. Then, since we were leaving for Everest the next morning, we all stood in line while a Sera lama touched our necks with a heavy stone that was thought to ward off illness and injury—good luck, perhaps, for a dangerous trip.

Early the next morning, I saw a Land Cruiser drive up to the hotel. The young Chinese driver sped the car through the parking lot, slammed on the brakes, and got out with a satisfied swagger. He was wearing a kind of tight-fitting gray teddy-boy suit—common to the young Chinese one sees in Lhasa—with a pair of what looked like high-heeled sandals, apparently the latest rage. A cigarette dangled from the corner of his mouth; he was the king of the road. I took an instantaneous dislike to him. His Land Cruiser seated six and baggage pretty comfortably. We divided up by generations. Dunaway, our British "ironman," Garry Daintry, and I, and two of the Sherpas, got into the machine with the teddy-boy driver, while the rest of the group got into the second Land Cruiser. We left Lhasa by the northern route, which connects to the Chinese heartland. This after a half-hour's delay, while our driver stopped for a mysterious errand. It later turned

2. It is not clear whether or not Wentz ever tried digging into the earth of the Tibetan plateau. Having done it on several occasions, when trying to erect tents, I can testify that it is like digging into concrete—another possible reason that earth burial is not popular.

out that he was trying unsuccessfully to talk another driver into taking his place—a measure of his enthusiasm for the trip.

As we left Lhasa, we encountered convoy after convoy of soldiers. Lhasa had been alive with rumors of an impending border war between the Chinese and Indians over the southern border of Tibet, the McMahon Line. The putative front was said to be two days' drive from Lhasa. People told us that the local hospitals had been cleared, the better to receive the possible casualties. Travelers had said that the flight from Chengdu was operating only on alternate days—the other days being used to fly in military personnel. During our visit to the Norbu Lingka, we had encountered what we were told was an entire squadron of fighter pilots who said they had come to Lhasa for a "vacation." Each day, on Garry Daintry's shortwave radio, we could listen to the Chinese and Indian "brotherly" conversations—in tones to make one's blood run cold. And now, as we left Lhasa, were those truckloads after truckloads of soldiers. For some reason, this seemed to unnerve our driver. He started passing cars with abandon. I heard Daintry say, "Don't even think of that." I looked up to see our driver pass a car, barely missing an oncoming truck. Daintry and I agreed that if the driver made one more dangerous maneuver, we would stop the car. No sooner said than done: The driver made a lunatic passing maneuver on a blind hill, and we stopped the car. The second Land Cruiser, which had been following us, also came to a stop. I went over to Kun and said that if our driver did not drive more carefully, one of us was going to take over the car. "Unfortunately," Kun began, "the driver has been on vacation in China and is now suffering from the altitude." What luck! Two million Tibetans to choose from and we have a Chinese driver with altitude sickness. Kun came into our car, trading places with one of the Sherpas. The petroleum engineers gave her a small stack of Joni Mitchell tapes to cheer her up. Kun spoke to the driver and informed us that he had apologized and promised to do better. We drove on over the plateau with no further incidents.

After another dreary night in the Shigatse Hotel, we headed east, in the direction of Nepal. Even though we were by now all of us Buddha'd out and eager to get to the mountains, Sonam Gyalpo said that it would be a great mistake if we did not make a side trip to visit the monastery of Sakya. He was right. Apart from the Jokhang and Mount Kailas, which I will describe in the next chapter, the Sakya monastery is the most extraordinary religious site I have seen in Tibet. From a distance, the village of Sakya seems untouched by modern life. Only when one gets closer does one notice a nearby Chinese hydroelectric power plant with the usual array of tin-roofed, concrete-block houses. But this has not affected the beauty of the monastery. There are, in fact, two monasteries—the North and the South. The North Monastery was largely destroyed in the Cultural Revolution, but the South Monastery appears to be intact. It dates from the Khans. Indeed, it was with the monks of Sakya that the Khans made their alliance, and preserved in the monastery is the parchment with its gold seal—the Seal of Kublai Khan—authorizing the monks of Sakya to rule all of Tibet. As we have seen, this is what lead to the institution of the Dalai Lamas. The statuary in the monastery has been beautifully preserved in the dry desert air, as has the fantastic library with its thousands of scrolls and *thangkas* (painted scrolls). Best of all, the monastery appears to be functioning as a real monastery. When we were there, we saw a group of young novices at prayer in the great chanting hall. This hall has a roof that is supported by forty huge tree-trunk columns. One of them is said to have been a gift of Kublai Khan himself. The effect is something like being in a giant, serene forest. If only all of Tibet were like this.

Our next stop was Xegar, the turnoff onto the road that leads to the Everest base camp. To get there we passed the town of Lhatse, and the fork in the highway—one branch of which leads west across Tibet, just north of the Himalayas, and then into Pakistan. It looked very inviting. Little did I know. I would find out seven years later. Toward evening, the Land Cruisers came to a bend in the road, near a river. I looked out the window and saw a delightful tent camp. The rest of our Sherpas had by now commandeered a truck, and they had already set up our camp and made tea. It was like coming home.

The next morning, our little caravan—two Land Cruisers and the truck with the tents and the food—headed for Everest. The road, which was at best a superannuated Jeep track, appeared first to climb aimlessly in the general direction of the Pang La—a pass at seventeen thousand feet. The terrain was bleak and fairly monotonous, and nothing prepared one for the view from the top of the pass. I have spent a good deal of my life in and among mountains, but I have never seen anything like the panorama from the top of that pass. It may be the only place on earth where the ordinary traveler—as opposed to a mountain climber—can see four eight-thousand-meter mountains in one sweep. From left to right, one sees—unobstructed—Makalu, Lhotse, Everest, and Cho Oyu. When one sees Everest from Nepal, it is usually obstructed by lesser and closer mountains. From the Pang La, it dominates the horizon, and there is absolutely no doubt that it is the king of the range. We could hardly tear ourselves away from the view.

The road then descended into a broad valley, and the mountains disappeared. The main obstacle was a river, the Dzakar Chu, which can be impossible to cross. Our caravan managed to do so, but only after one of the four-wheel-drive Land Cruisers towed the truck through it, attached to a climbing rope. The road then became worse and worse, and one jounced along hoping the vehicles would stay on it. Suddenly, with almost no warning, we were at the Rongbuk monastery, or at least what was then left of it. (There has since been some reconstruction.) The first thing that we noticed was the brightly colored stupa, and the second thing—the overwhelming thing—was Everest. This was the view that stunned the British when they first saw it in the 1920s. Everest fills the skyline. One can make out all the features that one has read about in the accounts of trying to climb it from this side. Above all are the yellow bands that streak across its north face. It looks unclimbable, but we knew that there had been several expeditions on that face, including a solo American who was later killed. The road now all but disappeared, and we made crude tracks through a bleak moraine until the vehicles, blocked by a rocky outcrop, could go no farther. This was the Everest base camp, at about seventeen thousand feet.

We set up our tents and the wind began to blow. The winds on Everest are notorious. The summit of the mountain is often in the jet stream, and a characteristic plume of snow perpetually blows off the summit. The Sherpas got a fire going, and over tea we plotted our next move. The idea was to make a high camp in the snow at about eighteen thousand six hundred feet, from which the fittest could spend a day trying to get to the Lho La, the high pass that leads into Nepal. (It was the place from which Mallory looked over to Nepal and claimed that Everest was unclimbable from the Nepalese side.) That was our plan. But everything rapidly became unstuck. Yaks were to carry all of our gear up to the camp. But it seemed that all of the yaks in the Rongbuk had been commandeered by a huge Swedish expedition whose neat camp was festooned with blue and yellow flags a few hundred yards from ours. Most of the Swedes were on the mountain, where they had rigged up some kind of satellite telecommunications system so that every night, they could talk to their wives and girlfriends in Sweden. They had been on the mountain for weeks, and had taken all the yaks. Sonam Gyalpo made several forays among the yak drivers, and each time had returned crestfallen. Just when we thought everything was lost, a remarkable compromise was reached: The yaks will not go, but the drivers will, and—for a high price—they can carry most of our stuff. We went back to our tents, the wind howling, and got ready for the next day.

The walk up to the high camp had an eerie beauty. The trail follows the moraine alongside the Rongbuk Glacier. In my mind's eye, I could see the map in Ullman's book—that map of the Everest region I looked at so often as a child. We were, for the time being, walking where Mallory must have walked. To our right, on the glacier, we could see the strange ice formations that look like monks at prayer—the French call them *"penitents."* From time to time, we could catch a glimpse of the north face of Everest. Mallory's route branched off from ours and continued onto the East Rongbuk Glacier. We kept climbing, up into the snow. The going got harder, and I began to feel the altitude dramatically. Everyone else had gotten ahead of me. By the time that I got to the camp, the Sherpas had already set up the tents. I flopped into mine, too exhausted to move. The next day, the weather was beautiful, but I was done for. The altitude had gotten me. While my coexpeditioners went off in the direction of the Lho La, I made a few forays up to where I could see Everest, and then returned, gasping, into my tent. Late that afternoon they came back, exhausted but exhilarated. It was time to go home.

The next day, we broke camp and made the long walk down to where we had left the vehicles. As much as I love the mountains, I was glad to see our base camp tents and the rest of the group. Poor Kun had spent the three days in her tent. "Unfortunately," she said, "I do not feel well." We asked her if she planned to come back to Everest. " No," she said, "never."

The next morning, we began the drive back to Nepal. This return trip was even more unreal than the one out. The weather was perfect, and while we had been gone the desert plateau had acquired a light tinge of green—green, turquoise blue, and brown—with the great mountains hovering on the horizon. The road suddenly dove between the mountains and we were dropped into the lush tropical splendor of Nepal. Tibet, only a few miles away, had vanished like a dream.

Epilogue

The first of October is celebrated by the Chinese in Tibet as a national day. It is the anniversary of the Chinese Communist Revolution and, coincidentally, marks the Chinese takeover of Tibet, which began in October of 1950. The observation that took place in October of 1987, some four months after we left Tibet, was different from previous ones. In the first place, a large number of foreign tourists was present. In the second, the celebration turned violent. According to eyewitness accounts by the tourists, somewhere between three thousand and five thousand Tibetans in Lhasa took part in anti-Chinese demonstrations. Many of the demonstrators were monks from the nearby Sera and Drepung monasteries. The monks carried the outlawed Tibetan flag, which depicts a pair of lions beneath a snow-capped mountain, and led crowds of pilgrims in a traditional circuit of the Jokhang temple. As they marched, the crowds chanted, "This is Tibet, a free and independent nation!" Four days earlier, in a much smaller demonstration outside the Jokhang, two dozen monks had been beaten and arrested; now, the crowds attacked a Chinese police station near the temple and burned it to the ground. The rioting continued over the next few days. At least fifteen people, nine of whom were Tibetans and the rest Chinese police, were killed, and thousands of additional Chinese security forces were flown into Tibet. The

Chinese accused the Dalai Lama, who had just visited the United States and met with members of the Congressional Human Rights Caucus, of making remarks during that visit that had incited the Tibetans to riot. The Tibetans, however, said that the demonstrations had been sparked, at least in part, by the execution of two Tibetan nationalists a week earlier. Given the despair that many Tibetans feel about the occupation of their country, the proximate cause of these particular demonstrations could have been anything. What was new was that these demonstrations were acknowledged publicly by the Chinese, who consider all Tibetan matters to be a purely internal Chinese affair—a view that has, unfortunately, also been the official policy of the United States government. As an apparent result of the strong reaction that the news reports of the clashes provoked in the West, the Chinese quickly reversed their policy of journalistic openness and expelled all foreign newspeople from Tibet. Tourism was also suspended until April 18, 1988, when the Chinese announced that they would allow tourists into Tibet on a restricted basis. No individual visas would be issued and all tourists would have to spend a minimum of one hundred yuan—about twenty-seven dollars—a day. In addition, all of these groups would be compelled to hire Chinese guides. Since 1988, the rules governing tourism in Tibet have been in a constant state of flux, but the general trend has been toward liberalization—at least for the present. In principle, it is still not possible to get a simple entry visa into Tibet for an individual. But it is possible to have oneself categorized as a one-person tour—although the details of such a "tour" must be approved and coordinated with a travel agent in Lhasa. My own experience suggests that one is much better off joining an organized tour. Incidentally, as I will recount in the next chapter, it is, at least as of this writing, no longer necessary to have a Chinese guide. But these things can change overnight—one way or another—in Tibet.

All of this raises a deep moral question—one that faces or should face any prospective traveler to Tibet: Should one go there at all under the present circumstances? An impressive argument for the negative was given in a newspaper op-ed column by John Avedon, the author of *In Exile from the Land of Snows,* a powerful indictment of the Chinese in Tibet. Mr. Avedon wrote, "In 1986, almost thirty thousand tourists visited Tibet. They exulted in the most rarefied air on Earth, marveled at the Potala . . . and enjoyed Tibetans' native kindness beside their nervous Chinese overlords. What most people failed to recognize was that the money paid to see 160 rebuilt monasteries [there are now many more] did not go to Tibetans. Instead, it directly subsidized the purveyors of Tibet's destruction, 32,000 of whom [now very likely many more] are working in Lhasa's service sector."

He concluded, "So a Communist regime is selling the supposedly antique society that its creed has pledged to erase. Another irony is Beijing's use of Tibetans to sponsor through the tourist trade their own demise."

Despite Mr. Avedon's strong arguments, and with a full awareness of what the Chinese are doing in Tibet, I would like to make the case that western tourists *should* visit Tibet. Tourists are the only window that lets light into the country. It was tourists, after all, who informed us of the events in Lhasa in the fall of 1987 after the journalists were expelled. But let me give three personal examples, based on my first trip to Tibet in 1987, of what I have in mind.

The first has to do with Tibetan artists. On the first of May, 1987, a new art gallery opened in Lhasa. A young Tibetan artist was given permission to use a large, loftlike structure to create an art gallery in which he was going to sell mainly modern Tibetan art. There is a long history of Tibetan art, which has traditionally been purely religious. As Giuseppe Tucci wrote in his book *Tibet*, "Tibetan art is essentially anonymous, and it is unusual for works of painting or sculpture to be signed. To paint or sculpt is an act of worship, and as such implies the negation of the person who performs it." Tucci would have been astounded at the art in this gallery. It is both personal and secular and represented the work of modern Tibetan artists. Its themes grow out of the natural, austere beauty of Tibet. Only tourists can afford to buy this work. If they do not, the gallery will disappear—and who will see these paintings?

My second example involves children. The incident occurred on our trip back to Nepal after having seen Everest. We were camped out one night by a river in what seemed like an isolated spot. But one thing one learns while traveling in Tibet is that, no matter how remote the site, people seem to materialize there. One has the sense that they emerge from the earth. No sooner had we pitched our tents than a small group of children appeared from somewhere. One young boy, who was carrying a book, spoke some English, meaning that he must have been doing his studies in Chinese rather than Tibetan. In fact, the book he was carrying was his geology schoolbook, written in Chinese—and, like schoolchildren everywhere, he wanted to show us what he had been learning, and so he recited his lessons to us.

The third example also involves a young Tibetan. It occurred just as we were leaving Tibet. We were at Zhangmu, early in the morning, waiting for the border to open. Alongside us was a long line of porters looking for work. Most of them looked not much older than school-children. One stepped slightly out of the line, and did not get back into it quickly enough to suit one of the Chinese soldiers supervising the lineup. The soldier went over and kicked the boy in the legs with his heavy boots. He was about to kick him again when he saw me watching him—and walked away. What would have happened if I had *not* been there to watch?

The kindness and good humor of the Tibetan people in the face of the most terrible sort of adversity is grounded in their faith. The meanest object can, for a Tibetan, become an object of veneration. In her book *Magic and Mystery in Tibet,* Alexandra David-Neel tells a Tibetan folk story about a trader who traveled every year from Tibet to India, where the Buddha had been born. Each year, he promised to bring back for his aged mother a relic from that holy land, and each year he forgot. But "this time the merchant remembered his promise before reaching his home and was much troubled at the idea of once more disappointing his aged mother's eager expectation."

Just as he was having these thoughts, he caught sight of a dog's jaw lying near the road. He got an idea.

He broke off a tooth of the bleached jaw-bone, wiped away the earth which covered it and wrapped it in a piece of silk. Then, having reached his house, he offered the old bone to his mother, declaring that it was a most precious relic, a tooth of the great Sariputra.

Overjoyed, her heart filled with veneration, the good woman placed the tooth in a casket on the altar of the family shrine. Each day she worshipped before it, lighting lamps and burning incense. Other devotees joined in the worship and, after time, rays of light shone from the dog's tooth, promoted [to a] holy relic.

Alexanda Neel concluded, "A popular Tibetan saying is born from the story:
Mos gus yod na
Kyi so od tung
which means, 'If there is veneration, even a dog's tooth emits light.'"

For all of these reasons, when Jaccoux proposed, seven years later, revisiting Tibet—to travel overland from Lhasa to Mount Kailas, the most sacred mountain in Tibet—I readily accepted.

8

Kailas

I

On the sixth of September, 1994, I found myself in the waiting room of the Tribhuvan International Airport in Kathmandu. There is not a great deal to do in this particular waiting room, so I had ample time to study my fellow waiters. One young woman caught my eye. She was a very pretty blond with that wholesome look one associates with football weekends at midwestern American universities. She was wearing a red T-shirt with a large white logo that read FREE TIBET. These are very common in Kathmandu, to say nothing of Greenwich Village and elsewhere. Two things came to my mind. The first was obvious. She was *not* waiting for the biweekly South West China Airlines flight from Kathmandu to Lhasa for which some two hundred of the rest of us *were* waiting. This is not the T-shirt one wants to wear while trying to clear customs at the Gonggar airfield—the sole commercial-aviation entry point into Tibet. The second thing that came to my mind was, What did *she* mean by this logo? What did she mean by "Free Tibet"? *Who* should free Tibet? and how? and at what cost? If I had had the chance to talk with her, I would have asked her.

The Chinese now call—cynically—the Tibet this woman wanted to free an "autonomous region." To guarantee its "autonomy," they have stationed what some estimates list as a million soldiers in the country—armed with the latest weapons. It is said that there are bases for intercontinental missiles in Tibet, at least three of which house nuclear weapons. Nuclear weapons have been tested close to the borders. There are military airfields all over the country, and many radar stations.

Now, it is difficult to get a reliable estimate of the number of Tibetans left in the country. About half the population is nomadic and not very easy to count. But a recent estimate, actually given by the Chinese, is about two million. There is then, roughly, one Chinese soldier per two Tibetans. In some of the population centers, such as Lhasa, as I have noted, the Chinese far outnumber the Tibetans. What, then, would it take to "Free Tibet"? If one is talking about a military intervention, one is talking about a nuclear war. The Chinese mean business here. Is this what the young woman with her T-shirt had in mind? Did she not understand that such a war would "free" all of us—body and soul—right into the next world? But before I had the chance to ask her, our flight to Lhasa was canceled for the day, and we were all bused back to Kathmandu to spend the night.

Let me explain how I came to be in this particular waiting room in Kathmandu, in September of 1994, on my way to Tibet. In the spring of 1993, there was a surprising development in Nepalese-Chinese relations, probably reflecting the confidence that the Chinese now had about the pacification of the Tibetans. The Chinese and Nepalese signed a treaty opening the border between the two countries to trekkers at one point in the extreme western part of both Nepal and Tibet. This made possible an entirely new kind of trip. The idea was the following: One would first fly from Kathmandu, southwest to the Indian frontier town of Nepalganj, where, unfortunately, one would have to spend the night. I say unfortunately because Nepalganj is like a sauna with mosquitoes, many of which carry malaria. It is not a place that one looks forward to spending time in. The next day, one would fly by either small plane or helicopter to Simikot, the administrative capital of the very remote Humla district in far western Nepal. There is a postage-stamp-sized airfield in Simikot. Realistically, there is no way to reach the place except by plane: Going there on foot from

Nepalganj would be a nightmare. From Simikot, however, one would trek five days north, finally crossing a fifteen-thousand-foot pass—the Nara Lagna—on the Tibetan border. To complete the next step, one would have to have prearranged a meeting at the border with a Tibetan tour group that was supplied with four-wheel-drive vehicles. No ordinary automobile could possibly deal with these roads.

If this worked out, one would then drive north for about two days, first to Lake Manasarovar, then to the village of Darchen at the base of the 21,850-foot Mount Kailas. Later, one would use the same vehicles to travel to Lhasa—about a week's drive—and then fly back to Kathmandu. That was the idea. But why Kailas? Kailas is one of the great focal points of all the eastern religions. For Hindus, it is the throne of Shiva—the worldly realization of the sacred Mount Meru. As the scripture said, "There is no mountain like Himachal; for in it are Kailas and Manasarovar. As the dew is dried up by the morning sun, so are the sins of the world dried up at the sight of Himachal." For Hindus, *Kailas* means "Crystal Shining." For Tibetan Buddhists, Kailas is called Kang Rinpoche—"Blessed Jewel of the Snow." The mountain was the abode of the legendary Buddhist sage Milarepa, who overcame Naro-Bon-chung—the priest of the Bon faith—in a series of contests of magic for possession of the mountain. For Jains, it is the sacred mountain Astapada. One circuit around the base of the mountain—one *kora*—will cleanse you of all your past sins, while 108 will take you straight to Nirvana. Within a hundred miles of the mountain, four of the great Indian subcontinental rivers have their headwaters. The Indus, the Karnali, the Brahmaputra, and the Satlej radiate from the region in the four cardinal directions, eventually ending up on opposite sides of the subcontinent.

This apart, there is the appeal of the remoteness of the place. It cannot be reached by any public transportation whatsoever. No trains, no airplanes, no buses—nothing. It is over a thousand miles from Lhasa. The roads, such as they are, leading to it from the capital cross several eighteen-thousand-foot passes. During the summer months, rains from the monsoons in the south spill over the Himalayas, swelling the rivers, making travel impossible. From November until spring, the passes are blocked by snow. A month or two in the fall, and the premonsoon period in the spring, are the only times one can make the trip. As far as anyone knows, the first westerner actually to have circled the mountain was the great Swedish explorer Sven Hedin, who did it in 1907, disguised as a Tibetan pilgrim. Between 1907 and 1985, when the region opened up to some extent to tourism, there seem to have been only sixteen westerners who managed the trip—many of them wearing disguises, too. A trip to Kailas, however one does it, clearly involves an expedition.

But expeditions are what "adventure-travel" companies specialize in, so it is not surprising that several of them, immediately after the agreement between Nepal and China had been signed, began proposing trips to Kailas. Among them was the small company owned and operated by my friend Claude Jaccoux—Jaccoux Voyages. Jaccoux had been to Tibet several times before 1994, primarily on climbing expeditions that he had organized, one of which was an attempt on Everest from the north. But he had never been to Kailas nor, indeed, anywhere in western Tibet. For him, and the rest of us, this would be an adventure into the unknown.

It takes many months to organize a trip like this, but by the early spring of 1994, Jaccoux had put the pieces together, and he had eight of us—all French with the exception of myself—signed up and ready to go. Jaccoux made nine; we were also taking a Sherpa named Pasang to help out. Everything was proceeding according to plan when, in late July, Jaccoux suddenly learned that the Chinese had had a change of heart. They had decided that the border between Tibet and Nepal at Sher—the crossing point in the west—was too open and unguarded to allow crossings, like ours, from Nepal into Tibet. However, they were willing to allow our group to make the trip in the opposite sense—starting in Lhasa, then crossing into Nepal *from* Tibet. The last major town in Tibet, Taklakot—also known as Purang—is essentially a military camp. The formalities needed for crossing the border would be performed in Taklakot. At least, so we were informed.

That is why we were in the Kathmandu airport that September day trying to fly to Lhasa, along with two hundred other people, some of whom were also planning to go to Kailas. After a pleasant night in the Yak and Yeti hotel in Kathmandu, at the expense of South West China

Airlines, we were informed that our flight would leave late in the morning—Nepalese time, three and a quarter hours earlier than Tibetan time. Indeed, only a few hours after the scheduled departure time, a spanking white Boeing 757 landed, bearing the logo—some sort of bird—of South West China Airlines. We were then herded on board.

The flight—some fifty-five minutes—was quite bizarre. The plane flies at about the altitude of the mountains—some twenty-nine thousand feet, in the case of Everest. I am sure the view would have been spectacular if only we could have seen it. But, apart from the odd tantalizing glimpse, the mountains were shrouded in monsoon clouds. So we wouldn't be bored, however, there was incessant "entertainment" on the movie screens. As we passed Everest, a rerun of one of "America's Funniest Home Videos" began. It was dubbed into Chinese. A young woman somewhere in Maine was shown with her bra being pulled off by an outboard motor. She was giggling and complaining in Chinese. The effect was uncanny—a lot funnier, I imagined, than the original. We were then served cookies and tea, after which we landed at the Gonggar airfield, some fifty miles southwest of Lhasa.

I do not know what my fellow travelers expected—some, I think, Shangri-la. Having been to Tibet before, I was not surprised by the bareness of the surrounding hills—the feeling of being almost in a desert. But there is also the altitude. Lhasa is at twelve thousand feet, meaning that one gains *seven thousand* feet coming up from Kathmandu. Upon landing, the interior pressure in the plane has to be adjusted to the *higher* altitude—that is, decreased—the opposite of the usual situation. When I got off the plane, I had the sense of moving in slow motion. To add to the general ambience, there were no amenities whatever. No luggage carts, no porters, no ground crew, nobody—just the two hundred of us, with our baggage, dumped on the tarmac. Fortunately, our group had packed expedition-style. We each had a duffel bag weighing—these were Jaccoux's rigorous instructions—no more than sixteen kilograms, as well as a backpack, as heavy as one was willing to carry. In addition, we had two large blue plastic barrels holding expeditionary gear, such as emergency oxygen.

There was a shed—the terminal building, one assumed—not too far from where the plane had landed. The two hundred of us—dragging our baggage—made for it. Once inside, the confusion was total. There was a small clutch of Chinese soldiers, some sitting behind a long table. They were examining passports. After receiving all sorts of conflicting advice, Jaccoux had finally determined that we would not need individual visas. But we had procured a *group* visa, containing all of our pictures, as well as our names, in Chinese, with English transliterations. The visa arbitrarily assigned us a numerical order. I was number 8, Jaccoux 9, and Pasang 10. At our group's turn at the long table, we were instructed to line up in a row by number. Whenever one of the soldiers asked us a question, the reply that seemed to work was "group." After our names were checked off against our passports, we were waived through. Oddly, no one had taken the slightest interest in our baggage. This was in sharp contrast to our experience in 1987, when our baggage had been searched from top to bottom. Each camera and watch had had to be declared, and accounted for when we left the country. This time, we just hauled our unexamined baggage past the table, out of the shed, and into Tibet—fifty miles from Lhasa.

It was not a very inspiring scene. The sky was gray and overcast. It had clearly been raining. There were a few cars and buses. What was supposed to happen next was not clear, but out of the confusion, several young men—Tibetans—emerged and introduced themselves. They turned out to be the drivers and guides who would make the trip with us—our companions-to-be for the next three weeks. The first thing that struck me was that they were *Tibetan*. In 1987, as I have explained, there were no Tibetan tour guides, and the Chinese guides we had were often so sullen and unhelpful that we did whatever we could to avoid their company. There were many complaints—which may have produced this welcome change.

Introductions over, we piled into three Land Cruisers for the three-hour drive to Lhasa. That it would take three hours to cover some fifty miles was no surprise to me, and these roads—the ones leading to the capital—were the *best* in Tibet. Our destination was one of the new hotels—the Himalaya—that have been constructed in

Lhasa since 1987. At that time, everyone who could afford it had put up at the Holiday Inn, the only modern hotel in the country, with its 486 rooms, and a color television in each one. The Himalaya was, according to Jaccoux, a much more modest affair, but it had the advantage of being close to the center of Lhasa—an important consideration in a city where public transportation is all but nonexistent.

The hotel was, at one and the same time, both new and run-down. Elevators, plumbing, hot water worked—but barely. It was operated and serviced entirely by the Chinese. By now, I was a bit giddy from the altitude, but I was determined not to waste the rest of the afternoon without exploring Lhasa. Our schedule had become a bit truncated because of the airplane delay. We were leaving for the west in two days. This gave me the rest of the afternoon and the following day to compare the impressions I had received seven years ago with those I would gain now. What would be the imprint of seven more years of Chinese occupation?

To find out, there is only one place to go in Lhasa—the Jokhang temple and its surrounding Barkhor, the open-air market, in the heart of the remaining Tibetan quarter of the city. The Potala palace is really only a memorial to a Tibetan society that is rapidly disappearing. The Jokhang and the Barkhor are like a breath of fresh air after the Potala. Whatever remains of traditional Tibetan life in Lhasa is there. To reach them from our hotel was an easy walk. At first, the streets were broad and tree-lined, with a good deal of traffic—again, mostly military. After walking a bit, I came to an intersection with a main thoroughfare where a uniformed Chinese policeman was directing traffic. I continued my walk, but then, more or less at random, I chose a small alleyway to wander into. I was immediately lost. I had entered another world—the world of the Tibetans.

The Tibetan quarter of Lhasa is a totally bewildering labyrinth of very narrow streets, crisscrossed by alleyways like the one I had turned into. The houses are low, stone, and stand "shoulder to shoulder." Although it was the fall, and we were at twelve thousand feet, it was still sufficiently warm that the doors of the houses were open. I could look into them. The furniture, from what I could see, was very sparse. Tibetans do not sleep on beds—at least not beds with mattresses and sheets. There were no beds in the houses, just what looked like benches covered with carpet. I did see a number of television sets. They seemed to be communal, with several families gathered around each one. They were on at full volume, and tuned to some sort of Chinese historical soap opera. The houses I saw did not seem to be especially dirty, nor especially clean. They did not look very affluent, although they were certainly more so than houses I have seen in many parts of Nepal, to say nothing of India. Early travelers to Lhasa always reported on its filth and squalor. That is not how the Tibetan quarter of Lhasa struck me, either on this visit, or on the one I had made in 1987. It is austere and modest, but it is not squalid.

However, something was dramatically different. This time, no one spoke to me. In 1987, one was approached constantly by Tibetans— some looking to sell things, others to ask questions, and some to invite you into their homes. But now I had the feeling of being almost invisible, or perhaps unwanted—alien—a dangerous presence. This was very likely the result of the seven additional years of Chinese occupation. See no evil. Hear no evil. Speak no evil—especially not to foreigners. I asked for directions to the Jokhang and got no response. In 1987, if one did that, often the Tibetan one asked would stop what he or she was doing and take you to your destination. Not today. But I was in no hurry, and was content to meander in what I thought was the general direction of the temple and the surrounding Barkhor.

Then, through the cracks between the houses, I saw the gilded cupolas of the Jokhang. To get to its front entrance I had to tour the Barkhor. It is a narrow, cobblestone alley that circles the perimeter of the Jokhang. It is just about wide enough for pedestrians to maneuver around the open-air stalls, from which everything imaginable is sold. There are stalls for cloth, food, earrings, hats, shoes, jewelry, household goods. God knows what else. The abundance is a bit overwhelming. Just before I reached the large open square that fronts the Jokhang, I came across a booth whose openly displayed contents really surprised me. The items were religious—photographs of Buddhas and temples, that sort of thing. But, and this was totally unexpected, there were also photographs of the Dalai Lama. In 1987, such a display would have been unthinkable. The "Dalai Lama pichu" was cherished contraband. Now, right in front of me, they were being sold openly. At the time, I thought that this was a good omen, but not long after my visit, it was reported that the Chinese had confiscated these pictures and once again stopped their sale—yet another example of their obsessive paranoia about Tibet.

The square in front of the Jokhang is one of the great people-watching places in the world. Tibetans are remarkable-looking. They have dark, ruddy faces, like those of Native North and South Americans. You can tell Tibetans from Chinese or Nepalese at a glance. What one does not see in the Jokhang are people who appear racially mixed. Although the occupation has lasted over forty years, there does not seem to have been much, if any, intermarriage between Tibetans and Chinese.

Tibetans love colorful clothing. The women usually wear long, dark, robelike dresses, made, one supposes, of yak wool. But across them they wear bright sashes that look like lightning bolts streaking a somber sky. They also wear "bowler" hats in colors like orange and red. The men carry ornamental daggers, often covered with semiprecious stones. Both men and women, but especially women, wear fantastically complicated necklaces. These are festooned with the wildest collection of objects imaginable. There are brightly colored orange and green corals, and blue semiprecious stones. There are teeth from animals, and coins. The more fortunate have one or more "Z-stones." These are narrow, cylindrical objects a few inches long. They look like little barrels. They are in black and white. Swirls in their designs resemble eyes; the value of the stone increases with the number of eyes. Where they come from, or how the "eyes" come to appear in them, or even what the material of the stones is, is entirely mysterious to me, although I have tried for years to find out. Every Tibetan or Sherpa I have asked has given me an explanation that involves magic—never the same magic. A several-eyed stone—if it is genuine and not a plastic replica—costs many thousands of dollars in Kathmandu. In Lhasa, it is cheaper to buy jade. The stones, which feel oddly dense and magnetic, bring the wearer good fortune. They are among the last possessions a Tibetan will sell.

One striking group of Tibetans that one sees in the Barkhor are the Khampas. They are somewhat taller than the usual mid-five-foot Tibetan men. Apart from their size, Khampa men have that very recognizable hairstyle: a kind of swirl, tied up with a red, ropelike ribbon. You cannot miss them. They have a reputation for being a pretty wild bunch. Therefore, it was not surprising to me that one of the two "police actions" I saw during my latest visits to the Barkhor involved a Khampa. (The other involved one of the street merchants; I gathered that she had not paid the required license fee for her stall.) The number of uniformed police—they seemed to be Tibetans—I saw in the Barkhor was minimal, a tiny handful, although there were, no doubt, many plainclothes police—*bian yi,* to use the Chinese name. This, too, seemed to contrast with what I had observed in 1987, when there were many uniformed Chinese soldiers patrolling the area. In any event, this particular Khampa, who seemed to have had a little too much to drink, had chosen a wall against which to micturate. Two uniformed officers came over to him and gave him a stern lecture. That was all. There was no arrest and no physical contact. I do not know what would have happened if I had not been there watching.

Finding my way to the Tibetan quarter had, at least until I got lost in the alleyways, been aided by a map I bought in Lhasa. It was the only map that any of us could find in either Kathmandu or Lhasa that showed western Tibet in any detail. But, if one knew how to read it, it also showed the dilemma that the Chinese now appear to be facing in Tibet. Before I come to this, let me describe the map itself. It was published in 1993 by the so-called Mapping Bureau of the Tibet Autonomous Region. The map itself, entitled China Tibet Tour Map, appears on one side, while the other is devoted to an "Introduction" to the country, written in English. This is what is interesting. Some of it is simply information that a tourist might find useful, such as "Needy Phone Numbers"—for hospitals and the like. But the introduction also casually rewrites the history of modern Tibet. It sums it all up in just two sentences: "After 1911 Revolution the Republic of China established a work-ing office in Lhasa to exercise its management over Tibet. In May 1951, concerning the method of liberation of Tibet, the 17-Point Agreement, was signed between the Central People's Government of China and the Local Government of Tibet which opened a new historical page over Tibet." That is it.

It would take a small book to deconstruct the absurdity of the first sentence. To take the simplest matter, the "working office" was, as I have noted, established in 1933, when the Chinese asked permission—*asked* permission—to send a delegation to the funeral of the thirteenth Dalai Lama. The delegation never left. However, the second sentence of this "history" is easily dealt with. The Seventeen-Point Agreement referred to was signed by the Tibetans in 1951, under duress. This is the agreement that included among its provisions one stating that the Chinese would not alter the "existing political system in Tibet." It went on to promise that "the central authorities [the Chinese] also will not alter the established status, functions and powers of the Dalai Lama." No sooner had this agreement been signed than the Chinese began their massive campaign of repression in Tibet. It is not surprising, considering the source, that there is no mention of the Dalai Lama anywhere in this introduction.

But it does contain an odd, very brief paragraph entitled RELIGION IN TIBET—which also does not mention the Dalai Lama. It is worth quoting in full, both for what it says, and for the way it says it. Here we can see the Chinese dilemma that I referred to earlier. The paragraph reads:

Buddhism, with an history of some 1,300 years since its penetration into Tibet, has shaped a unique form of "Lamaism." Tibetan history, culture and religion are mixed together and infiltrated on [sic] every aspect of social life. Tibetan religious arts have a distinctive style with adoption of Indian and Chinese Buddhist influence, thus forming itself a pearl of oriental art in Chinese Buddhism. Tibetan architecture is rich in shapes, sumptuous and full of noble aspirations. The Potala Palace is built on top of a hill and penetrates its dome into the sky. It's the king of Tibetan architectural structures. These architectural buildings include wonderful sculptures, carvings, murals, "thangkas" [painted scrolls] and skilled butter sculptures, and a vast accumulation of historical monuments which form a kind of religious art which are developed into a school of Tibetan tradition.

The author of this document has conveniently forgotten the fact that the Chinese did everything in their power to destroy the "wonderful sculptures, carvings, murals," and the rest, that were the glory of Tibetan art, to say nothing of the magnificent monastic structures and shrines. Nothing is said about this. No apology is offered. That aside, there is the choice of words. In them we find the Chinese dilemma. On the one hand, the actual religious inspiration for all of this art—no traditional Tibetan art is secular—is an anathema to the Chinese—Mao's "poison." But, on the other hand, to put it bluntly, tourism is the only producer of hard-currency income in Tibet. Economically, Tibet is a black hole. There does not appear to be a single substantial exportable asset. Such foreign trade as exists is in commodities such as salt and yak wool, and is with neighbors such as Nepal, equally strapped for foreign currency. But it has cost the Chinese *billions* to occupy Tibet. Everything has had to be imported— even the food to feed its Chinese population, to say nothing of what is needed to support a vast military machine. An entire infrastructure of roads, military bases, and airfields—to mention a few obvious items—had to be built from nothing—costing billions.

The only way the Chinese can recoup any of this money is through tourism. Hence, they are spending millions to attract tourists to Tibet. It is estimated, for example, that the Chinese have spent at least sixty-five million dollars since 1980 to rebuild the monasteries. But the last thing in the world they want to do is restore the full monastic life as it existed before their invasion of Tibet. From their point of view, these monasteries were, and still are, centers of subversion. Therefore, the number of monks and nuns allowed to enter monastic life is strictly controlled by the state. But why do the Chinese allow *any* monastic life or, indeed, any form of traditional Tibetan worship? Why not turn all the monasteries into museums like the Potala? I do not think that the decision to do this, or not to do it, would be influenced by what we, in the West, might think. We have made it clear enough that such human rights issues are readily submergible under a tidal wave of economic self-interest. My view is that the Chinese calculus here also has do with economic self-interest, and little else. They realize that, apart from the physical beauty of Tibet, it is the vision of traditional

Tibetan religious life that attracts tourists. That is clear from the map, which is full of religious sites. They must know that no tourist would spend five cents, let alone the well over a hundred dollars a day it actually costs, to see only the lumpen, dreary cities and towns—often little more than military bases—that the Chinese have imposed on this land. That is their dilemma: how to balance their commercial interests in Tibet with the revulsion they feel toward its underlying religious culture—the very thing that attracts tourists. This is why, in my view, the authors of the map use words and phrases like "architecture," "historical monuments," and "religious art." For Tibetans, a structure like the Jokhang is not "architecture" or "religious art," and still less a "historical" monument. It is life itself.

At the entrance to the Jokhang, there is a giant prayer wheel, turned constantly— day and night. Beside it is a small flagstone square, worn smooth by decades and decades—centuries—of pilgrims prostrating themselves on it, in prayer. They still do—Tibetans of all ages, not just the very old. The statue inside the Jokhang of the White Tara, or Drölma—no one knows whether the one now in the Jokhang is the original, or a total or partial reconstruction—is the most sacred icon in Tibetan Lamaistic Buddhism. Pilgrims pass before it in a state of total veneration. But it is not my favorite part of the Jokhang. Watching other people's religious ecstasy makes me very uneasy.

What I like to do is make my way to the roof of the Jokhang. From it, the view of Lhasa and its surroundings is magnificent. When I arrived at the temple on this visit it was late afternoon—well after the 11 A.M. end of the official visiting hour. But I waited at the front door and, when it opened to let some pilgrims out, I was able to walk in. I was followed by a young Tibetan who attached himself to me like a limpet. He kept hectoring me in English, of a sort. To get away from him, I climbed higher and higher on the wooden stairs that, I remembered, led to the roof. I had no idea who he was, or what he represented, but I was able to buy him off with a few yuan. By then, I had gotten lost in the maze of ladders and stairways. Somehow I had strayed into the monks' quarters. I heard an odd series of sounds. I did not know what to make of it at first. Then it dawned on me that it was the same television soap opera that I had seen on the televisions in the houses below. I followed the sounds. They led to a door that was slightly ajar. I was not prepared for the sight that greeted me as I opened it. I had walked into a kind of assembly room, large enough, I gathered, to hold the entire congregation of monks. There were about fifty in the room, of all ages, sitting on benches. I, too, took a seat on a bench. No one seemed to mind or, indeed, to pay much attention to me. On a table at the front of the room was a large television set. It was tuned to the soap opera. Three comic figures on the screen kept falling into some water. The monks were roaring with laughter. They were having the time of their lives. I could not help laughing, too. I watched with them for about a half-hour, and then found my way out of the room and onto the roof. The view was as lovely as I remembered. But there was a change. At the very edge of the Barkhor—the boundary of the Tibetan quarter—a loudspeaker had been mounted on a building with a Chinese flag. The speaker was whining and blaring Chinese. It drowned out everything—almost every private thought. I had no idea what the actual words of this rasping, shrieking, singsong voice meant. But the message was clear. You are ours—and never forget it.

II

While the rest of us were busy exploring Lhasa, Jaccoux and the Tibetans had been making detailed arrangements for the next part of our trip—the hard part. The evening before we left Lhasa, Jaccoux called a meeting to discuss the program. The first job was to get to Kailas. It turns out that there are two overland routes to western Tibet from Lhasa—both, of course, constructed by the Chinese. The most direct, by far, is the southern route, which skims Nepal, north of the Himalayas. If we had been able to take this route, it would have cut at least four days off of our driving time. But this route was impassable. The monsoon had been late in leaving in 1994 and, even into September, the rain-swollen rivers had not yet subsided. The southern route was cut by rivers in several places. Indeed, Jaccoux reported that he had talked to a leader of a group that had come back from Kailas by the other route; the man told him that the weather had been so bad that, not only had they not been able to make the kora circuit, but they had not even seen the mountain.

That left us with the northern route—the one this group had just come over. This route involves a long loop. First, we would head for the town of Lhatse on the Friendship Highway, which eventually leads to Nepal. This was the way we had come in 1987. At Lhatse, the Friendship Highway heads south; we would continue west. This intersection I saw in 1987, when I wondered what it would be like to follow the road west. Now I would find out. From Lhatse, we would drive to the point where the northern and southern routes diverge. Then we would head north until we come to the intersection with the road leading to western Tibet from central China. This road had served as one of the invasion routes in 1950, and had been used again by the Chinese in 1959 when they made incursions into Ladakh to rectify their grievances over the boundaries drawn up by McMahon at Simla. At this junction, we would head due west to the fortress town of Shiquanhe, also known as Ali. It is only a few miles from the frontier between Tibet and the Indian-held part of Kashmir. One cannot go any farther west in Tibet. In fact, we would have gone *past* Kailas, which is south of this road—cut off from view by high mountain ranges. From Ali, we would then head south and east, coming back to Kailas by the southern route. The whole operation would involve traveling over thirteen hundred miles. With a few sight-seeing detours, Jaccoux estimated that it would take us nine days of almost continual driving. This was assuming that, apart from a couple of half-days of sightseeing—and that no accidents occurred—we were prepared to drive for at least twelve hours a day.

This might seem absurd—unless one has actually driven in Tibet. It goes without saying that these roads—the principal highways in the country—are not paved. In fact, until the Chinese invaded Tibet, there was no reason for roads like this to exist at all. The nomadic people who inhabited this very isolated part of Tibet had no need to travel great distances; such traveling as they did, they did on foot or horseback. Hence, in many places, these are not roads at all. They are tracks—often multiple—made by the passing of cars and trucks. During the rains, the tracks get washed away, and finding one's way through the water is like running a maze. There are ditches and holes that would destroy an ordinary automobile. On top of everything else, all of this is at high altitude. On any given day, one can expect to cross one or more eighteen-thousand-foot passes, and one is never much below sixteen thousand feet. Driving on these roads at night would be madness. But, because of the time change, the sun does not set in Tibet until well after 9 P.M. Thus, if we were to start driving at seven in the morning—and nothing went wrong—we could cover enough distance before sunset to meet our schedule. We had to have a schedule because we had a firm date in Simikot, in Nepal, to be flown back to Kathmandu.

Our caravan was to consist of three Land Cruisers and a truck. Two of the Land Cruisers were four-passenger, and the third, three-passenger—ten of us, including Pasang, plus the Tibetan tour leader, Tashi. The truck was absolutely essential. Once we left Shigatse—which we expected to reach after two days—we had to be a self-contained unit. That meant we had to have with us all of our food; enough gasoline that we could get to Kailas, and the Tibetans back to Lhasa; our baggage; our camping gear; and an automobile repair shop. The extent of the latter was made evident one night when, after a day's driving, a welding set was brought out of the truck and the suspension in one of the Land Cruisers was replaced with a new one, which had also been carried in the truck. The camping gear was also a necessity. We expected to stay in hotels in Gyantse on the first night, then in Shigatse on the second, and then, a week later, in Ali. But for the rest of the trip, we planned to camp in tents. This was fine with me. I retained a vivid memory of the dreadful hotels in which we had stayed in 1987, in Shigatse and Gyantse, when the Chinese had refused to provide us with a truck, so we could not camp. The less time in these hotels, I thought, the better.

We were late in leaving Lhasa the following morning. Among other things, the driver of the Land Cruiser I was in had neglected to fill his tank with gasoline. This meant a further delay while we went to the gas station. There was, however, at least to me, something poignant about going to a gas station in the middle of Lhasa to tank up for a trip across the country. At a terrible cost, the Chinese have brought the Tibetans into the twentieth century. Here we were, in line at a gas station—the rest of the vehicles were military—about to perform a mundane twentieth-century act that, fifty years ago, would have been unthinkable in this country.

Our first stop was to be Gyantse. We could have avoided the town, which is off the main route to Shigatse, our second stop. But, since only Jaccoux and I had been to Tibet before, he felt that the rest of the group should be given the chance to see as much of the country as possible. I had been to Gyantse, but I was perfectly happy to repeat this very beautiful, albeit difficult, drive—which was as difficult and as beautiful as I remembered it. This time, Lake Yamdrok was a luminescent blue-green. But the real surprise was the hotel in Gyantse. In 1987, there had been no running water, and, of course, no plumbing; furthermore, we could not even get keys to our rooms. Now, we found a spanking new hotel. The plumbing worked; there was even a color television in my room. I was able to watch a little of the U.S. Open tennis tournament from Flushing Meadows— half a globe away. And we were given the keys to our rooms! There was yet another touch at dinner. In 1987, in every hotel dining room (except that of the Holiday Inn in Lhasa), one found only chopsticks. These are not for me, so I had used a soup spoon for everything. This time, I had armed myself with a little packet of camping utensils. No sooner had I opened the packet at dinner, however, than a waitress—Chinese—rushed over with a knife and fork.

The same hotel surprise was awaiting us the next day when we arrived in Shigatse. Here was yet another excellent hotel—even bigger, and entirely redone—another manifestation of the millions the Chinese are spending to attract tourists to Tibet. On my visit to Shigatse in 1987, the Tashilhunpo monastery—the home of the Panchen Lamas—was being restored. Now, in 1994, the work was nearly complete, and the results were magnificent. The life of the monastery was active—as the experience I am about to relate makes clear. I had noticed an announcement on a bulletin board at the hotel that there was to be a lama dance at the Tashilhunpo to celebrate the Tibetan harvest festival of Ongkor. In truth, I had seen so much monk-dancing since 1967 that I had more or less decided to skip this one. But I did want to visit the Tashilhunpo. So I went. It is such a maze of rooms that, once again, I got lost inside. Curiously, there did not seem to be any monks around to point out the exit. I was beginning to wonder if the monastery had been cleared of its occupants when I found a small door, which I opened. The sight that greeted me was remarkable. I had walked onto the back of the stage of an amphitheater. Out front, I could see an audience of Tibetans numbering in the hundreds. Near where I was, on a low balcony, sat a line of dignitaries in armchairs. Among them was a Chinese general, along with his two somewhat obese children. The general was dressed in a plain blue uniform and was smoking a cigarette through a long holder. I kept thinking of the Roman emperors. There are said to be several thousand Chinese troops in the Shigatse area, and he must have been their commander.

I made my way carefully behind these people and found a seat alongside the stage. For quite a while nothing happened. No one was on the stage. Then, through the door I had used, entered a procession of monks wearing yellow robes and yellow hats. They were carrying marvelous-looking musical instruments—huge horns, conch shells, and drums and gongs. They sat down and, after a short while, began to play. This is music that fills the soul. It seems at once very naive and very profound. Like the Tibetan language, it seems to have evolved to be heard over a high wind. Then came the dancers, also wearing yellow robes. There were so many that, with the musicians, they must have comprised the entire monastic community. They began to dance. What struck me was the power—the sheer physical power—of these dancers. I hesitate to read too much into what I saw, but it seemed to me that there was a message being conveyed both to the Tibetans in the audience, and to the Chinese "emperor": *Nothing* was going to break the spirit of Tibet.

When the dances were over, I tried to make my way to the street. The crowd was immense. Finally, I got to the front of the Tashilhunpo. The crowd was even denser. There were booths everywhere, from which food and drinks were being sold. I did not see a single Chinese soldier. These were Tibetans on holiday. I bought a mango drink at a stand. I was about to drink it when the gates of the Tashilhunpo opened and there came an eruption of yellow-robed monks from the inside. They were trying to clear a path for someone. We were in their way. They had whips. Suddenly I felt something sting my cheek. I had been hit by a whip. It did not draw blood, but it hurt. I crushed myself back into the crowd. Then I remembered something that I had read in Alexandra David-Neel's account of her journey to Lhasa. She found herself in a large crowd, waiting for the appearance of the Dalai Lama. She wrote, "Policemen, armed with long sticks and whips, growing more and more excited as the time of the Dalai Lama's coming approached, used their weapons indiscriminately against anybody. In the midst of this tumult, trying our best to guard ourselves against hustling and blows, we spent some lively moments." For just a moment or two, I felt that I had been transported back in time—to the real Tibet.

III

Our trip from Shigatse to Kailas was going to be so complex and so rich that I decided to keep a journal. Here are the entries.

Sunday, September 11: Somewhere Near Sangsang

Jaccoux has come up with a *truc*—a thingamajig, a device, a whatchamacallit, a trick. Jaccoux's *truc* is to continually rotate the nine of us among the three Land Cruisers. One Land Cruiser holds three passengers, and the other two, four. The remaining two places are taken by Pasang, our Sherpa, and Tashi, our tour guide. The idea is that we should not evolve cliques and cabals. All of us will share all of the Land Cruisers. A slight exception is Jaccoux's sister and her husband, who have come on the trip. They insist that they are inseparable and will only rotate as a unit. The other three women— we are four women and four men, plus Jaccoux—are quite willing to rotate as individuals. To someone who has not made a trip like this, Jaccoux's *truc* might appear absurd. But without having done it, it is difficult to imagine the strain of this kind of driving. We are only on our third day, but it is already beginning to show. One goes along a stretch of dirt track—which suddenly disappears, having been partially wiped out by the monsoon rains. There is then a backing and filling, up and down small ravines, to find a way through. When the road is dry, great clouds of dust fly off of it, and if one is not in the lead Land Cruiser one finds oneself breathing dirt. Having experienced some of this in 1987, I have prepared myself with a packet of surgical masks, one of which I put on whenever a window is open. Moreover, the road is full of holes. The Land Cruisers do not have functioning seat belts, so one must hang on by the straps on the roof in case one hits a hole. I estimate our average speed to be about thirty miles an hour. Since we have about a thousand miles to cover, the reason for Jaccoux's *truc* becomes clearer.

I am familiar with the first part of today's drive. It is along the route from Lhasa to Kathmandu that we followed in 1987. But our route today will turn northwest at the town of Lhatse. Before getting to Lhatse, there is a real surprise. Suddenly, with no warning, the road becomes paved. Just to make sure I am not dreaming it, I take a picture. This stretch is like driving on a cloud—for about twenty miles. If the entire road is ever paved, to match the new hotels, the drive from Kathmandu to Lhasa will be magnificent. For anyone who loves mountain scenery, there cannot be anything more beautiful.

But we are soon back in the dirt. Just beyond Lhatse, we turn off. The first obstacle is the Yarlung Tsangpo—a broad and very rapidly flowing river. An ancient-looking, but solid, ferryboat is visible on the far bank. There is nothing to do but wait until it returns to our side. Eventually, it does, and we cross. I now feel that I have left behind everything I am familiar with in this country. I feel both elated and depressed. I find some consolation in the fact that parallel to our dirt road is an endless string of telephone poles connected by wires. They are clearly leading somewhere. Our goal is the village of Sangsang, where we plan to camp. It takes us until eight-thirty at night to get there. It is still light, but we have traveled less than two hundred miles from Shigatse. It has taken us, with stops, over twelve hours.

Monday, September 12: Tsochen

And then there are the tents. When our truck, which had been following us, pulled in last night, the driver and his assistant, the three

Jeep drivers, as well as Tashi and Pasang, set to work unloading it. Our duffel bags were tossed out on the ground, along with several small, cylindrical, blue rip-cord miniduffels. These, it turned out, contained our tents—one to a person, with the exception, of course, of Jaccoux's sister and her husband, who were sharing. I had not mounted a tent since my Boy Scout days. When one treks with Sherpas, which I have done often since 1967, *they* mount the tents. They also bring you tea and "washing water" in the morning. The only Sherpa we have with us now is Pasang, and he has his hands full with, among other things, getting dinner ready. Pasang is also our cook.

I untie the string on my blue tent duffel and shake its contents out onto the ground. I do not have the slightest idea of what to do next. However, a few of my fellow travelers seem to know, and—like one of those apes that constructs model edifices by imitation—I set out to follow their examples. The first step is to lay out flat on the ground a yellow object, which, when erected, will allegedly turn into part of my tent. I see my companions proceed to hammer into the ground metal pickets, after having inserted them through straps at the bottoms of their yellow prototents. I attempt to do likewise, and immediately understand why they are hammering at their pickets with large rocks. The Tibetan plateau, into which we are trying to hammer, seems to be made of cement. I find a large rock and begin to hammer pickets. This completed, I then imitate my comrades by placing a collapsible pole inside the yellowish material and pushing inward. Lo and behold, something rises that looks like a tent! However, this, it turns out, is the easy part. There is a large blue nylon object that serves as the tent's wind- and rain screen. It goes over the top. At least, that is the theory. But, by now, the wind, which is notorious on the Tibetan plateau, has risen to gale force. I have all I can do to keep my windscreen from blowing away in the general direction of China—let alone get it onto the top of my tent. Fortunately, Pasang takes pity on me and stops what he is doing to help me. We finish the job, which includes driving in another dozen pickets to hold the windscreen. Just to make sure the whole thing does not blow away during the night, I erect a circle of heavy rocks on the bottom of the windscreen. This done, I put my sleeping bag and mattress inside the tent and prepare for the night.

In the morning, the whole process has to be reversed, but in the pitch dark, and in a strong, freezing wind. Since we are expecting another twelve-hour drive, we are determined to get away no later than eight. A few hours later we come to a bifurcation in the road; one fork heads north, one due west. Because of the flooded rivers, we have to go north. The road heads due north until it meets the east–west route coming down from Qinghai in China, part of the Chinese military network. In any event, this east–west road leads to the town of Shiquanhe, or Ali—the district capital of the province of Ngari, which Chinese people pronounce as *Ali*. Just before Ali, this road is met by one coming south from Kashgar, where it eventually joins up with the Karakoram highway into Pakistan.

Just at the intersection, there is a tiny tent with two bicycles parked in front of it. We stop to investigate and out of the tent comes a very rugged looking westerner. He turns out to be an Australian. He and his partner have just spent three months cycling down from Pakistan. They are on their way to Lhasa, which they hope to reach before their Tibetan visas run out. They have come by the southern route. It took them, he says, an entire day to find their way across one of the rivers. In another, a truck was stuck in the middle. I ask if they made the Kailas circuit. Yes, I am told, but the weather was so bad that they never saw the mountain. "A good walk," he says, which, translated from the Australian, means that it was bloody tough.

Then we head north. We now seem to be off the map—at least any map that any of us has. In particular, on the China Tibet Tour Map there is no indication of the remarkable hot springs we next come to. A very large geyser of hot water shoots into the air every few minutes. Next to it is a nomad camp. At least until recently, nearly half the Tibetan population was nomadic. One has the impression that the Chinese are trying to change this: It seems that a number of these nomadic people have been pressed into work on the strategic roads. But the people at the hot springs are true nomads—*dropkas*. They live in large tents made of yak hair. They are surrounded by goats and yaks. It is thought that there are about four million yaks in Tibet—

twice as many as people. In fact, in a certain sense, the Tibetan plateau is a giant pastureland. The hot springs nomads are neither very friendly nor very hostile. However, they make it clear that they do not want any pictures taken of them.

We continue north. Our destination is the garrison town of Tsochen. We arrive there just at sunset. It is a perfectly beautiful sunset. The whole place would be idyllic except for the radar tower and the loudspeaker blaring in Chinese. Where every prospect pleases.... The sun sets and the stars rise. In the clear Tibetan night there is as clear a view of the Big Dipper as I have ever seen.

Tuesday, September 13: Somewhere Beyond Gertse

This has been a nature day. We have several altimeters with us, and they all read over seventeen thousand feet most of the day, with occasional passes over eighteen. The mountains around us are several thousand feet higher, but we can't find a single one of them on the map. Imagine, twenty-thousand-foot mountains that do not even seem to have names! Moreover, we have passed several large and very beautiful lakes that also are not on the map. They must be salt lakes, since there are salt flats leading down to them that, from a distance, look like snowfields. I have not seen a single boat on any of these lakes. Tibetans are apparently not very aquatic. But we have seen several wonderful animals. There was a herd of wild asses—*kiang* in Tibetan. There were antelopes—*pantholops*—and wild sheep—*bharal*. There was the odd fox as well as a large number of giant rabbits—hares. They leapt among the tufts of grass like miniature kangaroos. Wheeling overhead from time to time were golden eagles. They live in the watershed of the mountains—the Himalayas to the south. From what I have read, this high country used to teem with these animals. They were apparently hunted out, often by Chinese soldiers.

We have seen almost no vehicular traffic—a few army trucks and a small truck convoy carrying salt. This used to be the only salt used in Nepal's high country. I do not know where this particular Tibetan salt is going. *We* are going past the town of Gertse. The town itself is exceedingly depressing. The Tibetans in it do not seem to have much to do, and hang out in the local bars. These are also pretty depressing, except for the fact that one can get imported beer. Pabst Blue Ribbon with Chinese labels is available in cans. It is a relief to get out of here. Our camp is by a beautiful salt lake—away from everybody.

Wednesday, September 14: Sixty Miles from Ali

This has been the worst driving day so far—absolutely interminable. We have covered about two hundred miles in something close to thirteen hours. The three Land Cruiser drivers have discovered a new game. It is called Land Cruiser racing. This is made possible by the fact that, often, our gravel-and-dirt-track road splits into several parallel branches—sometimes as many as six. They are all equally awful, but one can take one's pick. When this happens, the drivers race each other. There is no stopping them and one can only hang on and hope for the best. The only virtue in this activity, as far as I am concerned—apart from keeping the drivers awake—is that when we are going parallel, we do not throw dust into each other's vehicles. For some reason, Jaccoux's *truc* has left me in the same Land Cruiser with different occupants for the last three days. I have gotten to know the driver a little bit. His name is pronounced something like So-Do. He seems to be a very intelligent and very humorous man, as well as an extraordinarily good driver. I do not know how much English he speaks, but I think he understands a lot more than he lets on. However, if I try to talk to him about conditions in Tibet, his English vanishes. This is true of all of our Tibetans. They simply will not talk to us about what their lives are like. Their equilibrium with the Chinese is so delicate that they will not allow anything to endanger it.

One thing I do amuses So-Do enormously. He is easily the most daring of the three drivers, and carries out maneuvers that I did not think were possible with any automobile. During the course of one of them, I recited the Buddhist prayer mantra, *"Om mani padme hum"*—Hail to the jewel in the lotus. So-Do found this wonderfully funny. Now he performs even crazier maneuvers while we recite the mantra together. These roads are fairly close to the border with India. Their maintenance seems to be taken rather seriously. We see gangs of Tibetans under the supervision of Chinese officers working on them. One cannot imagine what they would be like if no one worked on them. Because of the difficulty of the driving, our drivers are given to taking long cigarette breaks every few hours. One can hardly blame them. Jaccoux has found a new *truc* to deal with this: We all start to walk in the general direction of our destination. This should help with our acclimatization to Kailas, since all of these walks take place at over seventeen thousand feet. But they have revealed an interesting optical phenomenon. I first noticed it when we stopped within what I took to be easy walking distance from a town. We decided to walk into it to get a beer. We walked for a half-hour. The town got no closer. Then we walked for another half-hour, and the town still did not get much closer. The air is so thin and clear on the plateau that one loses one's usual sense of distance. When the Land Cruisers picked us up, we still had a good half-hour's drive to the town. It is a miserable place. The Tibetans seem to live in hovels. The only thing that looks functional is the radar tower at the army base. There are soldiers everywhere.

When we make camp at sunset, the Tibetan crew gathers around the oldest of the three Land Cruisers. Its suspension has been showing signs of wear and tear, and today's activities have finished it off. This must have been anticipated, because a new suspension is taken out of the truck, along with some welding gear. In the middle of the field in which we are camping, a makeshift automobile repair shop is created. The Land Cruiser is jacked up and in rather short order a new suspension is welded in place. The ingenuity and ability of these drivers never ceases to amaze me. Tomorrow—Ali.

Thursday, September 15: Ali

As far as I am concerned, Ali has very few redeeming features. One of them is that it is only sixty miles from our last campsite. This means that we did not have to get up until eight. The sun was nearly up, and we could have breakfast without freezing. We get to Ali by noon and pull into the principal hotel. It is pretty much in the old mold. There is no running water. Hot water is available from a communal heater in the hall. We are not allowed to have keys to our rooms. But there is a color television in my room. It has a single channel—in Chinese, with Tibetan subtitles. I watch a program from Lhasa, which shows several Tibetans wearing blue suits with Mao jackets receiving medals from smiling Chinese officials. There are also a number of displays of electric generators. Nothing else is available on television.

The town itself is perfectly dreadful. It is located almost as far west as you can get in Tibet. The border with Indian Kashmir looks from the map to be some thirty miles away. Ali itself is at the junction of the Indus and Gar Rivers. It is eerie to think that if one put a paper boat in the Indus near Kailas, it might float past Ali, cross into Ladakh, then sail under the shadow of the Himalayas into Pakistan and, eventually, into the Arabian Sea—eighteen hundred miles and several civilizations away. Western visitors have only been allowed here since 1984. The place is basically a Chinese army fortress. The few Tibetans I see are wearing non-Tibetan dress. The young people are wearing T-shirts emblazoned with the logos of various rock bands. If this were all one were to see of Tibet, one would despair. In the center of the town, in the middle of a square, is a very large statue of a lion. In fact, the Tibetan name for the town is Senge Khabab—"Lion Town." This is very curious because there have been no lions in Tibet for centuries. The only lions on the Indian subcontinent can be found in Gujarat in northwestern India. Yet the lion is an important symbol in Tibetan iconography. Very odd. None of the guides can explain how Ali got this odd Tibetan name. Even So-Do who, he tells me, lived here for seven years, has no idea. Lions or no lions, I will be very glad to leave this place tomorrow.

Friday, September 16: Tholing

In the ninth century, Buddhism came under attack in central Tibet. Buddhists found refuge in a very isolated area in western Tibet near the Indian border and, in 866, the Kingdom of Gu-ge was established. By the next century, it became the focal point for the practice of Buddhism in Tibet. In 1042, the great Indian teacher Atisa was persuaded to come to Gu-ge. He is credited with the revival of Buddhism in all of Tibet. He spent two years in a monastery in Tholing, which, along with the neighboring monastery-fortress in Tsaparang, remained a great center of Tibetan Buddhism until the seventeenth century. For reasons that are not clear, the Gu-ge kingdom then disintegrated.

Today we are headed for Tholing. This takes us in a general southeasterly direction—toward Kailas—but it involves a detour. The roads, we are warned, will be the worst yet. However, all the guidebooks are in agreement that, having come this far, it would be inexcusable not to visit these sites. The first step involves a detour within a detour. The main route to Kailas follows the Indus River. If we simply followed this, we would have to make a long loop—an arc. That is what the truck will do. The drivers of the Land Cruisers have other ideas. They head directly south into the mountains. This involves crossing a river with the Land Cruisers half submerged. I am still with So-Do, and we are still doing our mantra. Then we climb to the summit of an eighteen-thousand-foot pass. When I look over the top, I am sure that it is some sort of joke. It is very hard to estimate the angle of these things, but I have been on enough ski slopes to know an advanced run when I see one. Jaccoux, who is in my Land Cruiser and is noted for his *sang-froid,* is heard to mutter "*Pas vrais!*" This does not seem to bother So-Do in the least. The slope is some kind of soft scree, and So-Do and the other drivers slalom down it, while we cling to our roof straps. We are observed by a family of golden eagles—raptors—I can understand why. So-Do tells me that when he makes the trip in the reverse order, he goes *up* this slope. I will believe it when I see it.

We can now join the main east–west road that follows the Indus. It is the best road we have seen since leaving the Kathmandu–Lhasa Friendship Highway. We must be averaging at least forty-five miles an hour. But not for long. We turn off and head south into the mountains on the wildest road I have yet seen. Not only is the road bad, but it also has hairpin turns, and in places it is partially washed out. There are two passes in the eighteen-thousand-four-hundred-foot range. After crossing the second, we get a view of the western Himalayas that is absolutely stunning. On the skyline, and dominating it, is one of the great Himlayan peaks—Nanda Devi. It is at 25,645 feet, and rises some five thousand feet above its neighboring peaks. At a fork in the road, So-Do comments that the western branch leads to a very large military base—one of the bases on the Indian frontier. We take the eastern branch.

In an hour or so, we come to something that, at least for me, is completely unexpected. The Satlej River has created a vast canyonland. Our road runs through the bottom of it, next to—and sometimes touching—the river. There are vertical walls on either side, and the water has carved out figures that in places look like giant human heads. There are caves that seem to have been inhabited in earlier days. After about forty miles of this, we emerge into an open space. It is surprisingly fertile. In fact, there are trees—essentially nonexistent on the plateau. Across the river, the town of Tholing is visible. It looks like a pleasant, tree-filled oasis. We drive through it and pull up in a field on the other side to camp. Before we can unload, Tashi—our Tibetan tour guide—insists that he and Jaccoux return to Tholing to get official permission from the Chinese police. He is adamant about this, so he and Jaccoux go off. We mill about on the grass while the rest of the Tibetan crew plays cards. In the middle of this, an army truck filled with Chinese soldiers passes by. They wave cheerfully at us, ignoring the Tibetans. The reaction is mutual. After another hour, Jaccoux and Tashi return. It has taken them a long time to locate the relevant official, who, after a certain amount of negotiating, has given us the necessary authorization. We go to sleep early. Tomorrow we will visit Tsaparang.

Saturday, September 17: Halfway to Darchen

I cannot imagine a more dramatic site than Tsaparang. It is about ten miles west of Tholing. The site does not become visible until one is almost on top of it. Then it is a bit difficult to believe what one is seeing. Tsaparang consists of a series of chapels set one above the other on a sheer rock face. On top of the cliff, outlined against the sky, is the palace of the Gu-ge kings. It looks completely inaccessible. In fact, one can only get to it by entering what was once a secret tunnel carved into the mountain, which contains a smoothly polished, very steep stone stairway. In the case of an attack, it could be easily blocked by an armory of stones kept on a balcony above the tunnel. On the way to the palace, one passes the White and Red Chapels. Neither of these chapels was seriously damaged by the Red Guard, although the Chinese did loot and destroy a great deal of the magnificent statuary.

There are several surrounding chapels in various states of ruin—attributable, it appears, to neglect and not vandalism.

Very fortunately, the glorious wall murals in the Red and White Chapels have been left nearly intact, their vivid colors preserved. Those in the White Chapel date from the fifteenth century and were painted by artists imported from Kashmir. The female deities and consorts have the sensuous, full bodies one so often sees in Indian art. The murals in the Red Chapel—so called because its exterior walls are painted an ocher color and leap out at you from the surrounding cliffs—were painted two centuries later, just as the Gu-ge kingdom was about to disappear. Although they are less fine, they are fascinating, because they depict scenes from daily life. Among other things, some of the scenes show foreign visitors to the kingdom. It is interesting that, in 1624, it was a Portuguese missionary, Antonio de Andrade, who was the first European to visit the Gu-ge kings. He founded the initial Christian church in Tibet, but a few years later all of the missionary churches were driven out in an invasion by the neighboring Buddhist Ladakhis, who were concerned by the intrusion of the new religion. This may well have been one of the reasons that the Gu-ge kingdom disintegrated.

We are shown around Tsaparang by a young Tibetan who seems totally devoted to the site and very knowledgeable. A handful of people live there and take care of it. Our guide is quite stern when it comes to the matter of photographs. None are allowed in the interior of the chapels—so as, he says, not to damage the murals. But, when he is asked a question about the detail in any of them, he touches the relevant place with his finger. Fortunately, Tsaparang is so remote that it does not get very many visitors, so his finger is not much used. During our visit, we do not see a single foreigner, either on the site or on any of the routes. It will surely be different when we get to Kailas tomorrow. At least three tour groups flew in with us planning on making this trip. In the early afternoon, we begin our drive. It takes us several hours to get clear of the canyonland and back close to the Indus, where we camp.

Sunday, September 18: Darchen

One never knows quite what to make of this country. Today it was the sacred and the profane. The sacred was our first view of Kailas.

We had put in another twelve-hour driving day, and it was not until late afternoon that we got our first glimpse of the mountain. It was cloudy so we could not see much until we were nearly at Darchen—the settlement at its base. Then the clouds dissipated, and the whole mountain was visible. The lower parts glowed purplish red in the setting sun; it was crowned by a halo of white snow. The mountain stands isolated by itself. Imagine an ocher pyramid, covered with a sheer white capuchin, rising eight thousand feet—eight Empire State Buildings—in isolation out of a flat plane. To add to the magic, across the broad prairie that leads to the base of the mountain came a group of pilgrims on horseback. They were in family groups, with tiny children riding on their mothers' backs. All were dressed in their very finest. They, too, were caught in the spell of the mountain and, to bask in it, had slowed the horses to a stately walk. The bells on the reins tintinnabulated in a slow march. The scene was enough to take one's breath away.

And then there was Darchen. Darchen is not, in fairness, something one can blame on the Chinese—unless one wants to blame the Chinese for opening this country up to the modern world. That probably would have happened anyway, although who can say what course it might have taken. There were, as far as I could see, no Chinese in Darchen. It seemed to be in the hands of various Tibetan entrepreneurs. Basically, Darchen is a base camp for pilgrims who are planning to circumnavigate the mountain. It consisted of a filthy, squalid tent community located next to an almost equally filthy and squalid compound for more affluent pilgrims. In the latter, rooms were available, five beds in each. They were miserable hovels that looked as if they had never been properly cleaned. Mangy dogs roamed around the courtyard feeding on slops. One look, and we insisted on mounting our own tents in the courtyard—which we were able to do, for a fee. Mine was located next to the "cabaret." This consisted of a large tent containing a disco amplifier and a television screen on which music videos were shown. The hostesses were young, heavily made up Tibetan women, dressed in tight-fitting jeans and leather boots with stiletto heels. Beer and other drinks were available. The noise of the amplifiers poured out of the tent until midnight, when the electric generator was shut off.

Since I could not sleep anyway, I took the opportunity to rearrange my gear for our three-day trek around the mountain. This required care. Everything had to be divided into three categories. In the first category were things I am going to carry on my back. I will need enough gear so that if, as sometimes happens, I am separated from whatever support group is carrying our heavy baggage—in this case, a train of yaks—I will be able to survive a night outdoors at high altitude. This means carrying, at the least, a down jacket, a wool hat, and heavy gloves, along with a "space blanket"—a metal foil that retains heat, which one can, in extremis, wrap around oneself. It also means carrying at least a liter of tea or other liquid, and some snack food. Even adding my camera and flashlight, I think I kept all of this to under fifteen pounds. Items like my down sleeping bag and changes of clothes, along with a medical kit, went into my duffel to be loaded on the back of a yak. The rest will stay in Darchen, locked in one of the Land Cruisers. Of our crew, only Tashi and Pasang will go with us around the mountain. By midnight, I have checked and rechecked everything and, with the help of a sleeping pill, drop off to the troubled night's sleep I always have before this kind of adventure.

Monday, September 19: The Drira Phuk Monastery

As far as anyone knows, no one has actually climbed Kailas. This has to do not with its difficulty, but with a taboo that has, so far, been respected by the Chinese authorities. The great Tyrollean climber Reinhold Messner came close to getting permission in 1985. While he was waiting, he sprinted around the thirty-two-mile kora circuit in twelve hours. Before permission could be granted, however, he learned—in Darchen—that one of his brothers had been killed in a climbing accident in Italy, so he left Tibet without making an attempt. The time normally required for a well-acclimatized party to make the kora is three days. Some guidebooks recommend four if the group has not already spent a good deal of time at high altitude. In our traverse across Tibet, we had spent much of our time at seventeen thousand feet, and above, so we were as acclimatized as we were going to get. Hence, we planned a three-day circuit.

Books have been written about this circuit. John Snelling, an English writer, in his *Sacred Mountain* describes what seems to be every trip ever taken by a westerner prior to the 1980s. In 1994, Stan Armington and Sushil Upadhyay published a brief guide—*Humla to Mount Kailas*—which we all bought in Kathmandu and are carrying with us. As if this were not enough, Victor Chan, in his monumental *Tibet Handbook* published in February of 1994, devotes twenty pages to describing the religious symbols and monuments one will encounter. There do not seem to be two feet of the kora that do not have deep religious significance for one eastern religion or another. All of these guides are in agreement that the first day of the tour is both relatively easy—if long—and very scenic. It is on the second day that the real difficulties begin. At least, that is the theory.

I am notoriously slow in my trekking pace, so to compensate I always start out an hour or two before everyone else. The general starting time was in fact quite unclear, since it depended on when the designated yaks could be rounded up and brought to the compound in Darchen. Hence, at about nine-thirty I simply started in the clockwise direction around the mountain. This is the sense taken by all pilgrims except the Bon-Po—the pre-Buddhist sect that has some adherents in this part of Tibet. It was a lovely day—bright and clear. As soon as I got away from Darchen, I could look south over the plains and see the iridescent blue of Lake Manasarovar and the Gurla Mandhata mountain massif behind it. In the distance I could even see the mountains of Nepal, as well as the Indian Himalayas. I found myself in the company of large numbers of pilgrims of all ages. They were mainly Tibetan, but a few had come from India. In 1981, the Chinese and Indians concluded a treaty that allows two hundred Indians a year to come to Kailas. They each pay a fee of ten thousand rupees—a fortune—to the Indian and Chinese governments for the privilege. There are so many applicants that they are chosen by lottery.

This was the time of the full moon, which is considered especially auspicious for making a pilgrimage. There were entire families with the smallest children on the backs of their parents. There was a wonderful-looking elderly woman with a prayer wheel she kept turning. There were a few westerners, some of whom I had met in Kathmandu or Lhasa. The greeting everyone used was *"tashee-de-lay"*—"good luck."

The path was broad and unmistakable. One gained altitude very slowly. After about an hour, the south face of Kailas came into view. This is the site of the first of four prostration stations. Devout pilgrims generally prostrate themselves twelve times—three in each of the four cardinal directions. After an hour or so, the Chuku monastery came into view across the river and above the trail. All the monasteries on the kora were destroyed by the Red Guards. The small Chuku monastery, like the others on the kora, was restored in the 1980s. The scenery became more alpine and I felt more remote. By this time, I had had lunch and was beginning to wonder what had happened to the rest of my group and the yaks. A few of them caught up with me, but they had no idea where the others were, either. We decided to keep walking. After another hour, we sat down by the path to figure out what to do next.

I had done enough reading, and talked to enough people about the kora, to know that in the worst case we could spend the night in the Drira Phuk monastery. It is at sixteen thousand feet, just before the real difficulties of the climb begin. It, or its environs, is the natural place to stop the first day. I was sure that we could get some food in the monastery, and find a bed of some sort. My companions were less sanguine. Finally, the group split in two. Two decided to stay where they were until the yaks arrived, while three of us decided to go on to the monastery. By this time the sun was beginning to set. I kept thinking that the monastery would be just around the next bend in the trail, but it never appeared. Whenever I came across a Tibetan, I would point hopefully up the trail and say, *"Gompa? Gompa?"* He or she would generally point somewhere in the direction of the horizon. Finally, I spotted the *gompa* across the river and above me. I had to make a wide detour to find a bridge over the river, but just before sunset I was able to open its front door.

Inside was a cheerful and reassuring sight. Around a yak-dung-fueled stove were several Tibetans. One detached himself—the guardian—and pointed out a place where I could sit. Shortly, my two companions came in and were also shown places. Since there was absolutely no sign of Jaccoux and the yaks, I began to make plans to bed down in the *gompa*'s rest house. The guardian understood a little English, and I was able to communicate with him that we wanted to rent one of his rooms. Actually, one has to rent the individual beds in a room, so I rented all the beds in one of the rooms. For a small additional fee, I was able to rent enough blankets for the three of us. They seemed a bit dusty but otherwise fairly presentable. Next I made various signs about being hungry. He brought out some boxes of powdered Tibetan noodle soup—a soup so thick that you can practically walk on it. He put some water into a pot and soon had a boiling cauldron of soup. It made a fine supper, and after it we bedded down in our room. There remained no sign of Jaccoux and the yaks, but we were safe and sound. Even with my down jacket, wool hat, and gloves, I was still cold. In any event, I was able to fall into a fitful sleep as the full moon rose over the north face of Kailas, just across the valley.

Tuesday, September 20: The Zutrul Phuk Monastery

This has been the hardest day of trekking I have ever had. I am so tired that before writing in my diary, I got violently sick. That has never happened to me in the mountains before. I now feel somewhat better, but exhausted. I knew that this was going to be a very tough day even before I started.

The Drira Phuk monastery, where we were last night, is at sixteen thousand feet. The pass—the Drölma La—is at 18,400 feet. Our final destination is the Zutrul Phuk monastery, which is at 15,400 feet. To see what this means, imagine putting the Empire State Building at sixteen thousand feet and climbing it two and a half times, then descending it three. That is the altitude change we dealt with. There was also the horizontal distance, which—judging from the map— was about fifteen miles. All of this might have been more manageable if I had been able to get a decent night's sleep. My sleeping pills were in my medical kit, which was on the back of a yak somewhere. After falling asleep fairly promptly at about nine, I woke up at eleven and, as far as I could tell, did not sleep at all for the rest of the night. My two companions, in their neighboring wooden beds, claimed that *I* had slept all night and that *they* had been awake. Whatever—about five in the morning, I gave up and went outside.

It was a clear morning, but very cold. The north face of Kailas glowed in the nascent sunrise. Out of the neighboring rooms in the *gompa*'s rest house came family after family of pilgrims—mostly Tibetan, some Indian. Silently, they headed up the trail. I watched them disappear into the distance. I then set out to find the guardian to buy some breakfast. I was not able to find anyone. In the meanwhile, my companions had arisen. They were sure that they could see our tents across the river. There were so many tents across the river that the ones I could see could have been anybody's. However, they decided to cross the river anyway, to look for the rest of the group. I found a little candy in my pack and ate it while I figured out what to do next. Finally, I decided to head up the trail, following the rest of the pilgrims, and to wait at the point just before it appeared the trail got really steep. I crossed the river on the bridge I had come over the evening before, and found a lovely spot in a meadow next to the trail. During the next hour, a seemingly never-ending stream of pilgrims passed me. There must have been several hundred. Finally, a New Zealand woman, whom I had met in Kathmandu and was with a British group making the kora, came along. She had two bits of welcome news. Firstly, Jaccoux and our yaks were not far behind her. Secondly, she had some extra candy she did not want. More breakfast. Then Pasang came racing up the trail. He had come to look for me. He had even more good news. He had brought *two* pack lunches for me—one of them for breakfast. Then came Jaccoux. He told me that our yaks had not shown up in Darchen until four in the afternoon! The group had not arrived at the campsite until after ten at night. No wonder we did not see them. Now the group was reunited and we could get to the business at hand—the climb.

The trail became quite steep and crossed a moraine. From there, Kailas looked very forbidding, with a heavily crevassed glacier guarding its approaches. This is taken by devout pilgrims as a glimpse of what hell might look like and is an important spiritual moment in the kora. There was a fork in the trail. Pilgrims who have made the kora twelve times are allowed to choose the branch that leads to a pass adjacent to the Drölma La. The rest of us must follow the main trail. At 17,500 feet, we came to a hillside known as the Siwatsal. This hillside is strewn with human artifacts—clothing, bones, parts of saddles, locks of human hair, and shoes, among other things. The tradition is to take something and leave something. It is symbolic of leaving one's past life and entering a new one. I was prepared to leave something, but it took a larger suspension of disbelief than I possess to take something from that bizarre collection.

At the top of the hill, the trail leveled off for a bit. I could see the next steep part, with a line of pilgrims making their way painfully up it. We now had about a thousand feet more of altitude to gain—the hardest thousand feet. For this Jaccoux had another *truc*. In his system, one climbed for fifteen minutes by the clock. At that point one sat down for exactly ten minutes, whether one was tired or not. It looked crazy to any observer who studied us, but it worked. It allowed us to gradually adapt to these very high altitudes. Jaccoux's sister agreed to be timekeeper. She was very rigorous about both the resting and walking times—not a minute more or less. I was very amused to compare our progress with that of two young Tibetans whom we kept passing. They would start out at practically a dead run. This would go on for about five minutes. Then they would collapse on the ground gasping for air. They did not seem to understand why we kept getting ahead of them. We made good progress and after an hour or so we could see the prayer flags marking the pass.

There is a big boulder at the pass that is said to be an image of the goddess Drölma—the Tara in Sanksrit. This is her pass. At the pass itself is an archway made up of hundreds of prayer flags. One walks under this arch to arrive at the summit of the pass. The act of passing under the arch cleanses one of all one's past sins. Animals that pass under the arch and complete the kora are given colorful braids to wear, indicating that they are never to be slaughtered. Once through the arch, the tradition is to have one's best meal of the kora on the other side. For this occasion Jaccoux took out of his rucksack a magnificent sausage brought from Chamonix and some cheese from the Savoie. We sat in a state of grace in the bright sunshine—until the *fire!* All of a sudden, an entire end of the arch of prayer flags burst into flames. A monk, whose intentions were completely obscure, had succeeded in setting it. Everyone—two hundred people—jumped up and began trying to douse the flames by pouring sand on them or by stomping them out with their feet. It was a close call—a demonic scene—but the arch was saved.

I took this as some sort of omen that I had better start down the other side. The wind had risen and was blowing in gale bursts. Coming up had not been too bad, but going down was murder. The trail was very steep and made up of loose rocks. The footing was tricky, and I had to take each step with great care so as not to twist an ankle or worse. Even when the trail leveled out, there were long stretches of boulder fields that had to be negotiated by climbing from one boulder to another. The going was painfully slow, and there were three thousand feet of altitude to lose. It simply did not end. The sun began to set and still it did not end. Just when I thought that I might have to walk the rest of the trail by flashlight, I saw the *gompa* below. It was all I could do to get there. Since the yaks had not yet arrived, I sank down on the grass too exhausted to move. When the yaks finally did appear, we then had to set up our tents. I did my best with mine, but Pasang had to help me. I crawled into it and became violently ill. Pasang brought me some soup and, after drinking it, in sort of a coma, I totally passed out.

Wednesday, September 21: Lake Manasarovar

This has been a rather easy day. It took me about four hours to walk the gently sloping trail back down to Darchen. It was more like sleepwalking than walking. When I arrived at the Guest House, I found a broken-down easy chair that someone had left under an eave. I sat down in it and promptly dozed off. When I awoke, it was early afternoon. Our drivers had put everything into the Land Cruisers and the truck, and we were off to Lake Manasarovar, which is visible from Darchen. It only took us a couple of hours to get there. I cannot imagine a more beautiful setting than this lake. It is a luminous blue and seems perfectly untouched. There is a sixty-mile circuit around the perimeter of the lake that is often taken by Hindu pilgrims. Some of the ashes of Mahatma Gandhi were scattered in the lake in August of 1948. For Hindus, it is a very sacred place. We set up our camp on a meadow with a wonderful view of both the lake and Kailas. It was sunny and warm and, after a fine dinner, I slept the sleep of the blessed.

Thursday, September 22: Ten Miles from Taklakot

This has been a strange day. It began and ended well enough, but there were some fireworks in the middle. We got off to a late start, since we did not have that far to go. Just before leaving, I went down to the shore of the lake, where about fifty Indian pilgrims were camped. They were chanting to the lake and the mountain in a state of religious ecstasy. Then they crammed themselves into two brightly decorated trucks and headed off in the direction of Kailas.

Last night we had carefully discussed today's program with Tashi. I was the official French–English interpreter, and had gone over everything several times to make sure that all was clear and agreed upon. The main point was that under no circumstances did we want to spend the night in the Guest House in Taklakot. It was obvious— sight unseen—that it would be at least as bad as the one in Darchen. Tashi said that there was a very nice farming village a few miles from Taklakot where we could camp. Then, the following day we could drive to Taklakot and make our arrangements for crossing the border out of Tibet. It sounded fine.

The drive south was very beautiful, passing close to the Gurla Mandhata and by the nearly adjacent sacred lake, Raksas Tal. There were several pilgrims making their way on foot or by horse toward Kailas. By the afternoon, the scenery had changed, and we were in a fertile farming area. We kept going and at one point were about to pass through the village in which we had agreed to camp. It became rapidly clear that we were being double-crossed. Jaccoux, who was in the same Land Cruiser as me, insisted that it stop. This brought to a halt the Land Cruiser behind us, which contained Tashi. In the meanwhile, the truck, which had also stopped, took off at high speed in the direction of Taklakot. It was obvious that the intention was to put us in the Guest House whether we liked it or not. However, Tashi and the others had not reckoned with Jaccoux's temper. He all but picked Tashi up and put him bodily into the Land Cruiser, which he then ordered to give chase to the truck. The two vehicles took off in a cloud of dust, leaving the rest of us in a field near the village.

While waiting for the denouement, I had an opportunity to look around the village. It was a model farming village—clean and prosperous. Something, however, seemed odd to me. Then I realized what it was. While the people were obviously Tibetans, everything Tibetan was missing. Even the clothing was Chinese. The men wore Mao jackets; the women, those padded jackets one sees all the time in pictures of Chinese farming communities. One wondered whether any of the traditional Tibetan values, including the veneration of the Dalai Lama, would have any meaning for these people. It was puzzling to find all of this in a part of Tibet as far from China as it is possible to be. I wondered whether the proximity to Taklakot might have something to do with it. It caused me to wonder whether the present generation of Chinese even know what they are doing in Tibet. Surely, no one believes that the Indians are going to try to reestablish the McMahon Line by force. Does it really require a million Chinese soldiers to suppress the Tibetans? Would it not be vastly less costly in every way to give the Tibetans real autonomy—to make them partners—to allow this beautiful, ancient culture to flourish?

Soon, Jaccoux returned with the irate truck driver, who grabbed our stuff out of the truck and hurled it onto the dirt. But peace was restored when Jaccoux said that, as far as he was concerned, all of them could spend the night in Taklakot. It was just that *he* was not going to spend the night there. This put everyone into a good mood, and the whole Tibetan crew went off to amuse themselves in the big city while we camped in our field.

Friday, September 23: Sher

Our crew returned this morning about eight, looking somewhat the worse for the wear. I asked So-Do about the big night and he rolled his eyes. We then drove to Taklakot, which was only a few miles away. Everything I had thought might be true of this place, was. It is basically a Chinese military garrison—a frontier post. There are hundreds of soldiers. It is also a trading post. There are bazaars run by Chinese and Nepalese, and one somewhat run-down bazaar run by Tibetans. There are also innumerable open-air billiard parlors. One has the impression that the local Tibetan men spend their days playing billiards and drinking beer. If this was all one saw of Tibet, one would conclude that it was a culture in ruins. Equally depressing was the Guest House. There were a number of forlorn Europeans who had been waiting for days to get rides back to Lhasa. Everywhere you looked papers and litter were on the ground, some being picked over by dogs. I looked into one of the rooms that we would have been put in if we had stayed there, and recoiled. I could hardly wait to get out of the place.

But before we could leave we, of course, had to clear the police formalities. This is the last post before the frontier. We all thought that the process might take hours. Here, we were in for a pleasant surprise. In fairly short order, a small group of Chinese officers marched into a building neighboring the Guest House. Tashi then marched us into the building. We were instructed to line up in the order in which our names appeared on our group visa—exactly the same protocol we had followed on entering the country. Jaccoux was then asked to produce our customs declaration. He had to explain that we did not have one. No one had given us one in Lhasa. Remarkably, this explanation seemed perfectly satisfactory. Then we marched past the officers seated at a table, one after the other. Our passports were studied, and the names compared with the list, and then a stamp was put on them. I had the only non-French passport in the group, and when the officer in charge saw my American document he gave me a sort of mischievous smile. Nothing was said, but it seemed a friendly enough gesture. Now we were free to leave Tibet. That was all there was to it.

One of the Land Cruisers had definitely collapsed and had to be replaced by another one belonging to our tour company. It took a couple of hours for this transaction to be completed, and then we could leave for the Nepalese border—a couple more hours away by car. But what a couple of hours! The road was impossible. I had noted the laconic commentary in the guide by Armington and Upadhyay—to the effect that, in July of 1993, a truck carrying two dozen Nepalese passengers on top of a load of salt turned over, killing thirteen of them. One could understand how this might have happened. The road runs along the Karnali River and is so narrow that one senses at least one of the tires is hanging over the edge at all times. One also senses this is a road that has never been maintained. After about an hour, we came to the second pleasant surprise of the day—the *gompa* at Khojarnath.

Nothing prepares one for the presence of this *gompa*. It seems to be in the middle of the wilderness. Perhaps that is why the Red Guards did not destroy it. It is so beautiful and so moving that even So-Do—as worldly as he seemed to be—offered prayers. There are two main chapels. The principal chapel contains statues of religious significance to both Buddhists and Hindus, and indeed, there were several Indian pilgrims in it. Softly glowing butter lamps illuminated the statues as well as the pictures of the Dalai Lama. The second chapel—in addition to having a number of side rooms with statues—also had stuffed animals suspended from the ceiling. There were a snow leopard, a tiger, and part of a yak, as well as other local animals. It is an uncanny display and adds to the mystery of the place. If this was all one saw of Tibet one would say that it was a culture that was flourishing.

Then we made for the border. I do not know what I expected—a kind of arcadia perhaps. Instead, what happens is that the road gets worse and worse and then stops. One simply runs out of road. When So-Do brought the Land Cruiser to a halt, I was sure that there must be some mistake. There was nothing. Or rather there was a cliff on the other side of the river with a very steep trail leading up it. There was no sign of civilization at all. No one was there to greet us—nothing. We unloaded all of our gear from the Land Cruisers and the truck and waited to see what would happen. Pasang took over and began to whistle in the ear-piercing way that Sherpas are able to achieve. About ten minutes later, there was an answering whistle from the top of the cliff. Then someone came down the trail. He turned out to be a Sherpa—part of Pasang's waiting crew. They had been waiting for us for six days, not knowing quite when we would appear. He told us that our camp was about an hour's walk away—across the Karnali River inside Nepal. He said that he would send a yak-train down to get our baggage. I put on my rucksack and went to thank So-Do. I gave him all my remaining yuan and told him to use it to buy everybody some beers. Our crew would soon start the trip back to Lhasa in the Land Cruisers. By now, the rivers had gone down, so they could take the southern route—only five days to Lhasa. I felt sorry to see them go. They had become part of our life.

Then I crossed the river and started up the trail. It was slow going and hard work in the afternoon sun. It was only at the top of the trail that I saw the village of Sher. It is still in Tibet, but barely. Sher is a local trading post where Nepalis bring produce such as rice to exchange for Tibetan salt. It took only a few minutes to walk through the village. Then the trail descends steeply down the other side, to the Karnali River. A rickety bridge crosses it, and just before the bridge is a stone pillar. That is the border—the pillar. There are no police, no customs officers, no soldiers—nobody. One simply walks out of Tibet as if it were not there. Not far from the river I could see our camp. Several Sherpas were working around it. There was a bright orange mat on the ground—which usually means tea will be served. When I got there, I was greeted by smiles and laughter—and tea.

Postscript

It took us five days to walk from Sher to Simikot. The first day was the hardest, since we had to cross the fifteen-thousand-foot Nara Lagna pass. Once one is over the pass, one is truly in Nepal—the verdant, fertile Nepal that one knows so well. There are fields and flowers and forests. Very few trekkers come on this route. At one police post, we were told that, in an entire year, they had seen only about two hundred westerners, passing in both directions. Because there were so few trekkers, we were a curiosity rather than objects to be exploited. It was like the old Nepal—the Nepal of the 1960s.

The trail to Simikot follows the Karnali River. Sometimes we were in deep gorges, sometimes high above the river. On the last day we crossed a pass and there was Simikot below us, the air-strip in full view. From that vantage point the town looked idyllic. It is only when one reaches it that the illusion fades. It embodies all of the problems of modern Nepal—overpopulation, poverty, lack of meaningful work, lack of medical facilities, lack of sanitation—all of the problems. But the one problem it does not have is occupation by an alien power. To see what that means, all one has to do is to walk five days to the north.

Part Three

BHUTAN

9

Druk Yol: The Kingdom of the Thunder Dragon

On a horribly humid September afternoon in 1988, I found myself in a non–air-conditioned taxicab in Calcutta, trying to instruct the driver on how to get to the South Park Street Cemetery. He seemed a very intelligent man with a lively command of English, but for some reason I was not able to get through to him the idea that I wanted to go to a place where dead bodies were buried. He appeared to think that I wanted to see a hospital, like that of Mother Theresa—a common destination for visitors to Calcutta. It suddenly dawned on me what the problem was. There are no real cemeteries in Calcutta. The dead are burned and their ashes are thrown in the Hooghly River. I then tried another tack and explained that I wanted to go to a place that English visitors would go to visit their ancestors. The response was immediate and, in short order, in a driving monsoon thunderburst, we pulled up in front of an ancient cemetery. The driver got out and spoke to the *chowkidar*—the watchman—who apparently lived in the cemetery with five assistants, all of them huddled under the eaves of a crypt to get out of the rain. The negotiations completed, I was allowed into the cemetery and given a tour of it under an umbrella held by the taxi driver and the *chowkidar*.

It is a lovely cemetery, as cemeteries go: an island of tranquillity in the Calcutta maelstrom. It was opened in 1767 and recently restored by the British Association of Cemeteries in Southern Asia. Some of the tombs are massive, some tiny. Some of the inscriptions appear newly carved and some are faded to illegibility. They collectively tell, at least implicitly, the history of British India. Charles Dickens's second son, Walter Landor Dickens, of the British army, is buried there, as is Richmond Thackeray, William's father. George Bogle, whom we met earlier and will meet again, is buried there. His monument contains the words IN SINCERE ATTACHMENT TO THE MEMORY OF MR. GEORGE BOGLE LATE AMBASSADOR TO TIBET WHO DIED 3RD OF APRIL, 1781. Soldiers, statesmen, women, and young children are all buried there, one of the last tangible reminders of the British raj. On the way back from the cemetery, through the cloacal Calcutta traffic, made even worse by the intermittent cloudbursts, which had turned the streets into a sort of malignant Venice, the driver asked me where I was going next. I told him, to Bhutan. "Bhutan," he said wistfully. "Bhutan is a nice place. You will like it there."

When told that one is going to Bhutan, unlike my Calcutta taxi driver, most people tend to look at one blankly. Where is it? What is it? To locate Bhutan, imagine shooting an arrow—archery is the national sport of Bhutan—north from Calcutta and slightly east, about five hundred miles, and then elevating it to about eight thousand feet above Calcutta's sea level. Properly aimed, it would land in the Changlimithang Sports Grounds in Thimphu, the capital of Bhutan. Sixty miles or so farther north it might hit the Kula Gangri, which at 24,784 feet is the highest mountain in Bhutan. It is part of the Himalayan wall that separates the country from Tibet. To the west of Bhutan lies the tiny protectorate of Sikkim, which received a certain amount of attention when the then-maharaja took as his consort the American socialite Hope Cook. (Subsequently they were divorced and the maharaja died and the country was basically taken over by India.) The rest of Bhutan, which is about the size of Switzerland, is bounded by India.

Bhutan, which the Ngalungs—Tibetans who migrated south centuries ago and who speak a language, Dzongkha, related to Tibetan—
refer to as Druk Yol (the "Thunder Dragon Land"), has been, at least
until recently, regarded as a kind of Shangri-la. In some ways it is.
While population statistics are incredibly difficult to come by, the best
guess is that the overall population is about a million. Of these—and
here the statistics are even worse—somewhere between 16 and 20
percent are Ngalungs. The rest of the population is divided into two
groups—the Sarchops, who migrated from eastern Tibet, and who
speak their own language and have their own religious and cultural
customs; and the Lhotshampa, who are Nepali-speaking Hindus and
live mainly in the south. The Nepali-speakers are variously estimated
as composing between 30 and 50 percent of the population, the
remainder being Sarchops. The significant thing, which I will come
back to, is that the Ngalungs, who are the Bhutanese who rule the
country and set its standards, are by all counts a minority in it. In any
event, taken as a whole, Bhutan is one of the few countries in Asia that
is actually underpopulated and has had to import "guest labor" to
perform some of its essential work, such as building and repairing
roads.

But this is not all. Bhutan is also one of the rare countries in Asia
that actually *exports* food—a situation that Nepal used to enjoy before
the size of its population got out of hand. Bhutanese fruit, grown
mainly in the semitropical southern part of the country, is famous for
its variety and quality. Bhutan is also the only Himalayan country
whose forests are basically intact—again in contrast to Nepal, where
the results of deforestation are visible everywhere. The conservation
of Bhutan's forests is not an accident. Wood products, such as plywood, are one of the country's principal exports. (Another is hydroelectric power from the Chukha Hydel Project in the south, which
sells power to India. Here, too, is a remarkable contrast to Nepal. In
August of 1995, the World Bank, in an unprecedented move, canceled
a $175-million loan that would have gone toward financing the $1
billion so-called Arun 3 hydroelectric power project in eastern Nepal.
The Bank argued that the project was going to cost some ten times
what comparable projects usually cost, and that the country simply

couldn't handle it.) Trees are considered such a precious resource that any Bhutanese who wants to build a house made in whole, or part, of wood must apply to the government for a permit, which states how many trees may be cut for that purpose. In Bhutan, education and medical services are free—at least to citizens. As I will discuss later, one of the agonies that the country is now confronting is just who is a citizen. At the time of my 1988 visit, there were no reported cases of AIDS in the country, and prostitution, if it existed, was invisible.

On my visit, I observed almost no begging in Bhutan—another stunning contrast to Nepal and India. Visitors—the two thousand or so visitors who are allowed in by the government each year—are not allowed to tip anyone. Nor are they allowed to enter the Buddhist monasteries—Buddhism is the state religion of Bhutan—for fear of disturbing the contemplation of the monks, some of whom have taken vows of silence that can last for several years. Again this contrasts to Nepal, and to a certain extent Tibet, where the monasteries have become yet another tourist attraction. Although, for reasons I will come to, the constitutional monarchy in Bhutan is now under challenge, it has been relatively stable. The king, Jigme Singye Wangchuk, the fourth hereditary monarch of the Wangchuk dynasty, who is in his early forties, has been very popular with at least the traditional elements of Bhutanese society. Many Bhutanese would like to believe that the king may have been misled by his advisers and that his own intentions have always been honorable. Others feel that he is as responsible as anyone else for the divisions that are now threatening the stability of the country.

Be that as it may, one thing that struck me during my visit was the basic honesty and decency of many of the people with whom I came into contact. Here is a perfect example. An American acquaintance of mine was about to take a grueling seven-hour bus trip from Thimphu south to the Indian border town of Phuntsholing, one of the entry or exit points for tourists. I, too, was going. To fortify ourselves, we stopped off at what is known as the Swiss Bakery in Thimphu. It is so called because it is owned and operated by a Swiss who married a Bhutanese woman and took out Bhutanese citizenship. The bakery features European-style pastries and westernized sandwiches, such as yak burgers, that relieve the tedium—at least to a westerner—of the traditional Bhutanese diet, which features rice and daal-lentils, with an admixture of usually strongly spiced green vegetables or potatoes. (The only memorable local dish that I had while in Bhutan was a melted-yak-cheese concoction laced with bits of peppers.) The owner must have had a certain nostalgia for his homeland, because near the front counter was a faded poster of the Matterhorn. In any event, my friend finished his pastries and coffee and we boarded the bus for Phuntsholing. Two hours later, he noticed that he had left an extremely expensive camera on the table at the bakery. He explained this to the bus driver. The driver stopped the next northbound tourist bus to Thimphu and explained the situation to its driver, who said that he would retrieve the camera and put it on the next bus south; that it would arrive in Phuntsholing that evening. Which it did. It never occurred to either driver that someone might simply make off with the camera. As a Bhutanese said to me, "No one will touch a visitor's property except maybe children, who don't know what it is."

Despite its appeal, one must never lose sight of the fact that, by western standards, Bhutan is a very poor country. A recent article by Bhutan's foreign minister, Lyonpo Dawa Tsering, noted that the country's annual per capita income rose from $140 in 1971 to $425— more than twice Nepal's—in 1991. Dawa Tsering also noted that 90 percent of what he referred to as "our people" have health coverage and 67 percent of the children are enrolled in school. The question, of course, is what is meant by "our people"—again something I will come back to. Despite the medical coverage, the life expectancy of the Bhutanese, at least in the early 1990s, was about forty-five years— lower than in Nepal or India. This very likely has to do with the uneven distribution of medical services in the country. People in Bhutan are dying from diseases such as tuberculosis and—in the south—malaria, which can be controlled or prevented by modern medical technology. No westerner can, for example, drink untreated water anywhere in Bhutan without running the risk of becoming seriously ill.

The Bhutanese people live with very little in the way of material comforts. I visited an apparently well-to-do farm family in western

Bhutan and was struck by the austere quality of their lifestyle. There were very few glass windows in the house, which, even on a sunny afternoon in early fall, was very cold. Cooking was done on a smoky fire. It is a commonplace of these Himalayan communities that people smell of smoke. There was no running water, no plumbing facilities, and no electric light. But there was a simple room with mats on the wooden floor, which had been set aside for monks in the event they needed a place to stay when passing through or performing rites for the family. There was, at least in this Ngalung family, a sense of a harmonious lifestyle, of people in tune with themselves and their surroundings.

My own interest in Bhutan was relatively recent. This is just as well, since no tourists were allowed into the country prior to 1974, the year of the present king's coronation. Indeed, air travel into the country was only begun on a commercial basis in February of 1983. Druk Air now operates flights between Calcutta and Paro, a town in eastern Bhutan located in one of the few valleys wide enough to provide space for a small airfield. This is how I entered the country. But now there are also flights from New Delhi and Kathmandu. (Indeed, visitors to the country are required, in an effort to support Druk Air, to fly at least in or out of the country.) I have not taken it, but I have been told that the flight from Kathmandu to Paro is simply magnificent. In any event, I first became interested in Bhutan because of one of those chance encounters with a historical figure, who, for one reason or another, becomes something of an obsession.

In this case, the historical figure was none other than the aforementioned George Bogle, whose tomb I had gone in search of in Calcutta. My first chance encounter with Bogle, as I have mentioned, was when I happened across his *Narratives of the Mission of George Bogle to Tibet* in a private library in Kathmandu. I was able to borrow it for only a couple of days. Since, at the time, I was mainly interested in Tibet, I largely skimmed over the parts of the *Narratives* that had to do with Bhutan. But when I returned from Tibet, I discovered that an inexpensive facsimile edition printed in India was available in Kathmandu, so I bought it and read the rest. Here are a few more facts about Bogle, who was—as far as anyone knows—the first westerner to visit Bhutan.

George Bogle was born on the twenty-sixth of November, 1746, in a place called Daldowie, Scotland, on the banks of the Clyde. He was the youngest of nine children, two of whom died in infancy. Throughout his adult life he expressed, especially in letters to his favorite sister Anne (known as Chuffles), his nostalgia for Daldowie, which—as it happened—he was never to see again once he left for India. It was decided early in his career that Bogle should become a merchant and, after a desultory education, in June of 1765 he entered his brother's "counting house" as a clerk. There he remained for the next four years, until—at age twenty-three—he received an appointment with the British East India Company in Calcutta. His arrival in Bengal coincided with a famine there, and he reported to his father that "there were sometimes 150 dead bodies picked up in a day and thrown into the river." Bogle was placed on the so-called Select Committee of the Company, an entity that transacted all of the company's political business on the subcontinent. He also mastered Persian, which was the language of diplomacy on the subcontinent—treaties were often written in it—in somewhat the same sense that French, at the time, was the diplomatic language of Europe.

After Bogle had been in Calcutta for eighteen months, Warren Hastings arrived from Madras to become the governor of Bengal. Hastings was a remarkable and controversial man. It was he who decided that the British must assume full responsibility for the actual governance of India, while at the same time preserving what was best in traditional Indian life. He instituted a number of reforms in the administration of Indian affairs, which led to serious conflicts with the local British establishment and, ultimately, to an impeachment trial before the House of Lords, which lasted from 1788 to 1795. He was eventually acquitted. Bogle's relationship with Hastings began in 1773, and the feeling of mutual admiration between the two men was established almost at once. To his father, Bogle wrote, "Mr. Hastings is a man who is every way fitted for the station which he holds. He possesses a steadiness, and at the same time a moderation of character; he is quick and assiduous in business, and has a fine style of language, a knowledge of the customs and dispositions of the natives whose tongue he understands and, although not affable, yet of the most ready access to all the world." As the feeling was mutual, it was quite natural that when, for reasons that we have already discussed, a mission to Tibet—which began in Bhutan—seemed desirable, Hastings turned to Bogle, who was only twenty-eight. The mission lasted an entire year, and when Bogle returned, he found Hastings in the middle of the imbroglio that finally led to his impeachment. In addition, Bogle learned that his beloved Daldowie was in financial jeopardy; much of his salary for the next few years went to help his father pay off his debts. In 1776, Hastings was restored as governor-general, and Bogle's relationship with him was reestablished. At the time of his death, at the age of thirty-four, in Calcutta, Bogle was engaged in the planning of a second mission to Bhutan, which he did not live to carry out.

These are the essentials of Bogle's brief life, but before I turn to a description of Bogle's mission to Bhutan, I would like to discuss the relation of Bogle, and other Englishmen of this period—the eighteenth century—to the native women of the subcontinent. This was to change radically in the next century, and many writers about the history of British India have speculated that the arrival of the memsahibs—British women either joining their husbands or, in some cases, looking for husbands—with all of their Victorian material and moral baggage, played a decisive role in the sharp class distinctions that developed between the British and the people of the subcontinent they governed. This, as we shall see, was certainly a very significant factor in the nineteenth-century British attitude toward the Bhutanese.

But during Bogle's era, it was a commonplace for a British man in India to take on a "beebee"—a native woman—with whom he would often have a family. In a fascinating memoir entitled "George Bogle and His Children," Hugh M. Richardson, who, as I have mentioned, was for the nine years preceding the Chinese takeover the head of the British mission in Lhasa, described the evidence that Bogle himself had had such a family—indeed, that he had had *two* such families. One was his liaison with a Tibetan woman, probably the Panchen Lama's sister, that produced the two daughters, Martha and Mary, who were educated in Scotland. Of the second liaison, little is known, except that it apparently produced sons. It seems clear to me that Bogle's intimate, and apparently quite open, connection with these native women was what made him such a sensitive and sympathetic observer of the subcontinental people he traveled among. Here, for example, is what he wrote about the Bhutanese in the *Narratives:* "The more I see of the Bhutanese the more I am pleased with them. The common people are good-humored, downright, and, I think, thoroughly trusty. The statesmen have some of the art which belongs to their profession. They are the best built race of men I ever saw; many of them very handsome with complexions as fair as the French." Contrast this with the evaluation of Ashley Eden, a bishop's son and a pillar of Victorian society who visited Bhutan on a similar mission in 1863. Here is Eden's approving commentary on the remarks of a somewhat earlier British visitor to Bhutan: "As a race their failings are very correctly described by Captain [R. B.] Pemberton [who had visited the country in 1837] in the following words: 'I sometimes saw some few persons in whom the demoralizing influences of such a state had yet left a trace of the image in which they were originally created and where the feelings of nature still exercised their accustomed influence, but the exceptions were indeed rare to universal demorality, and much as I have traveled and resided amongst savage tribes on our Frontiers, I have never yet known one so wholly degraded in morals as the Booteahs [Bhutanese].'" It is as if Bogle, Pemberton, and Eden had visited different countries, having in common only a geography.

Before returning to these visits, it is important that we understand the geography of Bhutan. I do not know any country in the Indian subcontinent where geography plays, and has played, such a powerful role in the unity—or lack of it—among the elements of its population. To understand this geography, imagine the level plains of Bengal and Assam, bordering on Bhutan from the south, as a sort of seafloor (when these plains flood—which they often do—this is very nearly true). If one follows these plains—the "seabed"—north, one suddenly runs into an abruptly rising "coastline." Seen from an airplane, it is as if one has run into a vertical cliff some seven thousand feet high. Apart from a narrow strip of flatland that merges with the Indian plain, these Himalayan foothills are the southern boundary of Bhutan. Not only are these foothills extremely steep, they are also covered by an all-but-impenetrable tropical rain forest. From the air, one cannot see the actual ground through the dense carpet of foliage. However, at precisely eighteen places, known as *duars*—a word akin to the English *door* and the Hindi *dwar,* or "gate"—river valleys cut through the mountains. All of the motor roads from the south pass through one of the eighteen duars; anyone controlling the duars would control almost all of the commerce in and out of the country. From time to time, invading bands of Bhutanese would sweep down through the duars to raid neighboring provinces, such as the princely state of Cooch Behar. Indeed, the first inkling the British had that there might be some kind of political entity, with possibly hostile intent, on their newly created northern borders seems to have occurred in 1772, when the Bhutanese invaded Cooch Behar through an adjacent duar and carried off both the maharaja and his brother.

However, in describing this historical event, one must be careful when one uses the term *the Bhutanese* as if one were describing, as early as 1772, the actions of a sovereign nation. Indeed, Bhutan was hardly a nation at all until the beginning of this century, but rather a collection of local fiefdoms located in isolated valleys and speaking their own languages. In particular, there was practically no contact with the Nepali-speaking people—the Lhotshampa, who lived below the duars, and the highland Ngalungs and Sarchops—who in turn had rather little contact with each other. The Lhotshampa probably engaged in a two-step migration, first traveling from southern Nepal to India, and then from India to southern Bhutan, over the course of a century, beginning in the 1850s. To all intents and purposes, they resemble the Nepalese of the Terai; the place where they live, in the south of Bhutan, also resembles the Terai, down to the malarial mosquitoes. Even in the 1950s, it is said, the only contact these people had with the Ngalungs who ruled the country from the north was an annual visit from the tax collector.

In any event, the Cooch Beharis appealed to the British to do something. The British dispatched four companies of Sepoys with two cannon under one Captain Jones, who proceeded to administer a good lesson to the intruders. In fact, it was such a good lesson that it thoroughly alarmed the Bhutanese. They, in turn, appealed to the Tibetans, who were at this juncture their patrons, to make peace. (The relationship of Tibet and Bhutan, like that of Tibet and China, alternated between periods of armed hostility and of patronage. At present, there is an uneasy truce with the Chinese in Tibet, who have made some territorial claims on the northern Bhutanese frontier.) This is what prompted the Panchen Lama to write the letter I quoted from earlier—the one that began, "The affairs of this quarter in every respect flourish. I am night and day employed in prayers for the increase of your happiness and prosperity. . . ." and on and on. This was the letter that inspired Hastings to send Bogle to Tibet.

As was to happen again and again in the next century, the British found it very difficult actually to lay their hands on the individual responsible for this raid. It seems that it was a dubious character named Deb Judhur, who had subsequently retreated to Tibet. The Panchen, who above all wanted to keep the British out of Tibet, attempted to reassure Hastings that the Deb was under control. He wrote, "I have reprimanded the Deb for his past conduct, and have admonished him to desist from his evil practices and to be submissive to you in all matters," adding, "as to my part I am but a Fakir and it is the custom of my sect, with the rosary in our hands, to pray for the welfare of mankind, and for the peace and happiness of the inhabitants of this country; and I do now, with my head uncovered, entreat that you may cease all hostilities against the Deb in future."

If Hastings had been a different sort of person, he might simply have left it at that. But, as we have seen, he took the Panchen's letter as an opportunity to explore a new territory. I have already described some of the instructions that Hastings gave to Bogle, but one of the most remarkable side effects of Bogle's mission was the introduction of the potato to Bhutan—something that the British were to do in Nepal in the middle of the nineteenth century.

As any traveler to Bhutan can testify, the potato is a common—if not relentless—part of one's diet. Indigenous to South America— Peru, Ecuador, Bolivia, and Chile—it was brought to Europe in the sixteenth century, and thence to Asia. There is no doubt it was Bogle's mission that introduced the potato to Bhutan. Hastings instructed Bogle to plant potatoes everywhere the mission camped, simply to introduce a new crop to Bhutan, out of curiosity as to what would happen. As Peter Collister wrote in his book *Bhutan and the British,* "At every halt Bogle carried out Warren Hastings' instructions to plant potatoes, the first batch being at a place called Jaigugu which consisted only of three houses. At Maridzong which they reached after a journey including many descents and steep climbs, passing three waterfalls, he planted fifteen." One wonders if historians looking back at the British legacy on the subcontinent will conclude that the two most important elements of it were the English language and the potato.

The route Bogle followed, as nearly as I can tell by studying the map, is essentially the same as the one taken by the remarkable Indian-engineered road that now leads from the border at Phuntsholing, through one of the duars, to Thimphu—a distance of about one hundred fifty miles, over very difficult terrain. One loses count of the hairpin turns. Bogle called his destination Tassisudon, but the modern transliteration of the Bhutanese name would usually be rendered Tashichodzong. The word *dzong* in Dzongkha (also Tibetan) refers to a fortresslike monastery, a structure that was usually placed at some strategic high point so as to dominate the countryside. Bhutan is dotted with such structures, many in ruins. The buildings that Bogle visited in the Tashichodzong are still standing. But they are a reconstruction made by the present king's father in 1961. The Tashichodzong, on the outskirts of Thimphu, is the largest structure in Bhutan. It is also next to the only golf course in the country—at the time of my visit, a nine-hole affair that also served as a cow pasture. The beasts appeared to move obligingly so as not to interfere with play.

Half of the Tashichodzong is an active monastery into which non-Buddhist visitors cannot enter. The rest of the dzong houses most of the present government. The King receives officially in a room on the second floor overlooking a magnificent courtyard. With special permission—which we managed to obtain—visitors can enter this courtyard after 5 P.M., when the government offices are closed. It is a lovely, tranquil place. Sitting in the courtyard, I tried to imagine the feelings Bogle must have had when he entered the same courtyard. I suspect the scenery was not radically different. However, on my entry I was not regarded by "3,000 spectators." Nor was I presented with "several copper platters with rice, butter, treacle, tea, walnuts, Kashmirian dates, apricots, cucumbers and other fruits . . . ." as was Bogle. But still.

There was, of course, no photography in Bogle's day, but there is a contemporary oil painting by one Tilly Kettle showing Bogle in what are described as "formal Bhutanese clothes." The hat he has on, which looks like an inverted flowerpot, does not resemble anything I saw worn in Bhutan, but the knee-length robe with its marsupial pockets known as a *gho*—pronounced *go*—is still the costume, worn above all by Ngalung men, in Bhutan. It seems to come in two varieties: an oxford gray version for formal occasions, and a tartan version worn every day. Bogle is shown barefoot in his gho, while a traditionally dressed Bhutanese would have worn high boots. It is more common now, however, to see men wearing a kind of knee-length argyle socks—like Scottish golfing socks—and some sort of western shoes, often sneakers or basketball shoes. Women usually wear dark-colored, ankle-length dresses called *kiras*. I never saw a Bhutanese woman, of any sort, wearing a short skirt or slacks, and western women are advised that shorts or tight-fitting clothes are not appropriate in Bhutan. The issue of whether all Bhutanese—Ngalungs, Sarchops, and Lhotshampas—should be *required* to wear ghos and kiras has, in the last few years, become a very divisive one. It would seem, at least to me, to be less than an ideal costume to wear in the stifling heat of the south, and indeed the Lhotshampa have put up a great deal of resistance to wearing it. In 1988, it was declared mandatory, leading to a good deal of civil resistance. It is said that the policy has now moderated to some extent, but no government official ever wears anything else, and certainly no Lhotshampa who hopes to settle in the north can afford to wear anything else, either.

There was, of course, a political entity in what is now Bhutan—or Druk Yol—before the British "discovered" it. Although the identity of the original inhabitants of the territory is unclear, it is generally agreed that by the ninth century A.D., the country had two distinct populations—the Sarchops in the east, and what were known as Bhotias—hence *Bhutan*—the ancestors of the Ngalungs, in the west. By the ninth century, the Bhotias were practicing a kind of Tantric

Buddhism that had been introduced into Tibet from India by the great eighth-century teacher Padma Sambhava, along with his disciples.

The Tibetans account for the rapid spread of this guru's vehicle with the notion that he was able to locomote from place to place on the back of the snow lion. In Bhutan, Padma Sambhava, so the legend goes, was able to make use of a winged tiger. The tiger landed in a place called Taktsang, not far from what is now the airfield in Paro. However, instead of landing on the flats, the tiger landed on a ledge that now supports a clutch of monastic structures—the Tiger's Nest— which cling impossibly to a cliff some three thousand feet above the valley floor. From below, it is impossible to imagine how *anything* could be transported to this monastery short of using a flying tiger. In fact, a reasonably comfortable path leads first to a tea house established by the government for tourists—the Taktsang is one of the prime tourist attractions in the country—and then, above the tea house, to the monastery itself. Fortunately, a wall of trees conceals from the pedestrian the fact that he or she has been navigating across the face of a sheer cliff with a drop of some three thousand feet. When one returns, and looks back up the cliff, it is still difficult to believe. One can approach to within a few hundred feet of the lower monastery, which, like the upper, is off-limits to non-Bhutanese visitors. At the time of my visit, there was a ceremony in progress involving, among other things, the eerie reverberations of conch horns and tambours. The monks waved cheerfully at us between rituals. The upper monastery has about thirty monks who have taken a vow of silence of three years, three months, three weeks, and three days. The ban on visiting them has been imposed partly so as not to disturb their contemplation, and partly because visitors were being sold antique artifacts from the monastery, a practice that has all but denuded the monasteries in Nepal of their great art treasures. Visitors who leave Bhutan are subject to a rigorous search of their baggage to make sure that no antiquities are being exported.

The Buddhism that is practiced in Bhutan shows traces of Bon, the proto-Buddhist animistic religion. For Bhutanese Buddhists, mountains and rivers embody living spirits. An interesting example is Chomo Lhari—pronounced *Jomolari*—a magnificent twenty-four-

thousand-foot peak on the Tibeto-Bhutanese frontier. Chomo Lhari
will never be climbed to the top, because this would offend the spirit
of the mountain. Climbing any peak in Bhutan requires permission
from the king, and to get permission to climb Chomo Lhari, one must
agree not to violate the summit. But that is not all. The spirit of the
mountain is offended by the sight of fire. Hence, one does not make
an open fire within sight of the mountain. If one does, and one burns,
say, refuse in it, there will surely be a terrible storm. I met a lovely
young Bhutanese woman who had come from a small village in the
east to take temporary work in the government tourist hotel in Thimphu. She spoke a serviceable and delightful English, and we spent
several hours discussing various things. She told me that it was very
dangerous to cook meat within the sight of Chomo Lhari. If one did,
one ran the risk of being taken off by a "gorilla." She told me that one
of the girls in her village had been taken off by a gorilla and had
become a gorilla bride. The men and boys in the village took their
bows and arrows and spears and went looking for her. They found her
in a cave and brought her back to the village. They got a lama from a
nearby monastery to come to the village and exorcise the spell that the
gorilla had cast upon the girl. Thereafter, she was simply a girl. I asked
my Bhutanese friend if she herself had talked to the girl. "No," she
answered solemnly, "but my mummy did." When I want trekking to
Chomo Lhari, I made sure that I lit no fires in sight of the mountain.

To return to the history, in 1616, fleeing from persecution in
Tibet, the lama Ngawang Namgyal came to Bhutan. In the next
thirty-five years, until his death in 1651, he succeeded in unifying
all of western Bhutan, making Buddhism the state religion. He
built the system of fortress dzongs, whose ruins one sees today
strategically placed in the valleys of Bhutan, and which were used
successfully to fend off invasions from both the Tibetans and the
Mongols. When he died, it is said that the secret of his death was
kept for fifty years. It is the country he created that Bogle visited in
1774. Following Bogle's mission were several others, including one
led by Captain Samuel Turner in 1783. What distinguished
Turner's mission from its predecessors was the presence of the artist
Samuel Davis. The watercolors painted by Davis captured the

sublime beauty of the Bhutanese countryside in a way that has never been excelled. Apart from a few roads and the odd telephone line, nothing much has changed in the countryside as Davis drew it.

None of these missions resolved the matter of the duars. Even the seizing of the seven Assam duars by the British in 1840 failed to stop raiding by the Bhutanese. A perfect microcosm of the controversy can be found in the affair of Mr. Pyne's elephant. The incident is described in the "Report on State of Bootan [sic]," by Ashley Eden, whom we met earlier when we quoted his acerbic views of the "Booteahs." Eden's mission in 1863–64 led to what became known as the Duar Wars of 1865. Of the elephant, he wrote, "Early in January 1861 the Bootan Frontier Office at Gopalgunge sent over men who stole a valuable elephant belonging to Mr. Pyne, the Manager of Messrs. Dear and Co. at Sillagooree [the northern Indian town of Siliguri, from which one can fly to Calcutta, or—by helicopter—to Darjeeling, if one exits Bhutan via Phuntsholing]. On Mr. Pyne's tracing the elephant and finding it to be in the Gopalgunge stockage, he asked the Booteah Officer to send it to him. The man acknowledged having it, but refused to deliver it up till he received a present of Rupees 300, a telescope, and a gun." A contemporary writer commented that the "Bootan people went on in their evil course, stole an elephant from a Mr. Pyne, another from a native, and with much effrontery allowed them to be frequently seen from our side of the river bank, so that the owners were sorely tempted to recover them by force or stratagem. It is recorded that Mr. Pyne 'altogether bears his loss with less equanimity than the native as is natural to a man with English blood in his veins.'"

Whatever else one may say of Ashley Eden, he was certainly a man of remarkable courage. With twenty-five soldiers and four British officers, and ten thousand rupees to be used to buy presents, he set out on the fourth of January, 1864, to compel some sort of treaty from the Bhutanese committing them to cease and desist from their hostile activities in the duars. After several weeks of marching through a variety of difficult terrain—varying from the malarial lowlands to waist-deep snow over the high passes—Eden arrived in Punakha in the east central part of Bhutan in mid-March. Punakha was, until a few years ago, the winter capital of Bhutan—now it is Thimphu. The distance between them as the crow flies is about forty miles, but the route is so circuitous and mountainous that it took us the better part of a day to complete it. The magnificent dzong where Eden was received still stands. (In 1986, a fire burned some of its interior. At the time of my visit, active restoration was under way.) Eden was received—if that is the word—by a local potentate known as the Tongsa Ponlop. This institution of ponlops—local regents—still exists, and before a king's son can claim the throne, he must have been appointed as either the Tongsa Ponlop or the Paro Ponlop. This ponlop did his best to humiliate Eden and his retinue. As Eden reported, "The Penlow [*sic*] took up a large piece of wet dough and began rubbing my face with it. He pulled my hair and slapped me on the back and generally conducted himself with great insolence. On my showing signs of impatience or remonstrating he smiled and deprecated my anger, pretending that it was the familiarity of friendship, much to the amusement of the large assemblage of bystanders." Eden was also compelled, under duress, to sign a treaty that gave the Bhutanese back the occupied duars before he and his party were allowed to return to India.

Eden was known to loathe the Bhutanese even before his mission, and his report is full of vitriolic comments upon all aspects of Bhutanese life—for example, the betel nut. The betel nut is the fruit of the areca or the betel nut palm tree. It is chewed throughout Asia. It is a bright red—at least in the Bhutanese version—and it is chewed while keeping some sort of calcium-carbonate-producing stone in the mouth, which turns the betel nut into a mild narcotic. It also turns the chewer's mouth red. To westerners, used to shiny white teeth, the sight of red teeth in a blood-red mouth is, to put it mildly, extremely disconcerting. It is comforting to know that these stains are readily washed off. To Eden, the chewing of the betel nut was one more illustration of Bhutanese depravity. He wrote, "The higher classes have their mouths filled with this disgusting stimulation: they almost live on it...." This gave him a brilliant idea for dealing with Bhutanese intransigence: "The occupation of the Dooars [*sic*], if it affects them in no other way, will by stopping their supply of betel soon bring them to reason." More substantially, Eden's contempt for the Bhutanese caused him to underestimate their abilities as soldiers, and this was soon to cost the British dearly. Eden wrote, "Their chief arms are stones, a long knife, a shield, and bows and arrows; the latter they can scarcely use." And he concluded, "They admit themselves to be the most despicable soldiers on the face of the earth; they told us that if one man was killed there was a fight for his body, but if in that another was killed they always ran away."

It is not for nothing that archery is the national sport of Bhutan. It is the only sport in which Bhutan was represented in both the Los Angeles and Seoul Olympics. (No medals were won.) Villages in Bhutan have spirited competitions with each other, and children of both sexes practice the sport from childhood. A Bhutanese specialty is long-distance archery. I watched a team of soldiers shoot—from a distance that looked to me like the length of a football field—at a small target. Their bows, which they showed me, were made of bamboo, and the bowstrings were made of the vine of the stinging nettle. They said that if they could afford them, they would use American bows and arrows—which, apparently, shoot even farther. In the national museum in Paro—a lovely place in which, as in most of the historical sites in Bhutan, no photography is allowed (for some reason, no motion-picture photography is allowed anywhere in the country, except with special permission)—there is a display of the kinds of bows and arrows that were used by Bhutanese soldiers in the last century. They have long, sinister-looking metal barbs, the ends of which were usually tipped with poison.

In December of 1865, a strong force of British mercenary Indian and Nepalese soldiers—Gurkhas, Assamis, and Punjabis—invaded the Bengal duars to settle, they hoped once and for all, the "outrages" that were being committed by the Bhutanese. They had six Armstrong guns, four eight-inch mortars, and several other heavy weapons. What ensued was described by a Major Macgregor, who reported that "We have been accustomed to regard these Bhutias [sic] as a despicable, pusillanimous race, and yet we see them with stones and arrows offering no contemptible defence to some 500 to 600 men with Armstrong guns and inflicting on them a loss of 58 killed and wounded. . . . I doubt . . . if we could have lost many more men if the enemy had been armed with muskets. The arrows are all sharp and pointed and fly with great precision, having penetration enough to go through a man's body."

The war continued with appalling losses on both sides—the British suffered several hundred casualties to disease, probably malaria—until the following fall, when the British compelled whatever authorities in Bhutan they could make contact with to sign the so-called Treaty of Sinchula (November 11, 1865). In this treaty, the British received the right to annex all of the Assam and Bengal duars, in return for which the Bhutanese were to receive a stipend that would eventually rise to fifty thousand rupees a year. There followed some twenty years of uneasy peace, with the Bhutanese in a state of near civil war, often over which faction should control the fifty-thousand-rupee stipend. This is where things stood until 1879, when Ugyen Wangchuk became the Tongsa Ponlop. On December 17, 1907, he was appointed the first king of Bhutan, founding the present hereditary Wangchuk dynasty.

Contemporary photographs of Ugyen Wangchuk show him to be a solidly built man with a broad, powerful face—someone who gave off an aura of no-nonsense authority. It took some seven years prior to his becoming king for him to consolidate his power within Bhutan—often by the use of force—and then he turned his attention to Bhutan's relations with its neighbors. It is not clear how much was chance and how much guile, but Wangchuk was able to take advantage of the almost paranoid fear the British had of the Russians and Chinese extending their influence south toward India—the Great Game. When the British and the Tibetans had an armed skirmish in 1888, Wangchuk very pointedly did not come to the aid of the Tibetans.

By 1903, the British were, after some backing and filling, able to enlist Wangchuk as a kind of diplomatic go-between for the Tibetans and the armed mission to Lhasa led by Francis Younghusband. Collister, in his book on the British in Bhutan, reports that Younghusband and his officers called Wangchuk "Alphonse"—"because of his rather Gallic appearance: short and well-built with a small 'imperial' beard, and usually sporting a gray Homburg hat." In 1905, one of Younghusband's former officers, John Claude White, led an official mission to Bhutan, the high point of which occurred when the mission reached the ancient capital of Punakha, and White was able to confer upon Wangchuk the insignia and warrant of Knight Companion of the Indian Empire, by means of which Wangchuk became Sir Ugyen. White later wrote, "It says a great deal for the change in conduct of affairs in Bhutan and the anxiety to show respect for the British government that they should have made the presentation of the decoration . . . the first occasion of so public and elaborate a ceremony."

On December 17, 1907, White was back in Bhutan to witness the signing of what has been called the "Magna Carta of Bhutan." The most significant part of the document read:

> *We, the undersigned abbots, lopons and the whole body of Lamas, the state councillors, the chiolas of the different districts, with all the subjects, having discussed and unanimously agreed to elect Sir Ugyen Wangchuk, Tongsa Ponlop, prime minister of Bhutan, as hereditary Maharajah of this state, having installed him in open durbar on the golden throne on this thirteenth day of the eleventh month of Sa-Tel year, corresponding to the 17th of December 1907, at Punakah[sic]-phodey* [The spelling of "Punakha," like the spelling of many Bhutanese place-names, seems to lie in the eye of the beholder. I have taken the spelling from present-day maps], *we now declare our allegiance to him and his heirs and with unchanging mind undertake to serve him and his heirs loyally and faithfully to the best of our ability. Should anyone not abide by this contract by saying this and that, he should altogether be turned out of our company. In witness thereto we affix our seals. . . ."*

Now that Bhutan was, in some sense, a princely state with a proper maharaja, the British had to decide how many "guns" it merited. In British India, there were 565 princely states. These were separated by the British into three divisions. The first consisted of "salute states"— the maharajas of which were allowed, on ceremonial occasions, to be saluted by the British army with the firing of a certain number of cannon. Two states got twenty-one guns, six had nineteen, thirteen had seventeen, and seventeen had fifteen. Bhutan was given fifteen.

King Ugyen Wangchuk ruled until 1926 when, upon his death, he was succeeded by his son Jigme Wangchuk, who ruled until 1952. One of the most important things that Jigme Wangchuk did was preside over the transition of Bhutan's status when India gained its independence in 1947. The role of Bhutan in the British Commonwealth had always been somewhat ambiguous. When it suited the British, they treated Bhutan like any other princely state, which meant that they kept control over Bhutan's foreign policy. But when, for example, it came to giving the Bhutanese large financial subsidies, the British tended to treat Bhutan as if it were an independent country. While this was frustrating for the Bhutanese, it probably saved the independence of Bhutan. In 1947, the British required its princely states to choose between India and Pakistan in the partition of India and Pakistan. Bhutan, because of its ambiguous status, never had to make that choice.

When India became independent, it agreed to assume the British role, which meant, in particular, that it would guide Bhutan's foreign policy. On the other hand, India has been the main benefactor of Bhutan. Among other things, the Indians have engineered the road system, trained the army, and provided Druk Air's first pilots. As it happened, my visit to Bhutan coincided with that of the late Rajiv Gandhi, who was then the prime minister of India. On this particular visit, Mr. Gandhi announced that he was donating one million nu—a *nu* is a Bhutanese rupee, and it is tied in value to the Indian rupee—for the construction and restoration of religious structures in central Bhutan. On the other hand, as a sort of declaration of their independence, the Bhutanese maintain their local time a half-hour ahead of the national Indian time.

The present king's father, Jigme Dorji Wangchuk, took over from his father in 1952. As a young man, he had paid a visit to London. He was, according to an account I read of the visit, feeling a little nostalgic for home on Bhutan's national day (which is celebrated on various calendar dates, depending on the augurs), and decided to shoot an arrow out of the window of the apartment where he was staying. It found its way through a neighbor's window, and the future king retrieved it by climbing like a cat burglar up a drainpipe and into the neighboring apartment. Fortunately for British-Bhutanese relations, he was not discovered. In any event, it is Jigme Dorji Wangchuk who is credited with initiating the process that is slowly bringing Bhutan into the modern world. In 1953, in a remarkable unilateral gesture, the king gave up the power of absolute veto over the legislature of Bhutan. He was prepared to defer to a national assembly of about one hundred fifty representatives, about two-thirds of whom were elected directly by the people for three-year terms. Ten were from monastic orders, and the rest were appointed by the king. In 1968, the king gave the assembly the power to force any future king to abdicate if it felt that he no longer served the interests of the country.

Until 1960, there were no proper roads in Bhutan; in that year the program was begun, in collaboration with India, that produced the remarkable network of vertiginous roads now joining the various pieces of the country. It is no easy matter, road or no road, to get from one place to another in Bhutan. Until 1968, there were no banks in the country—most transactions were by barter. In that year the Bank of Bhutan was established, along with a monetary system that has replaced barter. Until 1962, there was no postal system in Bhutan. In that year stamps were issued, and in 1969 Bhutan joined the Universal Postal Union. Like many small countries, Bhutan has realized that there is hard currency to be made if only one can convince foreign stamp collectors to buy one's stamps. The Bhutanese have made a successful effort to design unusual stamps. I saw a full display in the museum in Paro. It included a three-dimensional stamp; a series in which each stamp is also a small playable record; five triangular stamps that portray the yeti; and the world's first steel stamp, printed on a thousandth-of-an-inch-thick steel foil. It is not clear why anyone needs a steel stamp, but it certainly is pretty. In 1971, the year before the king died, by a unanimous decision of the General Assembly, Bhutan became a member of the United Nations, and opened up the Permanent Mission of the Kingdom of Bhutan to the UN in New York. By 1994, Bhutan had resident embassies in India, Bangladesh, and Kuwait, and UN missions in New York and Geneva. It had diplomatic relations with eighteen countries. By comparison, Nepal had diplomatic relations with more than eighty-one countries.

Like most visitors to Bhutan, I had to confine my travels to that part of the country where the Ngalung population lives—the west. As I have mentioned, we entered the country by the Paro airport, the only one in Bhutan. We then made the classic and wonderful trek that takes one to the base of Chomo Lhari, and on to Thimphu. From Thimphu, we traveled by bus to Punakha, and then somewhat east. But we never traveled far enough east to visit the Sarchops in their own land. That would have required a serious expedition—considering the state of the east–west roads—and more time than we had. We then exited the country by Phuntsholing in the south—the land of the Lhotshampas. I bring this up because the attitudes that I observed and recorded were those of the people in power—the Ngalungs; and, as events have shown—and I will discuss—they are not necessarily representative of the rest of the population—as it happens, of the majority of the population. That is part of the present dilemma.

There was no question that the people I spoke to—Ngalungs—had an affection and respect for the present king, Jigme Singye Wangchuk, that went beyond any sort of pro forma gesture. This was clear from the anecdotes told about him. The king, who was born on November 11, 1955—the Wood-Sheep year in the Bhutanese calendar—is both a sports fan and a sportsman. At the time of my visit, his favorite sport seemed to be basketball. He played every day with players from the army. (The Royal Bhutan Army was founded by the present king's father in 1959, and has about six thousand men. One of their missions is to control the smuggling that takes place across the Tibetan borders.) The king, at the time a Boston Celtics fan, played forward. (One of the members of our group, who was from Boston, attempted to send a message to the king offering to supply him with tickets should he ever come to Boston. I do not think that there was any response from the Royal Palace.) The king also used to play a good deal of soccer. His position was goalie. I asked a Bhutanese, who seemed to be knowledgeable about these matters, if other players were hesitant about scoring goals off the king. He said no, and he told me that in one game a player scored a particularly brilliant winning goal off the king in the last minute of the game. The king was so impressed that he asked the player after the game to show him how he had done it. When the king left the field, the player was approached by one of the king's aides, carrying a small envelope. Inside the envelope were five hundred rupees—a gift from the king.

One day, on the outskirts of Thimphu, I was shown, from a considerable distance, a fairly modest looking bungalow. I asked who lived there and was told, the king. I asked if he lived there alone. There was no answer. I then asked if he had a queen. There was still no answer. I decided to ask any Bhutanese I met if the king had a queen, with no response. Finally, one of them took me aside and told me, in the strictest confidence, the situation. The king, it appeared, had four queens! When I learned this in the early fall of 1988, it turned out that he had been privately married to four sisters for nine years and had had children with each of them—eight in all. Moreover, an eight-year-old son of the oldest sister, who was then twenty-nine, had been selected as the future king. (In a recent publication, the oldest sister is identified as "Her Majesty Ashi Sangay Choden Wangchuk." But then a photo caption on a previous page identifies another of the sisters as "Her Royal Highness Ashi Pem Pem." Both sisters look perfectly beautiful.) While all of this was apparently common knowledge to many Bhutanese, they impressed upon me that it was a sort of state secret. However, on October 30, 1988, the king announced it publicly, and a formal marriage celebration took place on the twenty-second day of the ninth month of the Earth-Dragon year—that is, on October 31, 1988. At the same ceremony, Prince Jigme Gesar Namgyal Wangchuk was named crown prince. At age eighteen, the young man will be designated Tongsa Ponlop, the essential prior step to his succession of his father.

As far as I can determine, there is, in general, no stigma to a child's having been born out of wedlock in Bhutan. There are, however—so I was told—strict rules about the support, financial and otherwise, that must be given to the child's mother during and after the pregnancy. There appears to be a fair amount of divorce in Bhutan, where first marriages—which are voluntary and not arranged—take place at about the age of eighteen.

The present king was first tutored privately in Bhutan, then sent to India and finally to Oxford to complete his education. He has been especially concerned about education in Bhutan. A survey completed in 1979 showed that there were 124 schools—104 primary schools, fourteen junior high schools, and six high schools. A university to be named after Ugyen Wangchuk was being planned. Many Bhutanese who have gone through the high school system go abroad for higher education. Nontraditional—Western-style—doctors, for example, are now trained in India and elsewhere. Traditional doctors, who practice herbal medicine, are trained in Bhutan. All education in Bhutan is free. At the time of my visit, the instruction was in English. However, the study of the national language, Dzongkha, was compulsory at all levels. But even in 1988, this pervasive use of English was already provoking a certain amount of conservative reaction in the country. I came across the following letter in the *Kuensel ("Enlightenment")*, a weekly national newspaper that was started in the mid-1980s with the help of a $93,000 grant from the United Nations Development Program, which has a large presence in Bhutan. The paper appears in three editions: Dzongkha, Nepali, and English. I quote the letter as it appeared in the English edition of Saturday, September 24, 1988. It was signed by Chen Chen of the Dzongkha Development Advisory Committee and read:

> *Although our country has her own rich culture, tradition and language as a sign of her sovereign independence it is observed that many people are accustomed to western language and style.*
>
> *They are more familiar with speaking English than dzongkha and even their babies are first taught to speak English, making them forget their mother tongue [a reference to the Lhotshampas and Sarchops] or the national language dzongkha.*
>
> *Due to this influence, even in the remote villages, the villagers try to teach their children to say uncle, aunty and mummy instead of the beautiful words, ashang, ahni and aai.*
>
> *It is the responsibility of every citizen to keep in mind their national language. I would say that a language has not merely a distinctive idiom but it also embodies distinctive patterns of thought and feeling. It is this idiom of the thought and feeling, if we can use such an expression, that often defies translation. It is the vehicle through which people can exchange their views, ideas and opinions and react with one another thus fostering a greater understanding that is responsible for peace, harmony and unity and side by side, increase economic development in the country.*
>
> *Therefore, I would request all concerned to afford their self*

interest in learning dzongkha which is the identity of our peaceful and religious kingdom.

A perfect illustration of the mixed feelings that the Bhutanese have about influences from the outside is the matter of tourism. Until 1974, there was essentially no tourism in the country. That year, in connection with the coronation of the present king, a number of hotels, guest houses, and cottages were built to accommodate visitors. They now accommodate tourists. The large hotels in places like Paro and Thimphu are built in traditional Bhutanese style: wood and stone, one or two stories, and without nails. They are very comfortable, but not, by western standards, luxurious. They are built far enough away from the communities they serve to not interfere with people's daily lives. The hotel near Thimphu—the Motithang—has in its lobby a small shrine dedicated to the eleventh-century Buddhist poet-saint Milarepa. Next to the shrine is a quotation from his verse that reflects the tranquil atmosphere of the hotel:

> The non-arising Mind Essence cannot
> Be described by metaphors or signs;
> Be extinguished is oft described
> By fools, but those who realize
> It, explain by itself
> Devoid of symbolized and symbolizer,
> It is a realm beyond all words and thought
> How wondrous is the blessing of my Lineage!

At present there are about four thousand tourists a year in Bhutan. Most come on tours arranged by foreign tour operators. As in Tibet, it is also possible to create a "private" tour, which must be arranged through the government—specifically, the Bhutan Tourism Corporation. In either case, the itinerary must be approved in advance. The fees are also fixed. They range between $120 and $200 per day, depending on one's activities. There are about fifteen hundred trekkers a year on all of the trekking routes—many of which, especially those in the north, are extremely challenging. One does not find, as one does in Nepal, tourists simply wandering around.

The Bhutanese got into the tourist business late enough that they were able to profit from the example of Nepal. As I have tried to make clear, the Nepalese went for mass tourism, and as a result put much of their culture and environment at risk. The Bhutanese are absolutely determined not to do this. While the Bhutanese economy can certainly use the hard currency that comes from tourism, I am quite certain that, if the government ever felt the integrity of their society were being threatened by tourism, they would not hesitate to end it.

Because there are so few trekkers, even if one is trekking with a small group, one often has the feeling that one is alone. This struck me forcibly one day when I was hiking by myself not far from Chomo Lhari. In the distance I saw a small caravan approaching: men in red robes, some walking and some riding the surefooted Bhutanese ponies that Bogle wrote about with such affection. The ponies had on bells, and their tinkling echoed across the valley. When they came closer, I could see that each man was armed with the very long knife Bhutanese men in the countryside use for everything from peeling fruit to trimming tree limbs. In some other country, I might have felt a sense of menace. But not here. I had no idea where these men had come from or where they were going. The parade might have been something out of the Middle Ages. When they approached me, they smiled and briefly waved. They did not seem to have any particular curiosity as to who this rucksack-carrying, eyeglass-wearing westerner was. They, and I, were simply well-intentioned travelers going our own ways. They seemed in perfect harmony with their surroundings and at peace with themselves. I thought of something that Bogle said about the Bhutanese people two hundred years ago. He wrote, "The resources of a light heart and a sound constitution are infinite." I wished that this would forever be Bhutan.

Epilogue

I have thought often of my visit to Bhutan in the last few years and, in view of what has happened since, wondered whether there were things that I saw in 1988 that I should have paid more attention to. One scene in particular comes back to me. We were traveling by bus from Thimphu to Punakha. I saw a group of people—men, women, and children—working on the road. They seemed to be trying to repair it with their hands. They bore no resemblance to any other Bhutanese I had seen, in either dress or facial characteristics. They seemed to be living in some sort of miserable, open shanties on the side of the road. I asked the driver of the bus who they were and he said, "Nepali people." I was going to ask more, but the driver suddenly stopped the bus. He pointed out the window. There, alongside the road, was the largest snake I have ever seen outside a reptile house in a zoo. It must have been fifteen feet long. It seemed to have a reddish coloring. I had, and have, no idea what kind it was. I asked the driver if it was dangerous. He said, "Very!" Being a Buddhist, it would never have occurred to him to run over the snake with the bus. He was quite content to let it go its way. But it occurred to me that these "Nepali people" were living in open huts in an area where there were snakes like this. It did not occur to me that this was the least of their problems.

A year later, I was back in Kathmandu. As it happened, my hotel was near both the Royal Palace and the Bhutanese mission. Every time I walked back to the hotel, I passed the mission. Outside it were people—Nepalese—picketing. They carried signs that advocated the freeing of the Lhotshampas. I had no idea what all this meant. The term Lhotshampa was at the time unfamiliar to me. I decided to try to find out. It has not been easy. Feelings run so high, and the points of view are so divergent, that it is difficult to get any agreement on the facts. It is even difficult to get any agreement on the basic numbers. But this is what I have been able to piece together.

Bhutan is a country that has had a chronic labor shortage. This has been especially true in the south, where much of the country's agriculture is practiced. One of the ways of dealing with this has been the imposition of a kind of compulsory civic labor service—the *goongda woola*. This was simply a part of what a Bhutanese citizen was expected to do. But it was far from sufficient. In addition, the Ngalung-dominated government encouraged the immigration of Nepalese to the south of Bhutan to perform the agricultural work. As

I have mentioned, the climactic conditions in the south, while comparable to those in southern Nepal, are totally different from those of the north. It is not a natural environment for mountain people to live and work in. Not only were the Nepalese immigrants encouraged to become citizens of Bhutan, they were even encouraged to intermarry with the northerners. There were Lhotshampas in the government and, despite the fact that they spoke a different language—Nepali—and practiced a different religion—Hinduism, they appeared to live in peace and harmony with their neighbors.

This changed almost overnight in the mid-1980s. What exactly happened is not clear. But it appears that the authorities in Thimphu—I use the word *authorities* quite deliberately, because one of the unresolved questions is the degree of responsibility that the king himself must bear for this—suddenly discovered, as the result of some kind of census, that the Lhotshampa population was larger than anyone had realized. Indeed, there were more Lhotshampas than Ngalungs; if there were ever anything like a one person–one vote policy in Bhutan, the Ngalungs could find themselves in the position of an embattled minority. The integrity of their culture—even the compulsory wearing of ghos and kiras—could be at risk. In the modern world, this is not an unfamiliar situation. We have only to look at ourselves. The Founding Fathers did not envision a United States where native English-speakers would be a minority. The reaction is also not unfamiliar: namely, to somehow get rid of the "foreigners," in this case, the relatively powerless Lhotshampas.

It turned out—and this is also not surprising in view of our own experience—that there were two groups of Lhotshampas. There were Lhotshampas who had been in Bhutan for generations and were as much citizens of the country—by any sensible definition—as anyone else. But there were also "illegal" immigrants. These were people who had come to Bhutan looking for work, crossing the porous borders that separate Nepal, India, and Bhutan, without attempting to become citizens. How many illegals there were is a matter of dispute, but there were certainly thousands. So long as their labor was needed, and they did not seem to be a threat to the Ngalungs, their presence was tolerated and a blind eye turned. In addition, some—again, how many is not clear—of the Lhotshampas resorted to acts of terrorism in order to, one gathers, try to create a separate Lhotshampa state in the south. These people, and the illegals, provided the government all the excuse that it needed to crack down on the Lhotshampa population in general.

The first thing that it did was make the dress code mandatory for anyone who wanted to be classified as a Bhutanese citizen. This, of course, provoked civil resistance. This, in turn, led the government— again, the king's role is murky—to begin a campaign to expel the Lhotshampas from Bhutan. How this was accomplished is also a matter of dispute. The government claims that the legal Lhotshampa citizens were offered adequate compensation for any property seized. The Lhotshampas claim that they were offered little or nothing by way of compensation, and that they were run out of the country by intimidation and brute force. The king claims that he made several trips to the south to encourage the people to stay. It appears that his power of persuasion—or the perception of his sincerity—was not great, because, in the event, what has been estimated as one hundred thousand Lhotshampas left Bhutan. The precise numbers have never been clearly established, but it is a significant fraction of what had been the Lhotshampa population in the country.

Their first destination was northern India. This is understandable, since India borders Bhutan to the south. It is also understandable that the Indians were less than pleased at having a population of some hundred thousand "foreigners" suddenly dumped upon them. The Indians have consistently taken the position that the Lhotshampas are not their problem. On the other hand, an unstable Bhutan would most certainly *become* their problem. The Indians have made it quite clear that they will not tolerate unstable regimes on their northern borders. It will be recalled that they were instrumental in the overthrow of the Ranas in Nepal when it became clear that a continuing Rana regime, with its attendant instability, might encourage some sort of Chinese move southward. Likewise, they used the excuse of instability in Sikkim to basically absorb it. Up to now, the king has been very skillful in keeping India from absorbing Bhutan—which it could certainly do if push ever came to shove. Therefore, in the interests of preserving their independence, the Bhutanese are, or should be, highly motivated not to let the matter of the Lhotshampas get further out of hand.

When the Lhotshampas discovered that they were not welcome in India, they naturally turned north to Nepal, thus reversing the migratory pattern that had brought them to Bhutan so many years before. But the Nepalese did not want them either, declaring that they were not Nepalese, but rather citizens of Bhutan. Thus, most of them have ended up in refugee camps in southern Nepal in conditions, so far as can be determined, that are at best primitive. The number of people in these camps is at least sixty thousand and very likely more—the rest having been absorbed in one way or another into either India or Nepal. What then to do? Clearly, what is needed is some sort of realistic dialogue between the government of Bhutan—the king and his representatives—and the government of Nepal, which, as it happens, is no longer subservient to the Nepalese king. This dialogue has to recognize that some of the displaced Lhotshampas truly are citizens of Bhutan, and have as much right to be there as anyone else. It is absurd to deny citizenship to an individual whose family has been in Bhutan legitimately for decades because he or she is unwilling to wear a robelike garment that may be both uncomfortable and contrary to custom and habit. On the other hand, the Nepalese government must acknowledge that some of the people in the camps are illegal immigrants to Bhutan. They are citizens of Nepal, and should remain there until they can legitimately migrate elsewhere if they choose. Once these general principles are recognized on a governmental level, then some outside agency can begin to go to the camps and to consider each situation on a case-by-case basis.

In fact, this process has gotten under way. Starting in 1993, the two governments began serious negotiations. In July of 1993, an entity called the Nepali-Bhutanese Ministerial Joint Committee was set up for precisely this purpose. By 1994, it had progressed enough to create what was called a Joint Verification Team, which would have been composed of five members from each side to carry out the case-by-case analysis. Some matters did need to be worked out when, in the fall of 1994, the government of Nepal was radically transformed. As I have noted, at that time, the United Marxist Leninist Party of Nepal won the general election, giving it the right to form a new government. Before the election, the party had taken the position that *everyone* in the camps was a Bhutanese citizen. This would, of course, have destroyed any chance for working out a compromise. But the government of Nepal changed again in the fall of 1995 and work of the Joint Committee was put on hold. One hopes it will soon get back on track. To all of us who have had a love affair with Bhutan, however brief, the idea that the independence and integrity of this lovely country could be lost is intolerable. To repeat the words of George Bogle: "The resources of a light heart and a sound constitution are infinite."

Selected Bibliography

Nepal

Anderson, John, ed. *Nepal: Insight Guides.* Singapore: Kok Wah Press, 1986.

Armington, Stan, *Trekking in the Nepal Himalaya.* Berkeley: Lonely Planet Publications, 1994. This book has a number of recent and useful references.

Bista, Dor Bhadur. *People of Nepal.* Kathmandu: Government of Nepal, Department of Publicity, 1967.

Buhler, Jean. *Nepal.* Lausanne: Editions Rencenive, 1964.

Chevalley, Gabriel, et al. *Avant Premières à l'Everest.* Paris: Arthaud, 1953.

Choegyal, Lisa. *Nepal: Insight Pocket Guides.* Boston: Houghton Mifflin Company, 1993.

Furer-Haimendorf, Cristoph von. *The Sherpas of Nepal.* London: J. Murray, 1964.

―――. *The Sherpas Transformed.* New Delhi: Sterling, 1984.

Gellner, David N. *Monk, Householder and Tantric Priest.* New York, Cambridge University Press, 1992.

Hagen, Tony. *Nepal.* Berne: Kummerly & Frey, 1961.

Hornbein, Thomas F. *Everest:The West Ridge.* London: Allen & Unwin, 1967.

Houston, Charles S. *Going High.* New York: American Alpine Club, 1980.

Hunt, Sir John. *The Ascent of Everest.* London: Hodder & Stoughton, 1953.

Joshi, Bhuwan L., and Leo Rose. *Democratic Innovations in Nepal.* Los Angeles: University of California Press, 1966.

Landon, Percival. *Nepal.* London: Constable, 1928.

Levi, Sylvain D. *Dans l'Inde.* Paris: F. Reider & Company, 1925.

Majupuria, T. C., and I. Majupuria. *The Complete Guide to Nepal.* Bangkok: Craftsman Press, 1983.

Matthiessen, Peter. *The Snow Leopard.* New Delhi: Harper Collins, 1989.

Mihaly, Eugene Bramer. *Foreign Aid and Politics in Nepal.* London: Oxford University Press, 1965.

Morris, John. *A Winter in Nepal.* London: Hart-Davis, 1963.

————. *Nepal and the Gurkhas.* London: Her Majesty's Stationery Office, 1965.

Peissel, Michel. *Tiger for Breakfast.* London: Hodder & Stoughton, 1967.

————. *Mustang: A Lost Tibetan Kingdom.* London: Collins, 1968.

Regmi, D.R. *A Century of Family Autocracy in Nepal.* Benares: Commercial Printing Works, 1950.

Rieffel, Robert. *Nepal: Namaste.* Kathmandu: Sahayagi Prakhashan, 1978.

Snellgrove, David L. *Buddhist Himalaya.* Oxford, England: Cassirer, 1957.

Swift, Hugh. *Trekking in Nepal, West Tibet and Bhutan.* San Francisco: Sierra Club, 1989.

Tucci, Giuseppe. *Nepal: In Search of the Malla.* New York: E. P. Dutton, 1952.

Ullman, James Ramsey. *Man of Everest: Tenzing.* London: George Harrap, 1956.

Unsworth, Walt. *Everest.* Boston: Houghton Mifflin, 1981.

I would like to put into a special category *Himal Magazine.* This bimonthly, nonprofit magazine is essential reading for anyone with an interest in this region. I have repeatedly been instructed by it. The magazine is published and edited in Kathmandu but can be ordered by writing to *Himal Magazine,* P.O. Box 470758, San Francisco, CA 94147-9801.

Tibet

Avedon, John F. *In Exile from the Land of Snows.* London: Michael Joseph, 1984.

Booz, Elisabeth B. *Tibet.* Lincolnwood: Passport Books, 1986.

Buckley, M., and R. Strauss. *Tibet: A Travel Survival Kit.* Berkeley: Lonely Planet Publications, 1986.

Chan, Victor. *Tibet Handbook.* Chico: Moon Publications Inc., 1994.

David-Neel, Alexandra. *Magic and Mystery in Tibet.* New York: Dover, 1971.

———. *My Journey to Lhasa* Boston: Beacon Press, 1983. (Reprint of 1927 edition.)

Feigon, Lee. *Demystifying Tibet.* Chicago: Ivan R. Dee, 1996.

Fleming, Peter. *Bayonets to Lhasa.* New York: Oxford University Press, 1985.

Foster, B., and M. Foster. *Forbidden Journey.* San Francisco: Harper and Row, 1987.

Harrer, Heinrich. *Seven Years in Tibet.* New York: Granada, 1984.

———. *Return to Tibet.* New York: Penguin, 1986.

Hopkirk, Peter. *Trespassers on the Top of the World.* Los Angeles: J. P. Tarcher, 1983.

———. *The Great Game.* New York: Kodansha America, 1994.

Markham, Clements R., ed. *Narratives of the Mission of George Bogle to Tibet.* 1774, 1879. Facsimile edition: New Delhi: Manjusri Publishing House, 1971.

Miller, Luree. *On Top of the World.* Seattle: The Mountaineers. 1985.

Richardson, Hugh M. *Tibet and Its History.* Boulder: Shambala, 1984.

Shakabpa, Tsepon W. D. *Tibet: A Political History.* New York: Potala Publications, 1984.

Snellgrove, D., and H. Richardson. *A Cultural History of Tibet.* Boulder: Shambhala, 1984.

Snelling, John. *The Sacred Mountain.* London: East West, 1983.

Thubten, T., and C. Turnbull. *Tibet.* New York: Penguin, 1987.

Tucci, Giuseppe. *Tibet: Land of Snows.* New York: Stein & Day, 1967.

Wentz, W. Y. Evans, ed. *The Tibetan Book of the Dead.* New York: Oxford University Press, 1985.

Bhutan

Collister, Peter. *Bhutan and the British.* London: Serindia Publications, 1987.

Crosette, Barbara. *So Close to Heaven.* New York: Knopf, 1995.

Eden, Ashley. *Political Missions to Bootan.* Facsimile edition: New Delhi: Manjusri Publishing House, 1972.

Edmunds, Tom Owen. *Bhutan.* London: Elm Tree Books, 1988.

Hickman, Katie. *Dreams of the Peaceful Dragon.* London: Victor Gollancz, 1987.

Steele, Peter. *Two and Two Halves to Bhutan.* London: Quality Book Club, 1970.

Index